Colonial Ambivalence, Cultural Authenticity, and the Limitations of Mimicry in French-Ruled West Africa, 1914–1956

FRANCOPHONE CULTURES AND LITERATURES

Michael G. Paulson & Tamara Alvarez-Detrell
General Editors

Vol. 45

PETER LANG
New York • Washington, D.C./Baltimore • Bern
Frankfurt am Main • Berlin • Brussels • Vienna • Oxford

James E. Genova

Colonial Ambivalence, Cultural Authenticity, and the Limitations of Mimicry in French-Ruled West Africa, 1914–1956

PETER LANG
New York • Washington, D.C./Baltimore • Bern
Frankfurt am Main • Berlin • Brussels • Vienna • Oxford

Library of Congress Cataloging-in-Publication Data

Genova, James Eskridge.
Colonial ambivalence, cultural authenticity, and the limitations of
mimicry in French-ruled West Africa, 1914–1956 / James E. Genova.
p. cm. — (Francophone cultures and literatures; v. 45)
Includes bibliographical references and index.
1. Africa, French-speaking West—History—1884–1960.
2. France—Colonies—Africa—History—20th century.
3. Decolonization—Africa, French-speaking
West—History. I. Title. II. Series.
DT352.5.G46   966.03'1'0917541—dc22   2003019578
ISBN 0–8204–6941–6
ISSN 1077–0186

Bibliographic information published by **Die Deutsche Bibliothek**.
Die Deutsche Bibliothek lists this publication in the "Deutsche
Nationalbibliografie"; detailed bibliographic data is available
on the Internet at http://dnb.ddb.de/.

© 2004 Peter Lang Publishing, Inc., New York
275 Seventh Avenue, 28th Floor, New York, NY 10001
www.peterlangusa.com

For Stephanie and Eva

Table of Contents

Acknowledgments

This book began as a dissertation at the State University of New York at Stony Brook, where the ideas advanced here first germinated. Since then, this project has metamorphosed several times as a result of the insightful critiques, generous assistance, probing questions, and informal intellectual exchanges provided by many people over the course of the last decade for which I am deeply grateful.

I wish to thank the following institutions and individuals for providing the support necessary to conduct the research for this book: The staff at *Le Centre des Archives d'Outre-mer* (CAOM) in Aix-en-Provence, France, whose able assistance and endless patience enabled much of the research to be accomplished, and in particular Françoise Durand-Evrard, director of the CAOM, for her kind aid in locating essential materials for this project; France's Ministry of Culture approved all of my requests for access to documents that were, at the time, incommunicable and were vital to the successful completion of the research for this book; and the staff of *Les Archives de la République du Sénégal* (ARS) in Dakar, Senegal, who offered friendship and a helping hand that enabled me to fruitfully navigate their invaluable holdings on French West Africa, and in particular to Saliou M'Baye, director of the ARS, who kindly set aside a generous portion of his time to engage in fascinating conversations about our mutual interests, this project, and to guide me through Dakar's extensive resources. Other institutions have provided financial support, accommodations, and a vibrant intellectual environment for the synthesizing and development of ideas for this book as well as its writing. The History Department at Stony Brook served as a second home for many years and its faculty and staff have been a real family to me, offering financial support, a semester's leave for research, a stimulating intellectual climate, and sincere friendship and support. I am, more than they will ever know, forever in their debt. Special thanks are due Ms. Margaret Creedon, graduate coordinator, and Ms. Susan Grumet, undergraduate coordinator, who had a miracle touch that solved problem and created a wonderfully pleasant atmosphere in which to study and work.

Indiana State University and its History Department have been invaluable for the completion of this project providing a comfortable work environment, stimulating conversation, and unfailing support. In particular Ms. Carolyn Greenwalt, the History Department's administrative assistant, deserves special thanks for all of her help in too many areas to mention. The Office of Sponsored Programs at Indiana State University furnished a generous grant for completion of the research for this book. The West African Research Center (WARC) kindly served as my host institution during research in Senegal and provided workspace and pleasant surroundings for relaxation and contemplation, while also helping to find accommodations during my stay. Wendy Wilson Fall, director of the WARC, took time out of her busy schedule to discuss the project and point me in productive directions. Ms. Nene N'diaye Diop, administrative assistant, guided me through the Center's resources. Ms. Amelia Drumond, manager of the Center's buvette, offered useful advice for navigating Dakar as well as exceptional provisions.

Many scholars and friends added immeasurably to this study with advice, insightful critiques, and guidance. Kathleen Wilson, Richard Kuisel, and Richard Harvey read and critiqued the dissertation, furnishing invaluable guidance as part of my Ph.D. committee. They have continued to offer advice and suggestions throughout the revision process and their support has been essential to its completion. Gary Marker helped launch the study, continually pressing for clarity and deeper probing of the basic questions it was to address. Fred Weinstein offered crucial insights concerning the psychoanalytical perspective on group identity formation. Fred Cooper provided cautionary advice on the use of post-colonial theory at an early stage of this project. Laura Lee Downs highlighted important themes to be pursued in the work. Lynn Hunt kindly read the book manuscript and offered suggestions for its revision and publication as well as encouraging support of the project. Gary Wilder has provided constant intellectual stimulation enabling a clearer development of ideas fundamental to this study. My editors at Peter Lang warrant acknowledgement: Heidi Burns for her continual interest in the manuscript; and Michael Paulson and Tamara Alvarez-Detrell for reading the final version of the manuscript and including it as part of their series.

I wish to make special mention of two intellectual debts that greatly shaped this project. Gene Lebovics and Femi Vaughan served as dissertation advisors, teachers, and friends. Gene Lebovics has been a sincere friend since my undergraduate days; his scholarship on French culture and identity has had the most profound impact on my own work; and the many informal conversations throughout the years became the workshop for the ideas developed here and have helped me grow as a person. Femi Vaughan's unbounded enthusiasm for scholarship and teaching was a wonderful example and inspiration; and his willingness to discuss in depth all issues pertaining to Africa and the world was an immeasurable resource. Without their scholarly contributions and personal friendship this book could not have been written.

All of my friends and family have contributed in myriad ways to the development of this study and deserve my most sincere thanks. I would like to thank in particular Tom Sauer, Dan Monk, Barbara Weinstein, Emmanuelle Saada, Eric Jennings, Young-sun Hong, Iona Man-Cheong, Toyin Falola, Marc Michel, Laurent Dubois, Mamadou Diouf, Sara Lipton, Claude Massu, John Soumilas, Herrick Chapman, Don Layton, Judith Wishnia, Joel Rosenthal, Susan Gauss, Brooke Larson, Karl Bottigheimer, Sally Kuisel, Jonathan Katz, Mavis Uberall, Alyssa Sepinwall, Phil Nord, Chris Olsen, Spencer Segalla, and Amanda Sackur. My greatest debts are to my wife and colleague Stephanie Smith and my daughter Eva Pietri. They have been my constant sources of inspiration throughout this project. Both have furnished wonderful insights, stimulating discussions, and crucial advice that enabled this book to be completed and greatly improved its quality. Stephanie has opened whole new perspectives on my work and life that have been invaluable to their development. I am eternally and deeply grateful to her and Eva.

Introduction
France and West Africa as a Field of Analysis

...[I]ncapable of entirely returning to our original traditions or of assimilating to Europe, we had the feeling we were forming a new race, mentally mixed, but which was not aware of its originality and had not become self-conscious. Uprooted? We were precisely to the degree that we had not yet defined our position in the world and [that] we were stranded between two societies, without recognized meaning in either one, foreigners to both.

> Alioune Diop, *Présence Africaine* (December 1947)[1]

Detaching themselves from the [colonial] masses [are] groups or individuals that in one sudden leap pass through all the stages [of evolution].... The evolved one (*évolué*) *appears* ill bred, not because he is black or yellow, but because he is evolved. The *évolués* have to be esteemed, but they [also] need to feel responsible. It is with the *évolués* that we (France) will succeed [in the colonies]. They are the ones, in every territory, that will be the scaffolding of the structure [we] are building there.

> Gov. Henri Laurentie, *Mensuel de Documentation* (March 1946)[2]

The statements reproduced above were made at a pivotal moment in the history of French rule in West Africa. France was flush with the optimism of liberation from Nazi occupation; a freedom achieved in no small measure thanks to the assistance of volunteers and conscripts from its colonies. Yet, the pronouncements also inaugurate a theme that would dominate political discourse for the next decade: the attempt by peoples long subjugated by colonial oppression to chart their own independent destiny, to (re)discover themselves in the world, and the concomitant effort by the imperial power, France, to recover/maintain its position as a world power while also reinventing itself in light of the recent calamities associated with the just-concluded war. Both statements point to the existence of a new social class produced out of the colonial encounters between France and its overseas possessions. Laurentie and Diop highlight the uniqueness of this community, straddling and blurring the boundaries between colonizers and colonized.

Each, in turn, suggests that the French-educated elite, labeled "*évolués*" by imperial administrators, had a special purpose or mission to fulfill with regard to both France and West Africa. However, the remarks also expose a tension in the imperial relationship, laying bare a struggle for authority that marked and shaped the colonial experience in both locales. Diop's language is one of alienation, dislocation, and an attempt to define this new community and its tasks in the imperial framework. His is an insurgent claim, asserting the latent power located within the *évolué* community by reason of its objective position *vis-à-vis* the structures of colonial rule. For Diop, the new elite is in control of its self-articulation. The ability to achieve meaning in the French and African contexts inheres within the *évolué* class. Moreover, Diop's statement implies a capacity to delineate the separate categories, French and African, in relation to which the new elite stands. While Laurentie acknowledges the importance of this group, it is in the context of its contribution to France's overseas mission, its *mission civilisatrice*. However, here too the ambiguous relations of power operable within the colonial relationship are revealed. France's objectives, left undefined by the colonial governor, can only be fulfilled through the cooperation and affinity of purpose of the *évolués*. This puts into relief the basic regime of power that characterized colonialism—the dominant position of the French colonizer—but also the limits to that authority—circumscribed by the responses and initiatives of the colonized. The fundamental purpose of this book is to explore how this numerically small class of French-educated West Africans came to be regarded by themselves and the colonial rulers as occupying such a strategic position in the imperial setting. How did they develop into a self-conscious social category, endowed with a unique identity upon which to base their claims to leadership in West Africa and their participation in French politics? What does the history of this community tell us about the nature of the colonial experience and its enduring legacies for the former metropole and ex-colonies?

This book is a particular history of how French colonialism came to an end in West Africa by 1960. Certainly, it is a narrative of the processes whereby the federation of French West Africa (AOF—*Afrique Occidentale française*) achieved political sovereignty as the eight states of Guinea, Senegal, Ivory Coast, Niger, Mali, Mauritania, Upper Volta (Burkina Faso), and Dahomey (Benin). But, it is also a history of some of the ways in which France was shaped as a political and cultural entity through its experience as a colonial power. As such, this project has a much broader purpose. It aspires to contribute to our understanding of the crises, social and political, which afflict both locales in the present. In recent years the state systems in many parts of sub-Saharan Africa have virtually collapsed, frequently accompanied by what is dismissed as "tribal" or "ethnic" violence. France, during the same period, has witnessed the emergence of influential, and at times murderous, anti-immigrant movements that participate in and exacerbate anxieties over the perceived loss of a distinctive French identity. At the center of the upheavals in Africa often stands the class of educated elite that assumed leadership of the former colonies at independence. The objects of anti-immigrant activity in France are almost invariably migrants from the former overseas possessions. An aura of fatalism usually accompanies acknowledgement of or engagement in the conflicts in both the former metropole and ex-colonies. They are presented for public consumption, and generally accepted, as somehow "natural" human responses when "different" cultures come into contact.[3] This work seeks to demonstrate how those patterns of social confrontation came to be "naturalized" in France and West Africa during the twentieth century and, in the process, to illustrate the perils inherent in claims to civil and political rights made on the basis of cultural difference or specificity.

A basic argument of this book is that anxieties over the loss of "national identity" in France[4] and the "crisis of institutions" that has afflicted much of sub-Saharan Africa in recent years are linked phenomena.[5] On one level they are joined in the sense that a collapse of state structures in Africa induces migration, generally in the direction of the former metropolitan power, which furnishes the targets for a politics of hate or exclusion in France. In another way, though, the crises in both places and the particular ways in which they are manifested—through language, social organization, and political practice—have emerged from and participate in a shared "political culture," defined by Lynn Hunt as "[t]he values, expectations, and implicit rules that expressed and shaped collective intentions and actions," that was forged in the colonial context.[6] In this work I attempt to map the emergence of political cultures in France and French-ruled West Africa between the First World War and 1956, when the metropole relinquished effective governance of the federation, that privileged notions of cultural authenticity and of essential differences between Europeans and Africans. Such an approach allows us to better understand why the negative reaction toward migrants to France from the former colonies takes the particular forms of a cultural defensiveness and concern with the protection of the French language from "corruption."[7] Moreover, it deepens our analysis of the bases for the disintegration of administrative systems throughout post-colonial sub-Saharan Africa that is marked by the ascendancy of local, ethno-tribal loyalties over and against the state.[8]

Consequently, this study "treat[s] metropole and colony as a single analytic field" and shares Ann Stoler's and Frederick Cooper's perspective that "Europe was made by its imperial projects, as much as colonial encounters were shaped by conflicts within Europe itself."[9] France and West Africa, during the period of imperial domination, comprised what Pierre Bourdieu calls a "field of production" where social identities, cultural meaning, and patterns of exchange and engagement were constituted that, in turn, delineated the limits of the field in terms of location and conceptual possibilities. Bourdieu describes the field as "a set of objective, historical relations between positions anchored in certain forms of power (of capital)." The participants enter a given field with a "habitus," which "consists of a set of historical relations 'deposited' within individual bodies in the form of mental or corporeal schemata of perception, apperception, and action." Yet, this habitus is also transformed through competition and struggle within the field, redefining the terms of engagement and the parameters of the field itself.[10] The fights within the French colonial field, comprised of the geopolitical entities France and AOF, centered on claims to leadership or the right to speak on behalf of particular communities, specifically the "French" and "African" people. Those confrontations increasingly situated control of the administrative structures in both regions and the ability to define the "true" Frenchman and "veritable" African as the core objectives of the contending forces.[11]

To conduct this investigation I have focused on the problematic place of the French-educated elite from West Africa, or *évolués*, in the colonial field. That social category was, I argue, pivotal in defining citizenship, constructions of French identity, and the production of *imaginaires* about the real African throughout the period under consideration here. In fact, Gov. Laurentie, cited above while he was minister for Overseas France in 1946, asserted, "[I]t is not an exaggeration to say that the *évolués* are the vital center of the colonial question."[12] The French-educated elite from AOF claimed a presence in the cultural worlds of both "Europe" and "Africa" while they helped to define the boundaries and substantive characteristics of each. As such, they met resistance from and were positioned in opposition to interested forces in both regions. Colonial administrators and many metropolitan officials viewed the *évolués* as dangerous and a threat to French identity, while they acknowledged the strategic importance of the new elite for the durability of France's presence (cultural and political) in West Africa. Concomitantly, the "traditional" or pre-colonial elite saw the *évolués* as rivals for the loyalties of the indigenous peoples of AOF and enemies of ancestral social structures and practices. Therefore, a study of that social category as it developed between 1914 and 1956 provides a unique means to explore how practices of colonial rule were conceived and the cultural frameworks in which the exercise of metropolitan authority was justified.[13]

The idea of a *mission civilisatrice* permeated the institutional and intellectual contexts of the colonial field.[14] Imperial administrators, metropolitan officials, the *évolués*, and the pre-colonial elite each came to embrace the sense that they had a particular mission to fulfill in relation to France and West Africa. In the course of their contacts and conflicts the content of the civilizing mission was continually re-defined. Those re-articulations contributed to the emergence of a pattern of erratic governmental praxis in France and West Africa, instabilities that reflected the fundamental tension embedded in French colonialism as experienced in AOF, what Stoler and Cooper describe as "the dialectics of inclusion and exclusion:" the need to maintain the distinction between ruler and ruled while permanently attaching the subject population to France.[15] The *évolués* operated at the core of that difficulty since they transcended the boundaries between citizen and subject, French and African, colonizer and colonized. They epitomized the contacts between France and West Africa and the possibility that the link between the two regions could be severed. This is what, in another context, Homi Bhabha calls the "*ambivalence* of mimicry" affected through "colonial discourse." He writes, "Mimicry is...the sign of a double articulation; a complex strategy of reform, regulation and discipline, which 'appropriates' the Other as it visualizes power. Mimicry is also the sign of the inappropriate...a difference or recalcitrance which coheres the dominant strategic function of colonial power, intensifies surveillance, and poses an immanent threat to both 'normalized' knowledges and disciplinary powers."[16] This work explores how that process works and its limitations in the specific context of French West Africa.

The study of *évolué* identity as it was articulated throughout the period of French rule in West Africa furnishes an important means by which to examine the historical production of certain notions of what it meant to be "French" or "African" as they circulated, were translated, and were re-produced throughout the colonial field. To conduct this inquiry, then, it is necessary to take discourse seriously as a tool of analysis. Michel Foucault explains, "It is in discourse that power and knowledge are joined.... Discourse transmits and produces power; it reinforces it, but also undermines and exposes it, renders it fragile and makes it possible to thwart it."[17] While Foucault's definition of discourse is a useful starting point, I suggest that his explication of it needs further elaboration. In Foucault's notion, discourse itself is made the actor. He uproots discourse from the social conditions in which it is articulated and presents it as an autonomous force acting upon unwitting Subjects constituted by this extra-societal framework. The present study demonstrates that certain discourses attain the power attributed to them through their connection to the historically specific relations that exist between and among social actors and is constituted by, while simultaneously constituting participants engaged in a common field of struggle. Bourdieu's discussion of language and symbolic power furnishes a way to reintegrate social actors in the constitution of the discursive framework through which they make sense of the world in which they live. According to Bourdieu, "For the philosopher's language to be granted the importance it claims, there has to be a convergence of the social conditions which enable it to secure from others a recognition of the importance which it attributes to itself."[18]

The language deployed by the players in the imperial framework reflected and helped to structure the relations of power operable in France and West Africa. Particular descriptions of "authentic" French and African cultures and forms of social organization that gained prominence in the colonial field not only expressed desired ends, they revealed conceits about the reality experienced in metropole and colony. Real "Frenchmen" and "Africans" were endowed with specific characteristics by which individuals were measured to determine their "proper" place in the geo-social context of French imperialism. Those criteria or models of cultural life were taken up by colonial administrators as well as the French-educated elite to make claims about the right to govern, to represent particular interests, and the correct relationship between France and West Africa. Accordingly, prevailing discourses informed practices of colonial rule as well as strategies of resistance to imperial domination and, as a result, they became arenas where the struggle for authority in the metropole and AOF unfolded.

The re-production of particular notions of the "authentic" France and Africa requires an analysis of why some discourses became dominant while others did not. Specifically, this study traces the process whereby the language used by ethnographers to portray French and African societies became hegemonic in the colonial field. According to Antonio Gramsci, the development of a hegemonic system entails a multi-dimensional exchange. At one level is "[t]he 'spontaneous' consent given by the great masses of the population to the general direction imposed on social life by the dominant fundamental group." But a second, necessary aspect is "[t]he apparatus of State coercive power which 'legally' enforces discipline on those groups who do not 'consent' either actively or passively."[19] For colonial administrators, the newly emergent discipline of ethnography provided a scientific justification for the elaboration of systems of command in West Africa, in this way furnishing a basis for consent to the new relationship of authority while the institutions of coercion were articulated. However, ethnography functioned ambiguously in the colonial field. Ethnographers provided information to imperial officials and metropolitan politicians about the people over whom France ruled that confirmed certain prejudices and challenged others. While the government general for AOF, based in Dakar, used the conclusions reached by ethnographers to justify colonial rule and its programs, *évolués* adapted those findings to challenge French dominance in the region and as a source for the articulation of their own particular identity. The new urban elite in AOF asserted that the existence of essential and immutable cultural differences between Africa and France, "proved" by ethnographers, revealed the futility of colonialism and argued for the metropole's withdrawal from the region. Moreover, ethnography provided a model of "traditional" African society that informed the political agendas and aspirations of the *évolués* as they became the dominant social class in West Africa by the end of the 1950s. Those archetypes prepared the foundation for tensions in the post-colonial societies of the federation as claims by labor and women, among others, clashed with the "authentic" Africa envisioned by the new ruling class.

The new urban elite from West Africa laid claims to being the organic intellectuals of the subject population in the colonies. At first asserting their prerogatives as a distinct social class in the imperial framework, the *évolués* sought to enhance their position through appeals to represent the interests of the colonized masses, a process analogous to that described by Partha Chatterjee in the case of Indian nationalism.[20] At that point they constituted a direct threat to the colonial administration, which imagined it had a special role in leading the "colonial natives" to a higher plane of existence. By the 1920s the broad outlines of a struggle between French officials and the urban educated elite to be regarded by the indigenous peoples of the colonies as the "natural leaders" of West Africa were visible. However, neither group was sufficiently large enough or endowed with recognized claims to historical precedent to make good their assertions alone. Consequently, they sought to forge "hegemonic blocs" with other social groups, particularly the "pre-colonial" or "native" elite, which did have some historical basis upon which to legitimate its position. As Jean-François Bayart observes, though, the "search for hegemony" was never entirely successful[21] as the terms of struggle and the relations of forces remained remarkably fluid throughout the period of French rule in West Africa. Other social groups (workers, peasants, and women) and international developments all intervened to shape the circumstances under which the colonial administrators and *évolués* carried out their battles. Nevertheless, certain patterns of struggle were articulated in the colonial context that gave rise to what Mahmood Mamdani describes as a "bifurcated State" where "two forms of power [existed] under a single hegemonic [framework]. Urban power spoke the language of civil society and civil rights, rural power of community and culture. Civil power claimed to protect rights, customary power pledged to enforce tradition." Both the urban and rural forms of power were experienced as "variants of despotism" where certain groups competed for ruling positions while others were continuously constrained or excluded from the possibilities of exercising authority, by both French officials and the new urban elite.[22]

Scholarly interest in the rise of the Western-educated elite throughout sub-Saharan Africa has increased over the past two decades. That scholarship has changed how we understand the end of imperial rule and the nature of post-colonial societies on the continent. It situates the Western-educated elite at the center of the decolonization process in ways that challenge earlier presentations of that social group as either a cluster of intellectuals at the head of mass parties or as unambiguous liberators of their people from foreign rule. More attention has been paid to the *évolués*, Anglicized Africans, or *assimilados* as a clearly defined social class with identifiable aspirations and self-interests. Much of the new work concludes that the (misguided) goals pursued by the Western-educated elite were largely responsible for the fate that has befallen African societies since independence. In fact, George Ayittey claims that Africa has suffered from a "far more insidious invasion" than that of the European colonizers. That incursion was perpetrated by "sons of Africa who briefly left to pursue studies overseas" and "came back with a vengeance to denigrate, to enslave, to destroy, and to colonize by imposing alien ideological systems upon the African people."[23]

Such work raises new questions about the importance of colonialism in shaping African societies. I agree with Mahmood Mamdani's assertion that "the colonial experience" was decisive in shaping the political cultures of Africa.[24] In fact, the objects of Ayittey's criticisms, the *évolués*, are the most obvious products of colonial encounters. However, he dismisses colonialism as a failed attempt to destroy "traditional" African institutions. As such, he concludes that autochthonous social and political structures "were left largely intact by colonial rule."[25] However, I argue that French rule in West Africa left an indelible mark on the patterns of political engagement, forms of social organization, and the conceptual possibilities for change that predominated after independence. The *évolués* were not foreign conquerors. The rhetoric and actions of both agents from the ex-metropole and among West African indigenous groups, which include the peasants and "chiefs" praised by Ayittey, valorized the French-educated elite as leaders of the new states. In fact, this study demonstrates that the pre-colonial elite benefited and suffered at the hands of colonial administrators and the *évolués* alike. However, they did not do so as passive agents, but as active participants in a protracted struggle for authority that they helped to shape.

Focus on the rise of the Western-educated African elite also points to the enduring connections between former metropole and ex-colonies. However, that aspect of the story has often been neglected by the recent work. The attempt to find "African" causes and solutions to "African" problems has elided the role that states such as France continue to play in the internal politics and cultural practices of Africa. One theme of this book is how France came to see itself as having a special connection with Africa and what that says about French identity.[26] Also, we need to understand how events in the former colonies impact the decision-making processes and cultural dynamics of the ex-metropoles in manners that help to sustain such perspectives. Within the Hexagon, the debates over France's ability to absorb migrants from its one-time overseas possessions into its national framework, and what that identity is to begin with indicates the degree to which the colonial question still haunts metropolitan life.[27] This project charts the ways in which a historical context was elaborated wherein the issues at the heart of current disputes over the nature of French culture and identity as well as the specific reactions to peoples from the ex-colonies took shape. Accordingly, it demonstrates that the educated elite from West Africa played important roles in French politics throughout the twentieth century and in the development of Gaullist foreign policy during the early Fifth Republic. In addition, they contributed in unintended ways to the articulation of a racial discourse in the metropole that receives its most extreme expression today in the rhetoric of the far right *Front National*. Those legacies, I contend, continue to be significant for understanding France today.

To explore those issues we must go back to the period of the First World War, a time when the dynamics of the colonial field began to take shape and the social forces forged with it coalesced into distinguishable and self-conscious communities. The imperial framework we are about to interrogate was a place of exchanges, movements, clashes, and compromises. The colonial field, bounded by the geographic spaces of France and French West Africa, was a fluid context that permitted a multitude of stances, but authorized few. Paul Gilroy's "image of ships in motion" is an appropriate one for this story.[28] Our narrative, much like the subjects of this work, moves back and forth between France and West Africa, and at times unfolds in both locations simultaneously. In the end France was no longer able to govern AOF, but that did not necessarily signal the end of their special relationship with each other or the colonized frameworks in which their peoples lived before decolonization. We begin, then, on the edge of a catastrophe, one that was formative for France and West Africa and, this study hopes to demonstrate, continues to be reflected in the forms and patterns of the crises that beset those regions today.

NOTES

1. Alioune Diop, "Niam n'goura: ou les raisons d'être de *Présence Africaine*," *Présence Africaine* Issue 1 (November-December 1947), p. 8.

2. Le Centre des Archives d'Outre-Mer (CAOM), 1/Affaires Politiques (AP)/2147, Governor Henri Laurentie, "Le Noeud du Problème Colonial: Les Évolués," in *Mensuel de Documentation*, February–March 1946. (Emphasis in the original.)

3. This is the basis of Samuel Huntington's theory of the "clash of civilizations." Huntington's argument helped to galvanize anti-immigrant rhetoric in the United States during the early and middle 1990s. Samuel P. Huntington, "The Clash of Civilizations?" in *Foreign Affairs* (Summer, 1993), pp. 22–49.

4. For discussions about public debates over the loss of or threats to French national identity see: Patrick Ireland, "*Vive le jacobinisme: Les étrangers* and the Durability of the Assimilationist Model in France," *French Politics and Society* 14:2 (Spring, 1996), pp. 33–46. See also in the same issue: Virginie Guiraudon, "The Reaffirmation of the Republican Model of Integration: Ten Years of Identity Politics in France," pp. 47–57; and Riva Kastoryano, "Immigration and Identities in France: The War of Words," pp. 58–66.

5. Basil Davidson, *The Black Man's Burden: Africa and the Curse of the Nation-State* (New York: Times Books, 1992), p. 10.

6. Lynn Hunt, *Politics, Culture, and Class in the French Revolution* (Berkeley: University of California Press, 1984), pp. 10–11.

7. Significant and insightful contributions to the study of cultural politics and identity, French and otherwise, in recent years include: Herman Lebovics, *Mona Lisa's Escort: André Malraux and the Reinvention of French Culture* (Ithaca and London: Cornell University Press, 1999); Herman Lebovics, *True France: The Wars over Cultural Identity, 1900-1945* (Ithaca and London: Cornell University Press, 1992); Kathleen Wilson, *The Sense of the People: Politics, Culture and Imperialism in England, 1715-1785* (Cambridge: Cambridge University Press, 1998); Richard F. Kuisel, *Seducing the French: The Dilemma of Americanization* (Berkeley: University of California Press, 1996); Victoria de Grazia, *How Fascism Ruled Women: Italy, 1922-1945* (Berkeley: University of California Press, 1992); Mary Louise Roberts, *Civilization Without Sexes: Reconstructing Gender in Postwar France, 1917-1927* (Chicago and London: The University of Chicago Press, 1994); and Thongchai Winichakul, *Siam Mapped: A History of the Geo-Body of a Nation* (Honolulu: University of Hawaii Press, 1994).

8. David Laitin's work on Nigeria is one of the best studies on that phenomenon in post-colonial African societies. David D. Laitin, *Hegemony and Culture: Politics and Religious Change among the Yoruba* (Chicago: The University of Chicago Press, 1986). Other important works on this subject include: Jean-François Bayart, *The State in Africa: The Politics of the Belly*, trans. Mary Harper, Christopher and Elizabeth Harrison (London and New York: Longman, 1993); and John Iliffe, *Africans: The History of a Continent* (Cambridge: Cambridge University Press, 1995).

9. Ann Laura Stoler and Frederick Cooper, "Between Metropole and Colony: Rethinking a Research Agenda," in Frederick Cooper and Ann Laura Stoler, eds.,

Tensions of Empire: Colonial Cultures in a Bourgeois World (Berkeley: University of California Press, 1997), pp. 4, 1.

10.   Pierre Bourdieu and Loïc J. D. Wacquant, *An Invitation to Reflexive Sociology* (Chicago: The University of Chicago Press, 1992), pp. 16, 103, 100, 101. For further discussion on the notion of a "field" and its corollary, the "habitus," see: Pierre Bourdieu, *Language and Symbolic Power*, trans. Gino Raymond and Matthew Adamson (Cambridge: Harvard University Press, 1991).

11.   For a discussion of the multifarious ways in which individuals or groups are "authorized" to speak on behalf of another individual or group see: Michel de Certeau, *Heterologies: Discourse on the Other*, trans. Brian Massumi (Minneapolis: University of Minnesota Press, 1986); Gayatri Chakravorty Spivak, "Can the Subaltern Speak?" in Cary Nelson and Larry Grossberg, eds., *Marxism and the Interpretation of Culture* (Urbana: University of Illinois Press, 1988); and Bourdieu, *Language and Symbolic Power*.

12.   CAOM, 1/ AP/2147, Governor Henri Laurentie, "Le Noeud du Problème Colonial: Les Évolués," in *Mensuel de Documentation*, February–March 1946.

13.   For important work on the "legitimization" process see: Terence Ranger and Olufemi Vaughan, eds., *Legitimacy and the State in Twentieth-Century Africa: Essays in Honour of A. H. M. Kirk-Greene* (Oxford: The Macmillan Press Ltd., 1993); Bayart, *The State in Africa*; Jürgen Habermas, *Jürgen Habermas on Society and Politics*, trans. and ed. Steven Seidman (Boston: Beacon Press, 1989); and Gayatri Chakravorty Spivak, "The Politics of Interpretations," in Gayatri Chakravorty Spivak, *In Other Worlds: Essays in Cultural Politics* (New York and London: Routledge, 1988).

14.   For a discussion of the ways in which the notion of *la mission civilisatrice* shaped imperial policy see: Alice L. Conklin, *A Mission to Civilize: The Republican Idea of Empire in France and West Africa, 1895–1930* (Stanford: Stanford University Press, 1997), pp. 2-3.

15.   Stoler and Cooper, "Between Metropole and Colony," in Cooper and Stoler, eds., *Tensions of Empire*, p. 3.

16.   Homi K. Bhabha, *The Location of Culture* (London and New York: Routledge, 1995), p. 86. (Emphasis in the original.)

17.   Michel Foucault, *The History of Sexuality: Volume I: An Introduction* (New York: Vintage Books, 1990), pp. 100, 101.

18.   Bourdieu, Language and Symbolic Power, pp. 72, 105.

19.   Antonio Gramsci, *Selections from the Prison Notebooks of Antonio Gramsci*, trans. and eds. Quintin Hoare and Geoffrey Nowell Smith (New York: International Publishers, 1992), p. 12.

20.   Partha Chatterjee, *Nationalist Thought and the Colonial World: A Derivative Discourse?* (Minneapolis: University of Minnesota Press, 1998).

21.   Bayart, *The State in Africa*, pp. 110–115.

22.   Mahmood Mamdani, *Citizen and Subject: Contemporary Africa and the Legacy of Late Colonialism* (Princeton, N.J.: Princeton University Press, 1996), p. 18.

23.   Important recent studies of the Western-educated elite, their ascendancy during the period of decolonization, and the connections to Africa's current crises include: Davidson, *The Black Man's Burden*; Achille Mbembe, "The Banality of Power and

the Aesthetics of Vulgarity in the Postcolony," *Public Culture* 4:2 (Spring 1992); Bayart, *The State in Africa*; Mamdani, *Citizen and Subject*; George B. N. Ayittey, *Africa Betrayed* (New York: St. Martin's Press, 1992); and George B. N. Ayittey, *Africa in Chaos* (New York: St. Martin's Griffin, 1999). The quote is taken from: Ayittey, *Africa Betrayed*, p. 7.

24.   Mamdani, Citizen and Subject, p. 3.

25.   Ayittey, *Africa Betrayed*, p. 94.

26.   This issue is also discussed in: John Chipman, *French Power in Africa* (Oxford: Basil Blackwell, 1989). Recent events in Côte d'Ivoire have provided striking evidence of that continued role. At the time of this writing, France has several thousand troops on the ground in that country ostensibly to preserve the peace following an as yet unresolved civil war that traces its origins to a 1999 military coup. France is also the primary broker of the peace accord that is designed to end the fighting between government forces and two main rebel groups. In the summer of 2003 France also took the lead in a peacekeeping operation in the Democratic Republic of Congo in an effort, as yet unsuccessful, to end that country's brutal and complex war dating to 1998.

27.   Some important works in the field of immigration include: Gérard Noiriel, *Le Creuset français: Histoire de l'immigration, XIXe—XXe siècles* (Paris: Seuil, 1988); Maxim Silverman, *Deconstructing the Nation: Immigration, Racism, and Citizenship in Modern France* (London and New York: Routledge, 1992); Alec G. Hargreaves, *Voices from the North African Immigrant Community in France: Immigration and Identity in Beur Fiction* (New York: Berg, 1991); Donald L. Horowitz and Gérard Noiriel, eds., *Immigrants in Two Democracies: French and American Experiences* (New York: New York University Press, 1992); and Yves Lequin, dir., *Histoire des étrangers et de l'immigration en France* (Paris: Larousse, 1992).

28.   Paul Gilroy, *The Black Atlantic: Modernity and Double Consciousness* (Cambridge: Harvard University Press, 1996), p. 4.

Chapter One
Escaping Their Milieu:
Colonial Transgressions and the Great War

In the waning months of the First World War, Gabriel Angoulvant, governor general of French West Africa, wrote, "The war, by its long duration and by the exigencies of the struggle, upset all our expectations; it inexorably accelerated the trajectory [and the] evolution [of colonial society] under conditions that no one could have predicted.... The war was for our West African colonies a veritable moral disaster."[1] That "moral disaster," though, was not calculated in the thousands of soldiers from the colonies who fell on European battlefields, nor was it measured in terms of economic dislocation and depressed world markets. Rather, colonial administrators, West African elites, and metropolitan politicians located the tragedy of the 1914–1918 war in the cultural disruption it was perceived to have induced not only in AOF, but in France as well. Mary Louise Roberts calls this a "discourse of cultural pessimism" that she argues was reflected in the debates on gender and sexuality in the post-war world. However, if gender issues were central to how the war experience was understood by those who lived through it and "certain images of female identity...provided the French with a compelling, accessible way to discuss the meaning of social and cultural change," alterations in the colonial dynamic also strongly informed post-war debates about French citizenship and what it meant—and took—to be culturally "French."[2]

This chapter explores several transformations within the French colonial field induced by wartime circumstances and the apperception of those experiences by the participants. One of the most significant of those changes was the coming into prominence in West Africa of a new social category—the *évolué* or French-educated elite. Blaise Diagne, elected to the French parliament as deputy from Senegal on the eve of the "Great War," symbolized the aspirations and rise of this new "class." His actions in the Chamber of Deputies during the conflict, backed by supporters in AOF and

France, profoundly influenced debates about French citizenship, systems of governance in the colonies, and the relationship between West Africa and the metropole. Concomitantly, they also tended to circumscribe the possibilities for resistance to colonial rule as opposition to Dakar's policies was mobilized and channeled in directions that were largely reflected in Diagne's perceptions of Africa and France. The emergence of this new elite during the war forced a rethinking of what it meant to be French—at what point one could be considered "fully" French—through their agitation to participate in the administration of AOF and France as citizens of a greater France.

However, as the *évolué* became an important factor in the colonial empire and a wave of threatening rural rebellions plagued the West African federation, some in the imperial hierarchy wondered if the *mission civilisatrice* ostensibly practiced to that point should not be reconsidered and reformulated.[3] The sense of "political disorder, economic disorder, social disorder, [and] administrative disorder"[4] growing numbers of colonialists attributed to misguided indigenous policies, contributed to the valorization of a new discourse of cultural authenticity that took root in AOF and the metropole at that time. This rhetoric not only informed administrative practice in West Africa, but in addition justified a retreat from wartime promises to extend citizenship rights to colonial subjects who served in the defense of France. However, the language of cultural authenticity also brought the question of the right to speak to the fore in the colonial field—of who is authorized to represent (in all the meanings of the term) the African colonial subject and the French citizen. As such, some among the *évolués* appropriated and rearticulated notions of the authentic African and the authentic European circulating throughout the imperial framework to challenge colonial rule and legitimate assertions to leadership in AOF as well as membership in the French national patrimony.

One's right to speak on behalf of the "real" African or a "true" France[5] was inextricably linked to the idea of "being from there" or of having issued from a given cultural milieu.[6] Prior to the 1914–1918 war, the colonial administrator possessed a near monopoly in the representation of the "real" France to the colonial subject. For the "indigenous" population of AOF, the French official was "France." Further, the colonist who returned to France after a sojourn overseas claimed the right to speak on behalf of and describe the "authentic" African to metropolitan audiences.[7] In fact, the French administrator also claimed the authority to determine the veritable African culture for the West African subject.[8]

The requirements of total war, however, inaugurated a period of massive border migrations and transgressions that challenged the colonist's exclusive privilege to speak. Hundreds of thousands of West Africans were enlisted—willingly or through coercion—in the war effort and gained a first-hand and unmediated experience of the metropole. According to police reports, the "indigenous" populations in the colonies and in the metropole regarded the veteran who returned to West Africa or the colonial subject who remained in France after the cessation of hostilities as a legitimate voice in discussions of the real France and the true nature of African society.[9] Thus, during the war years the circulation of ideas and bodies across borders—mental, physical, and social—widened in scope and significantly reconfigured the colonial field. Contemporaries often attributed the credit and the blame for these changes to one person—the deputy from Senegal, Blaise Diagne.[10] How did Diagne become a cultural signifier for the fundamental transformations that afflicted the French imperial framework? What implications did this and the changes outlined above have for the trajectory of French colonialism and the processes of decolonization? To address these questions our story must begin with a discussion of Diagne's rise as an organic intellectual of the new elite from AOF.

Citizens, Subjects, and the New Elite from AOF

Alice Conklin argues that French expansion in the late nineteenth century was bound up with the notion of a *mission civilisatrice*, which "rested upon certain fundamental assumptions about the superiority of French culture and the perfectibility of humankind.... [It also] assumed that the Third Republic had a duty and a right to remake 'primitive' cultures along lines inspired by the cultural, political, and economic development of France."[11] This was made explicit in 1885 by one of the most prominent figures in the annals of French imperialism, Prime Minister Jules Ferry. In a speech before the Chamber of Deputies justifying the colonial adventures initiated during his watch, Ferry explained, "There is for the superior races a right...[and] an obligation...to civilize the inferior races."[12] The ideology of a civilizing mission embraced by Ferry and subsequent generations of French colonialists left its deepest imprint in the "Four Communes" of Senegal—Gorée, Dakar, Rufisque, and St. Louis, the base from which the federation of French West Africa later grew. In those cities the residents were accorded the rights of French citizens, including the privilege of electing a deputy to the Chamber in Paris, had local governmental institutions, and were generally subject to metropolitan civil laws. G. Wesley Johnson describes Senegal as "a 'pilot' colony" that served as a testing ground for colonial policy throughout West

Africa and the empire as a whole.[13] However, what is striking is the extent to which policies—especially with regard to civic rights and citizenship—implemented in Senegal were *not* extended to the rest of the empire. The Four Communes became an increasingly special case in the French colonial field and it is that specialness that provided the institutional context for it being an originating space for leaders of the anti-colonial movements during France's rule in West Africa. Thus, the residents of the Four Communes were uniquely situated in the imperial framework to have a decisive impact on the trajectory of decolonization and in shaping post-colonial West Africa and France. Finally, the inhabitants of those cities were more likely to be immediately effected by the decisions and acts of colonial administrators and the currents within the political culture of the metropole.

The special status of the Four Communes dated to 1790 when the revolutionary government in Paris passed a law that "authorized" residents of all France's overseas territories "to make known their views on the constitution [then being drafted], [as well as] legislation and administrative matters that concern[ed] them."[14] However, it was the law of 16 pluviôse An II (4 February 1794) that raised and linked the issues of citizenship, anti-colonialism, and republicanism. That act, passed by the Committee of Public Safety, not only abolished slavery throughout the French empire, it also declared all freed slaves—in fact all residents of territory under French administration—citizens of an undivided republic entitled to equal rights and full representation in the central government.[15] Even though Napoléon reinstated slavery in 1802, placed the colonies under special laws, and rescinded their right to participate in metropolitan government, each subsequent return of republican rule to France brought the reinstatement of some form of citizenship and representation to the overseas territories.[16] With the advent of the Third French Republic in 1870 Senegal was again accorded a deputy to the French parliament, a post continuously filled from 1879.[17]

What distinguished the *originaires*—the term that denoted those born in the Four Communes—from other West Africans, however, was not the rights accorded to them, since those enabling acts were extended to all residents of overseas territories at the time, but the failure to extend those privileges to others as they were brought under French control. Thus, while the population of AOF (administratively established in 1895) exceeded 12 million by 1914, less than 100,000 residents of that vast territory were accorded the basic rights of French citizens—either as settlers from the metropole or as "indigenous citizens," a euphemism for *originaires*. Despite their small numbers, though, developments among the new urban elite in the federation strongly configured the cultural framework for devising systems of colonial rule, structuring resistance to those regimes of power, and articulating French and African identities.[18] In other words, they were a constituency viewed as vital to and exemplary of the success of French colonialism. Moreover, they had knowledge of and practical experience with the rules of metropolitan and colonial politics. As such, they engaged with French officials and colonial administrators in ways that others in Senegal or West Africa could not.

Nonetheless, while the *originaires* possessed the ability to elect a deputy to the Chamber and participate in local politics, their status as citizens of France remained ambiguous in the early 1900s. If a resident of the Four Communes migrated to the metropole or any other part of the colonial empire, did he (women were still excluded from most civic rights in France and the colonies) retain his rights as a citizen? Could a native of Senegal continue to participate in politics and enjoy judicial protection under French law outside the Four Communes?

In an attempt to settle those questions and define the status of the *évolué* within the colonial field William Ponty, governor-general of AOF, issued an order in May 1912 that enflamed political passions in the Four Communes and contributed to Diagne's electoral success two years later. The *arrêté* promulgated on 25 May 1912 declared that the "accession of indigenous peoples of French West Africa to the status of French citizen" had to be an individual act, not, as previously assumed and practiced the fate of birth. In addition, the order stipulated that naturalization could not take place unless the applicant had met the following conditions: "1. To have proved devotion to French interests or to have occupied, with distinction, for a period of at least ten years, a position in a public or private French enterprise. 2. To know how to read and write in French. 3. To have a stable means of support and to be of good morals and lead a clean life." The language requirement could be waved if the applicant was decorated with the *Légion d'honneur*, a military medal, and those who it was determined had rendered valuable service to France or the colony.[19] Through this act Ponty sought to standardize the naturalization process and establish an "objective" and "rational" basis for the determination of who could and could not be considered "French." In addition, it conformed to widely held notions of French identity—dedication to the nation, individualism, and rational order—in the period prior to the First World War.

However, Ponty's act unintentionally helped to precipitate the emergence of the *évolués* as a self-conscious and autonomous social category within the colonial field and provoked the first serious challenges to France's authority in the region since the subjugation of Samori Touré in 1898. Furthermore, the *arrêté* influenced a pattern of debate about French identity and the relationship between citizens and subjects that was intensified and broadened during the 1914-1918 war.[20] Ponty's order led to thousands of *originaires* being struck off the electoral rolls. Also, it meant that those *originaires* who ventured outside the administrative limits of the Four Communes were subject to the *indigénat* law code, as well as "tribal" justice. The *indigénat* permitted overseas administrators to imprison colonial subjects without charge for up to five days for any offense—real or imagined—deemed detrimental to imperial government. Those transgressions included, "any crime committed by an African employed in the administration or against such an agent; offenses committed by African soldiers in complicity with civilians; usurpation of title or function; illegal wearing, with harmful intent, of uniforms belonging to agents of public authority; breach of public ordinances; any offense prejudicial to the state, colony, or public administration."[21] In other words, Dakar asserted that the protection and rights accorded Africans born in Dakar, St. Louis, Gorée, and Rufisque were geographically situated, not individually held—unless the individual had undergone a rigorous naturalization process. Such a claim actually contradicted the individualism said to be fundamental to French culture and identity. However, colonialists justified the creation of what amounted to two tiers of Frenchness on the grounds of the unique conditions found in the imperial context. Commenting on the 1912 order, Minister of Colonies Albert Lebrun explained, "It seemed to us that this status of French citizenship had to be able to be accorded, through these kinds of measures, to the natives of this Colony who have been brought close to us by their education, who have adopted our civilization and our mores or who have been noted by their services."[22] In other words, they were close to being French, but still distinct.

The 1912 *arrêté* was designed to eliminate the ambiguity of the *originaires'* status by erecting two rigid categories within the colonial field. One status was that of citizen with the full range of rights guaranteed by the Third Republic's constitution. The other was that of the subject where the person designated as such possessed no rights with regard to France and was under the arbitrary and authoritarian rule of colonial administrators, or their agents—described as traditional or tribal authorities. This is a pattern of imperial rule Mamdani argues was common to the colonial experience in Africa, creating what he terms the "bifurcated State."[23] However, we should not read the intentions of colonial authorities as accomplished facts. While the administrations in AOF and Paris attempted to erect two legal categories—the much-discussed "Colonizer" and "Colonized"—this was more part of a continuous project of defining categories by all participants engaged in the colonial field than it ever was an actualized structure. As Gyan Prakash writes, "[I]f the colonial rulers enacted their authority by constituting the 'native' as their inverse image, then surely the 'native' exercised a pressure on the identification of the colonizer. I refer here not to a dialectic but to the dissemination of the self and the other that ensued as the identity and authority of the colonizer were instituted in the language and the figure of the 'native.'"[24]

While French *colons*—those residents of the Four Communes who had migrated from the metropole—and the offspring of French and West Africans (*assimilés* or *métis*) were unaffected by Ponty's decision and did not have to submit to an individual naturalization process, those *originaires* of "pure African" descent were suddenly threatened with the loss of their special status in the colonial field and of being subsumed in the pool of millions of *sujets* of the empire. In effect, by stripping the African *originaires* of their historic rights, the 1912 order contributed to the formation of the *évolués'* sense of themselves as a distinct social category within the colonial framework. By targeting those without a "blood" connection to France, the *arrêté* also provided a conceptual space for the articulation of a separate "African" identity that would later be exploited by French colonialists and more immediately by prominent figures among the French-educated elite.

The transformation of the *originaires* into a source of opposition to Dakar's policies undermined established imaginings of the place occupied by the *évolués* in France's imperial mission. As the institutions of colonial government were erected in the late nineteenth and early twentieth centuries in West Africa, French authorities were confronted with a lack of personnel to fill the federation's growing bureaucratic needs. Therefore, the administration tended to rely upon local people that had been instructed in the French language, familiarized with France's legal codes, and integrated into the money economy increasingly dominated by the industrial capitalist societies of Europe and North America. The French colonizers ascribed the label "*évolué*" to this category of schoolteachers, interpreters, clerks, and intermediaries who maintained connections with "native" cultures, societies, and frequently the Islamic faith.[25] The term itself reflected the permeation of social Darwinist discourse throughout European societies by the late nineteenth century. The belief that some cultures were more "civilized" than or superior to others and that history had a progressive dimension—moving from primitive to advanced—constituted an intrinsic part of French national identity as propounded by the Third Republic's leaders. This idea animated France's overseas expansion in the last decades of the 1800s and provided an ideological framework through which to legitimize the fact of imperial rule. Consequently, those people the French colonizers decided had made the first steps out of their initial state toward becoming French were said to have "evolved" in comparison to their countrymen. Yet, what perhaps most distinguished the *évolué* from the rest of West African society was their place of residence. The French-trained elite was an urban social group, but one with strong familial and historic links to rural AOF. Catherine Coquery-Vidrovitch describes African cities as geographic spaces of colonization. Urban centers served as meeting points between cultures, as well as sites of cultural production. Thus, the Western-educated elite with connections that transcended the discursive boundaries of "Europe" and "Africa," was uniquely situated as an agent of cross-colonization. She writes, "Part integrated with the new society, they navigate between the two cultures, daily inventing the modes of adaptation that implicitly give advantage to the strongest of the two." Consequently, the *évolué* can be said to have occupied a separate physical space from that of the native subject, yet only part way between metropolitan and indigenous life.[26]

The 1912 order required that the *évolué*, to become a naturalized citizen of France, renounce those personal and historical connections to their cultures of origin, and take on a French identity defined by colonial authorities. At the same time the language of the *arrêté* recast the new urban elite as still fundamentally "African" and in need of further "civilization" by France. At best the *évolués* could be regarded as "half-French" and, therefore, ineligible to participate in the decision-making processes that directly affected their lives.[27] As a result, Ponty's act contributed to the articulation of *évolué* self-identity as belonging to both "French" and "African" cultures, and necessarily precluded the delineation of neatly separated categories of citizen and subject.

The order also exposed the political vulnerability of the French-educated elite within the colonial field. Even though black Africans were a substantial majority of electors in the Four Communes, local government and the deputyship were controlled by a coalition of *colons* and *assimilés*. In 1912, however, a small group of *évolués*, among them a young lawyer named Lamine Guèye, answered Ponty's order with the establishment Senegal's first indigenous political organization, the *Jeunes Sénégalais*. A year later, the journal *La Démocratie du Sénégal* was founded as a voice for the *évolué* community in the Four Communes while it organized the discontent elicited by Ponty's act and mobilized the *originaires* as a community with shared and unique interests.[28]

Confronted with growing agitation among the new urban elite, and with legislative elections due in just over a year, Ponty issued a new order in 1913 that explicitly exempted the *originaires* from the *indigénat* and permitted them to participate in electoral politics within the Four Communes.[29] However, Ponty's attempt to defuse the political crisis came too late and was too limited in scope. While the *originaires* were protected from the *indigénat* even outside the Four Communes and were recognized as electors, their status as citizens of France remained unsettled. By the time Ponty revised his 1912 proclamation, the circles around *Jeunes Sénégalais* and *La Démocratie du Sénégal* had resolved to put up a candidate in the campaign for Senegal's representative to the Chamber of Deputies that would defend the traditional rights of the *originaires* from present and future infringements. After much wrangling, *La Démocratie du Sénégal* endorsed a little-known customs official, Blaise Diagne, as their candidate in 1914 to contest the seat occupied by the *métis* François Carpot.

While Diagne lacked the political experience of his campaign manager Galandou Diouf, who in 1909 became the first black African to win a seat on a municipal council, and the legal acumen of Lamine Guèye, the native of Gorée was an articulate voice for the frustrations and discontent of the *évolué* community. Born in 1872 on the island of Gorée, off the coast of present-day Senegal, Diagne's early biography exemplifies the processes through which the new French-educated elite in AOF was constituted. As an *originaire* Diagne was automatically placed among an elite within the colonial field. He was educated in French colonial schools and, for a brief period, in the metropole. After terminating his studies, Diagne was employed in the customs service of the empire where he served for over twenty years. That vocation took him to the French possessions of Dahomey, French Congo, Gabon, Réunion, Madagascar, and, finally, French Guyana. Throughout his career, Diagne openly expressed his frustration at the lack of social mobility within the civil service for those who were not natives of the metropole. The willingness to voice his displeasure to imperial officials contributed to Diagne's frequent reassignment. However, it also brought him to the attention of those in the Four Communes who were searching for a spokesperson when the administration in French West Africa appeared to be further restricting opportunities for the *évolués*.[30]

According to Diagne, the "program of 1914 asserted for my racial brothers the full quality of French citizens, with all its prerogatives and also all its responsibilities. One can be French and Muslim," he argued.[31] As Diagne traveled throughout the Four Communes, the former customs agent insisted that the *originaires* be endowed with full French citizenship, a quality that traveled with the individual, not one that was geographically restricted. However, Diagne's campaign went further than simply asserting the rights of the *originaires*. He insisted that citizenship entailed obligations upon the *évolué* as well. For Diagne, the most important obligation of citizenship was military service. But, he maintained that, as full citizens of France, the *originaires* should serve in the regular French armed forces, not the separate colonial army.[32]

To the surprise of officials in Dakar, Diagne defeated his rivals and ended the dominance of Senegalese politics by the *métis* and *colons*. While the government in Paris hardly took notice of the events in West Africa, those developments soon had an important impact in France because less than a month after Diagne took his seat as the first black African elected to the Chamber of Deputies the metropole found itself at war. If the conflict did not exactly "furnish the occasion to definitively establish" the *évolués'* status as citizens, it did lend added importance to Diagne's electoral triumph, a prominence the new deputy wasted no time in exploiting.[33]

The idea of colonial subjects contributing to the defense of France was not new in 1914. In fact, one of the early justifications for French expansion was the need to augment a population falling further behind that of Germany. West Africa, according to some well-placed French officers, was uniquely suited to close the perceived manpower gap because it was said to possess a vast "reserve of military forces" whose place in the event of war would be "on the frontline."[34] France had the "right to appeal" to its colonies, it was argued, because the metropole had "brought to our colonies prosperity and peace. We have delivered them from epidemics, raids, periodic famines, and civil wars. We have shed the most precious of our blood to ward off the great invaders and the slave merchants."[35] This declaration is striking in several regards. First, it was a clear statement of the *mission civilisatrice*, presented here as already an unmitigated success. Second, the proclamation masked the violence and dislocation induced by colonial expansion itself. In the name of bringing civilization to the "backward peoples" of Africa and delivering them from internecine warfare, France embarked on a conquest that profoundly disrupted African societies and created the conditions for new conflicts. Now, in the name of having brought peace to Africa, France appealed to its colonial subjects to participate in war. Yet, that appeal was couched in the language of reciprocal obligations. Since, it was claimed, France brought a measure of "civilization" to Africa the colonized must share in the defense of that civilization at a time when it was imperiled. This rhetoric dovetailed with that practiced by Diagne during the 1914 campaign and opened a conceptual space for the new deputy to press the claims of the *évolué* to full citizenship through demonstrating their loyalty to France.[36]

When war broke out in the summer of 1914, Diagne conveyed to the ministry of colonies his confidence "in the patriotism of [his] indigenous compatriots" and asked that the government, "by decree," authorize the electors of Senegal to participate "for the duration of the war" as equals in the French military.[37] However, if there was a general consensus on using colonials to defend France, there was strong disagreement on whether they should—or could—be integrated with the regular French military. Stung by Diagne's surprising electoral triumph, Ponty objected to Diagne's attempt to have the *originaires* serve as regular French soldiers. He wrote, "I am of the opinion to accept [their service] only on the condition [that they form] distinct companies administratively attached to the colonial infantry battalions of AOF."[38] The ministry of war added the further objection that incorporation of the *originaires* in the same units as "full" French citizens would foster divisions among the indigenous populations of AOF and, thereby, weaken France's hold on the territory.[39]

The disagreement between Ponty and Diagne over how to deploy recruits from AOF pointed to the growing rivalry for leadership of the subject populations between the colonial administration and the new urban elite of the Four Communes. Both the governor general and the Senegalese deputy understood that the outcome of that debate would have a direct impact on the status of the *originaires* within the imperial framework. Their integration into the regular French military would add legitimacy to the claims of the *évolués* to full citizenship. On the other hand, should Ponty's position prevail, the *originaires* would be administratively linked with the *sujets* and once again confront the loss of their special position within the colonial field.

When the war bogged down in the trenches of northern France by early 1915, the need for reinforcements from AOF became more urgent. This made it imperative that a decision be reached as to the proper deployment of recruits from the Four Communes. In order to resolve the dispute, Diagne proposed a law that stipulated the *originaires* be integrated in the regular French military. In addition, the law declared unequivocally that natives of the Four Communes were "French citizens and enjoy all the rights assured by the Constitution."[40] However, the proposal only widened the growing rift between the colonial administration in AOF and its native auxiliaries, since Dakar interpreted Diagne's actions as a usurpation of the colonial administration's ability to command in West Africa.[41] This dispute highlighted the unique structural conditions operable in the field of engagement constituted by AOF and France. The presence in France of an elected representative for the indigenous population of West Africa precluded Dakar from acting unilaterally on questions of governance in the federation, at least with regard to the Four Communes. Furthermore, Diagne's measure contributed to disagreements mounting between Dakar and Paris over colonial policy, differences exacerbated by the Chamber's support of the legislation.

To many in the metropole, Diagne offered eloquent testimony to the success and benevolence of France's *mission civilisatrice*. The deputy from Senegal ceaselessly insisted on his Frenchness and the loyalty of those under France's tutelage.[42] Further, he did this in a language familiar to metropolitan citizens and republican politicians alike—the universalist rhetoric of the 1789 Revolution. Paris legitimized this discourse by casting the war as a struggle to defend "civilization, [which was] threatened by our enemies." France and its overseas empire, the government claimed, were united in a common struggle "to save...humanity."[43]

In an atmosphere of military necessity and republican enthusiasm, the Chamber overwhelmingly passed Diagne's law on 19 October 1915. However, the struggle within the colonial field over authority and specifically the place of the *évolué* therein only intensified.[44] While Diagne viewed the 1915 law as a means for consolidating the *évolués'* status as citizens of France, entitled to the full range of rights stipulated in the constitution,[45] others in the colonial administration saw the act in strictly military terms.[46] According to the latter, the only significant aspect of the new law concerned the deployment of *originaires* in regular French military units. Ponty's 1912 order still, consequently, served as the organic text determining citizenship in French West Africa.

Ponty's replacement in Dakar after 1914, François-Joseph Clozel, believed that according the new urban elite equality with metropolitan citizens threatened to undermine France's authority among the indigenous populations of AOF by creating a rival voice in the colonial field endowed with the same rights and prerogatives as those of the administration.[47] Angoulvant, at the time governor general of French Equatorial Africa (*Afrique Équatoriale française*—AEF), went even further and viewed Diagne's law as a prelude to the end of French rule in the colonies. He protested that once the "door was opened," the "35 million subjects" of the empire would not hesitate "to take advantage of the equal civil and political rights...to throw us into the sea."[48] Still others, while supporting Diagne's desire for equality, argued the 1915 law undermined France's commitment to govern all under its tutelage without distinction. Diagne's act, one official wrote, created an elite within AOF that aroused the animosity and jealousy of others who might aspire to similar rights or see their own position in West African society undermined. As such, "this law which in France appeared as an egalitarian measure, appeared in AOF as a measure contrary to all our principles of equality."[49]

Another point of contention centered on the meaning of *"originaire."* The 1915 law made all *originaires* citizens, but did not define exactly whom that was. Were children born to indigenous citizens outside the Four Communes automatically granted the same status as their parents? Also, what was the status of children produced by relationships between natives of the Four Communes and *sujets?*[50] Adhering to precedent, Dakar insisted that only those born in Dakar, Rufisque, Gorée, and St. Louis were entitled to protection under the 1915 law.[51] Such a reading suggested there were two types of French citizenship, one for metropolitan France and another for the Four Communes since children born of metropolitan citizens anywhere were automatically accorded the rights of their parents.

The controversy over the 1915 law revealed the reluctance of the colonial administration to ever accept West Africans as equal French citizens, no matter the level of "cultural attainment" or service rendered the nation. In addition, Dakar's refusal to embrace the *évolué* as fully "French" opened a space for the new urban elite to bid for the loyalty and leadership of the millions of West African subjects. Since the colonial state appeared reticent to extend the rights enjoyed by Frenchmen to Africans, the *évolué* was now in a position to claim it alone could deliver the "liberty" and "emancipation" promised by France's *mission civilisatrice.*[52] Some French politicians noted the retreat from Republican values evident in the actions of colonial officials. For example, one senator lamented, "Is it not regrettable that the administration of Senegal—the civil as well as the military—believed it could…hold certain racial prejudices or [privilege] certain interests of caste…in the pure and simple application of the [1915] law, [to impose] restrictions and limitations…contrary to the spirit [and the] letter of the texts voted" by the Chamber?[53]

To overcome Dakar's obstruction, Diagne proposed a new piece of legislation, made law on 29 September 1916, declaring "the natives of the *communes de plein exercice* of Senegal *and their descendents*" complete and equal citizens of France with those from the metropole.[54] As such, the *originaires* and all their children were to be considered citizens at all times, in any geographic location. Diagne's supporters in the Four Communes and among the colonials serving in the military deluged the Chamber with letters backing the new measure. "We are very happy to spill our blood for France, country of justice and liberty," Diouf wrote after participating in the Somme offensive.[55] Other communications indicated the growing influence of Diagne and the urban elite of the Four Communes among the *sujet* population, which was also shedding its blood in the defense of France. "We value this quality of French citizen they possess and [to which] we [too] have attached our blood," read one message.[56]

The 1916 Diagne law made it possible for non-*originaires* to attain citizenship rights through marriage to a native of the Four Communes and eliminated the requirement for the children of such relationships to undergo a tedious and often unsuccessful naturalization process. In addition, by declaring the *originaires* citizens no matter where they happened to be, the new law protected the political activities of the *évolué*, affording him or her the safety needed for effective oppositional activity. In other words, not only had the actions of the colonial government opened a space wherein the new urban elite could claim moral leadership in the fight for equality for all under French rule, but also, through Diagne's leadership, the *évolué* had attained the legal sanction to contest for political leadership in AOF.

That point was not lost on those within the imperial hierarchy. Accordingly, colonial officials asked Paris to consider the "very dangerous" implications of the measure.[57] Angoulvant claimed the privileges of the *originaires* engendered animosity throughout sub-Saharan Africa and led the *sujet* population to ask, "Why them and not us?" In addition, he argued, the law was bad for France. It "introduced in the French body politic, along side those quite honorable individuals, an immense majority of natives devoid of all French culture and all French mentality, and even some completely undesirable individuals." However, the strongest objection was that it undermined the authority of the "natural leaders of [Africa]" by "creating a new elite issuing from a population that is living in direct contact with the Europeans." This violated France's "promise to respect [the natives'] traditions, their beliefs, and their laws."[58]

The colonial state's concern that the new rights of the *originaires* "would shake the ancestral customs of these new French citizens [and African society] from the foundation to the summit" reflected the burgeoning of a new discourse of cultural authenticity then gaining sway in the colonial field.[59] Not only was the *évolué* a threat to French rule in West Africa, the new urban elite also posed a danger to their "true" selves, a peril from which Dakar was prepared to save them. However, if events in Paris worried overseas administrators, their worst fears seemed to be confirmed by the crises that engulfed AOF in 1915 and 1916.

Conscription, Rebellion, and the Language of Cultural Authenticity

In late 1916 Maurice Delafosse, noted ethnographer and director of political affairs in French West Africa, reported "grave political troubles" throughout the federation.[60] Those disturbances ranged from insubordination among recruits to full-scale armed rebellion against France.[61] According to Dakar, the erosion of French authority was induced by two wartime developments: the direct contact with the metropole gained by soldiers who had served in France and were now returning to the colonies, and recruitment itself.[62] Those circumstances "generated disorder" by undermining "the traditional [political and administrative] order of things" in the region. Moreover, they subverted redefined notions of France's colonial mission, which was increasingly couched in terms of "safeguarding native traditions," foremost among them being the institution of chieftaincy.[63]

As the Tricolor was carried further inland from the coast of Senegal in the late nineteenth century, France signed a number of treaties with local rulers that protected their position in return for fealty to the new colonial power.[64] Thus, while the official discourse of the intrepid colonizers claimed France was bringing the concepts of *Liberté, Égalité, Fraternité* to lands suffering under "tyranny without control...disorder...and anarchy,"[65] practical questions of rule forced often-unwilling administrators into deals with established native authorities. The celebrated colonialist Joseph Simon Gallieni devised the practice of leaving some of the pre-colonial elite in positions of authority and termed it *"la politique des races,"* a policy he claimed acknowledged the cultural and political differences between the various ethnic groups, and respected the "real authority" of the established elite.[66] More of an expediency than a commitment to multiculturalism, this method of rule provided the basis for the system of governance as it was organized at the end of the nineteenth century in West Africa.

The institutional command structure in the federation functioned as follows. The village or canton was at the base of the power hierarchy and was headed by an indigenous "chief." Several villages were grouped into subdivisions usually directed by an official of the colonial state, although occasionally a native authority might hold this position. Subdivisions were grouped in *cercles*, of which there were 108 in French West Africa, frequently governed by military officers. The *cercles* were subsumed in regions and supervised by colonial officials. Regions, in turn, were brought together to form a colony headed by a governor and colonies were united in the federation of AOF directed by the governor general based in the capital, Dakar.[67]

While "indigenous chiefs" were not accorded much legal power by the colonial government, the lack of a palpable French presence in many areas of AOF provided great latitude for the pre-colonial elite to exercise real authority in the "bush."[68] One of the most important duties, and powers, of the "traditional" elite was providing troops for the colonial army. When France went to war in 1914, this responsibility made them an important element of the metropole's combat plans. Consequently, to secure the forces France believed it needed from West Africa in order to compensate for its numerical weakness *vis–à–vis* Germany, Dakar had to rely upon the loyalty and effectiveness of the village chiefs. As encouragement, chiefs received financial compensation for each man taken away to serve on the Front. Such fiduciary incentives produced the desired results early, but later chiefs deliberately sent unfit men to the recruitment offices to gain payment from the colonial government, while keeping the fit males home to work in the fields they controlled.[69]

The *"armée noire"* was to be composed of both volunteers and conscripts.[70] However, the West African response to France's call to arms was disappointing.[71] In fact, Clozel reported that "the native electors of the Four Communes *de plein exercice* of Senegal have not contributed a single volunteer."[72] The failure of the *originaires* to sign up for military service in greater numbers prompted Clozel to make two important assertions in a letter written to the ministry of colonies in early 1916. The first was a criticism of the *évolués* who were pressing claims for citizenship, but remained reluctant to volunteer to defend France. Accordingly, the failure of the urban elite to rally to the flag in the metropole's time of need indicated their unworthiness for full citizenship rights. However, it should be recalled that the status of the *originaire* in the defense structure of France had not yet been settled. Until the question of their enlistment was resolved in favor of full integration in regular French units with the Diagne laws discussed above, the urban elite was unwilling to risk being assigned to units of the colonial army. Therefore, Clozel's claims reflected a dissonance in the perceived order of things as maintained by colonial administrators and the *évolués*.

The second point Clozel made was an argument in favor of the *voie d'appel*, as conscription was called in AOF.[73] In the *voie d'appel*, Dakar imposed quotas upon "tribal chiefs" of men to be delivered to a local *commission de recrutement* for enlistment. AOF delivered only 29,720 troops, volunteers and conscripts inclusive, in the war's first year.[74] This fell well short of Paris' earlier estimates of West Africa's potential in this regard. Compounding the disappointment with these results was the growing sense that there was no end in sight to the fighting.[75] These factors led the government general to increasingly turn to the *voie d'appel* to make up the shortfall of volunteers and to increase the quotas exacted on the various politico-ethnic units of the federation. As Marc Michel observes, this process tended "to restore the prestige and power of the chiefs" in the colonial field since they were situated as vital to the success of France's recruitment efforts in AOF.[76]

However, the increased use of forced conscription also induced rebellion throughout large areas of West Africa and nearly culminated in the collapse of French authority in the region. Despite the protests of some local administrators who regarded conscription as a "dangerous idea for the future of our domination,"[77] Clozel asserted AOF could still realize its imagined manpower potential and ordered a new levy of 50,000 troops at the end of 1915.[78] When word spread of the new "blood tax,"[79] as recruitment was labeled by veterans from AOF, hostility grew among the colonized populations. This discontent was "manifested by the evacuation of villages before our [recruitment] agents [arrived], by evasion of the best men, by self-inflicted mutilations or suicides and in the end by the efforts of the population to liberate by force the convoys of those recruited."[80] One official noted, "From the moment recruitment was announced the villages emptied from numerous points, either in part, or in total and the inhabitants took refuge far in the countryside or among the trees of the forest, waiting until all danger of being enlisted had passed. To bring them back, we had to negotiate for a long time or imprison the Chiefs and to impose upon them full punishment or judicial condemnation."[81]

By the summer of 1916 France faced insurrections that involved over 300,000 rebels.[82] Most of the uprisings were quickly put down by colonial troops that were better armed and organized than were the rebels. The operation against Bandiagara *cercle* in present-day Mali is exemplary of the methods used to quell the rebellions. At first, the colonial government allowed the revolt to run its course, during which several villages were razed by the rebels. Once the scope of the uprising had been determined and sufficient force was mustered, a police column moved into the trouble spot and methodically retook each village, driving the rebels further from their base of operations and food supply. Within two months, the rebels were exhausted and subdued. In all, 15 villages were destroyed, two pitched battles occurred, and hundreds were left homeless and relocated into internment camps.[83]

However, the government general faced an even greater threat to the federation's future: the mass exodus of populations from AOF to neighboring colonies, especially those controlled by Britain. The British colonies of

Nigeria and Gold Coast were the principal beneficiaries of the cross-border migration because the United Kingdom did not conscript its African subjects for duty in the trenches of Western Europe and wages paid for labor were generally higher and more regularly dispensed than was the case in AOF. For the authorities in Dakar, the movement of large numbers of *sujets* to the British colonies was a disaster that could cripple the future economic exploitation of the colony. Since the colonies were supposed to be self-sufficient and contribute not just soldiers, but economic resources to the metropole, the decline in population in AOF constituted a matter of grave concern in Paris and the federation.[84] Further, the migration to neighboring British colonies undermined France's claim that its method of colonial rule was more humanitarian and produced greater loyalty among the native population than that of its chief imperial rival.[85]

However, it was not until the arrival of Joost Van Vollenhoven in AOF as governor general in early 1917 that the protests of "bush administrators" against continuing recruitment gained a sympathetic ear. With Van Vollenhoven's appointment conscription was temporarily halted and the government general for AOF moved in a decidedly different direction in its conception of imperial rule and the relationship between colonizers and colonized.[86] For the new governor general, the "root of the discontent" afflicting the indigenous populations was the imposition of principles "incompatible" with African society. The application of these notions emanating from France, he claimed, "has disorganized native society and profoundly disturbed the populations" of AOF. The result was widespread "disillusion" with French rule as recruitment seemed to betray the colonizer's pledge to help "native society evolve according to its own traditions and its own statutes."[87] Further, Van Vollenhoven, advised by Delafosse, interpreted the convulsions of the previous years as evidence of the chiefs' importance in the colonial framework and the pre-colonial elite's legitimate authority within indigenous society. Acting on this reading of the situation in AOF, the governor general issued a circular on 15 August 1917 that "reestablished" the institution of chieftaincy throughout the federation and authorized the creation of a "council of notables" to assist the "traditional" rulers.[88]

The problem Dakar confronted in implementing this institutional reform was that where France received the most protracted resistance during the period of conquest indigenous power structures were dismantled and direct colonial administration was established. That meant Van Vollenhoven's circular put the colonial state in the position of having to create chiefs and (re)invent native tradition.[89] The actions of the administration, therefore, produced the structural space that necessitated and valorized the work of ethnographers in formulating colonial policy. In order to "rediscover" the "true" nature of African social organization, as well as the legitimate authorities to be entrusted with the title of chief, officials relied on ethnographic studies by people like Delafosse. The colonial government also appointed ethnographers as principle advisors in "native" and political affairs. Delafosse and his followers were henceforward provided with a state-sanctioned platform that privileged their vision of the veritable African and authentic indigenous society, a vision discussed in subsequent chapters.

In Van Vollenhoven's justification for the new administrative measures, he offered a revealing glance at the intense struggle for leadership then materializing in AOF. The explanatory note that accompanied the circular also provides an early indication of new conceptions of "authentic" African and French culture then being articulated in the colonial field. After crediting Delafosse as the "authority" in all "matters of native policy," the governor general advised:

> A colony is not an object in a laboratory and one cannot isolate French West Africa from the rest of the world in waiting to discover the methods that permit it to integrate with the rest of the world without danger.... There is a native policy...from which [it is asserted that] one cannot leave indigenous society to develop according to its own traditions and its own statutes.... [Accordingly] we have given the status of French citizen to several thousand Senegalese.... These, who are an elite, have learned from us how to speak of civilization and have been dazzled by our marvelous tales.... [However,] the black needs to feel secure in his family, in his village, in his traditions.... They live in collective societies where the individual does not have any rights and where, as a result, personalities are atrophied.... I think that we must clearly distinguish what must be done for the mass, which has to pursue its evolution in its own milieu, and what must be done for the elite, which needs to evolve increasingly in our milieu.... The auxiliaries of our administration are no longer natives; they live more [as Europeans than Africans].... This elite that is separated from its native milieu and to which it cannot return must be recognized by us and be better oriented by us.[90]

In the above statement Van Vollenhoven made three arguments that are significant for our purposes. First, he asserted that France had to reassess its relationship with West Africa and reconsider the premises of the *mission civilisatrice*.[91] The earlier policy of "substituting" metropolitan institutions for indigenous "customs," he argued, was misguided and in need of revision.[92] This assertion reflected the ongoing dispute between Paris and Dakar over which set of officials knew the "true" African and could best fulfill his or her needs evidenced in the earlier debate over the Diagne laws.

Second, Africa, it was discovered, had its own autochthonous forms of social organization that should be nurtured and respected. The effectiveness and scope of native challenges to French rule in 1915 and 1916 seemed to have proved that point. The fundamental institution of West African society as indicated in the 1917 circular was the chieftaincy. The "chief" was claimed to be the natural and legitimate head of distinct tribal groups, the boundaries between which would be determined by the colonial state. This assertion presented the pre-colonial elite as the only indigenous African leadership possible in the colonies and, therefore, they were the true auxiliaries of the imperial administration. Correspondingly, the change in administrative policy was a direct challenge to the *évolués'* expanding pretensions to leadership of the colonized populations as demonstrated through the activities and rhetoric of Diagne and his followers. In fact, the governor general contended that the *évolués* were no longer even African. Neither were they yet "truly" French and this justified the need for continued colonial rule of the *originaires* as well as the *sujets*. This is what Bhabha calls a process of "colonial mimicry," which he defines as "the desire [by the colonizer] for a reformed, recognizable Other, *as a subject of a difference that is almost the same, but not quite....* [It] is a discursive process by which the excess or slippage produced by the *ambivalence* of mimicry (almost the same, *but not quite*) does not merely 'rupture' the discourse, but becomes transformed into an uncertainty which fixes the colonial subject as a 'partial' presence."[93] Yet, the present study suggests that the "partial presence" that unsettles the hoped for colonial project is a privileged space of the educated elite, not of all "colonial subjects." In this way we can see how the binary formulation of colonizer and colonized is inadequate to describe the imperial relationship.

The third point of Van Vollenhoven's circular was the need to keep the new urban elite separate from the masses of West Africa. Included in this stratum were the veterans returning to AOF from the trenches of northern France. Since the colonials were often placed in the most dangerous circumstances of combat, many survivors received military decorations.[94] According to the terms of the 1915 and 1916 Diagne laws, those decorated veterans were eligible for citizenship, without having to satisfy the most stringent cultural requirements. Further, the *voie d'appel* took West African peasants and inserted them in a context where they acquired a working knowledge of French and were provided direct access to the ideas and customs of the metropole, something not possible at that time in rural AOF. One deputy described the process as follows, "In appealing to our subjects to cooperate in a military effort without precedent on the fields of battle in Europe, [the war] provokes the expatriation, then the return of the natives who have been in contact with European populations, with superior civilizations...." In conclusion, he expressed the hope that this contact did not lead to the spread of "pernicious ideas."[95]

Dangerous Liaisons: Diagne's 1918 Recruitment Campaign

By the end of 1917, however, the needs of Paris outweighed the desires of Dakar and a new levy of troops from AOF was announced.[96] The new appeal to West Africa was of an entirely different order than those that preceded it. First, all recruits were ostensibly to be volunteers. The *voie d'appel* was eliminated because of the troubles it was professed to have caused in 1915 and 1916. Second, and most significant, the campaign was to be led by the deputy from Senegal, Blaise Diagne, as "*Commissaire de la République*" with a stature and authority equal to that of the governor general in West and Equatorial Africa.[97] The changed nature of recruitment in 1918, itself the result of confrontations within the colonial field and their apperception by the agents involved, fundamentally altered the parameters and essence of the emergent struggles for authority in the imperial context. Because of the 1918 mobilization effort in AOF, the links between the patterns of social engagement in France and West Africa were deepened and transformed. Diagne's actions increased the impact of metropolitan politics and disputes on social life in the colonies, while it also expanded the affect of encounters overseas, and the issues that dominated public debate in those territories, on struggles within France. These changes were manifested in the intensified movement of bodies across borders as West Africans in large numbers were brought to the metropole to fight in defense of "French" civilization. There they established new relationships as well as a pattern of migration and physical exchange that persisted long after the war ended.

The "payment of a [new] blood tax"[98] was required because of the "prolongation of hostilities" in Europe and the fear of a new German offensive in the West. In addition, the recent revolutions in Russia had undermined the stability and military effectiveness of France's erstwhile ally in the East. "To obtain sufficient results [from the drive] without compromising the future of our colonial expansion," Prime Minister Georges Clemenceau made clear, "it appeared necessary to us to boldly resort to new methods." Diagne was chosen to head this vital mission because he "already represents an important fraction of West Africa which has proved its passionate devotion [to France]" and also because of "the strong influence he can personally exercise on his racial brothers."[99]

The decrees authorizing Diagne's 1918 mission point to the important position attained by the *évolués* within the colonial field. As a significant part of West African society, Paris asserted that the French-educated elite could not be ignored in matters concerning the federation. This challenged Van Vollenhoven's contention that the *évolué* was no longer connected to African society and should be kept apart from indigenous affairs. Further, Paris recognized Diagne as the public symbol of the new urban elite. In other words, the state sanctioned the deputy from Senegal as the spokesperson for this burgeoning social stratum and valorized his actions and discourse within the colonial framework. As such, the 1918 recruitment campaign highlighted increased tensions between administrators in French West Africa and Parisian officials over proper governance in the colonies. Those differences indicate the complexities of the colonial experience and caution against a monolithic reading of imperialism.[100] Lastly, by according the new Commissaire of the Republic powers commensurate with those of the governors general in Dakar and Brazzaville, the French government subsequently intensified the struggle for power unfolding in sub-Saharan Africa between colonial administrators, *évolués*, and the recently strengthened pre-colonial elite. Paris had effectively, and unintentionally, intervened in a fight of which it had paid little attention to that point. Moreover, Clemenceau's administration had, through the 1918 recruitment appeal, made the metropolitan state a legitimate arena wherein colonial confrontations could be played out.

However, even the government in Paris realized that Diagne's appeal as "a racial brother" was not enough to secure the results expected and demanded by the metropole. Thus, the Commissaire of the Republic arrived in Dakar in February backed by a series of reforms and promises directed at those non-citizens who were expected to respond to his appeal. The nature of those pledges further legitimated the *évolués'* bid for leadership in AOF by making the response to Diagne's call the condition for ameliorating the circumstances of the subjects' daily lives. Among the benefits offered was a blanket exemption from the *indigénat* not only for those who volunteered, but also "their wives and children" (article 1). In addition, access to French citizenship was opened and made easier for the recruits and their families (article 3). The naturalization procedure was refined to where a decorated soldier need only present himself before the *commandant de cercle* and formally renounce his personal status and accept French civil law to receive citizenship status. For his family, the veteran simply had to declare their willingness to be naturalized (article 4). The regional administrator then researched the "moral" background of the candidate and forwarded his findings to the lieutenant governor (article 5). The lieutenant governor subsequently issued his opinion and sent the entire application file to the governor general in Dakar who added his perspective and shipped the assembled documents to the ministry of colonies. All this had to take place within six months of the original request, significantly shortening the bureaucratic process and potentially allowing for a more rapid expansion of citizenship rights in West Africa (article 6).[101]

The powers accorded Diagne and the accompanying reform package created a furor throughout the administrative hierarchy of the federation. At the end of January 1918 Van Vollenhoven resigned in protest "because he did not believe that the governor general could share the powers and prerogatives of office with anyone else...within the colonial administration."[102] In addition, the state's sanctioning of Diagne's, and by implication the *évolués'* place in West African society ran counter to his conception of the "authentic" African and assertion that the pre-colonial elites were the natural leaders of the indigenous communities. Van Vollenhoven's replacement, Gabriel Angoulvant, proved a more enthusiastic partner in the tasks confronting the Commissaire of the Republic, despite his earlier opposition to Diagne's citizenship laws in 1915 and 1916.[103]

With the unequivocal support of Paris, the cooperation of the new leadership in Dakar, and 300,000 francs to cover expenses, Diagne began his mission among friendly crowds in the Four Communes in February 1918.[104] At a meeting in Rufisque at the end of that month over 10,000 people turned out to greet the new Commissaire of the Republic.[105] Throughout the cities of Dakar, Rufisque, Gorée, and St. Louis, Diagne was received as a hero. The population recognized the significance of an *originaire* who had attained a stature equivalent to that of the governor general. Diagne embodied, for a time, the possibilities for inclusion in the French national patrimony contained within a certain conception of the *mission civilisatrice*. His presence emboldened the *évolués* in their struggle with the colonial administration since he represented what could be attained through resistance.[106] By 1918 no one in West Africa possessed greater prestige or authority than the deputy from Senegal. However, the most striking aspect of Diagne's tour was not so much the enthusiasm with which his constituents welcomed him, rather it was his success in the "bush," among the rural communities of the federation. In fact, the deputy from Senegal made a concerted and calculated endeavor to bridge the widening gap between urban and rural populations in West Africa.

Diagne agreed with Van Vollenhoven's appraisal "that the revolts of [1915 and] 1916 were singly caused by political errors."[107] However, the

Commissaire of the Republic did not agree that the solution was reinforcing the authority of the pre-colonial elite and isolating the *évolués* within the colonial field. Rather, Diagne suggested that proper government in AOF rested upon establishing greater links between the new urban elite and the village chiefs.[108] For the deputy from Senegal, his tour of French West Africa demonstrated that he knew the "true" African better than the colonial administration. As one of them, a point Diagne never tired of making in his appeals, he could better communicate with the indigenous populations. He understood their fears and could overcome the West African native's reticence to fight on European battlefields. At the same time, Diagne presented himself, and by implication the *évolué*, as the essential link between France and West Africa. Being both "French" and "African," the *évolués* occupied a privileged position in the colonial field that enabled them to effectively represent French interests to the indigenous population while also conveying the concern of "Africans" to the metropolitan government. Diagne criticized both Van Vollenhoven and Delafosse for their "dangerous" and misguided image of Africa. He further urged the ministry of colonies to reject the ethnographer's request to be appointed governor of a West African colony, a petition accepted in Paris, the result of which was the termination of Delafosse's formal career in the colonies and a life-long bitter dispute between the two protagonists. Accordingly, Diagne's tour directly challenged the colonial administration's claim to a monopoly on the right to speak on behalf of the "African" and on behalf of the metropole.[109] The actual recruitment of large numbers of soldiers from the federation and their transport to France further weakened one of the earliest and most fundamental bases of colonial legitimacy: the assertion that Europeans alone could carry out the work of the "civilizing" mission.

Throughout his campaign Diagne utilized a two-pronged approach in appealing to the *sujet* population. One method was the mass meeting where he dealt directly with the West African people. The second technique was to secure the collaboration of village chiefs beforehand and make a joint entreaty on behalf of France and the local ethnic or tribal community.[110] Diagne's liaisons with the chiefs reflected the impact the rebellions of 1915 and 1916, as well as the shift in government policy and discourse under Van Vollenhoven, had had even on the new urban elite. Instead of posing as the replacement or implacable foe of the pre-colonial elite, the *évolués*, or at least some of them, were prepared to participate as partners with the chiefs in directing West African society.[111] This directly contradicted Dakar's claim to be the federation's co-administrator with the "traditional" authorities and undermined the effectiveness of Van Vollenhoven's reforms of the previous year, especially with regard to their political objectives internal to the federation.

Diagne's strategy produced results that exceeded even the most optimistic predictions. By the time the deputy from Senegal had returned to France in the summer of 1918, Angoulvant reported the levy had raised 73,230 troops for the war effort, well over the 50,000 set as a "high goal."[112] There was no question in the governor general's opinion that "a large part of this result comes back to the personal action of M. Diagne, to the moral authority that he exercises on his compatriots."[113] Diagne succeeded in 1918 where Dakar failed in 1915 and 1916. Instead of rebellion, the call up produced genuine enthusiasm, much of it based on a confidence in Diagne's ability to achieve redress of grievances held by the colonized population and the promises for social advancement made in connection to the appeal. Thus, the Commissaire of the Republic's tour contributed a large portion of the nearly 300,000 West Africans that served as soldiers for France in the war, of which over 30,000 died.[114]

Yet, even as Diagne worked his way across West Africa in the spring of 1918, opposition to the campaign within the federation mounted. Some wondered if the short-term expediency of sending thousands of West Africans to fight in Europe might not produce "dangerous" results in the future.[115] Even colonial administrators who were required to fulfill all Diagne's needs obstructed his efforts. Complaints surfaced about returning veterans that refused "to recognize any authority, neither that of the *chef de canton* nor even more so that of the village chief, nor even that of the administrator."[116] Others pointed to the "disastrous influence of M. Diagne in AOF"[117] and even Angoulvant commented on the "ideological movements" ostensibly inspired by Diagne.[118]

The protests against Diagne's campaign became more vehement and frequent in the spring and summer of 1918, after the new Bolshevik government in Russia signed a treaty ending its involvement in the First World War, a circumstance that I suggest was not coincidental. Anxieties surfaced in Dakar and Paris at that time that the "mental" stability of the West African soldiers was imperiled by exposure to subversive ideas developed in "a country quite different than that where they have spent the greater part of their existence."[119] Subjects whose previous contact, if any, with the colonial power had been through the person of an administrator or officer had now been to the metropole and formed their own opinions of France without the mediation of the colonial state. In addition, the recruit from AOF also offered an alternative perspective of West African society to the metropolitan citizen without the filter of colonial officials, ethnographers, or visiting representatives of the pre-colonial elite. This contributed, as we shall see later, to the elaboration of new anti-colonial movements and alternative imaginings of the "authentic" African.[120] The production and dissemination of knowledge about "France" and "Africa" was escaping the bounds imposed by imperial rulers in ways that called into question the established justifications for colonialism. Correspondingly, the hostility expressed toward Diagne's tour by some officials suggested not only that the civilizing mission had to be re-defined, but also the direction in which it was to be re-cast.

Contact with "alien" ideas, though, was not the sole source of consternation for imperial officials. The recruitment campaign of 1918 in AOF facilitated and magnified the constant movement across borders— physical, mental, and social—that shaped and transformed the colonial field. Administrators in Dakar and increasingly in Paris, viewed the transgression of the boundaries that separated metropole and colony as threats to the long-term stability of the overseas empire and, ultimately, to the metropole itself.[121] Mary Louise Roberts provides a convincing argument of how the "blurring of gender boundaries" in France during the post-war period reflected deep-seated anxieties about the future of French civilization.[122] However, the notion of "French civilization" was closely interwoven with colonial expansion and rule as well. If women crossing presumed sexual borders represented one preoccupation of 1920s France, colonial subjects who "have escaped their milieu and who, thus, find themselves at once on the margin of autochthonous society and that in which [they have] been placed" provided another site for cultural trepidation.[123]

To avoid potential "catastrophes" that could result from direct contact between colonial subjects and metropolitan society, officials in Dakar suggested returning veterans "retake their place...within their village, their caste and their family, under the voluntarily-accepted authority of their chiefs, of their instructors or their parents."[124] As Delafosse put it, the time had arrived at the close of hostilities in November 1918 "to re-Senegalize" the *tirailleurs*.[125] This meant, in addition, that France "repeal the decrees of 14 January 1918" that motivated many of the *sujets* to respond to Diagne's tour.[126] Thus, the immediate post-war years were not only characterized by attempts within the metropole to restore an imagined pre-war *belle époque*, it also involved a resurgence of a discourse of cultural authenticity that we observed being formulated during the Van Vollenhoven administration in Dakar. By the end of the Great War, then, the struggle to define the "true" nature of French and West African society, and who properly qualified for membership in each, had become a dominant motif of engagement in the colonial field and would remain so throughout the period of French rule in West Africa.

Conclusion

The conflict over what it meant to be "African" or "French" that became prevalent in AOF and the metropole by 1918 indicates the extent to which the 1914–1918 war transfigured the colonial field. By 1918 the *évolués* had emerged as an important social category within the imperial framework. Led by their elected representative Blaise Diagne, the new urban elite engaged with the colonial and metropolitan states to shape definitions of citizenship and what it meant to be French. Further, they insisted that "in return" for a "blood tax" colonial subjects should be accorded easier access to the rights of French citizens.[127] This marked a bid on the part of the *originaires* for leadership of the rural *sujet* population that challenged Dakar's claim to be the sole legitimate authority in the federation.

The colonial administration responded to that development not by welcoming "the assimilation of new Frenchmen,"[128] but by questioning both the "Africanness" and "Frenchness" of the new urban elite. According expanded citizenship rights to the colonized peoples of West Africa, some argued, represented "the negation of our (France's) social organization, of our civilization, of our genius and, if it is not the end of France, it is in any case the origin of terrifying conflicts" to come.[129] The rebellions of 1915 and 1916, while they threatened French control in large parts of the region, also provided a basis for dealing with the challenge of the *évolués* since the uprisings suggested that the pre-colonial elite remained a powerful force in West African society.[130] In fact, under Van Vollenhoven and Delafosse in 1917 Dakar was prepared to reassess the very bases of colonial rule and make the "chiefs" the primary collaborators in governing AOF. This was justified on the grounds that African society was fundamentally different from that of Europe. Each must develop according to "its own traditions" and in "their own milieu."[131]

Yet, France's perceived needs during the war and its preconception of West Africa's relationship with the metropole brought hundreds of thousands of colonial subjects out of their "traditional" milieus and placed them in direct association with the culture and society of the colonizer. The physical and mental transgression of the boundaries between colony and metropole undermined the privilege of the colonial authority to singly determine the image of Africa presented to France and the portrait of the colonial power offered for consumption to the *sujet* in AOF. Moreover, it further enhanced the stature of the *évolué* within the colonial field and provided the bases for larger numbers of West Africans to demand an increased say in administering their own lives. In essence, the physical migration from the federation to France as a soldier opened new intellectual vistas for the recruit and also laid the foundation for crossing social boundaries from *sujet* to *citoyen*.

The actions of Dakar and Paris when the need for troops ended in 1918, though, blocked the possibility for that social migration and trapped the veterans in an ambiguous space between colonizers and colonized. Calls by officials in West Africa and France to repeal the reforms promised in conjunction with Diagne's mission further focused attention on the unique place of the *évolué* within the colonial field, a social category that grew in the *imaginaires* of the colonial administration and the new elite to include the veterans of the war. In addition, it created the bases for a greater distancing of the new urban elite from France. If France had "abandoned" the veteran from the colonies then he would look elsewhere for liberation from "oppression."[132] Many found this new source of liberation in the ideologies associated with the 1917 Russian Revolution and the Communist movements then forming in Europe. It is to this radicalization of the *évolué* class that our story now turns.

NOTES

1. CAOM, 1/AP/170/3, letter of Governor General Gabriel Angoulvant to the ministry of colonies, "Évolution des milieux indigènes," 16 May 1918.

2. Roberts, *Civilization Without Sexes*, pp. 3, 7.

3. Scholars generally agree that the First World War was marked by a shift in colonial policy from what has been too conveniently and too schematically labeled as "assimilation" to "association." See Raymond F. Betts, *Assimilation and Association in French Colonial Theory, 1890–1914* (New York: Columbia University Press, 1961); William B. Cohen, *Rulers of Empire: The French Colonial Service in Africa* (Stanford, Cal.: Hoover Institution Press, 1971); and Philippe Dewitte, *Les Mouvements nègres en France, 1919–1939* (Paris: L'Harmattan, 1985). Recent studies of French colonial rule in West Africa have provided a more nuanced reading of indigenous policy and have forced a rethinking of the categories previously used to explain the history of France's overseas empire. See: Conklin, *A Mission to Civilize*.

4. CAOM, 1/AP/3037, Ernest Haudos, deputy from the Marne, "La conscription chez les noirs," in *Les Annales Coloniales*, September 1919.

5. The emergence of the idea of a "true" France during this period is explored in: Lebovics, *True France*.

6. The idea of "being from there" as a source of authority and legitimacy is examined in: de Certeau, *Heterologies*, p. 69.

7. This is a process of constituting a power relationship and legitimating one's authority within that relationship described in: Edward W. Said, *Orientalism* (New York: Vintage, 1979), p. 3.

8. The colonial administrator's assertion of the prerogative to instruct the African in his or her genuine culture was the ideological basis for the *mission civilisatrice* as practiced by France in West Africa. See Conklin, *A Mission to Civilize*, p. 75; and Raoul Girardet, *L'Idée coloniale en France de 1871 à 1962* (Paris: La Table Ronde, 1972).

9. CAOM, 3/Service de Liaison entre les Originaires des Territoires d'Outre-mer (SLOTFOM)/35, unsigned report, mid-1920s.

10. CAOM, 1/AP/3037, article in *La Démocratie Nouvelle*, 26 September 1919, signed XXX. It is generally accepted that the prominent French ethnographer and colonial administrator Maurice Delafosse was "XXX." CAOM, 1/AP/3036, telegram from Diagne to the ministry of colonies, 26 April 1918.

11. Conklin, *A Mission to Civilize*, pp.1–2.

12. Paul Robiquet, editor, *Jules Ferry: Discours et Opinions*, Vol. 5 (Paris: Armand Colin, 1896), pp. 189-190; speech of 28 July 1885.

13. G. Wesley Johnson, jr., *The Emergence of Black Politics in Senegal: The Struggle for Power in the Four Communes, 1900–1920* (Stanford: Stanford University Press, 1971), p. 75. For additional discussion of assimilation in French West Africa see: Michael Crowder, *Senegal: A Study in French Assimilation Policy* (London: Methuen, 1967).

14. CAOM, Généralities (Gén)/237, "Rapport sur un projet de loi organique du gouvernement et de l'administration dans les colonies," March 1850.

15. CAOM, Gén/666 "Situation des colonies au premier Thermidor de l'an 5." There is an extensive and rich body of scholarship on the history of "republicanism" in

France, most of which centers on developments during the Third Republic. Important recent works include: Gary Wilder, "Framing Greater France Between the Wars," *Journal of Historical Sociology* 14:2 (June 2001); Laurent Dubois, "*La République Metisée*: Citizenship, Colonialism, and the Borders of French History," *Cultural Studies* 14:1 (2000); Philip Nord, *The Republican Moment: Struggles for Democracy in Nineteenth-Century France* (Cambridge: Harvard University Press, 1995); Maurice Agulhon, *The French Republic 1879–1992*, trans. Antonia Nevill (Cambridge: Blackwell, 1993); Judith F. Stone, *Sons of the Revolution: Radical Democrats in France, 1862–1914* (Baton Rouge: Louisiana State University Press, 1996); Pamela M. Pilbeam, *Republicanism in Nineteenth-Century France, 1814–1871* (New York: St. Martin's Press, 1995); and Claude Nicolet, *L'Idée républicaine en France, 1789–1924: Essai d'histoire critique* (Paris: Gallimard, 1982).

16. CAOM, Gén/237; and CAOM, Gén/277, see the letters of 8 September and 12 October 1848 from the abolition commission that discussed Senegal's representation in the Constituent Assembly of the Second Republic. See also: CAOM, Gén/119, the 27 April 1848 decree abolishing slavery; and: CAOM, Gén/162, "Les élections dans les colonies en éxecution du Décret du 5 mars 1848."

17. Johnson, *The Emergence of Black Politics in Senegal*, pp. 39, 45, 51–52.

18. See: G. Wesley Johnson, "The Ascendancy of Blaise Diagne and the Beginnings of African Politics in Senegal," in *Africa*: No. 3: (July 1966), p. 235. Also: François Manschuelle, "Assimilé ou patriotes africains? Naissance du nationalisme culturel en Afrique française (1853-1931)," in *Cahiers d'Études Africaines*: Nos. 2-3: (1995), p. 337; and Catherine Coquery-Vidrovitch, "Villes Coloniales et Histoire des Africains," in *XXe Siècle*: 20: (October-December 1988), p. 53.

19. CAOM, 1/AP/170/3, "Arrêté promulgué en AOF fixant les conditions d'accession des indigènes de l'Afrique Occidentale française à la qualité de citoyen français," published in the *Journal Officiel de l'Afrique Occidentale française*, 22 June 1912, signed by William Ponty.

20. On the importance of the 1912 *arrêté* see: Johnson, "The Ascendancy of Blaise Diagne," pp. 245–247; Johnson, *The Emergence of Black Politics in Senegal*, p. 84; and Conklin, *A Mission to Civilize*, pp. 151–154.

21. Archives de la République du Senegal (ARS), circular from the government general to the lieutenant governors of AOF, "a.s. des pouvoirs disciplinaires," in *Journal Officiel d'A.O.F.*, 28 September 1913.

22. CAOM, 1/AP/170/3, letter from Albert Lebrun to the President of the Republic, "La France d'Outre-Mer," 25 September 1913.

23. Mamdani, *Citizen and Subject*.

24. Gyan Prakash, "Introduction," in Gyan Prakash, editor, *After Colonialism: Imperial Histories and Postcolonial Displacements* (Princeton: Princeton University Press, 1995), p. 3.

25. Conklin, *A Mission to Civilize*, pp. 151–152.

26. Coquery-Vidrovitch, "Villes Coloniales et Histoire des Africains," p. 62.

27. CAOM, 1/AP/1638, letter from Albert Sarraut, minister of colonies, to the office of the prime minister, 19 June 1923.

28. Johnson, *The Emergence of Black Politics in Senegal*, pp. 149, 104.

29. CAOM, 1/AP/145, letter from the ministry of colonies to the governor general of AOF, "Régime de l'indigénat," 17 June 1913; and, "Projets de décrets relatifs au

statut personnel des indigènes de l'Afrique Occidentale française et notamment des Sénégalaise des 4 Communes," 21 January 1914.

30. For biographical information on Diagne see, Johnson, "The Ascendancy of Blaise Diagne," pp. 237, 246.

31. CAOM, 1/AP/595, "Profession de foi de citoyen Blaise Diagne," 20 November 1919, in *L'Ouest-Africain français*.

32. CAOM, 1/AP/534/18, letter from Diagne to the ministry of colonies, 3 August 1914; CAOM, 1/AP/534/18, debate in the Chamber of Deputies on military service, 8 July 1915; and CAOM, 1/AP/534/18, note by Diagne dated 3 July 1915.

33. Marc Michel, "Citoyenneté et Service militaire dans les quatre Communes du Sénégal au cours de la Première Guerre Mondiale," in *Perspectives Nouvelles sur le Passé de l'Afrique Noire et de Madagascar* (Paris: Publications de la Sorbonne, 1974), p. 314.

34. Lieutenant-Colonel Charles Mangin, *La Force Noire* (Paris: Librairie Hachette et Cie., 1910), pp. 225, 92.

35. CAOM, 1/AP/3034, "Proposition de loi No. 1246," presented to the Chamber of Deputies on 16 September 1915 by MM. Pierre Masse, Ajam, and Maurice Bernard.

36. This point is also emphasized in: Robert W. July, *The Origins of Modern African Thought: Its Development in West Africa During the Nineteenth and Twentieth Centuries* (New York: Frederick A. Praeger, 1967), p. 398. For further discussion see: Jacques Thobie, Gilbert Meynier, Catherine Coquery-Vidrovitch, and Charles-Robert Ageron, *Histoire de la France Coloniale*, Vol 2, (Paris: A. Colin, 1990), p.79.

37. CAOM, 1/AP/534/18, letter from Diagne to the ministry of colonies, 3 August 1914.

38. CAOM, 1/AP/534/18, letter from Ponty to the ministry of colonies, 7 August 1914.

39. CAOM, 1/AP/534/18, letter from the ministry of war to the ministry of colonies (service of AOF), "Incorporation des Sénégalais des communes de plein exercise," 5 December 1914. See also: ARS, Tribunaux et Judiciaires (M)/87, letter from the governor general to the ministry of colonies, 2 February 1916.

40. CAOM, 1/AP/534/18, note by Diagne 3 July 1915; CAOM, 1/AP/534/2, note on a discussion in the Chamber of Deputies in 1916 interpreting the 1915 Diagne law.

41. CAOM, 1/AP/170/5, "Note pour le Ministre 'Situation des Sénégalais originaires des communes de plein exercise—Discussion au Sénat du rapport de M. Berenger," unsigned, written in late 1915.

42. CAOM, 1/AP/3036, telegram from Diagne to the ministry of colonies, 19 February 1918.

43. CAOM, 1/AP/3036, "Circulaire ministérielle relative au recrutement dans chacun des groupes des Colonies de l'Afrique Occidentale et de l'Afrique Équatoriale française," signed by the Minister of Colonies Henry Simon, 14 January 1918.

44. Diagne anticipated the controversy the new law would create in AOF and immediately embarked on a tour of the Four Communes to lobby for full implementation of the act. CAOM, 1/AP/551, letter from Diagne to the President of the Republic requesting the voyage, 21 October 1915. See also the telegram from Diagne to the ministry of colonies, 24 October 1915, explaining the need for the excursion, CAOM, 1/AP/551.

45. CAOM, 1/AP/170/5, letter from Diagne to the ministry of colonies, 20 October 1919.

46. CAOM, 1/AP/534/18, letter from François-Joseph Clozel, governor general of AOF, to the ministry of colonies, 5 January 1916.

47. CAOM, 1/AP/534/18, letter from Clozel to the ministry of colonies, 5 January 1916.

48. CAOM, 1/AP/599, letter from Angoulvant to the Chamber of Deputies, "A.S. de la proposition de loi tendant à faire accorder la qualité de citoyen français aux natifs des communes de plein exercise du Sénégal," 3 September 1916.

49. CAOM, 1/AP/534/18, letter from R. Antonetti, lieutenant-governor of Senegal, to Clozel, 2 January 1916.

50. CAOM, 1/AP/534/18, letter from the ministry of colonies to the governor general of AOF, 30 December 1915, "Jugements supplétifs d'actes de naissance et statut des indigènes du Sénégal."

51. CAOM, 1/AP/534/18, dispatch from Clozel to lieutenant governors of AOF, 9 December 1915.

52. CAOM, 1/AP/595, declaration of Diagne in *L'Ouest-Africain français*, 29 November 1919.

53. CAOM, 1/AP/534/2, letter of Senator H. Bérenger to the ministry of colonies, September 1916.

54. CAOM, 1/AP/539/13, law of 29 September 1916 sponsored by Blaise Diagne, Deputy from Senegal. (Emphasis in the original.)

55. CAOM, 1/AP/534/2, letter from Diouf to the Chamber, 10 September 1916.

56. CAOM, 1/AP/534/2, letter signed by Dakhourou-Koulynguidiane, a "jeune Sénégalais mobilisé," and read before the Senate on 14 September 1916. The letter was also printed in *Presse Coloniale*, 13 September 1916.

57. CAOM, 1/AP/534/1, article in *La Depêche Coloniale et Maritime*, 12 September 1916, signed, F. Jourdier, entitled, "De Nouveaux Citoyens Français."

58. CAOM, 1/AP/599, Angoulvant to the Chamber of Deputies, "A.S. de la proposition de loi tendant à faire accorder la qualité de citoyen français aux natifs des communes de plein exercise du Sénégal," 3 September 1916. See also: CAOM, 1/AP/192/5, "Note sur les Métis en Afrique Occidentale Française (État de la Question en 1917)," October 1917, François de Coutouly; and CAOM, 1/AP/534/2, Maurice Viollette, 8 July 1916.

59. CAOM, 1/AP/534/2, unsigned article in *L'A.O.F.*, 29 November 1916, "Sont ils ou ne sont ils pas citoyens français."

60. CAOM, 1/AP/159, "Projet d'arrêté portant internement de Côte d'Ivoire d'indigènes du Haut-Sénégal-Niger ayant participé à des troubles politiques graves," signed by Delafosse, 21 September 1916.

61. CAOM, 1/AP/3034, letter from the lieutenant-governor of Guinea to the governor general of AOF, "A.S.—Incidents de Kindia," 19 April 1916; and CAOM, 1/AP/3035, "Rapport sur les opérations du recrutement dans la Colonie de Haut-Sénégal-Niger," 22 January 1916. See also: ARS, Affaires Militaires (4D)/88.

62. CAOM, 1/AP/3037, unsigned report of 17 June 1918 from Dakar; and CAOM, 1/AP/3036, letter from General Pineau to the lieutenant-governor of Côte d'Ivoire, 8 June 1916.

63. CAOM, 1/AP/3037, Gabriel Cambrouze, deputy from Gironde, "Un Peu de Politique Indigène; Les tirailleurs libérés: Leur situation et ses conséquences," in *Les Annales Coloniales*, December 1918.

64. For a discussion of the impact on West African leadership systems during the period of colonial expansion see: Catherine Coquery-Vidrovitch, *Afrique Noire: Permanences et Ruptures* (Paris: Payot, 1985), p. 123; Michael Crowder and Obaro

Ikime, eds., *West African Chiefs: Their Changing Status under Colonial Rule and Independence* (New York: Africana Publishing Corporation. 1970), p. XVII; and Cohen, *Rulers of Empire*, p. 12. The aforementioned scholars share Cohen's assertion that the indigenous authorities were transformed "from independent political forces into subordinate instruments of the French administration," a position with which I also concur. Olufemi Vaughan's insightful essay, "Assessing Grassroots Politics and Community Development in Nigeria," in *African Affairs*: 94 (1995), pp. 501–518, provides a corrective to earlier scholarship that "fail[ed] to comprehend fully the complex role of local actors" in shaping the societies in which they live.

65. Général Joseph Gallieni, *Neuf ans à Madagascar* (Paris: Librairie Hachette et Cie., 1908), p. 27.

66. Général Joseph Gallieni, *Gallieni au Tonkin (1892–1896)* (Paris: Éditions Berger-Levrault, 1941), p. 91.

67. CAOM, Commission Guernut (CG)/47, "Note sur l'organisation administrative de l'Afrique noire," signed by Hubert Deschamps, 23 February 1938.

68. CAOM, 1/AP/145, "Arrêté rapportant les arrêtés des 31 mars et 18 avril 1917, déterminant en Afrique Occidentale française l'exercice des pouvoirs disciplinaires et portant énumération des infractions spéciales passibles de punitions disciplinaires dans les Territoires du Niger et de la Mauritanie," signed by Joost Van Vollenhoven, governor general of AOF, 21 August 1917.

69. CAOM, 1/AP/3034, letter from the government general for AOF to ministry of colonies, "Recrutement de tirailleurs en A.O.F.," 21 November 1915.

70. CAOM, 1/AP/3034, letter from the government general for AOF to the ministry of colonies, 16 July 1915; For an analysis of recruitment techniques and discussions of the use of colonial troops in European wars see: Marc Michel, *L'Appel à l'Afrique: Contributions et réactions à l'effort de guerre en A.O.F. 1914–1919* (Paris: Publications de la Sorbonne, 1982), pp. 22–27; Conklin, *A Mission to Civilize*, p. 143; and Joe Lunn, *Memoirs of the Maelstrom: A Senegalese Oral History of the First World War* (Portsmouth, N.H.: Heinemann, 1999), pp. 34–41.

71. ARS, 4D/65; and ARS, 4D/55. Only a few thousand of the expected tens of thousands were found.

72. CAOM, 1/AP/3034, letter from Clozel to the ministry of colonies, 16 July 1915. "J'ajouterai cependant que les indigènes électeurs des quatre communes de plein exercice du Sénégal n'ont pas donné un seul voluntaire." While the statement is an exaggeration, it nonetheless reflects the reticence of the *originaires* to serve in a war without clear recognition of their status as equal citizens.

73. CAOM, 1/AP/534/18, letter from Clozel to ministry of colonies, 5 January 1916.

74. CAOM, 1/AP/3034. The recruitment system in AOF is outlined in a letter from the lieutenant-governor of Côte d'Ivoire to the government general for AOF, 4 September 1915, entitled, "Recrutement;" and ARS, 4D, which contains recruitment figures.

75. How the experience of World War One gave rise to the idea of an endless war is discussed in: Paul Fussell, *The Great War and Modern Memory* (London: Oxford University Press, 1977), pp. 71–74.

76. Michel, *L'Appel à l'Afrique*, pp. 127–128.

77. CAOM, 1/AP/3034, letter from the lieutenant-governor of Côte d'Ivoire to the government general in Dakar, "Recrutement," 4 September 1915.

78. CAOM, 1/AP/3034, "Telegramme circulaire No. 84," 6 October 1915, signed by Clozel.

79. CAOM, 1/SLOTFOM/2, Fernand Gouttenoire de Toury, "Le Paria ne demande que la justice," in *Le Paria: Tribune des populations des colonies*, 1 April 1922. The phrase was increasingly used in the later stages of the war and throughout the 1920s by veterans from AOF aggrieved at the failure of France to deliver on its wartime promises of citizenship and increased benefits.

80. CAOM, 1/AP/3035, "Rapport sur les opérations du recrutement dans la Colonie du Haut-Sénégal-Niger," 22 January 1916; and ARS, 4D/65.

81. CAOM, 1/AP/3036, letter from Inspector General of Colonies Picanon, head of the inspection mission in French West Africa, to the ministry of colonies, "Recrutement des Indigènes," 27 November 1916.

82. CAOM, 1/AP/3035, "Rapport sur les opérations du recrutement dans la Colonie du Haut-Sénégal-Niger," 22 January 1916. See also Delafosse's reports on Haut-Sénégal-Niger contained in CAOM, 1/AP/159; CAOM, 1/AP/3035, "Rapport sur le recrutement des troupes noires," 25 September 1917; and, in the same carton, letter from the government general for AOF to the ministry of colonies, "A.S. du recrutement indigène en A.O.F.," 25 May 1917.

83. CAOM, 1/AP/159.

84. Girardet, *L'Idée coloniale en France*, p. 54; Conklin, *A Mission to Civilize*, p. 23.

85. CAOM, 1/Télégrammes (Tél)/243, cable from the cabinet in Paris to Dakar acknowledging receipt of protests against recruitment from colonial administrators in AOF, 27 September 1915. The most frequent complaint was on the exiting of subject populations to neighboring British colonies.

86. CAOM, 1/AP/534/1. letter from Diagne to the ministry of colonies, 11 February 1917.

87. CAOM, 1/AP/170, letter from Van Vollenhoven to the ministry of colonies, "Situation politique de la colonie," 20 December 1917.

88. The circular is cited in Georges Hardy, *L'Afrique Occidentale française* (Paris: Librairie Renouard, 1937), pp. 205-207; and in: CAOM, 1/AP/170, letter from Van Vollenhoven to the ministry of colonies, 20 December 1917.

89. CAOM, 1/AP/542, sentiment expressed in a letter from Diagne to the ministry of colonies, 8 July 1922. This later became a source of controversy between the AOF administration and Diagne as they clashed over who was qualified to be the "true" chief of certain ethno-tribal groups.

90. CAOM, 1/AP/170, letter from Van Vollenhoven to the ministry of colonies, 20 December 1917.

91. Scholars generally agree on the important changes French colonial policy underwent during the First World War. In this regard see: Conklin, *A Mission to Civilize*, pp. 142-143; Michel, *L'Appel à l'Afrique*, p. IX; Gilbert Comte, *L'Empire Triomphante (1871–1936): 1. Afrique occidentale et équatoriale* (Paris: Denoël, 1988); Henri Grimal, *Decolonization: The British, French, Dutch, and Belgian Empires 1919– 1963* (Boulder: Westview Press, 1978), p. 5; Dewitte, *Les Mouvements nègres en France*, p. 9; and July, *The Origins of Modern African Thought*, p. 398; and Cooper, *Decolonization and African Society: The Labor Question in French and British Africa* (Cambridge: Cambridge University Press, 1996).

92. CAOM, 1/AP/170, letter from Diagne to the ministry of colonies, 20 October 1919.

93. Bhabha, *The Location of Culture*, p. 86. (Emphasis in the original.)

94. CAOM, 1/AP/192/5. This dossier contains listings of the AOF veterans decorated for service during the 1914–1918 war.

95. CAOM, 1/AP/3037, Gabriel Cambrouze, "Un peu de Politique Indigène; Les tirailleurs libérés, Leur situation et ses conséquences," in *Les Annales Coloniales*, December 1918.

96. CAOM, 1/AP/3036, "Un Nouveau Recrutement en Afrique Occidentale," in *La Dépêche Coloniale et Maritime*, 22 January 1918. The announcement is also recorded in the *Journal Officiel de l'Afrique Occidentale française*, 17 January 1918.

97. CAOM, 1/AP/3036, "Décret portant d'une mission chargée d'intensifier le recrutement en Afrique Occidentale et Équatoriale française," signed by Prime Minister Georges Clemenceau, 14 January 1918.

98. CAOM, 1/AP/ 3036, "Circulaire ministerielle relative au recrutement dans chacun des groupes des Colonies de l'Afrique Occidentale et de l'Afrique Équatoriale française," signed by Henry Simon, minister of colonies, 14 January 1918.

99. CAOM, 1/AP/3036, "Rapport au Président de la République Française, suivi d'un décret portant organisation d'une mission chargée d'intensifier le recrutement en Afrique Occidentale et Équatoriale française," signed by Clemenceau, Simon, and L.-L. Klotz, minister of finances, 14 January 1918; and CAOM, 1/AP/3036, "Circulaire ministerielle," signed by Simon, 14 January 1918.

100. Recent studies of colonialism, French or otherwise, have begun to treat that relationship as more complex and multifaceted than works produced much earlier. Some of the important contributions to the field in the past decade or two include: Conklin, *A Mission to Civilize*; Cooper, *Decolonization and African Society*; Cooper and Stoler, eds., *Tensions of Empire*; Robert J. C. Young, *Colonial Desire: Hybridity in Theory, Culture and Race* (London and New York: Routledge, 1995); and Mamdani, *Citizen and Subject*.

101. CAOM, 1/AP/1638, "Décret relatif aux conditions d'accession à la qualité de citoyen français de certains militaires indigènes de l'Afrique Occidentale française et de l'Afrique Équatoriale française, et de leur famille," signed by Raymond Poincaré, president of France, 14 January 1918.

102. Conklin, *A Mission to Civilize*, p. 180.

103. CAOM, 1/AP/3036. Angoulvant arrived in Dakar on 18 February 1918.

104. CAOM, 1/AP/3036, Clemenceau, "Décret portant organisation d'une mission chargée d'intensifier le recrutement en Afrique Occidentale et Équatoriale française," 14 January 1918.

105. CAOM, 1/AP/3036, "Rufisque en fête; Brillante réception faite par la population à l'occasion du passage de M. le Commissaire de la République," in *Le Petit Sénégalais*, 28 February 1918.

106. CAOM, 1/AP/3037. This carton contains extensive documentation of Diagne's 1918 recruitment tour, including a breakdown of the numbers of volunteers at each gathering orchestrated by the Commissaire of the Republic. The file also holds the communications between Angoulvant and the ministry of colonies on the "loyalisme" proclaimed to France and Diagne during the campaign.

107. CAOM, 1/AP/3036, telegram from Diagne to the ministry of colonies, 17 March 1918. He also made this charge in a letter to the ministry of colonies on 16 February 1918, contained in the same carton, where he mentioned "des graves erreurs

accumulées par la haute administration en matière de politique indigène" as the source of the federation's difficulties.

108. CAOM, 1/AP/3037. Diagne expressed this position in a telegram to the ministry of colonies, 22 April 1918. See also: ARS, Affaires Politiques (17G)/15, letters from Diagne to local chiefs; and ARS, 4D/83, letters from Diagne to the Muslim elite of Senegal.

109. CAOM, 1/AP/3036, report from Diagne to the ministry of colonies, "Compte rendu de l'action de la mission au Sénégal," 23 March 1918.

110. For examples of the cooperation between Diagne and the chiefs see: CAOM, 1/AP/3036, letter from M'Bakhane Diop, chef de province du Keur Bacine, to Diagne, 19 February 1918; "Compte rendu de l'action de la mission au Sénégal," Diagne to the ministry of colonies, 23 March 1918; telegram from Diagne to the ministry of colonies, 15 February 1918; telegram from Diagne to the ministry of colonies, 17 March 1918; and CAOM, 1/AP/3037, letter from Angoulvant to the ministry of colonies, 13 May 1918.

111. Comte, *L'Empire Triomphante*, p. 234.

112. CAOM, 1/Tel/336, telegram from Diagne to Dakar alerting the government general of his intention to leave AOF, 7 June 1918; and CAOM, 1/AP/3037, telegram from Angoulvant to the ministry of colonies, 17 August 1918.

113. CAOM, 1/AP/3037, telegram from Angoulvant to the ministry of colonies, "Compte-rendu des opérations de recrutement au Sénégal," 18 July 1918.

114. CAOM, 1/AP/192/1, "Les Colonies Françaises en 1918," in *La Dépêche Coloniale*, 3 January 1919. Several scholars have corroborated these figures, including: Conklin, *A Mission to Civilize*, p. 143; and Michel, *L'Appel à l'Afrique*. For figures of Senegal's contribution see: Lunn, *Memoirs of the Maelstrom*.

115. CAOM, 1/AP/3037, unsigned report from AOF to the ministry of colonies, 17 June 1918.

116. CAOM, 1/AP/3036, letter from Angoulvant to the ministry of colonies, "A.S. de l'attitude de M. de Lahitolle lors de la visite à Conakry du Commissaire de la République," 29 June 1918; and CAOM, 1/AP/3037, Delafosse, "Le Point Noir de l'armée noire; Tirailleurs libérés; La rentrée dans leurs foyers des tirailleurs libérés s'accompagne de circonstances qu'il ne faut pas négliger," in *La Depêche Coloniale et Maritime*, 4 November 1919.

117. CAOM, 1/AP/3037, "Le Gachis de l'Afrique Occidentale Française; M. Diagne politicien," signed XXX, in *La Démocratie Nouvelle*, 26 September 1919.

118. CAOM, 1/AP/170/3, letter from Angoulvant to the ministry of colonies, "Evolution des milieux indigènes," 16 May 1918.

119. CAOM, 1/AP/1638, letter from Nores, inspector general of colonies, to the ministry of colonies, undated.

120. CAOM, 1/AP/192/1. This point is confirmed in a letter from Binet-Valmer, president of the League of Heads of Section and Fighting Soldiers, to the ministry of colonies, 12 May 1927, "Notes pour Monsieur Raymond Poincaré et Monsieur le Ministre des Colonies."

121. CAOM, 1/AP/3037, unsigned report produced in French West Africa and forwarded to the ministry of colonies, 17 June 1918. See also: CAOM, 1/AP/1638, letter from Nores to the ministry of colonies, written in either late 1918 or early 1919.

122. Roberts, *Civilization Without Sexes*, p. 73.

123. CAOM, 1/AP/2147, Pierre Herbot, "Le problème des indigènes 'détribalisés,'" in *Bulletin du Comité de l'Afrique Française*, December 1937.
124. CAOM, 1/AP/3037, Cambrouze, "Un peu de Politique Indigène," in *Les Annales Coloniales*, December 1918.
125. CAOM, 1/AP/3037, Delafosse, "Le Point Noir de l'armée noire," in *La Depêche Coloniale et Maritime*, 4 November 1919.
126. CAOM, 1/AP/3037, Cambrouze, "Un peu de Politique Indigène," in *Les Annales Coloniales*, December 1918.
127. CAOM, 1/AP/170/5, letter from Diagne to the ministry of colonies, 20 October 1919.
128. Mangin, *La Force Noire*, p. 308.
129. CAOM, 1/AP/170/5, letter from Angoulvant to the ministry of colonies, "A.S. de la population ici tendant à faire accorder la qualité de citoyens français aux natifs des communes de plein exercice du Sénégal," 3 September 1916.
130. CAOM, 1/AP/3035, "Rapport sur les opérations du recrutement dans la Colonie du Haut-Sénégal-Niger," 22 January 1916.
131. CAOM, 1/AP/170, letter from Van Vollenhoven to the ministry of colonies, "Situation politique de la colonie," 20 December 1917.
132. CAOM, 1/SLOTFOM/2, Fernand Gouttenoire de Toury, "Le Paria demande que la justice," in *Le Paria*, 1 April 1922.

Chapter Two

Between Two Worlds: Radical Politics and the *Évolué* in 1920s France

After the armistice of 11 November 1918 social and political upheavals afflicted France and its colonies alike. Dakar reported a wave of strikes among "native personnel," dockworkers, and other laborers vital to the functioning of the colonial system that lasted into the early 1920s.[1] In France, disputes between labor and capital after the war culminated in a general strike in 1920.[2] Those convulsions, combined with the political turmoil afflicting many European states at the time, heightened the anxieties of overseas administrators who claimed the wartime changes in the colonial field had "compromised the security [and stability] of AOF."[3] The greatest source of that insecurity, according to police informers who followed migrants from the colonies that settled in France, was the class of "semi-civilized" from West Africa that was "susceptible" to the appeal of "professional agitators…[from] the Communist Party."[4]

Officials in Dakar and Paris were particularly sensitive to the threat posed by the new Bolshevik government in Russia and the revolutionary movements that drew inspiration from it because of the devastating effects the war had had on France. The metropole emerged from the conflict a greatly weakened power, albeit a victorious one. About ten percent of France's adult male population was killed during the war, with many more partially or entirely incapacitated. Since the fighting was fixed in the country's northern industrial zone throughout most of the conflict, France experienced a 60 percent decline in prewar production levels. Culturally, Roberts notes that the 1914–1918 cataclysm induced a "profound crisis in Western humanist values, to which the notion of 'civilization' was closely bound."[5] And, as the famed psychoanalyst Sigmund Freud observed at the time, some intellectuals of the post-war years held that "civilization [was] largely responsible for [Europe's] misery."[6]

Yet, the idea of "civilization" was deeply rooted in France's conception of its colonial mission.[7] Thus, any reevaluation of the cultural bases of Western society necessarily involved an examination of imperialism and the future of the overseas empire in the wake of the recent carnage in Europe. This chapter discusses how new, radical critiques of imperial rule, most of which were associated with Marxist philosophy and the recently-founded French Communist Party (PCF—*Parti Communiste Français*), contributed to shaping the ongoing struggles within the colonial field and provided the ideological bases for *évolué* political organizations that became active during the 1920s in the metropole itself. The nascent Communist movement and related anti-colonial ideologies tended to further "abolish the artificial distance which seem[ed] to separate"[8] colony from metropole, citizen from subject by binding the struggle for liberty in the colonies to liberationist projects in the metropole.[9] However, aspects of this revolutionary discourse and the activities of the PCF also reinforced trends toward elaborating a politics of difference that sustained certain notions of an "authentic" Africa and "real" France promoted at the time by colonial administrators and, increasingly, metropolitan officials.[10]

The decision by many *évolués* to rally "under the communist banner," though, involved more than a "turning of the theoretical arms of the French Revolution against the society which officially claimed it" as its own legacy.[11] It also influenced the emerging self-identity of this social class, a representation increasingly centered on the claim of participating in the societies of West Africa and France while being alienated from both. According to Prakash, "From Latin America to India, the colonized shifted the terrain of engagement by occupying and carving out positions placed in between the powerful command of authority and the powerless silence of the victim."[12] However, as the present study demonstrates, it was not the "colonized" as an undifferentiated bloc that carved out this "in between" position. Rather, a specific and elite social category originating among the colonized populations claimed this space and was socially and discursively available to occupy it. The space between is not a location of the mass, but of the elite. Further, it is a condition dependent upon sustaining the poles of "command" and "victim." The power of the in-between space stems from its mediating function, a function that requires the perpetuation of difference.[13]

Beyond providing organizational training and a political home for displaced West Africans, Communism offered a means for describing the colonial condition at odds with that embraced by the overseas administration or that of the circle around Diagne. Much of the scholarship on the relationship between the French-educated elite from the colonies and the

PCF emphasizes the political skills and organizational experience the metropolitan party imparted to those from the overseas possessions. However, this often produces the impression that the West African arrived in the Communist movement with a pre-established and fixed self-identity and departed it unaffected in their sense of themselves. In addition, this approach elides the important ways in which the colonial subjects and events in the empire shaped Communist politics.[14] One theme of this chapter is the ways in which the *évolués* and events in the colonies shaped the Communist Party's praxis and discourse in a manner that created the conditions whereby an internationalist and class-based ideology gave rise to and sponsored "nationalist" and race-oriented movements. In other words, we will explore the ways that the emergence of French Communism influenced the dynamics of the colonial field and, in turn, how the Party and its associated movements were shaped through their engagement therein. As Bourdieu relates, "[T]he political field…produces an effect of censorship by limiting the universe of political discourse, and thereby the universe of what is politically thinkable, to the finite space of discourses capable of being produced or reproduced within the limits of the political *problematic* understood as a space of stances effectively adopted within the field—i.e., stances that are socio-logically possible given the laws that determine entry into the field."[15] While the field circumscribes the possibilities for engagement within it, the nature of the field itself is at stake in the contest among the interested parties. Therefore, it is entirely possible for new elements to enter the field, thereby redefining the nature of both the field and the new element(s). However, the success of those new elements is dependent in large measure upon their being recognized as players by those previously engaged within the field. Our attention, therefore, now turns to a discussion of how Communist discourse and praxis became an accepted and important part of the French colonial field.

From Citizens to Mimics: The Marginalization of the *Évolué*

"For several years," a report produced for the government general in French West Africa noted, "a number of natives have traveled to France and returned to their homeland [where they served] as intermediaries and propagators…of subversive ideas among the masses."[16] Colonial administrators asserted that the subject population responded favorably to this "propaganda" because of the "notoriety" conferred on those who had spent time in the metropole.[17] As we saw in the previous chapter, this circumstance undermined one of the legitimating devices of colonial rule: the monopoly of imperial officials to represent France to the *sujets* of the federation as well as their exclusive prerogative to portray "authentic" Africa to audiences in the metropole. Now, the *évolué* also claimed the special authority to speak on behalf of and to both metropolitan and colonial communities. Of even greater concern to Dakar, the numbers of people who were labeled as belonging to or saw themselves as being part of that social category had greatly expanded and their geographic place of origin had substantially diversified during the war through the citizenship laws and recruitment efforts of their elected deputy, Blaise Diagne.[18]

In fact, the end of hostilities in Europe opened a new stage in the struggle for authority within the colonial field. The armistice of 1918 eliminated the conditions that produced a temporary working relationship between *évolués*, colonial administrators, and the pre-colonial elite during Diagne's recruitment campaign by ending France's need for troops from the colonies. Even as the Commissaire of the Republic prepared to return to Paris in the summer of 1918, sniping between the deputy and officials of AOF began. Anonymous reports were sent from throughout French West Africa to Dakar warning of the "dangerous" and even "treacherous" implications of Diagne's recently completed mission.[19] Other colonialists appealed openly for the *tirailleurs* to be repatriated without delay and for the 14 January 1918 decrees to be repealed because of the threat creating so many new citizens posed to the ability of the administration in Dakar to command and to the prestige of the pre-colonial elite.[20]

Diagne, however, insisted that the 1918 decrees and the citizenship laws of 1915 and 1916 be enforced, despite the reticence of some in the imperial hierarchy. The deputy from Senegal reminded his colleagues in the Chamber of the "blood tax" paid by thousands of West Africans in return for the promises of protection from the *indigénat* and easier access to citizenship. Diagne maintained that since France had "imposed certain metropolitan customs in place of some held by [the natives]," there was only one direction in which to move—toward granting full citizenship and increasing the cultural affinity between the metropole and its overseas territories. To renege or prevaricate on the public declarations made by Clemenceau would, according to Diagne, invite strife and permanently damage France's prestige in West Africa.[21]

The debate over interpretation of the Diagne laws and implementation of the 1918 decrees was made more urgent since 1919 was an election year in France and the Four Communes of Senegal. The themes of citizenship and equality between *originaires* and metropolitans dominated the campaign.

However, whereas Diagne entered the last contest an unknown and the candidate of a loosely organized coalition of *évolués*, in 1919 he exercised the power of incumbency, had a strong record of promoting the interests of his constituency, and led a more self-conscious and better organized strata within AOF. While the issues debated in the press centered on the actual meaning of the citizenship laws and their relevance after the war, the campaign reflected competing visions of French identity and African society. Responding to allegations that certain customary practices, especially polygamous traditions associated with Islam, barred the path to assimilation, Diagne asserted in unequivocal terms, "One could be both French and Muslim."[22] The deputy proclaimed that he spoke in the "name of one common country" comprising the metropole and its colonies.[23] For Diagne, citizenship was a status that provided for equal treatment before the law with corresponding rights and duties. Accordingly, the title *"citoyen"* was not meant to denote certain essential cultural traits that marked one off as distinct from others. Rather, Diagne claimed there was room in the Republic for many cultural practices. Thus, for the native from Gorée the goal of the *évolué* class was to disappear in the matrix of citizenry, not to maintain a permanent position between citizen and subject as Dakar appeared to prefer through its hesitation and obstruction in matters of naturalization for West Africans. According to François Manschuelle, "[Diagne's positions] seemed to suggest that the movements and political personalities interested in political assimilation could also have desired the preservation of African cultures."[24] That being the case, Johnson's claim that the deputy from Senegal was "an incipient nationalist" seems untenable.[25] To make that point one would have to dismiss the "assimilationist" rhetoric espoused by Diagne throughout his tenure in office. Diagne ceaselessly insisted on his own Frenchness as well as that of the *originaires*. Johnson misses the particular vision of French identity Diagne presented. For him, national belonging was not culturally based. Rather, in the tradition of the French Revolution, the deputy from Senegal insisted on a legalistic reading of citizenship. It was about rights and obligations and equality before the law, not the specific cultural practices of day-to-day life. Therefore, it is perfectly legitimate to claim assimilation into the body politic of France while also insisting on maintaining one's cultural heritage. One need not be a "separatist" to hold that position, a charge increasingly leveled at Diagne by Dakar in 1919.

The replacement of Gabriel Angoulvant in 1919 by Martial Merlin as governor general of French West Africa added to the erosion of cooperation between *évolués* and the colonial state at the end of the war. Under Merlin, the government general advanced notions of what it meant to be French and the proper organization of African society sharply at odds with those espoused by Diagne. For the political opposition in 1919, backed by Dakar, direct "contact between the natives [of West Africa] and the metropolitan population" had induced "mental confusion" among the recruits from AOF. Their exposure to "a country very different from that in which they had spent most of their lives," some colonialists advised, would only lead to "trouble." French and West African societies were fundamentally distinct, Dakar argued, a circumstance that should be preserved, not undermined by extending citizenship to those deemed "unfit" for entry into the metropolitan national patrimony.[26]

In fact, the government general and the ministry of colonies had expressed concern throughout the war about sending subjects from AOF to fight in the trenches of northern Europe. Those apprehensions led to the establishment of a Service of Assistance and Surveillance of Senegalese Troops that monitored the activities and contacts of the *tirailleurs* during their period of active duty in France.[27] This wartime agency was the precursor of the *Service de Contrôle et d'Assistance en France des Indigènes des Colonies* (CAI) that infiltrated and disrupted the activities of many organizations founded by migrants from the colonies that settled in France during the 1920s and 1930s.[28]

Despite the attempts by Dakar and Paris to regulate contact between *sujets* and *citoyens*, as early as 1916 informants were reporting a "real change in the spirit" of recruits from the colonies. "This new mentality," one agent related, posed a "danger for the post-war period" in that "the distance which otherwise existed between [French citizens] and [colonized subjects] had diminished." Accordingly, the *tirailleurs* had "now [become] conscious of rights of which they were entirely ignorant before their arrival [in France]."[29] That new consciousness meant it would be difficult, if not unwise, to "reintegrate" the returning soldiers "within their village, their caste [or] their family."[30] Early attempts to do just that ended in difficulties for the colonial administration as demobilized *tirailleurs*, according to the lieutenant governor of Guinea, "treated the colonies as conquered lands and some of them even posed as [the] saviors of [France]."[31] Delafosse observed that the veterans were so confident in their new standing within the colonial field that they refused "to recognize any authority...neither that of the village chief, not that of the administrator."[32]

The inability of the demobilized *tirailleurs*, and all other *évolués* to be seamlessly reincorporated within an "authentic" African society "guided by the authority of elders [and] the traditions and habits of their race"[33] did not indicate to Dakar that they had "become French," though.[34] Instead, the government general increasingly attempted to discredit the *évolués* among both the native populations of West Africa and the authorities in Paris. In the dichotomized world of the colonial state where there was only room for *citoyens* of France and *sujets* of the empire, the returning soldier was deemed to have no place. Having "received [only] the imprint of [French] civilization," officials of the empire claimed the veteran was driven "to conquer all the advantages of citizenship" without "any preparation for the liberties" attached to that status.[35] Furthermore, officials in Paris and West Africa asserted that the returning soldier who had "evolved" out of his previous milieu was "uprooted" and "detribalized," with a "simple mind" that was unable to comprehend the great events which he had just witnessed. Lost in the world, this "marginal individual" was, accordingly, easy prey for "subversive ideas" and capable of "disruptive acts."[36]

Such "uprooted" or "detribalized" individuals, Dakar argued, had to be blocked from attaining the rights guaranteed by the 1918 decrees because they represented a danger not only to West African society, but France as well. What troubled colonial administrators is that citizenship would protect the political activities of those returning veterans by providing the cover of French civil law, thus making the *évolués* as a class more effective in the developing contest for power with the government general by limiting the state's ability to act against "subversives."[37] Consequently, Dakar limited the numbers of those who could effectively participate in the political struggles in the colonial field by obstructing the naturalization process. This marked an attempt to recoup some of the authority the colonial administration felt it had lost to Diagne and the *évolués* during the war. By 1921 the naturalization rate had slowed to such a degree throughout the empire that Albert Sarraut, minister of colonies, ordered the governors general to take "more favorable action" in the cases of veterans.[38]

The rhetoric practiced by the government general in relation to the disputes over naturalization indicated a shift in official conceptualizations of the *évolué* within the colonial field. Whereas Van Vollenhoven argued in 1917 that the *évolué* was no longer "African" and, therefore, had to be kept separate from "native" society, he still suggested it was possible for the new elite to be incorporated into French society, even if they were still in need of further civilizing.[39] However, under Merlin, Dakar practiced a slightly different discourse, one that still insisted upon the binary division between "colonizers" and "colonized,"[40] but now placed the *évolué* out of the French as well as the African cultural and social framework. As such, the noted colonialist Georges Hardy explained, the introduction of "European ways" to Africa has created a group of people who are "declassed" and have "deformed characters" which lead them to "rebellion" and "impatience." The French-educated elite, therefore, was unable to speak on behalf of the "real" African because he had been tainted by contact with European civilization. On the other hand, this social group was not capable of "accurately" representing French society or enjoying the rights held by citizens because the *évolué* would always "be drawn back to [his] traditions" and a mental framework that led to misconceptions about the "true" nature of France.[41]

Despite the inhibiting actions of Dakar, the returning *tirailleurs* demanded that the 1918 decrees be honored and that they be accorded the rights of citizens. Throughout the 1919 election campaign and into the 1920s veterans from West Africa complained of mistreatment by Dakar and Paris' failure to enforce its wartime promises.[42] Metropolitan organizations such as the League for the Defense of the Rights of Man and Citizen took up the cause of these former soldiers and brought the actions of Dakar to the attention of the government in Paris. One such case became something of a *cause célèbre* in the early 1920s and illustrates the measures that Dakar was prepared to take in denying citizenship to its returning veterans. Salla Dialo, who in 1921 was still on active duty as part of the army of occupation in western Germany, had applied for naturalization several times, but had been denied on each occasion without any explanation from the government general. He had renounced his personal status, accepted French civil law, and had been decorated numerous times for bravery in the 1914–1918 war as well as in earlier combat in the protectorate of Morocco and the colony of Mauritania. As the League for the Defense of the Rights of Man and Citizen pointed out in a letter to the president of the Republic, Dialo had met all the criteria, and more, stipulated by the 14 January 1918 decrees issued by Clemenceau. Yet, Dakar still refused to grant this soldier citizenship and failed to provide a reason for that decision. Even Diagne's appeals on his behalf could not loosen Merlin's resolve.[43] In fact, few *sujets* who served in the defense of France during the 1914–1918 war were accorded citizenship.[44]

Diagne warned officials in Paris that France's failure to uphold the pledges made to those who volunteered in 1918 was creating "agents of revolt against French rule in our overseas possessions."[45] Yet, the political climate in France had changed markedly since Diagne was named Commissaire of the Republic in 1918. While voters in the Four Communes returned Diagne to the Chamber with an overwhelming majority, elsewhere the French electorate had produced a government dominated by the political right grouped under the *"Bloc National."* The new government's conception of the relationship between France and its colonies accorded more with the emerging views of the government general in Dakar and left Diagne and the *évolués* little room to maneuver within the structures of the French or colonial states.

From 1919 to 1923 the "Blue Horizon Chamber," so named because of the significant numbers of veterans elected in 1919, took two important actions that indicated a changing conception of the relationship between France and its colonies in the post-war period. First, in 1920 the deputies passed a bill that "impose[d] stiff penalties for any form of propaganda...that encouraged abortion and the use of contraceptive devices." As Roberts argues, the bill "sought specifically to bring women's sexual practices under legislative control by attacking abortion and female forms of contraception."[46] However, it also reflected new notions about the role of the empire for France and anxieties over changes in the colonial field induced by wartime pressures. The solution to France's demographic weakness *vis-à-vis* Germany, which was exacerbated during the war, was now to be found in the reproduction of "Europeans," not as previously suggested by turning colonial subjects into "Frenchmen."[47] Thus, one of the bases upon which Diagne had built the *originaires'* claims to citizenship was diminished within the changed political culture of 1920s France.

The shift in demographic strategies suggests the increasing influence of racial discourses within the colonial field. Not only had troops from overseas come into contact with dangerous ideas in the metropole, some of them also married French women. Such relationships, some in the imperial hierarchy urged, should be hidden from the *sujet* population in the colonies because of their potentially destabilizing effect on the delicate separation between rulers and ruled. To that end, governors general implored the ministry of colonies to keep those demobilized soldiers "in France" because their presence in the colonies "would have a disastrous effect" on the mentality of those under the metropole's tutelage. Such liaisons in Europe were frequently viewed with suspicion by imperial administrators and the women involved were castigated by at least one colonial official as invariably "prostitutes."[48] Thus, in addition to an increased concern with (re)defining gender categories in post-war France identified by Roberts, this period also included a heightened race consciousness that reinforced trends within the colonial field that construed Africans and Europeans as essentially different and, therefore, in need of managed separation. Ann Stoler notes a similar concern over the growth of the *métis* populations in Dutch and French-controlled Southeast Asia. According to Stoler, "such mixing [between French or Dutch and colonized natives] called into question the very criteria by which Europeanness could be identified, citizenship should be accorded, and nationality assigned."[49] In turn those that failed to adequately maintain the

distance between colonizers and colonized were viewed with distrust and
fear.

The second significant act of the *Bloc National* government was the
defeat of Sarraut's economic development plan for West Africa in 1923. In
1921 Albert Sarraut, as minister of colonies, presented a financial program
for the federation that included "more than one billion francs…for
investment in railways, ports, and irrigation in West Africa, as well as
schools, health care, and research facilities."[50] However, in addition to
Sarraut's inability to account for the source of funding for the project, the
program raised concerns in Dakar and Paris that it would contribute to the
"proletarianization" of AOF, precisely what neither the government general
nor the cabinet wanted. The strikes of 1919 to 1921 in West Africa
convinced Dakar that the federation's *sujets* were unsuited for "salaried
labor" as it was practiced in Europe. The strikers demanded equal pay with
their metropolitan counterparts and the same work rules as applied to citizens
of France. Such terms reinforced the emerging conception among colonialists
that the slightest contact with metropolitan ways produced impatience for
reforms among the new urban elite of West Africa. This impatience indicated
to some imperial officials that the mentality of the *évolué* was more like that
of "children" who never seemed to reach adulthood.[51] That perpetual
"immaturity" provided the grounds on which the colonial administration
justified its use of forced labor for public works projects and for making
unsalaried Africans available for disposal by private businesses.[52]
Furthermore, the government general claimed the West African was at heart
"a peasant" who merely "put on the clothes of a European." Upon doing so,
the urban worker in AOF introduced "disarray in his own family" and
became vulnerable to "xenophobic propaganda." This state of affairs, Dakar
argued, put the "native salaried laborer" at the center of "political and social
dangers."[53]

To prevent the growth of a "discontented working class" in AOF, the
government general informed Paris that money earmarked for the colonies
should be deployed to "intensify traditional production," especially that of
cash crops.[54] In other words, the reformulated *mission civilisatrice* involved,
as Herman Lebovics argues, a return to "traditional" sources in the colonies,
which meant intensifying plantation-style production in the "bush" under the
watchful eyes of the pre-colonial elite and French businesses, coinciding with
a trend in France wherein "folklorists began to discover the passing of a
failed rural France."[55]

However, the changes in the conception of the "proper" form of African
social organization as well as concerns in France over a disappearing

metropolitan peasantry took place within a political culture where workers throughout the colonial field had become more aggressive in asserting their demands. Politically, this new vigor was expressed in the growth of Communist movements and the spread of a Marxist discourse that offered alternative analyses of what produced the cataclysm of 1914–1918 and how to cope with its effects. During Diagne's bid for reelection in 1919, he seized on the popular attraction of the Russian Revolution. He called for support as "the candidate of all the African Proletariat."[56] And in a striking reproduction of the language emanating from the Bolshevik government in Moscow and its newly founded Communist International (Comintern), Diagne declared, "Tomorrow! Will witness the decisive Victory of the African Proletariat over the forces of reaction."[57]

Despite Diagne's triumph, frustration mounted among his constituents, especially the veterans who felt abandoned by Paris and unable to secure redress of their grievances through appeals to their elected representative. By the early 1920s, Diagne's position as the preeminent spokesperson of the *évolués* had slipped. Confronted with a hostile administration in Dakar, an increasingly antagonistic political culture in France, and "the object of a particularly severe surveillance" by authorities in France and West Africa,[58] the *évolué* was conceptually and politically marginalized within the colonial field. As such, growing numbers of the French-educated elite adopted more radical responses to their condition.

In fact, many veterans blamed Diagne for their plight as much as Paris or the colonial administration. He had promised citizenship and exemption from the *indigénat* in return for a "blood tax" that ostensibly demonstrated the volunteers' preparedness for entry into the "French family."[59] Instead, at war's end the *tirailleur* was greeted with mistrust and attempts to return him to the authority of chiefs and work on the peanut and cocoa plantations in the "bush." Many among the new elite became convinced that liberty could no longer be attained by proving their loyalty to France or pleading with an unreceptive colonial government for their rights as citizens. Rather, a rising chorus developed claiming the only path to "equality before the law" and "liberty from oppression" was through "the indispensable transformation [of a] social revolution" like that which had recently taken place in Russia.[60] Thus, if officials in Dakar and Paris claimed that the *évolué* was by nature susceptible to "subversive" propaganda, their actions in failing to enforce the decrees on citizenship helped to shape the context in which revolutionary politics became a viable option for many of the French-educated elite from West Africa.[61]

Common Enemies:
Marxism, the *Évolués*, and the *L'Union Intercoloniale*

By 1920 migrants from the colonies had founded two organizations in the metropole that provided the earliest institutional bases for *évolué* politics in France. Soldiers from the French possession of Indochina who were sent to fight in Europe established the *Association des Patriotes Annamites* (APA) in 1914 to agitate within the military for citizenship rights along the lines of those being won at that time by Diagne and the *originaires* from West Africa. By 1915 Nguyen Ai Quoc, later better known as Ho Chi Minh, had emerged as the most prominent leader of the APA and began his long association with radical political currents in France and East Asia.[62] In 1920, veterans from Madagascar held the first public meeting in Paris of the *Ligue pour l'Accession des Indigènes de Madagascar aux Droits de Citoyen Français* (LMDC) under the leadership of Max Bloncourt and the honorary presidency of the noted sociologist Charles Gide.[63] The LMDC, like the APA and Diagne, also campaigned for the extension of citizenship to veterans from Madagascar and complete integration into French society, a program that prompted one military official to urge that "Malgache troops be prevented from joining this group."[64]

However, 1920 was also the year of the Tours Congress of the French socialist party (SFIO) at which the majority of delegates voted to adhere to the Third (Communist) International founded by the Bolshevik leader V. I. Lenin in 1919. By that decision the French Communist Party (PCF) was formed. The decision to join the Comintern, though, represented more than a political alliance within the divided international socialist movement, or support for the Communist experiment then underway in Russia, although these were certainly important factors. Attachment to the Comintern meant acceptance of and participation in forging a worldview that had a considerable impact in shaping the colonial field. Communist discourse presented new perspectives on the relationship between metropole and colonies, helped to fashion the self-identities of those engaged in the imperial framework, and provided the ideological context for the development of new forms of struggle in France and West Africa. In fact, the "colonial question" was an essential element of the new Communist movements and helped to distinguish the ideology emerging from the Bolshevik Revolution from previous socialist tendencies. Early socialist and Marxist theories held that "imperialism [was] an inevitable by-product of capitalism" because production tended to exceed "national needs" which, in turn, forced a relentless search for "new markets" to avoid economic crises in the industrial centers. Thus, the period of rapid colonial expansion in the last quarter of the nineteenth century was explained as being an effect of the deep depression that gripped Europe from approximately 1873 to 1896. Colonialism was also viewed by Marxists of the late nineteenth and early twentieth centuries as an additional "means of suppressing the proletarian movement" that was becoming an important force in social struggles taking place within industrial societies at the time. According to that analysis, the colonized populations of Asia and Africa provided a new source of laborers who lacked the class-consciousness of European workers, which made it easier to exploit the subject peoples. In addition, imperial conquest strengthened the military power of the colonizing states by providing experience for soldiers, a testing ground for new tactics and weapons, and increased wealth to finance the coercive mechanisms of capitalist society.[65]

However, this reading of imperialism continued the Marxist tradition of concentrating the struggle against capitalism in the industrial societies of Europe and North America. By presenting imperialism as a natural outgrowth of capitalist development, early Marxists subsumed the fight against imperialism under the paramount effort to overthrow capitalism and, thus, colonialism as a special form of oppression received only marginal attention from the Socialist International throughout much of its history. In fact, many socialists in France prior to the First World War adopted a version of the *mission civilisatrice* and declared themselves in favor "of the penetration of French culture [in the colonies] through the propagation of the French language." That perspective corresponded with the objectives of the SFIO on the colonial question in 1914 that called for the "peaceful conquest of the semi-barbaric peoples by attracting them to progress and civilization."[66] Any liberation of the colonized populations, the argument went, would result from a socialist revolution in the metropoles.

Lenin's theory of imperialism, which served as the basis for the Comintern's doctrine on the colonial question, provided a different perspective on the nature of imperialism and the place of anti-colonialism in the confrontation between labor and capital. For the Bolshevik leader, the colonized populations were not "backward" and in need of tutelage by Europeans. In terms of the class struggle, they were actually more "advanced" and at the forefront of the conflict.[67] Accordingly, the PCF declared in 1924, "It would be erroneous to believe that it is necessary to wait for the European revolution in order to liberate the colonies [from] under the imperialist yoke." The advent of the imperialist stage of capitalism meant, in Leninist terms, that the colonized societies had been "brusquely ushered into the modern capitalist economy." Therefore, as in all capitalist societies, "there are capitalists and proletarians" each with their own "class consciousness." In fact, the PCF asserted, "...the natives of the colonies [were] capable of more energetic action [against capitalism] than their European brothers" because they were more severely exploited than were workers in the imperial centers.[68]

For Lenin, imperialism was a new stage in world history. "Capitalism," the future leader of the Russian Revolution wrote, "has been transformed into imperialism." Two processes were involved in this transmutation: concentration and globalization. Following a theory advanced earlier by J. A. Hobson, Lenin argued that competition inherent in the capitalist mode of production led to the formation of cartels—associations of businesses that divided markets between them and controlled all aspects of the production process. These cartels eventually gave way to outright monopolies. However, modern banking systems, or finance capital, arose alongside this transformation and became increasingly indispensable to the further expansion of profits and the development of industry. Eventually, monopolies developed in the financial sector as well. At a certain point in the process these financial oligarchies dominated all other forms of capital, including production capital, and generalized and intensified the "socialization of production" already characteristic of capitalism.[69]

Furthermore, Lenin continued, these processes were not restricted by the boundaries between states. Rather, "under capitalism the home market [was] inevitably bound up with the foreign market. Capitalism long ago created a world market." As a result, competition ensued between the monopolies tied to one Great Power with those of another, which led, invariably, to the conquest of new markets in Asia and Africa. In other words, colonialism, the Bolshevik leader argued, was the political expression of the triumph of monopoly throughout the world. It signaled the complete division of all known and "unknown" markets by a handful of powerful oligarchies that controlled and manipulated the political practices of a few major powers.[70]

Since imperialism had brought the capitalist mode of production to every part of the world and the dominant class was centered in Europe, the PCF concluded, "the French proletarians and the colonial workers have a common interest [and] will work to realize a unique front against capitalism." To forge this "unique front," though, it was necessary to "facilitate the training of natives for revolutionary struggle [for the time when] they returned to their native lands."[71] The PCF went even further and stated that the organization of the "reserve army of labor," as colonial subjects were sometimes labeled, was a means "to transforming and pushing the metropolitan proletariat" toward revolutionary action.[72] Instead of marginalizing the effort to achieve liberty in the colonies, Communist discourse placed the plight of imperial subjects at the center of an international socialist revolution and even made that transformation dependent upon liberation of the *sujet* population in the overseas territories.

For increasing numbers of *évolués* from AOF, marginalized within the colonial field after the war, the Communist Party's message was compelling.[73] Furthermore, whereas Paris and Dakar attempted to undermine the influence of the new urban elite in West Africa, the PCF regarded the *évolués* as future leaders of "a movement against capitalism and in favor of Communism in the colonies" as well as in the metropole.[74] Yet, both the government general and the Communists highlighted the same attributes as marking the French-educated elite's special place within the colonial field—their participation in the cultural worlds of both Europe and Africa. For Dakar, this disqualified the urban elite from AOF for membership in, let alone leadership of both communities and made them dangerous. However, the PCF reinforced the *évolués'* own emerging self-identity by citing this quality as precisely what legitimated the new elite's claims to speak on behalf of the *sujet* populations as well as participate as equals in metropolitan society. In effect, the PCF took up the political aspirations of the *évolués*, which Diagne seemed increasingly unable to satisfy, and pushed them in more radical directions.

In 1922 the Communist Party provided an organizational context for the discontent welling up among the *évolués* by merging such groups as the LMDC and APA into the *Union Intercoloniale* (UIC).[75] The PCF, at the insistence of the Comintern,[76] argued that the colonized population required its own associations, separate from the party's regular committees, because colonial subjects were "doubly exploited: as workers and as natives."[77] By creating distinct organizational space for people subject to colonial rule, the PCF also furnished the means, financial and institutional, whereby an alternative leadership emerged among the new urban elite from West Africa that challenged Diagne's authority. For while Diagne was prepared to blame the government general for the miseries of his constituents, he was unwilling to break with Paris or even the pre-colonial elite in West Africa with which he had forged alliances during the 1918 recruitment campaign. In fact, by 1923 Diagne had even made peace with the government general and thenceforth relied upon the support of Dakar to retain his seat in the Chamber.[78]

The UIC tarred the deputy from Senegal as a "traitor" who had sold out his own people for the sake of favors from the Parisian political establishment.[79] The Communist organization reminded the *tirailleurs* of how they had "suffered at the front" and that "when the war was over the natives of the colonies…were neglected [and] abandoned."[80] In light of the disappointment experienced by many recruits from the federation upon demobilization, the alliance that was forged during the Commissaire of the Republic's 1918 tour between Diagne, the government general, Paris, and the pre-colonial elite in AOF took on a sinister appearance. By 1924 rumors were circulating among *évolué* circles that the deputy from Senegal had received a commission for each African recruited in 1918. This, according to the celebrated novelist René Maran, explained Diagne's reluctance to break with Paris and take more energetic action on behalf of his constituents.[81]

In fact, it was Maran that forced the simmering disputes among the *évolués* into the public light. A former official of the colonial empire, Maran's life in many ways was similar to that of his rival, Diagne. Born in 1887 in French Guyana, Maran was educated in French schools and rose through the ranks of the colonial administration, eventually holding important posts in French Equatorial Africa during the First World War. This stay in Central Africa provided the experiences that brought Maran into direct conflict with the imperial state. Using notes accumulated during inspection tours of the French possession Oubangui-Chari, today the Central African Republic, Maran published *Batouala* in 1921 to draw attention to the plight of those under French rule in Africa. That year, his book was awarded the *Prix Goncourt* for literature, which made *Batouala* an instant success among the French-educated elite from overseas and metropolitan intellectuals alike.[82]

Maran's story of a tribal chief in a remote part of France's African empire attacked what the author perceived as the hypocrisy of the *mission civilisatrice*. Instead of railroads, education, health care, and economic development, Maran presented a picture of French-ruled Africa as a caldron of discontent and misery. Rather than liberate the African from "custom," France had stripped tradition of its meaning while leaving the colonial subjects under the authority of "guardians" of the old ways. Maran had Batouala, a chief in the colony, lament, "the young and…all those who served the whites [that now] looked on custom with derision." This produced hostility among the pre-colonial elite who wished that France "be beaten by the Germans" during the 1914–1918 war, and more depressingly, meant that the African hoped for death as the sole release from colonial rule.[83]

Maran's book earned him immediate dismissal from the colonial service, which meant he was free to engage in the more radical political currents then emerging among the new educated elite, a step Diagne never took despite his own periodic contacts with members of revolutionary organizations in

Paris.[84] While there is no evidence that Maran ever joined the PCF, he did associate with the UIC and was an activist in many Communist-sponsored organizations of colonial migrants in France during the 1920s. In fact, a series of meetings between Maran, at the time writing for the Pan-Africanist journal *Les Continents*, and the UIC produced a decision to publish an article that systematically catalogued Diagne's collaboration with the French government.[85] The article, published on 24 October 1924 in *Les Continents*, accused the deputy from Senegal of deliberately lying to those whom he recruited in 1918 and of participating in a conspiracy to increase the "economic exploitation of Africa."[86] This cabal was said to involve officials in Paris, the government general in Dakar, and "the tyrants [who are] native chiefs" in West Africa, the very coalition that brought success to Diagne's mission in 1918.[87] The alliance forged between the deputy from Senegal and the pre-colonial elite came in for particular criticism by the burgeoning legions of opponents to Diagne among his constituents. This, according to some radical *évolués*, was the clearest indication that Diagne, the onetime champion of citizenship rights for all colonial subjects, had abandoned his supporters and their cause for personal financial and political gain.[88]

In response to those accusations, Diagne filed a slander suit against Maran and *Les Continents*. The two-day trial that began on 24 November 1924 was a showcase of the growing cleavages within the urban elite from AOF and brought new leaders of the *évolués* to the fore. In a sense, the struggle for authority within the colonial field was, for a brief moment, concentrated in a Parisian courtroom.[89] Witnesses on Diagne's behalf included Georges Clemenceau, and for the defense Maran presented many of the veterans who had volunteered during Diagne's 1918 tour of West Africa. The suit came as a surprise to the circle of *évolués* around the UIC and *Les Continents*. A correspondent for the latter pointed out that "for a long time an intermittent campaign has been waged against him (Diagne) in various sections of the French Press, and accusations equally or even more damaging than the present one have been hurled at him, but he ignored them all."[90] However, the deputy from Senegal sensed the high stakes involved in accusations that originated among his constituents. He suggested that it was one matter to take on "some [among] the administration in the colonies [who] by their actions were doing great harm to the glorious reputation of the nation (France)," but a power struggle among the new elite from West Africa was of an entirely different order. At stake in this trial was the authority to represent the interests of the *évolués* within the colonial field who in turn were staking claims to leadership of the colonized populations in general. In other words, Diagne regarded attacks from colonial officials as a source of unity and strength for the new elite from AOF because they helped to galvanize opposition to the government general. However, rebellion within the ranks of the French-educated elite, Diagne reasoned, undermined what he saw as the primary goal for the *évolués*—to accede to complete equality in citizenship rights and become thoroughly integrated within the French political system. Therefore, Diagne told the court that he brought the trial "for the sole reason that my countrymen in Africa should not be left under the impression that it was for my personal interest that they have been sacrificed."[91]

In a reversal of his 1919 posturing, during the trial Diagne catered to the anti-Communist apprehensions of the court and said the accusations made against him "were really directed against France." Diagne said his interest was to create the conditions whereby more of his constituents would be touched by French civilization. This necessarily involved certain reforms in the colonial administration, but also patience and respect for the native cultures of the federation, including the institution of chieftaincy. His opponents, the former Commissaire of the Republic argued, deserved "an exemplary sentence...so that...the corrupting influence from foreign Negroes might be brought to an end."[92] The court ruled in the deputy's favor and fined Maran and *Les Continents* 1,500 francs for the cost of the trial and awarded 2,000 francs in damages to Diagne. In addition, the judge gave Maran a six-month suspended prison sentence.[93]

While Diagne won his suit, his standing among the *évolués* faltered. The trial indicated how closely tied he had become to the political establishment in Paris. It further revealed his unwillingness to challenge the authority of the pre-colonial elite who many veterans held responsible for their being forcibly recruited during the early years of the First World War. In addition, Diagne publicly associated himself with the business interests accused of fostering forced labor throughout the colonial empire.

Yet, changes also occurred among the opposition to Diagne after the trial. The fines levied against *Les Continents* were enough to destroy that journal. Within a month of the verdict, it had ceased publication and its supporters affiliated with other organizations and publications, with many, including Maran, joining the UIC.[94] The disappearance of *Les Continents* eliminated the most powerful voice in favor of the nascent pan-African and pro-Garveyite movements in France, although pan-Africanism received a new and different life in 1930s Paris, discussed in chapter four. Now only the PCF seemed to have the financial and organizational resources to effectively oppose Diagne and his allies in the colonial field. In fact, by 1925 informants for the CAI reported the UIC held regular meetings in Paris at which over

3,000 people attended.[95] According to secret reports prepared for the ministry of colonies, the UIC's journal, *Le Paria*, "receive[d] communications from [throughout] the empire," a testament to the reach of the PCF in the colonies and to the complex networks being established by *évolués* across vast geographical spaces.[96]

As mentioned above, the trial also provided the context for the emergence of new leaders among the French-educated elite from AOF. One such figure was Lamine Senghor who was a witness on Maran's behalf. Lamine Senghor, no relation to the poet Léopold Sédar Senghor, was born in the French colony of Senegal in 1889. He was drafted in 1915 and remained on active duty throughout the remainder of the conflict. Wounded during the battle of Verdun in 1916, Lamine Senghor also contracted tuberculosis, a disease that contributed to his death in 1927. Demobilized in 1919, Lamine Senghor joined thousands of other veterans who remained in France where he picked up work in the docks of the Midi. An admitted early supporter of Diagne, Lamine Senghor became disillusioned over the deputy's cordial relationship with the French government at a time when many veterans from West Africa were denied pensions, citizenship, and other rights they had been promised.[97]

According to Robert Cornevin, Lamine Senghor's political baptism occurred during the proceedings brought by Diagne against Maran in 1924.[98] In a Parisian court Lamine Senghor confronted the man he held responsible for his plight and that of his comrades-in-arms from AOF. For the veteran from Senegal there was no doubt after the ruling that Diagne was more interested in preserving his friendship with the Parisian political establishment than in fighting on behalf of those who "were conquered by violence" and were used "to feed [France's] industry."[99] Within months of the verdict informants for the CAI noted that Lamine Senghor had emerged as one of the most important figures in the UIC and had attracted a large following among West Africans living in the metropole.[100]

However, as the UIC became more successful within the colonial field, it too underwent changes reflecting accommodations affected through participation in those struggles: defining and being defined by the rules of the game. While Lamine Senghor was the most prominent figure within the Intercolonial Union from West Africa, Nguyen Ai Quoc from Indochina was recognized as the most influential member of the organization's leadership. He edited its newspaper and was the Communist Party's preferred delegate from the empire to the Comintern's international congresses.[101] As the confrontations between Communists and Nationalists intensified in China, the Soviet government concentrated more of the international Communist movement's energy on "anti-imperialist" activities in East Asia. This invariably contributed to orienting the PCF's colonial politics more toward issues affecting Indochina at the expense, some in the UIC asserted, of struggles underway in other parts of the French colonial empire.[102] By the end of 1925 factions had developed along ethnic lines within the UIC and the organization was slowly succumbing to the pull of diverging interests between those from Indochina, North Africa, and West Africa. The discontent of the West Africans crystallized during the Rif War in Morocco as the PCF ordered all energy to be devoted to that struggle. Lamine Senghor and others from AOF and Indochina questioned the Party's assertions of the revolutionary character rebellion's leader Abd el-Krim.[103]

The divisions that emerged within the Intercolonial Union during 1925 were not uniquely generated within the Communist movement, though. They also reflected the discourse of cultural difference that pervaded the colonial field at the time. The language of distinction between the "true" French and "authentic" African societies that the government general deployed as part of a strategy to marginalize the *évolués* also, as discussed above, informed policy decisions that contributed to shaping forms of production and social engagement in West Africa. Thus, the defeat of Sarraut's economic plan, the *mise en valeur*, in 1923 abetted a process whereby the development of a recognizable and self-conscious urban proletariat was truncated in the federation. In addition, Dakar and Paris increasingly channeled resources—cultural, political, and economic—to rural West Africa, which further valorized the authority of the pre-colonial elite and tribal forms of community organization.[104] For the Communist Party and its supporters to be effective in the political contests unfolding in French West Africa, its message had to correspond to a reality that was recognizable to the participants. By the mid-1920s the wave of strikes that had afflicted Dakar at the beginning of the decade had subsided. As the prospect of a "proletarianized" West Africa receded, the language of international class struggle increasingly gave way among anti-colonialists in the federation to the rhetoric of "national self-determination" that was oriented around definitions of racial difference. Yet, the decision by the PCF to "prioritize the national struggle," manifested in the campaigns around the Rif War, not only reflected the cultural context in which it participated and the influence of its supporters from AOF on the Party, it also helped to fashion that political culture and to legitimate notions of racial and cultural difference among the radical *évolués*.[105]

From Proletarians to Africans: The LDRN and the Politics of Culture

An integral aspect of Communist discourse was the idea of "complete equality [between] nations [and] the right of nations to self-determination." However, the idea that each national community could dispose of its own fortunes was linked to the "unity of the workers of all nations" which was to be the driving force and sustaining principle of national independence.[106] While Lenin claimed wars of "national liberation" were "inevitable," he asserted that these struggles "would be engaged against imperialism."[107] Since Communist discourse held that imperialism was monopoly capitalism, the fight for independence in the colonies was an expression of the international socialist revolution. In other words, anti-colonialism was simultaneously anti-capitalism and opposition to capital implied a concurrent fight for liberation of the colonized populations.

By the mid-1920s, though, the fights against colonialism and for socialism had become separated in both the rhetoric and practices of the PCF. Whereas the Intercolonial Union's original program asserted the "natives" from overseas were "men with the same title, exactly, as the inhabitants of France" and, therefore, should "enjoy...the same rights as French citizens,"[108] within three years the PCF was insisting on a "struggle by any means and without conditions for the total independence of the colonies."[109] However, national independence required specific organizations to lead the separate struggles. To that end, the UIC suggested groups be formed "that would be responsible to work within their own milieu."[110]

The idea behind the proposal was that the new groups would grow out of and continue to be a part of the UIC. Each geographically specific organization was to remain under the overall administration of the Intercolonial Union. Lamine Senghor nonetheless interpreted this suggestion as an opportunity "to create, outside of all political influence, an association that brings together blacks from all the different colonies, with the goal of defending their interests. His intention," one observer commented, "is to assemble his comrades within a society [that is] purely African."[111] When other leaders of the UIC learned in April 1926 that Lamine Senghor had founded the *Comité de Défense de la Race Nègre* (CDRN) without consulting the Communist Party, the simmering racial and ethnic disputes within the organization reached the breaking point. As a result, the Intercolonial Union decided it had no choice but to dissolve into "three sections: one for the North Africans, one for the Antilles [and all other blacks] and one for the Indochinese."[112] That schism, it later turned out, had momentous consequences for the future of nationalist and anti-colonialist politics in the French colonial field. In addition to the CDRN, the UIC fractured into the *Étoile Nord-Africaine* (ENA) led by Messali Hadj and the *Parti Annamite de l'Indépendance* (PAI) headed by Nguyen Ai Quoc and Nguyen The Truyen. The ENA was the precursor to later Algerian nationalist movements, while the PAI eventually developed into the Indochinese and later Vietnamese Communist Party.

Although still affiliated with the Communist Party, the CDRN insisted on its own internal autonomy. In fact, many within Lamine Senghor's new organization doubted the usefulness of maintaining any links with the PCF since their objective was supposed to be national independence, not socialist revolution. Within a year those among Lamine Senghor's associates who were still willing to work with the Communists as the "natural allies" of the colonized peoples had abandoned the CDRN and formed the *Ligue de Défense de la Race Nègre* (LDRN). The new organization had one stated goal: "The complete emancipation of the Negro race" which required "violent [struggle] against colonization in general and against France in particular."[113]

In addition to Maran, who was soon disenchanted with the LDRN, Garan Tiémoko Kouyaté, a schoolteacher from French Soudan (Mali) joined Lamine Senghor in the new organization's leadership. Born on 27 April 1902 in Ségou, Kouyaté was too young to have participated in the First World War. A graduate of the École William Ponty in 1921, Kouyaté served as a teacher in Côte d'Ivoire between 1921 and 1923 before leaving for France to attend the École Normale Coloniale in Aix-en-Provence. On 5 October 1925 he, along with some classmates, was expelled from school for "insolence" and "indiscipline." The report on his dismissal noted, "He expressed sentiments of hostility against the French administration in AOF." This included the authoring of a letter to the government general calling for reforms and family pensions for Africans.[114] Since he was not an *originaire* from the Four Communes of Senegal, Kouyaté was not endowed with the rights of French citizenship and as such, he was representative of a new generation of *évolués* from West Africa that had gained little from Diagne's early successes and was not confident or especially desirous of being integrated into French society.

Whereas Diagne accepted the notion of cultural difference and the importance of respecting these distinctions, he argued that this did not preclude the enjoyment of equal citizenship rights under French rule. For Kouyaté, Lamine Senghor, and others in the LDRN the idea that West African societies were fundamentally different from that of France provided the conceptual justification for the independence of the colonies. According to the *Ligue* the "people of France" were "posed with a dilemma: The assimilation *en bloc* of all natives [in the colonies] without restrictions, with all the logical political consequences which that entailed; or acceptance of the national question of our peoples by way of creating self-governing States."[115] In other words, one could not be both French and Muslim as Diagne argued. Either one had to be "truly French" and surrender the notion of cultural distinction, or one had to live according to one's "own traditions" as a sovereign people.[116] The LDRN considered it unlikely and undesirable to be completely assimilated into French society. Furthermore, throughout the 1920s the colonial administration advocated the "association of peoples" as the guiding framework for governance of the subject population and the rate of naturalizations continued to decline into the 1930s.[117] Even a law proposed by Prime Minister Edouard Daladier in 1924, designed to streamline the naturalization process and take it out of the hands of colonial administrators, was defeated in the Chamber of Deputies.[118]

The LDRN concentrated its efforts at "constituting a Negro State in black Africa" and was supported in this by the PCF, which by then had also dropped its endeavors to secure equal citizenship rights for the subject populations.[119] By the late 1920s the Communist Party regarded the liberation of the colonies as a pre-condition for the overthrow of capitalism in France, reversing the pre-Leninist conceptions of the colonial question within the socialist movement. At a 1927 international anti-colonial congress in Brussels Lamine Senghor explained that the goal of the "struggle...against imperialist capitalism" was "for national independence."[120] Once "the citizens of each country directed the government of their own State," Lamine Senghor wrote, "they would form *a fraternal alliance of free countries*."[121] The international community Lenin argued would result from a global struggle against imperialism by a united working class was in the late 1920s imagined by leaders of the PCF and the Party's supporters from overseas as the product of an association between independent States, each with their own national traditions.

Armed with a program that called for "the political emancipation of the Negro race," the support of the PCF, and practicing a discourse familiar to colonial administrators and those over whom Dakar ruled, the *Ligue's* influence spread rapidly throughout West Africa and among migrants from the colonies in France.[122] Sections of the organization were established in every colony of the federation and throughout the metropole. Lamine Senghor and Kouyaté, aided by Communist trade unions, traveled frequently between France and West Africa, and information was disseminated and actions planned by way of an expanding network of supporters and family members dispersed across the federation.[123] By the time Lamine Senghor had succumbed in late 1927 to complications from tuberculosis contracted during the 1914–1918 war, Kouyaté was regarded by CAI agents and many West Africans as the preeminent figure among those *évolués* opposed to Diagne and his path of conciliation with the government general. One CAI agent noted that Kouyaté "exercise[d] a remarkable influence and an incontestable authority among his compatriots [in France and West Africa]."[124]

While Kouyaté's stature among the *évolués* improved, Diagne was increasingly isolated from his constituents. The deputy from Senegal rarely traveled to West Africa and when he did it was only in the months prior to an election campaign. By 1928 the former Commissaire of the Republic was an entrenched figure among the Parisian political establishment and a staunch ally of the government general for French West Africa, then headed by Jules Carde.[125] Diagne recognized Kouyaté's influence among the *évolués* and attempted to diffuse any challenge to his authority within that community. On several occasions early in 1928 the deputy contacted the LDRN to request meetings with Kouyaté. However, each time they failed to agree on the bases for cooperation. Kouyaté insisted on a struggle founded upon "racial unity" with the goal of complete independence for Africa. Diagne, on the other hand, persisted in his assertion that colonialism was not entirely negative and the paramount goal for the *évolués* was the gradual extension of French citizenship and civilization in the overseas territories.[126]

The dispute between the leader of the *Ligue* and the deputy from Senegal was emblematic of conflicts among *évolués* over their self-identity as a recognizable social category within the French colonial field. While Diagne and his supporters viewed their destiny as being agents of the French *mission civilisatrice* among the *sujet* population, the *Ligue* described its role as "on the one hand making known to the Negroes the true republican France with its noble traditions, and on the other, expressing the true sentiments of the Negroes ... to the true France." Kouyaté and his associates avowed that "our evolution [would] find its inspiration in the possession of liberties guaranteed by ... our own traditions."[127]

When negotiations between Diagne and Kouyaté broke down, both camps mobilized their supporters for a showdown in the upcoming legislative elections. However, Kouyaté could not run against Diagne because he was not a citizen or an *originaire* from the Four Communes of Senegal. Nevertheless, the *Ligue* had forged close working relationships with two of Diagne's most influential early supporters who had since broken with the deputy: Galandou Diouf and Lamine Guèye, and the LDRN chose Diouf as its standard bearer in 1928.[128]

Governor General Carde informed Paris that "all measures have been taken in the sense you (the ministry of colonies) indicated" to disrupt the Diouf campaign and the activities of his supporters. Those measures included interdiction of the LDRN's newspaper *La Race Nègre* and arrest, under terms of the *indigénat*, of those non-citizens who made seditious statements against the government general or France.[129] The result of the vote, although close, was a foregone conclusion. Diagne retained his seat by virtue of the dubious assistance provided by the government general. The *Ligue* and Diouf's supporters in the Four Communes filed several protests demanding a new vote, but no investigation into allegations of ballot tempering was ever undertaken.[130]

Kouyaté and the *Ligue* also faced opposition from another quarter during and after the 1928 election. The Communist Party expressed concerns that "Kouyaté...[was] refusing any control by the Party of his organization," the LDRN.[131] In fact, disputes over the relationship between the PCF and the *Ligue* intensified within the LDRN and between it and the Party as the practices and rhetoric of the Communist movement increasingly gave priority to national independence over socialist revolution in the colonies. Even before the 1928 election Maran complained that the *Ligue's* work toward the emancipation of "their race" was hampered by the internal politics of the PCF and the Party's attempt to direct the LDRN's activities.[132] As a result, the novelist argued, the *Ligue* "had done nothing for the defense of the black race."[133]

The pressures within the LDRN contributed to the widening distance between it and the Party. The PCF expressed dismay at the meetings between Kouyaté and Diagne in 1928 and was apprehensive that a deal with Diagne would marginalize the Party as a force in the contests for authority within West Africa. In addition, as Kouyaté pushed for racial solidarity and national independence as bases for the struggle against colonialism, the Comintern reassessed its colonial policy in ways that partially undermined the *Ligue's* program. Following the Sixth Congress of the Communist International in 1928, the Communist Party stridently denounced calls for racial unity. Instead, its supporters among the colonized populations were instructed "to group together the entire working class, without distinction of language or skin color." The rhetoric of a "unique front" between the subject peoples and metropolitan workers was revived. Further, the Communists embraced an approach that decried "bourgeois nationalism" and "class collaboration" because the needs and objectives of the "revolutionary workers movement" had to be placed "before all other considerations."[134]

However, this sudden about face in Communist rhetoric and tactics included an appeal for "a cultural revolution" that was deemed "an integral part of all the work necessary for the socialist reconstruction" of colonies and metropole alike.[135] Kouyaté was attracted to the idea of a cultural revolution. He reasoned that the idea of national independence carried with it the notion of "cultural development." Emancipation of the nation, Kouyaté asserted, could only take place once the people had come to identify themselves as part of a recognizable national community. Therefore, Kouyaté argued that the *Ligue* should direct all its efforts toward the "cultural" revival of West African society in preparation for the independence struggle. [136]

By the early 1930s many *évolués* shared the LDRN's assertion that their task in the colonial field was to lead a "cultural renaissance" in West Africa. Colonialism, one *évolué* newspaper declared, had "brusquely stopped the development of the African people, and their civilization which, in several ways, had attained a high level of advancement, was almost completely destroyed."[137] Thus, "for the militant [*évolués*], the most urgent task [consisted] in proving to the world the reality and originality of African civilization."[138]

While the Communist Party endorsed the idea of a cultural revolution in West Africa, it balked at Kouyaté's continued appeals for racial solidarity or the idea that this transformation in culture could be based on anything other than class unity. In 1933 the conflicts between Kouyaté and the PCF reached the breaking point. That year Kouyaté accused the Party of failing to provide adequate support for the efforts of West Africans in the anti-colonial struggle, a pattern he traced back to the declining years of the UIC in 1925 and 1926. In turn, the Communist Party expelled the *évolué* leader on grounds of associating with "bourgeois nationalists," in particular the former British Communist George Padmore. By 1935 the PCF had lost most of its influence among West Africans and had become a marginal presence in the continuing contest for authority in the federation.[139]

Conclusion

If the PCF receded as a force among the new West African elite in the 1930s, through the Communist movement the *évolués* had found alternative ways to combat Dakar's attempt to marginalize them within the colonial field. Demobilized *tirailleurs* were attracted to the new Communist organization after the 1914-1918 war because the Party appeared as the only association capable of or willing to continue the fight for extending the rights of citizenship that had been a central part of the *évolués'* political agenda during the conflict. Whereas the government general castigated the French-educated elite as social misfits because they had "escaped their milieu" and were "tainted" by French civilization,[140] the PCF regarded those attributes as a means whereby the struggle against imperialism could be coordinated throughout the empire. For the Party, the *évolués* were destined to be the leaders of the revolutionary struggle against imperialist capitalism precisely because they straddled the boundary between colony and metropole.[141]

While Diagne won reelection to the Chamber in 1919 as the "candidate of the African proletariat,"[142] his influence among the *évolués* waned thereafter. Many of his former supporters accused the deputy from Senegal of having convinced the *sujets* of West Africa to aid the metropole's war effort with false promises. By the 1930s Diagne's political career had become dependent upon the aid of friends in the government general, alliances with the pre-colonial elite in West Africa, and benefactors within the metropolitan government. In fact, by that time the discourse Diagne practiced lacked meaning in the colonial field. His continued self-identification as "French" did not mobilize or inspire a French-educated elite that, for the most part, was blocked from the rights of citizenship and lacked a means of participating in decisions that directly affected their lives.

By the time of Diagne's death in 1934, new leaders had emerged within the *évolué* community who effectively challenged the deputy's preeminence within that class. Through figures such as Lamine Senghor and Garan Kouyaté new terms of debate entered the colonial field. Cut off from the institutions of state power in West Africa and France, and isolated from the tribal power structures that the government general was at that time strengthening, many *évolués* adopted a language of social revolution in the contest for authority in the federation. As such, the radical *évolués* presented the pre-colonial elite and colonial administration as having constituted an alliance between "feudalists and bourgeois" arrayed against the extension of citizenship rights to the *sujet* populations in order to more easily exploit West African laborers.[143] Thus, the radical anti-colonialist politics of the *évolués* continued the process whereby they asserted claims to leadership in the federation and provided new grounds by which to engage in the struggle for authority in West Africa. If Diagne had become a "traitor to his race," as radical *évolués* stated, others among the French-educated elite were prepared to continue the fight for an end to "colonial oppression."[144]

However, the Communist Party's entry into the colonial field also had transformative effects on Communist discourse and practices in the 1920s. When the strikes of the early post-war years faded and the Chamber had defeated Sarraut's *mise en valeur* prospects receded for an expanding West African proletariat upon which to base calls for a socialist revolution. Yet, the Leninist analysis of imperialist capitalism also provided for agitation in the name of national self-determination. If socialist revolution was not the "order of the day," many radical *évolués* and leaders of the PCF concluded, then the self-appointed representatives of each "national" community required separate organizations that directly addressed the needs of that group. Therefore, Communist discourse ultimately participated in a process that valorized notions of cultural difference between France and West Africa within the colonial field. The legitimization of the idea that French and West African societies were essentially different enhanced *évolué* claims to authority in the imperial framework as a unique social category straddling the borders between the cultures. As such, the new elite from the federation was particularly qualified to speak on behalf of the "authentic" Africa and the "true" France.[145]

Such discussions, though, repositioned the struggle for authority in the colonial field as one centered on delineating the essential attributes of metropolitan and West African societies. For Kouyaté and his associates, the urgent task confronting the *évolués* was to lead a cultural renaissance in the federation while appealing to France to remain true to its traditions. The "revival" of African traditions, members of the *Ligue* and other radical *évolués* asserted, was a precondition to the "total emancipation of the black race."[146] However, not only had colonialism "arrested the development of African society and nearly destroyed its civilization," but many *évolués* also reached the conclusion that Communist politics were "retarding the general evolution of the colonial populations."[147] Therefore, the battle for independence had to be won through the assertion of national cultures against all influences deemed to be alien to "traditional" African societies. These were terms familiar to the government general, which also viewed its mission as inducing a "cultural renaissance" that would satisfy "the African's need of a country."[148] In fact, the *évolués'* turn toward a politics oriented around certain notions of an authentic African culture partly reflected changes in the *mission civilisatrice* as practiced and articulated by Dakar. It is to a discussion of those changes, justified through the language of ethnography, that we now direct our narrative.

NOTES

1. CAOM, 7/Affaires Économiques (AE)/46, telegram from Dakar to the ministry of colonies, 31 January 1921; telegram from the ministry of pensions to the under-secretary of state for posts and telegraphs, "Au sujet grève Dakar," 23 August 1920; and telegram from Dakar to the ministry of colonies, 7 August 1920. Colonial administrators reported strikes throughout the empire during these same years. For examples see: telegrams from Pondicherry to the ministry of colonies, 27 March 1920, and from Basse Terre to the ministry of colonies, April 1920.

2. There is a rich tradition of scholarship on the history of the French labor movement that includes such recent contributions as: Lenard R. Berlanstein, "The Distinctiveness of the Nineteenth-Century French Labor Movement," in *Journal of Modern History* 64 (December 1992); Herrick Chapman, *State Capitalism and Working-Class Radicalism in the French Aircraft Industry* (Berkeley: University of California Press, 1991); Gérard Noiriel, *Workers in French Society in the 19th and 20th Centuries* (New York: Berg, 1990); and William H. Sewell, jr., "Uneven Development, the Autonomy of Politics, and the Dockworkers of Nineteenth-Century Marseilles," in *The American Historical Review* 19:3 (June 1988).

3. CAOM, 1/AP/3037, "Le Diagnisme; La désorganisation militaire," unsigned, in *Le Soir*, 23 September 1919.

4. CAOM, 3/SLOTFOM/101, anonymous report of 15 March 1923.

5. Roberts, *Civilization Without Sexes*, p. 2.

6. Sigmund Freud, *Civilization and its Discontents* ed. and trans. James Strachey, (New York: W.W. Norton and Company, 1989), p. 38.

7. There are several important studies of France's colonial ideology and the place of "civilization" within that cultural framework. Among the most valuable are: Conklin, *A Mission to Civilize*; Girardet, *L'Idée coloniale en France*; Jean Ganiage, *L'Expansion coloniale de la France sous la Troisième République (1871-1914)* (Paris: Payot, 1968); Agnes Murphy, *The Ideology of French Imperialism 1871-1881* (New York: Howard Fertig, 1968); and Comte, *L'Empire Triomphant*.

8. CAOM, 1/SLOTFOM/2, open letter from "Steffany" to his "comrades," 1 February 1922. Steffany was a veteran of the First World War and an early supporter of the PCF from Madagascar.

9. CAOM, 3/SLOTFOM/101, "Note sur la propagande revolutionnaire interessant les pays d'outre-mer," stamped "secret," 31 January 1924.

10. CAOM, 3/SLOTFOM/78, letter from the *Ligue de Défense de la Race Nègre* (LDRN) to the office of the prime minister, 26 April 1928.

11. Dewitte, *Les Mouvements nègres en France*, p. 116, 181. See also: G. E. Von Grunebaum, *French African Literature: Some Cultural Implications* (London: Mouton and Company, 1964), p. 9; and Raymond F. Betts, *France and Decolonization 1900-1960* (New York: St. Martin's Press, 1991), p. 34.

12. Prakash, "Introduction," in Prakash, ed., *After Colonialism*, p. 9.

13. Theorists such as Julia Kristeva and Georg Simmel in their discussions of the "stranger" examine the idea of mediating positions serving as a source of power. See: Julia Kristeva, *Strangers to Ourselves* (New York: Columbia University Press, 1991); and Georg Simmel, *The Sociology of Georg Simmel* trans. Kurt H. Wolff (New York: The Free Press of Glencoe, 1964).

14.   For works on the connections between colonized populations and the PCF see: Dewitte, *Les Mouvements nègres en France*; Claude Liauzu, *Aux Origines des Tiers-Mondismes: Colonisés et Anticolonialistes en France (1919–1939)* (Paris: Éditions L'Harmattan, 1982); Charles H. Cutter, "The Genesis of a Nationalist Elite: The Role of the Popular Front in the French Soudan (1936–1939)," in G. Wesley Johnson, ed., *Double Impact: France and Africa in the Age of Imperialism* (Westport, Conn.: Greenwood Press, 1985); Cooper, *Decolonizaton and African Society*; Betts, *France and Decolonization 1900-1960*; Jean-Pierre Biondi (avec Giles Marin), *Les Anticolonialistes (1881-1962)* (Paris: Robert Laffont, 1992); and Jakob Monéta, *La Politique du parti communiste français dans la question coloniale, 1920-1963* (Paris: F. Maspéro, 1971).

15.   Bourdieu, *Language and Symbolic Power*, p. 172. (Emphasis in the original.)

16.   CAOM, 1/AP/539/3, "Rapport Annuel 1934."

17.   CAOM, 3/SLOTFOM/2, letter from R. Antonetti, governor general of AEF, to the ministry of colonies, "A/S du refoulement dans leur pays d'origine de certains indigènes habitant la metropole," 8 July 1929.

18.   CAOM, 3/SLOTFOM/2, letter from the government general for AOF to the ministry of colonies, "A.S. du projet de loi destiné à réprimer les atteintes à l'integrité du territoire national," December 1928.

19.   CAOM, 1/AP/3037, unsigned report to Dakar from an inspector of colonies, AOF, 17 June 1918.

20.   CAOM, 1/AP/3037, Cambrouze, "Un peu de Politique Indigène," in *Les Annales Coloniales*, December 1918.

21.   CAOM, 1/AP/170/5, letter from Diagne to the ministry of colonies, 20 October 1919, responding to an article published in *Le Temps*, 2 October 1919, that demanded the 1916 law be interpreted as a wartime contingency, not a civil act that held force after the war ended.

22.   CAOM, 1/AP/595, "Profession de foi de Citoyen Blaise Diagne," in *L'Ouest-Africain français*, 29 November 1919.

23.   CAOM, 1/AP/595, election poster of Diagne's 1919 campaign.

24.   François Manschuelle, "Assimilé ou patriotes africains?" in *Cahiers d'Études Africaines*, 1995, p. 337.

25.   Johnson, "The Ascendancy of Blaise Diagne," in *Africa*, p. 235.

26.   CAOM, 1/AP/542, letter from Diagne to the ministry of colonies, "Délégues des Notables de la ville de Rufisque," 8 September 1921; CAOM, 1/AP/192/5, letter from Diagne to the ministry of colonies, 22 January 1919; CAOM, 1/AP/3036, report from "Julia," officer second class in charge of the Service of Assistance and Surveillance of the Senegalese Troops stationed in Fréjus, to the commander of the 15th military region, 30 November 1916; CAOM, 1/AP/3037, Gabriel Cambrouze, "Un peu de Politique Indigène," in *Les Annales Coloniales*, December 1918; CAOM, 1/AP/1638, letter from "Nores," inspector general of the colonies, to the ministry of colonies, 1919; and CAOM, 3/SLOTFOM/101, anonymous report of an agent of the *Service de Contrôle et d'Assistance en France des Indigènes des Colonies* (CAI), 15 June 1923.

27.   CAOM, 1/AP/3036, report from Julia, 30 November 1916.

28.   CAOM, 6/SLOTFOM/9, report by the CAI, 29 November 1926, in which the informant "Duchêne" states that the agency, directed out of the ministry of colonies,

was established by decree on 12 December 1923, but the actual functioning of an intelligence service directed at colonial subjects in France dates to the wartime deployment of troops and laborers from overseas in the metropole. For more information on the history of the CAI see: J. Dion, "Historique du Slotfom," in the catalogue for SLOTFOM at CAOM. Also see: Lebovics, *True France*, p. 102.

29. CAOM, 1/AP/3036, report from Julia to the commander of the 15th Military Region, 25 November 1916.

30. CAOM, 1/AP/3037, Cambrouze, "Un peu de Politique Indigène," in *Les Annales Coloniales*, December 1918.

31. CAOM, 1/AP/3034, letter from the lieutenant governor of Guinea to the government general for AOF, 19 April 1916.

32. CAOM, 1/AP/3037, Delafosse, "Le Point Noir de l'armée noire," in *La Depêche Coloniale et Maritime*, 4 November 1919.

33. CAOM, 3/SLOTFOM/2, letter from R. Antonetti, governor general of AEF, to the ministry of colonies, "A/S du refoulement dans leur pays d'origine de certains indigènes habitant la Métropole," 8 July 1929.

34. CAOM, 1/AP/192/1, letter from Binet-Valmer, president of the League of Heads of Section and Veterans, to the ministry of colonies, 12 May 1927.

35. CAOM, 3/SLOTFOM/101, anonymous report of the CAI, 15 June 1923; and CAOM, 3/SLOTFOM/2, letter from Antonetti to the ministry of colonies, 8 July 1929.

36. These sentiments were expressed by colonial government officials, officers in the French military, and metropolitan politicians throughout the 1920s and later. For examples see: CAOM, 1/AP/2147, Pierre Herbot, "Le problème des indigènes détribalisés," in *Bulletin du Comité de l'Afrique Française*, December 1937; CAOM, 1/AP/3037, "Emploi des Sénégalais dans les territoires ennemis occupés," unsigned, 31 December 1918; and CAOM, CG/60, "Rapport Politique et Administratif de l'A.O.F.," 1931, unsigned.

37. CAOM, 3/SLOTFOM/101, anonymous report of the CAI, 15 June 1923.

38. CAOM, 1/AP/2759, letter from the government general for Madagascar to the governors general of AOF and AEF, 18 December 1930; and CAOM, 1/AP/1638, letter from Albert Sarraut, minister of colonies, to the government general of Indochina, 15 June 1921. In 1920, for example, only three veterans were naturalized out of the nearly 120,000 that served from Indochina during the Great War.

39. CAOM, 1/AP/170, letter from Van Vollenhoven to the ministry of colonies, 20 December 1917.

40. There has been a lot of debate and scholarship on the dichotomous relationship of "colonizer" and "colonized." Among the most insightful early works is Albert Memmi's *The Colonizer and the Colonized* (Boston: Beacon Press, 1991). Other important contributions include: Gyan Prakash, ed., *After Colonialism*; Cooper and Stoler, eds., *Tensions of Empire*; Homi Bhabha, ed., *Nation and Narration* (London: Routledge, 1995); V.Y. Mudimbe, *The Invention of Africa: Gnosis, Philosophy, and the Order of Knowledge* (Bloomington and Indianapolis: Indiana University Press, 1988); Bill Ashcroft, Gareth Griffiths, and Helen Tiffin, eds., *The Post-Colonial Studies Reader* (London: Routledge, 1995); Bhabha, *The Location of Culture*; Said, *Orientalism*; and Frantz Fanon, *Black Skin, White Masks* trans. Charles Lam Markmann (New York: Grove Press, 1967), p. 197.

41.   Georges Hardy, *Nos Grands Problèmes Coloniaux* (Paris: Librairie Armand Colin, 1929), pp. 136, 195, 47, 74.

42.   CAOM, 1/AP/192/1, letter from E. Pieussergues to the governor of Côte d'Ivoire, "Mutilé Doua-bi-Daouan Réjet de Pension," 9 March 1927. In this correspondence, the wounded veteran Doua-bi-Daouan was named as an example of someone who had been mistreated by the government general and Paris. He was denied a military pension despite having had both his hands and feet amputated from complications following the 1914–1918 war.

43.   CAOM, 1/AP/2759, letter from the League for the Defense of the Rights of Man and Citizen to the office of the prime minister, 28 January 1921; letter from Diagne to the office of the prime minister and the office of the ministry of foreign affairs, 2 March 1921; letter from the League for the Defense of the Rights of Man and Citizen to the President of the Republic, 18 February 1921.

44.   CAOM, 1/AP/2759. This carton contains numerous files on those who applied for citizenship after the war. The League for the Defense of the Rights of Man and Citizen noted only 22 naturalizations in its letter to the President of the Republic, 18 February 1921.

45.   CAOM, 1/AP/2759, letter from Diagne to the office of prime minister and the office of the ministry of foreign affairs, 2 March 1921.

46.   Roberts, *Civilization Without Sexes*, p. 93, 96.

47.   For a discussion of how questions of reproduction were bound up with the formation of French national identities, see: Ann Laura Stoler, "Sexual Affronts and Racial Frontiers; European Identities and the Cultural Politics of Exclusion in Colonial Southeast Asia," in Cooper and Stoler, eds., *Tensions of Empire*, pp. 198-237. The idea that colonial subjects were to be made into Frenchmen is expounded upon in Arthur Girault, *Principes de colonisation et de législation coloniale*, seconde édition, Tome I (Paris: Librairie de la Société du recueil Gal. des lois et des arrêts, 1904), p. 7.

48.   CAOM, 12/SLOTFOM/3, letter from Administrator in Chief Berthier to the ministry of colonies, "Circulaire interministerielle du 4 avril 1919. Libération en France des militaires et tirailleurs indigènes," 27 June 1919.

49.   Stoler, "Sexual Affronts and Racial Frontiers," in Cooper and Stoler, eds., *Tensions of Empire*, p. 199.

50.   Conklin, *A Mission to Civilize*, p. 217.

51.   CAOM, 1/AP/3037, anonymous article in *Les Annales Coloniales*, 17 September 1918, "Le Recrutement Indigène."

52.   The question of forced labor in French-ruled sub-Saharan Africa has been explored by several scholars, including: Conklin, *A Mission to Civilize*; Cooper, *Decolonization and African Society*; and Jean Suret-Canale, *L'Afrique noire: L'Ère coloniale 1900–1945* (Paris: Éditions Sociales, 1962).

53.   CAOM, 7/AE/46, report prepared for the government general for AOF, "La Production Agricole et Pastorale en Afrique Occidentale Française," November 1930.

54.   CAOM, 7/AE/46, report prepared for the government general for AOF, "La Production Agricole et Pastorale en Afrique Occidentale Française," November 1930.

55.   Lebovics, *True France*, pp. 110–117, 133. For a thorough discussion of the economic transformations of Francophone sub-Saharan Africa see: Suret-Canale, *L'Afrique noire*.

56. CAOM, 1/AP/595, Diagne in *L'Ouest-Africain français*, 29 November 1919.

57. CAOM, 1/AP/595, election poster of 1919 produced by Diagne's electoral committee.

58. CAOM, 1/SLOTFOM/2, open letter from the Malgache veteran and Communist Steffany to his fellow *tirailleurs*, 1 February 1922. The records of those who conducted that activity confirm Steffany's assertion that he and his compatriots were under constant watch by agents of the colonial state in the metropole and overseas. See the letter signed "Benoit," minister of pensions, to the ministry of war, 29 December 1921, in the same carton, and also the unsigned note, "A.S. de la propagande internationale antimilitariste," 7 November 1921, also in that carton.

59. CAOM, 1/AP/2759, letter from the French League for the Defense of the Rights of Man and Citizen to the office of the prime minister, 28 January 1921.

60. CAOM, 1/SLOTFOM/2, Gouttenoire de Toury, "Le Paria ne demande que la justice," in *Le Paria*, 1 April 1922.

61. Dewitte, *Les Mouvements nègres en France*, p. 33.

62. CAOM, 3/SLOTFOM/3, "Note de l'Agent Désiré," 16 December 1921. This carton also contains several other documents pertaining to the beginnings of organized Indochinese politics in the metropole. See, for example, "Note sur les associations d'Indochinois à Paris," 14 June 1923; "Note de l'agent de Villier" 23 February 1923; and "Note de Monsieur Deveze," 11 June 1921.

63. CAOM, 3/SLOTFOM/3, "Note de l'Agent Désiré," 16 December 1921; and CAOM, 3/SLOTFOM/71, report on the first open meeting of the LMDC held on 21 December 1920 in Paris.

64. CAOM, 1/AP/1638, letter from the Commissaire Général of Black Troops to the ministry of colonies, 19 January 1921.

65. Wolfgang J. Mommsen, *Theories of Imperialism* trans. P. S. Falla (Chicago: University of Chicago Press, 1982), pp. 33, 32, 34.

66. Charles Dumas, *Libérez les indigènes ou renoncez aux colonies* (Paris: Eugène Figuière et Cie., 1914), pp. 175, 161-162. Dumas was a socialist deputy in the Chamber and wrote this book as a final report on conditions in the colonies he was commissioned by the French parliament to produce.

67. V. I. Lenin, "L'Europe Arriérée et l'Asie Avancée," in *Pravda* 31:18 (May 1913), reprinted in V. I. Lenine, *L'Imperialisme et la Lutte des Peuples Coloniaux* (Alger: Éditions Liberté, no copyright date), pp. 7-9.

68. CAOM, 5/SLOTFOM/11, El-Djazairi, "Plus d'Attention à la Question Coloniale," in *Bulletin Communiste* (organ of the PCF), 13 June 1924.

69. V. I. Lenin, *Imperialism, the Highest Stage of Capitalism: A Popular Outline* (Peking: Foreign Languages Press, 1975), pp. 20, 12, 31, 69, 24.

70. Ibid., pp. 79, 89.

71. CAOM, 3/SLOTFOM/101, statement published in *Cahiers du Bolshevisme*, No. 36, 21 January 1926.

72. CAOM, 3/SLOTFOM/101, "Note sur la propagande revolutionnaire interessant les pays d'outre-mer," 31 January 1924, stamped secret by the CAI.

73. Charles H. Cutter, "The Genesis of a Nationalist Elite," in Johnson, ed., *Double Impact*, p. 107.

74. CAOM, 1/SLOTFOM/2, notes of a meeting of the *Comité d'Études Coloniales* (CEC), 18 February 1922.

75.   CAOM, 3/SLOTFOM/3, "Note sur les associations d'Indochinois à Paris," 14 June 1923. There is some discrepancy in the archival records over the exact date the UIC was formed. While scholars generally accept spring 1922 as the date for the UIC's first meeting and the first issue of its journal *Le Paria* was published in April of that year, other documents contained in this same carton suggest that the UIC could have been founded as early as July 1921. In any event, it is the appearance of *Le Paria* that marked the UIC's entrance as an important force in the colonial field. See also CAOM, 3/SLOTFOM/24, "Réunion de l'Union Intercoloniale," note by agent "Désiré," 2 December 1924, in which the informant claims Max Bloncourt, one of the early leaders of the UIC, noted 1921 as the year the organization was founded.

76.   CAOM, 3/SLOTFOM/101. For an example of the pressure the Comintern exerted on the PCF to take more action on the colonial question see the letter from Gregory Zinoviev to the Third Congress of the PCF at Lyon, 12 January 1924.

77.   CAOM, 3/SLOTFOM/109, "Aux Indigènes des Colonies," by the CEC, reprinted in "Note sur la propagande révolutionnaire intéressant les pays d'outre-mer," 6 November 1922.

78.   For discussions of the process whereby Diagne came to a settlement with the government general for AOF and even became an ardent apologist for colonialism see: G. Wesley Johnson, "The Impact of the Senegalese Elite upon the French," in Johnson, ed., *Double Impact*, p. 173; and Conklin, *A Mission to Civilize*, pp. 157-158.

79.   CAOM, 3/SLOTFOM/3, letter from the ministry of colonies to the government general for AOF, 28 March 1924, quoting passages from the 5 March 1924 edition of the PCF newspaper, *L'Humanité*.

80.   CAOM, 1/SLOTFOM/2, Gouttenoire de Toury, "Le Paria ne demande que la justice," in *Le Paria*, 1 April 1922. The theme of abandonment at the end of the war was common in the literature of radical organizations among the *évolués* in the 1920s. For examples see: CAOM, 3/SLOTFOM/3, "Note de l'Agent Désiré," 2 March 1924, which reports that Bloncourt blamed Diagne for that abandonment; and CAOM, 3/SLOTFOM/24, "Note" from agent Désiré, 2 December 1924, which records that leaders of the UIC attributed the founding of their organization to the failure of Diagne's wartime promises to be realized after the conflict's resolution.

81.   CAOM, 3/SLOTFOM/6, editorial by René Maran in *Les Continents*, 24 October 1924.

82.   For discussions of the importance of *Batouala* in African, colonial, French, and "black" history see: Lylian Kesteloot, *Intellectual Origins of the African Revolution* (Washington, D.C.: Black Orpheus Press, 1972), pp. 14–16; Adriana Moro, *Négritude e Cultura Francese. Surrealismo Chiave della Négritude?* (Torino: Edizioni dell'Orso, 1992), pp. 34–35; Lylian Kesteloot, *Black Writers in French: A Literary History of Negritude* trans. Ellen Conroy Kennedy (Philadelphia: Temple University Press, 1974), p. 75.

83.   René Maran, *Batouala; A True Black Novel* (Washington, D.C.: Black Orpheus Press, 1972), pp. 74, 72, 23, 70, 93, 144.

84.   Prior to the 1928 legislative elections, Diagne requested several meetings with prominent Communists from AOF in an attempt at reconciliation. Those meetings proved fruitless and the African revolutionaries endorsed Diagne's opponent and one-time campaign manager, Galandou Diouf, in the election. Diagne was barely reelected in what is generally believed by scholars to have been a rigged vote. See

CAOM, 2/SLOTFOM/5, reports by agents of the CAI of 3 February 1928, 3 June 1928, 5 June 1928, and 9 January 1928.

85. CAOM, 3/SLOTFOM/3, "Note de l'Agent Désiré," 18 July 1924, in which the informant reproduces a letter addressed from Maran to the UIC that discussed planning meetings over how to challenge Diagne. See also: "Note de l'Agent Désiré," 3 December 1924.

86. CAOM, 5/SLOTFOM/6, "Nous n'avons pas à discréditer M. Diagne. Qu'il le veuille ou non, il se suffit à lui-même," in the 15 November—1 December 1924 issue of *Les Continents*.

87. For references to this combination of forces as a source of the misery experienced by the colonial subjects see: CAOM, 1/SLOTFOM/2, letter from Sarotte, an early leader of the UIC, "À nos frères indigènes," 2 January 1922; CAOM, 3/SLOTFOM/15, article, "La guerre imperialiste et les Parias coloniaux," in *L'Humanité*, 30 July 1924; CAOM, 3/SLOTFOM/24, "Note de l'Agent Désiré," "Réunion de l'Union Intercoloniale," 4, 6 December 1924; and CAOM, 2/SLOTFOM/5, anonymous report of a CAI agent on a speech delivered by Lamine Senghor, a prominent West African Communist, 14 February 1927.

88. CAOM, 1/SLOTFOM/2, letter from Sarotte, "À nos frères indigènes," 2 January 1922.

89. Robert Cornevin, "Du Sénégal à la Provence: Lamine Senghor (1889-1927) pionnier de la Négritude," in *Provence Historique*, January-March 1975, p. 71.

90. CAOM, 5/SLOTFOM/6, N.-S. Russel, "M. Diagne prosecutes 'Les Continents'; Maranism Versus Diagnism," in *Les Continents*, 15 November—1 December 1924.

91. CAOM, 5/SLOTFOM/6, N.-S. Russel, "M. Diagne prosecutes 'Les Continents'; Maranism Versus Diagnism," in *Les Continents*, 15 November—1 December 1924.

92. CAOM, 5/SLOTFOM/6, N.-S. Russel, "M. Diagne prosecutes 'Les Continents'; Maranism Versus Diagnism," in *Les Continents*, 15 November—1 December 1924. These "foreign Negroes" included not only the Garveyites from the U.S., but also those who had joined the PCF who were regarded by Diagne and other French politicians as agents of a foreign power—the Soviet Union.

93. CAOM, 5/SLOTFOM/6, N.-S. Russel, "M. Diagne prosecutes 'Les Continents'; Maranism Versus Diagnism," in *Les Continents*, 15 November—1 December 1924.

94. CAOM, 3/SLOTFOM/101, "Note sur la propagande révolutionnaire interessant les pays d'outre-mer," 31 December 1924.

95. CAOM, 3/SLOTFOM/3, "Note de l'agent Désiré," 22 July 1924. For other information on the early successes of the UIC in attracting large memberships and extensive circulation of its paper, *Le Paria*, see the reports of agent "Désiré" of 9 and 12 July and 12 May 1925 in CAOM, 1/SLOTFOM/2.

96. CAOM, 3/SLOTFOM/101, anonymous report of 20 July 1923. The CAI also noted that the Communist trade union federation CGTU, through its transportation workers union, "assurée" the links between the PCF and its anticolonial activities overseas. Resolution of the PCF's Commission Coloniale, February 1925, noted in "Action du Gouvernement Sovietique et du Komintern pour la Bolshevisation des Colonies Françaises," 1928, in the same carton. The ministry of colonies had become so concerned with the PCF's activities in the overseas territories that it had a law passed in July 1928 that extended the CAI's reach to monitoring the activities of colonial

subjects who returned to their geographic places of origin. See CAOM, 3/SLOTFOM/2, report of the CAI, 19 January 1929.

97.   CAOM, 3/SLOTFOM/144, CAI report of 30 June 1925 in which the informant records Lamine Senghor's description of his experience as a soldier. Lamine Senghor spent much of the 1920s in legal battles with the French government to secure a disability pension he was due under the terms of the 14 January 1918 decrees.

98.   Cornevin, "Du Sénégal à la Provence," in *Provence Historique*, January–March 1975, pp. 69-77.

99.   CAOM, 3/SLOTFOM/3, "Note de l'agent Désiré," 31 March 1925, recording a speech by Lamine Senghor before a meeting of the UIC on 29 March 1925.

100.   CAOM, 3/SLOTFOM/3, Report by Désiré of 4 June 1925. Lamine Senghor was also put in charge of the PCF's organization of veterans and was sent to international conferences sponsored by the Comintern as a representative of West Africa.

101.   CAOM, 3/SLOTFOM/101, "Note sur la propagande révolutionnaire interessant les pays d'outre-mer," 29 February 1924.

102.   CAOM, 3/SLOTFOM/24, report by agent "Désiré," 8 October 1926.

103.   CAOM, 3/SLOTFOM/3, "Note de l'agent Désiré," 24 October 1925.

104.   CAOM, 7/AE/46, "La Production Agricole et Pastorale en Afrique Occidentale Française," November 1930.

105.   CAOM, 3/SLOTFOM/101, letter from Zinoviev to the PCF, 12 January 1924, in which the Comintern leader urges the French Communists to put "l'indépendance des colonies" at the front of all their activities in the overseas empire. The PCF at first resisted the Comintern's pressure and held to the notion that it was possible to win the demands for complete equality between citizens and subjects. However, just over a year later the PCF changed its position and lessened its agitation for the extension of citizenship to the colonized populations.

106.   V. I. Lenin, "Du droit des nations à Disposer d'elles-mêmes," originally published in *Prosvechtchénie*, 1914, and reprinted in *L'Imperialisme et la Lutte des Peuples Coloniaux*, p. 9.

107.   V. I. Lenin, "Des guerres justes sont possibles," written in October 1916 and reprinted in *L'Imperialisme et la Lutte de Peuples Coloniaux*, p. 43.

108.   CAOM, 1/SLOTFOM/2, Gouttenoire de Toury, "Le Paria ne demande que la justice," in *Le Paria*, 1 April 1922.

109.   CAOM, 3/SLOTFOM/101, report by the CAI, 30 November 1924, in which were reprinted resolutions of the PCF in preparation for a Congress of Colonial Peoples scheduled for December 1925.

110.   ARS, 21G/27 (17), "Circulaire envoyée par la Commission Centrale Coloniale au Comité Directeur du parti communiste," 23 March 1925; and CAOM, 3/SLOTFOM/144, anonymous report of a CAI informant that provides an account of a UIC meeting held in Paris, 28 February 1926.

111.   ARS, 21G/27 (17), "Note de l'Agent Desiré" on founding of CDRN, 21 April 1926; in the same carton see: UIC declaration on the formation of a committee "des vieilles Colonies et Peuples Noirs," 10 July 1926, and "Note de l'Agent Desiré," on CDRN founding meeting, 22 July 1926; and CAOM, 3/SLOTFOM/144, anonymous report of the CAI that cites Senghor's speech at the founding of the *Comité de Défense de la Race Nègre* (CDRN), 31 March 1926.

112. CAOM, 3/SLOTFOM/27, "Note de l'Agent Désiré," 16 April 1926, in which the informant records the decision of a UIC meeting held three days earlier.

113. CAOM, 5/SLOTFOM/3, CAI report of November 1927 and Lamine Senghor's article, "Debout les Nègres," in the first issue of the LDRN's newspaper, *La Race Nègre*, June 1927.

114. ARS, 21G/28 (17), biographical report on Kouyaté filed with the government general on 2 April 1927, which includes the report of school administration in Aix-en-Provence.

115. CAOM, 2/SLOTFOM/5, leaflet of the LDRN, "Au Peuple de France," June 1928.

116. CAOM, 3/SLOTFOM/78, letter from the LDRN to the office of the prime minister, 26 April 1928.

117. Pierre Alexandre, "Chiefs, *Commandants* and Clerks: Their Relationship from Conquest to Decolonization in French West Africa," in Crowder and Ikime, eds., *West African Chiefs*.

118. CAOM, 1/AP/1638, law proposed by Daladier before the Chamber on 24 November 1924.

119. CAOM, 3/SLOTFOM/111, letter from Kouyaté to the U.S. activist W.E.B. Du Bois, 29 April 1929.

120. CAOM, 3/SLOTFOM/47, speech of Lamine Senghor at the "Congrès internationale de Bruxelles contre l'oppression coloniale et l'imperialisme," February 1927.

121. CAOM, 5/SLOTFOM/19, from Lamine Senghor, *La Violation d'un Pays* (Paris: Bureau d'Éditions de Diffusion et de Publicité, 1927).

122. CAOM, 3/SLOTFOM/111, Kouyaté, "Appel aux Nègres," 19 March 1930; and CAOM, 5/SLOTFOM/3, report of "Désiré," 22 February 1929.

123. ARS, 21G/44 (17), note in the security files of AOF on sections of the LDRN throughout the federation and travel between metropole and colonies of anticolonialists; and ARS 21G/27 (17), "Note de l'Agent Desiré," 29 October 1926, on the role of navigators as intermediaries.

124. CAOM, 3/SLOTFOM/36, anonymous report, "Syndicat des marins nègres de Bordeaux," 15 April 1930. The government general also noted the prestige Kouyaté held in AOF in a message to the ministry of colonies contained in CAOM, CG/60, 1928; and ARS, 21G/44 (17), note in security files of AOF, 18 June 1931.

125. Carde replaced Merlin in 1924 in an administrative shake up in which Diagne had a hand. As noted earlier, Merlin aggressively sought to curtail the deputy's influence among the *sujets* and obstructed enforcement of the 14 January 1918 decrees on citizenship. After Diagne made peace with colonial business interests in 1923 and solidified his alliance with Paris during the proceedings against Maran in 1924, Paris removed Merlin and replaced him with the more amenable Carde with whom the deputy maintained a close association.

126. CAOM, 3/SLOTFOM/144, letter from Diagne to Kouyaté, 20 February 1928. For other information on the meetings between the leader of the LDRN and the deputy from Senegal see: CAOM, 2/SLOTFOM/5, anonymous report of the CAI, 3 February 1928.

127. CAOM, 3/SLOTFOM/78, letter from the LDRN to the office of the prime minister, 26 April 1928.

128.　CAOM, 3/SLOTFOM/144, report of the CAI, 4 June 1928; CAOM, 3/SLOTFOM/78, letter from Kouyaté to Diouf, 27 October 1928; and CAOM, 2/SLOTFOM/5, CAI report, 3 June 1928.

129.　CAOM, 1/AP/595, telegram from Carde to the ministry of colonies, 28 March 1928.

130.　CAOM, 5/SLOTFOM/3, letter from Kouyaté to the ministry of colonies, 3 June 1928.

131.　CAOM, 5/SLOTFOM/3, CAI report of 1 November 1929 on discussions between representatives of the PCF's Central Committee and Kouyaté.

132.　CAOM, 3/SLOTFOM/144, CAI report of an LDRN meeting, 31 March 1927. Shortly after that gathering Maran ended his active participation in the League.

133.　CAOM, 2/SLOTFOM/5, letter from Maran to Kouyaté, 31 August 1927.

134.　CAOM, 5/SLOTFOM/45, *Methodes et Tactiques Revolutionnaires: Thèses et Resolutions du 5e Congrès de l'I.S.R.* Moscou: Septembre 1930.

135.　CAOM, 5/SLOTFOM/45, "Methodes et Tactiques Revolutionnaires; Theses et Resolutions du 5e Congrès de l'I.S.R., Moscou, Septembre 1930."

136.　CAOM, 3/SLOTFOM/53, reports by agent "Joe," 27 June 1932, 27 August 1932, 29 August 1932, and 5 September 1932. These documents also reflect a transition underway in the LDRN during which the League changed its name to the *Union des Travailleurs Nègres* (UTN).

137.　CAOM, 5/SLOTFOM/11, "Le Congrès de Bruxelles," in *Le Courrier des Noirs*, November 1927.

138.　Dewitte, *Les Mouvements nègres*, p. 318.

139.　CAOM, 3/SLOTFOM/53, "Rapport de Joe," 30 September 1933. See, in the same carton, "Rapport de Paul," 7 March 1933, "Rapport de Joe," 7 October 1932, and "Les Critiques de Kouyaté," 7 February 1935.

140.　CAOM, 1/AP/2147, Pierre Herbot, "Le problème des indigènes 'détribalisés'," in *Bulletin du Comité de l'Afrique Française*, December 1937.

141.　CAOM, 3/SLOTFOM/101, "Cahiers du bolshevisme," No. 36, 21 January 1926.

142.　CAOM, 1/AP/595, statement by Diagne in *L'Ouest-Africain français*, 29 November 1919.

143.　CAOM, 5/SLOTFOM/49, *Bulletin Colonial*, March-April 1931.

144.　CAOM. 3/SLOTFOM/53, "Rapport de Joe," 7 October 1932.

145.　Several scholars have produced work on the rise of a "nationalist" elite in French West Africa that argue the access this new force had to both African and French societies was indispensable to the emergence of anti-colonial politics in AOF. For example see: Grimal, *Decolonization*, p. 412; Betts, *France and Decolonization*, pp. 34, 120; G. Wesley Johnson, "The Triumph of Nationalism in French West Africa; or, the Change from Assimilation to Nationalism as a Secular Faith for West African Elites," in *Décolonisations européenes: Actes du colloque international 'Décolonisations comparées', Aix-en-Provence, 30 Septembre–3 Octobre 1993* (Aix-en-Provence: Publications de l'Université de Provence, 1995), p. 311; G. Wesley Johnson, "Les Élites au Sénégal pendant la période d'indépendance," in Charles-Robert Ageron and Marc Michel, eds., *L'Afrique Noire Française: L'heure des independances: actes du colloque 'La France et les indépendances des pays d'Afrique noire et de Madagascar' Aix-en-Provence 26-29 Avril 1990* (Paris: CNRS Éditions, 1992), p. 27; Comte, *L'Empire Triomphant*, p. 234; and Dewitte, *Les Mouvements nègres*, p. 248.

146. CAOM, 3/SLOTFOM/78, letter from the LDRN to the office of the prime minister, 26 April 1928; and CAOM, 3/SLOTFOM/111, Kouyaté, "Appel aux Nègres," 19 March 1930.

147. CAOM, 5/SLOTFOM/11, "Congrès Mondial," in *Le Courrier des Noirs*, November 1927; and CAOM, 3/SLOTFOM/24, statement by Maurice Satineau, 30 March 1927, over his split with Lamine Senghor and the CDRN.

148. CAOM, CG/52, "L'Enseignement et l'Education en A.O.F.," report by Inspector General of Colonies Charton, 5 July 1936.

Chapter Three

The Authority of Tradition: Ethnography and Colonial Governance in Interwar AOF

In 1929 Kouyaté, as general secretary of the LDRN, called on "all Negroes to reflect, to free their conscience of all moral and intellectual servitude." He reiterated that the one goal of his organization was "to prepare, with the shortest delay, our country for national independence." In this letter addressed to Chief M'Ba of the Pahouins in Libreville, Gabon (AEF), the schoolteacher from French Soudan denounced "assimilation [as an] instrument of division among the natives." He asserted, "We want to remain African, to safeguard our national traditions and our values, to reconquer those rights that have been usurped [by the French]." Further, Kouyaté proclaimed that "naturalization" was the greatest threat to achieving not only independence but also the intellectual awakening he deemed a necessary prelude to liberation from France.[1]

The language Kouyaté used in his appeal to Chief M'Ba closely resembled that deployed by the government general in Dakar to justify the system of rule devised in French West Africa during the 1920s and 1930s. In the *évolués'* fight to counter the imperial administration's attempt to marginalize them in the colonial field, the French-educated elite had become engaged in what David Laitin describes as a "dominant cultural framework" that was oriented around the articulation of certain essential differences between African and French societies. According to Laitin, "The 'political culture' of a society can be thought of as a function of the 'points of concern' embedded in the dominant cultural subsystem. Political elites in any society will act strategically and ideologically in the hope of defining and delimiting which strands of their society's culture should become dominant. Those who are successful in establishing a dominant cultural framework form a 'hegemonic bloc.' The dominant cultural subsystem, once chosen, spins political life into a 'web of significance,' which grasps elites and masses alike."[2]

This chapter examines the development of a political culture in the colonial field that privileged notions of racial and ethnic identity, and, in so doing, circumscribed the possibilities for effective resistance to imperial rule.[3] By obstructing the naturalization process and restructuring the institutional bases of colonial power, the government general effectively limited the means whereby the new urban elite could meaningfully engage in the contest for authority in West Africa. Furthermore, Dakar assiduously cultivated and strengthened the position of "traditional rulers" in the federation as an alternative to the French-educated elite who the government general deemed a threat to imperial rule in West Africa.[4] In the process a hegemonic bloc was forged among the pre-colonial elite and colonial administrators that valorized certain notions of "authentic" African society and situated tribal communities at the base of the colonial state in the federation.

Kouyaté's petition to M'Ba suggests that the *évolués* recognized the important place of the pre-colonial elite in the imperial framework and were prepared to offer themselves as more natural allies than France in the administration of AOF.[5] Furthermore, the LDRN's gesture toward the "traditional rulers" of sub-Saharan Africa denoted the degree to which some *évolués* had accepted and reproduced conceptions of "authentic" African society used by the colonial rulers to justify continued French domination of the *sujet* populations. While the government general castigated the *évolués* as a "threat" to both West African and French societies,[6] it suggested that "ignorance of local institutions" and "customs" had led Dakar to enact "dangerous [and] erroneous" policies that produced this disgruntled new elite.[7] To overcome that lack of knowledge, colonial administrators turned to the new discipline of ethnography, which provided a scientific language for talking about "authentic" African society as well as the framework for making decisions that concerned the structure of rule in the colonies. While ethnography predated the 1914–1918 war, the transformations of the colonial field during that conflict and their apperception by French rulers in AOF furnished a context wherein the discourse practiced by researchers such as Maurice Delafosse became hegemonic throughout the imperial administration. In addition, ethnography offered a means by which overseas officials challenged official French Republican principles and, in reconfiguring the *mission civilisatrice*, contributed to the emergence of far right political ideologies in the metropole in the ensuing decades.[8]

In West Africa ethnography functioned as a vehicle through which racist imaginings of African society received the legitimating veneer of science. Echoing the work of Gustave Le Bon, Georges Hardy informed his students at the École Coloniale that "it is not simply by the color of their skin that the African Black is distinguished from the other human races…[but] they are also identified by [certain] psychological traits."[9] The "discovery" and delineation of the mental differences between Europeans and Africans by Delafosse and others informed decisions by the government general about how to order West African society and afforded the ideological basis for the alliance forged by colonial administrators with the pre-colonial elite. Thus, following the 1914–1918 war Dakar set about restoring the "natural authority" of "chiefs" and "elders" who colonial administrators claimed were the "indispensable intermediar[ies]" of France's mission overseas.[10] In this way, the colonial state presented itself as the guardian of African "tradition" while creating the institutional and cultural bases for distancing indigenous society from that of Europe.

However, Dakar did not limit its actions to restructuring the political and juridical framework of governance in West Africa. In a speech before officials of the federation in 1935, Governor General Jules Brévié asserted that France had the task to bring about a "cultural renaissance" throughout the federation.[11] This was to be accomplished, the government general argued, by teaching the *sujet* populations how to live according to "authentic African traditions." Throughout West Africa, the colonial administration founded "rural popular schools" to train Africans in their "ancestral morals [and] culture" which had the added benefit of further "consolidating the traditional authority [of the chiefs]."[12] Dakar's attempt to revive African culture corresponded with the agenda of some far-right political tendencies in the metropole that sought to regenerate "the spiritual and moral forces of the [French] nation" threatened by the ideological left and the "decadence" of the Third Republic itself.[13] Furthermore, since Dakar grouped the *évolués* among those "subversive" elements tearing at the fabric of French civilization, the solidification of chiefly authority and the "re-invention" of African culture was meant to create the structural bases whereby the influence of the French-educated elite in the colonial field would be minimized. V. Y. Mudimbe notes that this legitimization process was a common feature of European rule throughout Africa. He writes, "They (colonialists) speak about neither Africa nor Africans, but rather justify the process of inventing and conquering a continent and naming its 'primitiveness' or 'disorder,' as well as the subsequent means of its exploitation and methods for its 'regeneration.'"[14]

Yet, the ethnographers' presentation of African and French societies as fundamentally and irremediably distinct further reinforced the self-identity of the *évolués* as a unique social group within the imperial context. As the conceptual and institutional gap between European and West African society was widened through the actions and rhetoric of the government general, the French-educated elite from AOF more forcefully asserted itself as the only means by which the connections between France and the native populations could be meaningfully sustained. Thus, while Kouyaté appealed to the pre-colonial elite on the basis of "racial" solidarity in the name of creating an independent African state, he also later suggested that the *évolués* could serve as "educators" of the "rural populations" and assist France's mission of reconstructing traditional African culture.[15] As we will see, these positions were not logically incongruous as they emanated from a single discursive genealogy. By the late 1930s much of the new elite from AOF and the government general shared the aspiration to regenerate "authentic" African culture, even if each claimed the prerogative to do so. In addition, both Dakar and the *évolués* looked to ethnography, especially the work of Delafosse, as the source for knowledge about "traditional" native society as well as models for its reconstruction. What, then, was this ethnographic vision of African society and how did it become hegemonic in our field of analysis?

The Negro-African Civilization:
Ethnography and the *Mission Civilisatrice*

In 1917 Van Vollenhoven proclaimed, "The judgments of M. Delafosse are preeminent in [all] matters of native policy."[16] In that report to the ministry of colonies Van Vollenhoven used the findings and advice of Delafosse to justify the decision in August of that year to reestablish the administrative authority of the "chiefs" in AOF. Fourteen years later Brévié cited Delafosse's work as having provided the scientific basis for according the pre-colonial elite additional influence in local juridical affairs.[17] In fact, the symbiotic relationship between Delafosse and the government general in Dakar dated to the earliest days of French rule in West Africa and left an indelible mark on the structures of rule and patterns of social engagement in the region.[18]

Maurice Delafosse was born in Sancergues, France, on 20 December 1870. By his eighteenth birthday he had successfully completed *baccalauréats* in letters, philosophy, and sciences. However, these were also years of rapid overseas expansion by the Third Republic. Delafosse was among many intellectuals of his generation who believed the colonies offered a laboratory in which to study the human condition in close proximity to the "state of nature." In 1894 the young researcher set sail for Africa in order to quench his curiosity about France's new possessions and there decided to dedicate his life to the study of those peoples who had recently been made *sujets* of the Republic's empire.[19]

At the turn of the century Delafosse was employed by the colonial administration as a low-level functionary, an assignment that was decisive for his future career. As a "bush administrator" the young ethnographer was in direct and daily contact with the local population. In 1909 François-Joseph Clozel, then governor of the colony Haut-Sénégal-Niger, commissioned Delafosse to study the customs of the populations native to the region so that the colonial government could devise policies "appropriate to their mentality and their state of society."[20] The result was a massive three-volume work that made Delafosse the most widely recognized authority within the colonial field on West African traditions and society. The 1909 circular authorizing Delafosse's mission deepened a pattern whereby colonial officials employed ethnographers with the explicit purpose of aiding imperial rule. Earlier, Gallieni explained, "The study of the races that occupy a region...determines the political organization" necessary "for [the] pacification" of the native populations and the development of systems of rule most appropriate to the territory under the colonial administrator's authority.[21] However, Gallieni's *la politique des races* was designed as an expedient means of ruling over recently conquered populations during which time French culture was supposed to penetrate and transform native society. Administrators like Gallieni, therefore, did not view the purpose of the studies produced by early ethnographers as delineating the characteristics of native societies that had to be preserved from all outside influence, including that of France. By the time of Delafosse's work on Haut-Sénégal-Niger, though, ethnography was being used by some colonial officials to provide a scientific basis for challenges to the assimilationist aspects of the *mission civilisatrice* and the knowledge produced by ethnographers became a weapon in struggles within the imperial hierarchy.

During his tenure in the colonies of Côte d'Ivoire, Haut-Sénégal-Niger, and French Soudan, Delafosse forged a close relationship with the pre-colonial elite. That experience led him to conclude before many in Dakar or Paris that there "exist[ed] a clearly defined Negro-African culture" that produced its own natural leaders, which the ethnographer identified as "chiefs."[22] Delafosse disdained the "Europeanized natives" whom he believed "did not have any ability to speak in the name of the true natives." Rather, he asserted, "the canton or tribal chiefs represent[ed] the real thought and opinion of the indigenous masses."[23] Consequently, the ethnographer's assertions placed him in opposition to the government general prior to the 1914–1918 war, and challenged the then-prevalent premises of the *mission civilisatrice* by valorizing autochthonous traditions and political structures, even claiming that some were "more humane and more defensible" than European ways.[24]

Clozel shared Delafosse's perspectives. As a bush commander himself in the early years of the twentieth century, Clozel, like Delafosse, had developed close working relationships with the pre-colonial elite. Delafosse's study of Haut-Sénégal-Niger, first published in 1912, confirmed for Clozel the conviction that an alliance between French administrators and the pre-colonial elite constituted the most appropriate means of governance for the federation. Thus, by the time Clozel replaced Ponty as governor general of AOF in 1915 he had embraced a model of the "true" nature of African society and France's mission overseas that disputed claims by the *évolués* to be the legitimate representatives of the *sujet* population's aspirations. This provided a justification for denying the new elite the rights of French citizens at a time when Diagne, supported by his colleagues in Paris, had pushed through legislation securing those privileges for the *originaires* of Senegal.

Although Clozel's tenure as governor general lasted just two years, it provided the context wherein the ethnographic archetype of African society mapped by Delafosse emerged as a potent alternative to previously ascendant notions of the colonial project and the nature of indigenous peoples and societies. In the process the conflict intensified between Dakar and Paris over the proper means of ruling the colonies and the essence of France's mission overseas, a clash that established the federation as a place where republican assumptions about "universal man" and social equality were routinely called into question and undermined. Delafosse joined Clozel in Dakar as director of political affairs for French West Africa; a position he continued to occupy under Van Vollenhoven until the latter's resignation at the end of 1917. As the chief political officer of the federation Delafosse was responsible for "native policy," which meant orchestrating Dakar's command over the *sujet* populations and defining France's mission in the region. The ethnographer, therefore, was directly engaged in defining the terms of the struggle for authority then taking shape between the *évolués*, Paris, Dakar, and the pre-colonial elite. In addition to Delafosse's appointment, Clozel founded the Committee of Historical and Scientific Studies of French West Africa. The new committee was not only funded by the government general, but was established with the stated purpose of abetting France's mission overseas.[25] Throughout the next two decades ethnographers and overseas administrators forged closer ties in a mutually beneficial relationship through which the practices of imperial rule were legitimated while researchers received invaluable financial and organizational resources to conduct their studies and publish their findings.[26]

A common concern to ethnographers and colonial administrators was the place of the *évolué* in the colonial field. For the government general, the new elite posed a political challenge to the authority of metropolitan officials in West Africa. Ethnographers, however, viewed the French-educated elite as an unsettling presence that called into question their basic assumptions about the real nature of native societies as well as claims about the immutability of cultures. Consequently, many prominent ethnographers cooperated with the colonial government in an attempt to marginalize and discredit the *évolués* while offering new definitions of the "true" African that sanctioned tribal identities in contradistinction to the universalist pretensions of French republicanism.

Delafosse argued that the *évolués* were unworthy representatives of "their race" since they had been "uprooted" from certain essential "material, intellectual, and social characteristics" of "Negro-African Civilization" that the ethnographer identified as indispensable for the harmonious functioning of West African society. According to Delafosse, "The family was at the base of native society" and it guaranteed social stability as well as cultural continuity.[27] However, it was not a family that resembled the model being propagated in the metropole at the same time.[28] Rather, Delafosse described the African family as comprising all "the descendents of a common ancestor living in the same place" in addition to the ancestors themselves.[29] Thus, the family was at the center of religious practice and was best understood as an ever-expanding network that irrevocably tied the living to the dead through the obligation to uphold and continue the mores, traditions, and structures of social organization elaborated in the primordial past.

The African family, according to Delafosse, was patriarchal and, as such, male members of the clan, tribe, or ethnic group exercised exclusive authority. Upon marriage, the control of women passed from fathers to husbands, a transaction viewed by Delafosse and other ethnographers of the period as fundamentally commercial in nature. One official in Dakar asked rhetorically, "What place does woman hold in native society? Without doubt none." The anonymous author of the aforementioned note went on to explain that the government general's hands were, therefore, tied with regard to ameliorating the condition of West African women. "We are obligated," the author maintained, "to respect the customs and the institutions of the peoples who are under our authority."[30] Among the customs Dakar argued it was compelled to respect was the use of women to pay off debts one male owed to another. While Governor General Marcel de Coppet acknowledged in

1937 that "this custom [was] not in accord with [French] principles," he reminded Paris, "are not our native policies based upon the respect of traditional customs."[31]

Several families linked through blood and marriage comprised a "clan or tribe" led by a "chief" who guaranteed the "political unity" of African society since he was the direct link with the ancestors of a given tribal community.[32] By the 1920s many prominent ethnographers in France agreed with Delafosse that West African tribal groups functioned as "collectivities" that precluded the development of individual personalities or the easy accommodation of the *sujet* populations to doctrines of personal rights and socio-political systems based upon such concepts.[33] The "primitive," according to Lucien Lévy-Bruhl, did not have the psychological ability to make decisions independent from the collectivity; the ultimate form of which he argued was "the tribe."[34] In fact, the "authentic" African was presented as "ferociously...ethnic" and endowed with a "tribal" mentality that precluded the possibility of the native populations to develop a national consciousness without the aid of European colonizers.[35] The will of this tribal collectivity was embodied in the person of the chief whose authority was not based on heredity, though, since he was "elected" by a "council of elders or notables" that functioned as "a sort of legislative assembly."[36] As such, many ethnographers deemed chieftaincy as consistent with the democratic principles of France while such a reading also provided officials in Dakar with the scientific justification for denying basic civil and political rights to the *sujet* populations of West Africa that were otherwise guaranteed to citizens by the Republic's constitution.[37]

Furthermore, the model of "Negro-African Civilization" mapped by ethnographers in the 1920s and 1930s and embraced by colonial administrators was that of a "peasant society" deeply "attached to rural life."[38] Accordingly, Van Vollenhoven, in addition to restoring some of the administrative authority of the chiefs in 1917 also issued orders that encouraged the intensification of cash crop production for export to Europe. Large plantations were organized along "tribal" lines and were generally supervised by "chiefs."[39] Thus, the government general enhanced the prestige and authority of the pre-colonial elite by placing greater economic resources at their disposal, including control of the labor supply.

Since the West African was by nature a "peasant," ethnographers and administrators argued, he lacked the intellectual capacity for handling his own wages. Therefore, wages owed to the agricultural workers and other laborers provided to the colonial administration for public works projects were paid to the tribal authority that then dispensed the money, usually after taking a substantial cut, to those who performed the work.[40] "Having become employed in a European firm," one official asserted, "the native peasant does not hesitate to degrade himself. [Abandoning his culture] he wears European clothes, in particular those of the rich, if he is able...[while] respect for his parents and his ancestors disappears [as well]. Even his [immediate] family is disorganized. Confused and isolated, the satisfied and honest farmer of old is nothing more than a discontented worker, solely guided by his desire for idleness and plunder. Should he be exposed to xenophobic propaganda, [the former peasant] immediately lends his support." The solution, according to this official, was "to intensify traditional [agricultural] production."[41] This argument justified forced labor since the "African" would only work if compelled to do so and remunerated labor "was unknown" to the region "before the arrival of the European."[42]

This reading of African society led Delafosse and his associates to view the introduction of industrial production processes and the development of urban centers as threats to the foundations of West African society that disrupted the "natural evolution" of native culture.[43] The rebellions that plagued the federation during the 1914–1918 war and the rise of the *évolué* class as an influential force in the colonial field confirmed for officials in Dakar the need to "preserve intact [the] armature" of African society.[44] For ethnographers and officials of AOF alike the *évolué* symbolized the dangers of imposing a European archetype of society on the federation. The French-educated elite was urban, educated, and employed in bureaucratic or capitalist enterprises. These factors combined with the "native's" supposed inability to grasp concepts such as "individuality" and "responsibility" induced mental "confusion" among the *évolués*. This state of mind prevented the new elite from appreciating the nature and importance of France's *mission civilisatrice*, which Dakar increasingly defined in the 1920s and 1930s as the protection of indigenous forms of social organization and the revival of "authentic" African cultures.[45]

Natural Leaders: The Revival of the Pre-colonial Elite in AOF

In 1929 Governor General Carde issued a circular in which he described the "native chief" as the "indispensable intermediary" in France's relationship with the *sujet* populations. He noted that "it [was] remarkable that [even] in Senegal, where the colonial authority encounters some particular difficulties inherent in the character of the people, the local administration has managed to keep the authority of the native chiefs intact and even to reinforce it."

Carde observed that this administrative structure had withstood the challenge of "the *évolués*" who had attempted to usurp the prerogatives of the pre-colonial elite "without possessing their natural authority."[46]

However, Carde's statement reveals a tension in Dakar's conception of native governance that plagued the colonial administration's transformation of indigenous administrative structures in the years between the two world wars. While Dakar pointed to the decisive contribution the government general had made to preserving and enhancing the position of "native authorities," Carde continued to insist that the "chief's" authority was "natural" and derived singly from the "authentic traditions" of the *sujet* populations. Yet, by the time Dakar had concluded that "native" authorities were legitimate rulers and constituted the best allies of France in governing West Africa, over two decades of official hostility toward the pre-colonial elite had undermined the effectiveness and credibility of autochthonous systems of power and social organization.[47] Therefore, the government general confronted the dual task of restoring an idealized version of pre-colonial African command structures while also infusing them with a measure of eminence that would induce "the 'spontaneous' consent … of the great masses of the population" to the new hegemonic order.[48]

During the 1914–1918 conflict the government general's ability to reshape authority and redefine France's mission in West Africa was constrained by Paris' wartime needs. When the hostilities ended so did the impediments acting against those that favored a revision of the *mission civilisatrice* and a fundamental reordering of imperial government along lines mapped by ethnographers like Delafosse. Furthermore, political changes in the metropole after the war provided administrators like Merlin, governor general of AOF from 1919 to 1923, with the support from Paris that revisionists in the colonial hierarchy lacked during the 1914–1918 conflict. The conservative governments that dominated metropolitan politics in the early 1920s sympathized with the colonial policies espoused by Van Vollenhoven, Carde, and Delafosse in opposition to those pushed by Diagne and Angoulvant. In 1920 Paris named Delafosse "honorary governor of colonies…[and] professor of West African languages and customs at the École Coloniale" over the objections of Diagne and Angoulvant who both asserted that the ethnographer's view of indigenous society was inimical to the universal and egalitarian traditions of France.[49]

Delafosse's appointment at the École Coloniale, where future overseas administrators were trained, indicated that Paris had accepted the ethnographer's understanding of West African society as accurate and his opinions on colonial governance as consistent with state policy. Furthermore, it signaled a shift in official conceptions of France's purpose overseas and the relationship between the metropole and its colonies.[50] Accordingly, one highly placed official declared, "The evolution of the natives in our African colonies within their ethnic communities is the order of the day. The disorganization of the tribes, and also that of the family, the only institution ... that survived the ruin of the great and small black States, is the present condition against which we are fighting."[51] While the ministry of colonies realized it could not ignore the "*évolués*" and, therefore, had to devise a special policy for that community, France's "paramount concern" was the development of a system of rule centered on the various "ethnic groups" then being defined by the colonial administration. In fact, if forced to choose between according greater influence to the *évolués* or to the pre-colonial elite, Paris informed administrators in sub-Saharan Africa that "only the natural leaders, traditionally recognized, are capable of acquiring firm and durable authority and of permitting us to succeed in reorganizing the [colonial] community."[52]

Many of those in the imperial hierarchy who favored the reorganization of colonial governance also advocated a restructuring of the metropolitan order and often viewed the overseas possessions as proving grounds for political projects ultimately prescribed for France itself. It was not uncommon to find former colonial officials or officers of the colonial army among the leading ranks of metropolitan fascist and conservative movements in the 1920s and 1930s.[53] Luminaries such as Delafosse, Pierre Drieu La Rochelle, Marshal Lyautey, and Louis Maran deemed the cultures of France and the colonized societies as threatened by the corrupting influences of "cosmopolitan" and "internationalist" forces that had gained influence as a result of the cataclysm of the First World War. Critics of the *mission civilisatrice* as understood before the 1914-1918 conflict, as well as the universalist aspects of French republicanism associated with that mission were united in their desire to defend what they perceived as the purity of French culture born "from twenty centuries of ancestors living in the same country." That same motivation led Jacques Doriot, a former Communist and prominent crusader against imperialism in the 1920s, to declare in 1938 that France's purpose overseas was "not to 'transform Moslems into Frenchmen' but to permit old civilizations to develop under French authority."[54] While many metropolitan fascists and conservatives declared that Jews, feminists, and Bolsheviks constituted the greatest threat to French culture in Europe, officials overseas regarded the *évolués* as the leading nemesis to native West African tradition. For the government general in the 1920s, the French-educated elite possessed all the undesirable characteristics of "cosmopolitanism," a propensity toward radical or "Bolshevik" politics, and femininity attributed to Jews and other ethnic communities in Europe by right-wing politicians and theorists.

To meet the threat Dakar claimed the *évolués* posed, while also concerned to offset further rural rebellions in the federation, the government general embarked on a radical restructuring of administrative authority that accorded greater influence to "purely native" rulers.[55] Of primary concern in this reordering of power was the provision of a legal basis for the authority of "indigenous chiefs." While ethnographers and imperial administrators agreed that the pre-colonial elite attained their prerogatives by virtue of "tradition," the colonial state maintained that such authority could only be preserved if it were provided a firm legal basis and if such customs were codified in a statutory code.[56] In 1921 Merlin issued an *arrêté* that charged the chiefs with assuring the execution of administrative authority, the maintenance of order and public peace, monitoring public hygiene, the preparation of military recruitment lists, tax collection, and the oversight of all markets in their areas of jurisdiction. Those jurisdictions were defined according to "tribal" groups identified by ethnographers.[57] Merlin's reforms of the command structure in West Africa situated the "tribe" at the base and as the foundation of governance in the federation. Accordingly, Dakar incorporated as a fundamental aspect of its mission the demarcation and preservation of tribal communities. In addition, Merlin's modifications of imperial rule invested the government general with the responsibility to appoint chiefs where they had been eliminated by France in the decades before 1914 and involved the colonial administration directly in power struggles within those societies.[58] While this order was designed to restore some of the power colonial administrators and ethnographers claimed chiefs exercised prior to the European conquest, in effect it transformed the pre-colonial elite into agents of the colonial state whose position was sustained only through the continued support of the government general.[59]

Those administrative reforms also tied the future of France's presence in West Africa to the loyalty and cooperation of the pre-colonial elite, a fealty that was not always readily forthcoming. In fact, Merlin met increasing resistance from some among the pre-colonial elite who insisted that the "chiefs" be made equal partners with the government general in the administration of the federation, not merely functionaries of the colonial administration. The dispute between the autochthonous rulers and Dakar centered on the delineation of the boundaries between tribal communities. While Merlin wanted to restore some authority to the pre-colonial elite, he did not want the chiefs to emerge as a powerful and autonomous element within the colonial field that could serve as a new site of resistance to French rule. Since many chiefs ruled populations spread over a wide geographic space and in numbers that exceeded the limits Dakar found acceptable, the government general designated "new" chiefs even among communities that had an established pre-colonial hierarchy in place. Also, Merlin established guidelines that limited the size of each community over which the new village or canton chief could exercise authority. Should the population of a given tribe exceed the pre-set limit the group would be divided and a new tribal unit created with its separate "chief."[60] Consequently, discontent spread among those proclaimed as the new indispensable allies of French colonialism in West Africa.

That tension became acute when Merlin appointed several new Lebou and Wolof chiefs in Senegal in the early 1920s. In response, representatives of the pre-colonial elite brought the dispute to Paris, as Diagne had done for the *originaires* in 1914. Several "notables" of Senegal complained to the ministry of colonies in 1921 that "Merlin does not like blacks and even less those of Senegal." The spokespeople of the pre-colonial elite accused the governor general of "practicing the politics of disunion with the aim of dividing us."[61] Even Diagne joined the Senegalese chiefs in their opposition to Merlin's policies, although for decidedly different reasons. The deputy from Senegal hand-delivered the "notables'" petition to the ministry of colonies and urged Paris not to recognize the delegation Merlin selected to represent the natives of West Africa at the 1922 colonial exposition in Marseilles on the grounds that the governor general's appointees were not "legitimate."[62]

However, the government general, following the image of "authentic" African society mapped by ethnographers, argued that the legitimacy of the chiefs did not derive from heredity or familial connections but rather from the people of each tribal group who had "democratically" selected the chiefs "following local custom."[63] In fact, Merlin issued a series of orders in 1919 that required the establishment of a "Council of Notables" for each ethnic community in the federation.[64] According to the government general, the new assembly was to be composed of the "elders" or "respected members" of the tribe who, in turn, would elect one among them that would serve as "chief." Of course, Dakar reserved the right to either approve or annul the decision of the council based on whether the colonial administration deemed the choice to be in the best interest of the community. In addition, the government general often appointed the members of the newly founded councils so that the choices for leadership of the tribe were restricted to those who Dakar had already approved.[65]

While some West African societies like the Lebou of Senegal had a tradition whereby the chief or leader was chosen through a deliberative process, many others did not. Thus, Merlin's reforms pointed to the continued tendency among French colonizers to promulgate uniform policies for the entire *sujet* population despite claims that the government general aimed to protect and respect autochthonous traditions. Moreover, Dakar found justification for this approach in the work of ethnographers who argued that African societies were fundamentally similar to one another and shared a common origin in the primordial past. According to Delafosse, "It is undeniable that the Negro-African populations, whatever differences the superficial observer sees among them, present between them a united character, which without doubt derives from the commonality of their ethnic origins and from the relative similarity of their physical, economic and social milieu from which they at first emerged and have, subsequently, evolved."[66]

The assertion of the existence of a "Negro-African Civilization" that provided the underlying basis for all African societies took on canonical status among French ethnographers from the 1920s into the 1950s. The Society of Africanists, founded in 1931 following the International Colonial Exposition in Paris, saw the idea of a Negro-African Civilization as a legitimating factor in fostering the study of "Africa" as a unified and recognizable socio-geographic space. In fact, by then ethnographers had come to accept ancient Egypt as an originating source for the Negro-African Civilization, a notion that would become widely reproduced in the period of formal decolonization.[67]

Yet, if African societies were basically alike, they remained profoundly different from those of Europe. Dakar asserted, therefore, that notions of justice or individual rights that were important components of metropolitan law could not be applied to AOF for fear of "disrupting tradition" and undermining the "harmony" of the federation.[68] The demise of Sarraut's program for the development of the overseas possessions in 1923 cleared the path for the intensification of plantation production in the federation while it also firmly situated the colonies as places of extraction to fuel the metropolitan economy. During the two decades between the world wars the government general dropped its rhetoric about "developing" the West African economy. Instead, it characterized its mission as increasing "production" among the native population in order to assist the metropolitan economy to recover from the devastation of the 1914–1918 war.[69] By production Dakar meant increasing the yield of cash crops and the tonnage of mined minerals, all of which was destined for export to the metropole. To achieve the desired results, French firms and the government general opted not to introduce more advanced technology, but to rely upon "customary techniques" which were labor intensive.[70]

In order to procure the necessary supply of workers without creating a class of discontented proletarians that might become attracted to Communist or other revolutionary ideas, the government general attempted to reorganize the labor market along tribal lines and made the chiefs responsible for the provision of manpower. This responsibility was not limited to the rural areas where the institution of chieftaincy was more firmly entrenched. In a direct challenge to the leadership role assumed by the *évolués* in the cities and commercial centers of West Africa, Dakar required that even urban workers long accustomed to autonomy *vis-à-vis* tribal hierarchies and pre-colonial systems of command "submit to the authority of the chief."[71] In this manner the government general sought to repair what it perceived as the damage done by earlier colonial administrators who had created a class of "detribalized" and "uprooted" Africans.[72]

Unwilling to permit the *sujets* to "become French," and anxious to prevent the emergence of political struggles along class lines, the imperial administration offered the "tribe" as the only valid frame of reference for political and social consciousness. Furthermore, while Dakar denied the right to free association for the *sujets* it forged the legal and structural basis that sanctioned ethnicity as the sole basis upon which Africans could engage meaningfully with the colonial state and through which non-citizens could struggle for reforms.[73] However, as Jean Suret-Canale observes, while the tribe or chieftaincy retained the appearances of "tradition" it "had a fundamentally new character [by the 1930s]. The traditional chiefdom gave way to the administrative chiefdom."[74] Thus, while the government general legally attached all *sujets* to a tribal authority and had infused the pre-colonial elite with some authority and numerous obligations, the revived native leadership lacked legitimacy not only in the urban centers, but in rural West Africa as well. Far from an independent agent in the colonial field, the chief was an imperial tax collector and gendarme of the government general. Even if Dakar required allies among the conquered populations in order to sustain French rule the overseas administration was careful not to allow the pre-colonial elite any significant ability to make decisions. Rather, the chiefs functioned as a conduit for orders decided upon in Paris or the federation capital. Should the indigenous authority fail to meet its obligations, Dakar did not hesitate to imprison, publicly humiliate, or even replace the chief.[75]

While the export market remained stable and *évolué* contact with the rural masses was effectively checked, the pre-colonial elite maintained the outward appearances of control and local sovereignty. Yet, when the global economic crisis of the 1930s reached West Africa the hollowness of chiefly authority and the lack of popular attachment to tribal leadership was exposed in a wave of discontent that threatened to undermine French rule in the federation. The decline in production that beset France in the first years of the Depression translated into reduced demand for the raw materials and produce generated in the colonies. In addition, to temporarily shield French workers from unemployment, laborers from the overseas territories were repatriated to their geographic places of origin, where no work awaited them.[76] Moreover, since the empire was contained within a protectionist wall that maintained the colonies as safe markets for French goods such as textiles, France compensated for the collapse of its trade with the United States and Europe by mandating increased prices on goods exported to its overseas possessions. Those price increases placed basic manufactured goods out of the reach of most West Africans, even the urban workers whose standard of living far out-paced that of the *sujets* in rural areas. Furthermore, the tariff wall, first erected in 1894, precluded access to manufactured goods produced outside the French imperial framework.[77] Thus, France had constructed a relationship that made the economic wellbeing of the *sujets* in the federation entirely dependent upon the health and stability of the metropolitan economy. When the European economy turned sour West Africans were reduced to extreme destitution.[78]

The collapse of the world economy in the early 1930s undermined the tenuous position of the pre-colonial elite in West Africa as the need for labor declined and the peasants were no longer able to pay taxes and meet other financial obligations imposed by Dakar. The government general, despite the crisis, insisted that the chiefs fulfill their function and return the same revenues to the state as prior to the Depression. In turn, the chiefs applied greater pressure on their population and used more brutal and arbitrary means to extract wealth from the *sujets*.[79] The rural masses initially expressed their discontent in the form of massive migration across colonial borders, generally in the direction of the British colonies of Gold Coast and Nigeria. Thus, over the decade from 1925 to 1936 the total population of the federation increased only slightly from 13,242,336 to 14,716,202. In 1932 the population of French West Africa declined by 100,000 and in the following year it fell by a further 70,000, most of which was attributed to cross border migration.[80]

In most instances, these migrations were not led, as in the past, by tribal authorities. Rather, those "elders" and "chiefs" that accompanied the movement to Nigeria, Gold Coast, or Sierra Leone did so under pressure from peasants who balked at forced labor and were in search of higher wages and greater accessibility to manufactured goods in the British colonies.[81] In other cases the Depression exacerbated tensions between the indigenous communities and incidents of tribal conflict were noted throughout the mid-1930s. Some groups took advantage of the widespread population movements to expand their areas of control to other lands, like the Islamic Mouride Brotherhood of Senegal that forced some communities off their territory and occupied areas abandoned by others. Consequently, the relations of influence between the local communities changed during the economic crisis enabling some groups to emerge as more strategically placed to intervene in matters of colonial governance while others saw their status erode. All this points to the profoundly destabilizing effect of the Depression on West African society.[82]

However, the government general confronted another problem associated with migration that produced even greater anxiety than the loss of population to British colonies: the movement of peasants to the cities in search of work. "The pauperization of the countryside" during the Depression induced many plantation laborers to "escape" the control of their tribal leaders and seek better fortunes in the cities and assistance from urban relatives.[83] Once there, the migrants from rural West Africa found little aid and no work. Instead, they augmented the growing ranks of urban unemployed and as such contributed to an upsurge in strike activity and the further development of organized politics in the federation.[84] As early as 1932 M. Chevanal of the Chamber of Commerce in Senegal observed that "the patience of the blacks...could have its limit." Up to that point, the representative of French business asserted, "our natives of AOF have supported with fatalism the terrible situation induced by the economic crisis." However, a time was fast approaching, he warned, when this "fatalism" would give way to disaffection "exploited by certain agitators."[85] Again the specter of radical *évolués* fomenting Communist revolution in West Africa haunted the government general. At a meeting of the Government Council for AOF in 1932 Brévié explained to his associates that French authority in West Africa was compromised by the shortsighted actions taken by Paris to confront the Depression; decisions the sole beneficiary of which was the European economy.[86] Thus, the dispute between metropolitan officials and overseas administrators on proper colonial policy received a new impetus under the strain of economic crisis.

Brévié's anger with Paris, though, did not represent a deep concern for the welfare of his subjects. Rather, the government general's exasperation was directed explicitly at the left-center government elected that year and headed by the Radical politician Edouard Daladier. Officials in Dakar interpreted the 1932 election, which brought socialists and radicals together in a new *cartel des gauches*, as a menace to the order the government general had so carefully cultivated in the 1920s. Over the next two years Brévié and his associates in West Africa added their voices to those of the increasingly numerous and belligerent far-right political movements in the colonial field who denounced parliamentary weakness in the face of the "Bolshevik danger." The publications of radical *évolué* organizations based in the metropole like Kouyaté's LDRN circulated freely in West Africa and attracted larger audiences as the economic crisis deepened.[87] Daladier, whose position depended upon socialist support, disregarded the pleas of colonial officials who wanted to restrict the press freedoms of French citizens from the colonies. Only when Daladier resigned following the fascist disturbances of 6 February 1934 did the metropolitan government, under the direction of Pierre Laval, issue the "Régnier-Rollin" decrees. Those orders allowed harsh penalties to be imposed on "anyone who, by publications of any kind whatever, incites resistance to the application of laws, decrees, regulations or orders of public authority."[88]

However, Dakar did not confine its actions to written protests directed at the left-center government between 1932 and 1934. After Brévié quoted several comparative prices for cotton and clothing to indicate the difficulty his *sujets* had in purchasing such products, the governor general declared in 1932 that West Africa had to become self-reliant in such products. In other words, the colonial administration was prepared to sponsor the development of "local industry" to provide basic necessities for the native population in violation of metropolitan orders that prohibited the production of certain manufactured goods in the colonies.[89] Yet, since Brévié accepted the arguments advanced by ethnographers like Delafosse and Henri Labouret that it was futile and dangerous to impose European models of economic development on "primitive societies," his call for greater local production was not synonymous with a plea for the industrialization of West African society. Rather he understood self-reliance to mean the revival of "traditional artisanal skills" and production techniques.[90] For the government general the malaise afflicting West African society did not result from the onerous exactions of the colonial administration and its allies among the pre-colonial elite. Nor did it emanate from low wages, lack of indigenous participation in decisions that effected their lives, or the failure of France and the colonial state to adequately develop and diversify the local economy. Instead, Brévié asserted that while Dakar had successfully reanimated "authentic" African political structures and associated the "legitimate" native rulers with the colonial mission, the *sujets* still sought to emulate "European ways" and standards of living because metropolitan society was held up as the model of civilization.[91] This contributed, Dakar argued, to the disrepute in which the rural population held many of their "chiefs" and the attraction exercised by radical *évolués* on urban workers. What Africa needed, Brévié suggested, was "a cultural renaissance" that would add legitimacy to the "traditional" political structures already in place. As a result, the governor general expected, the native would become content with his or her circumstances and more "willingly" accept French rule.[92]

From Primitives to Africans:
The Politicization of Culture in French West Africa

The "problem," as Brévié and others in the federal administration saw it, was rooted in the education system established during the early years of French rule. According to the inspector general for education in West Africa, M. Charton, the schools founded by the governors general prior to the Great War "had formed a new enlightened and educated class, a kind of native bourgeoisie whose existence poses difficulties for the social and political order" of AOF. Furthermore, since colonial instruction was oriented toward the formation of auxiliaries for France's mission overseas, it did not reach the "rural masses" who remained "ignorant" and lacked "basic skills." The dilemma, as the government general perceived it, was to reorganize and extend education in such a way as to prevent the generation of "Europeanized *évolués*" while increasing the productive aptitude of the indigenous masses. The solution, Charton proclaimed, was to steer instruction "in another direction, a more traditional one." "Education," Charton insisted, had to be "general and practical." It should be carried out "in light of the African experience" and must reinforce "the authority of the traditional chiefs."[93]

In fact, the chiefs themselves had to be sent to school to learn about "African culture" and the "ways of the ancestors."[94] According to Dakar, the pre-colonial elite was partly to blame for the lack of esteem in which the *sujets* held them because the chiefs were deficient in basic knowledge about their own "ethnic" or "tribal" heritage. Therefore, they could not inspire the kind of devotion and respect ethnographers suggested traditional leaders had done before the European conquest. To overcome that inadequacy, the pre-colonial elite and their charges were to be sent to "rural popular schools" where they would study "historical and ethnographic works, examples of native art, and research [done] on African folklore and music."[95] In other words, the government general decided that West Africans had to be taught how to be "authentically" African.

This "reindigenization" of the colonized populations under French rule was a general phenomenon throughout the colonial field in the 1930s. In the case of Indochina Lebovics argues, "Down to the village level...they (French administrators) hoped ultimately to implant their own dependent Vietnamese mandarin-teachers to frustrate the development of rebellious organic intellectuals."[96] Even metropolitan politicians claimed the need to reindigenize French society. According to the former Communist turned fascist Jacques Doriot, "A nationalism only understands itself if it finds its sources in the old traditions of the French provinces."[97]

The idea that France was authorized and even duty-bound to instruct the subject populations in their own culture perpetuated the underlying assumptions of the *mission civilisatrice* that claimed for the colonizing power the prerogative to mold and guide the societies which it had conquered. The fundamental change was in the goals of the mission, not the presumption that France represented a superior civilization or had a "right" to rule in Africa or Asia. With the establishment of the bureaucratic structures of the federation of French West Africa came the elaboration of an educational system designed "to guarantee [the formation of] the literate auxiliary personnel" needed for governance to introduce what were deemed by the colonial administration as the basic elements of France's civilization.[98] "Elementary education" was organized in village, regional, and urban schools where *sujets* received instruction in the French language as well as "hygiene, moral conduct, agricultural techniques, administration, and commercial skills." The regional schools serviced those rural areas that lacked a central village. At the next level, the colonial administration offered "higher and professional primary education" that further trained students in agriculture, administration, and commerce. If the pupil was selected by their teachers and local officials of the colony to continue beyond the primary level, then he (only rarely she) was tracked into either "education for technical training" or "secondary education." For technical training the government general had constructed four schools in all of West Africa: The famed École William Ponty, the École des Pupilles Mecaniciens de la Marine, the École de Medecine de Dakar, and the École Veterinaire de Bamako. These institutions were designed to produce cadre that would assist France in bringing the rudiments of "civilized society" to the native population such as medical care, hygiene, veterinary care to improve livestock, and technical skills used in road, railroad, and port development. For those very few students permitted entry into the secondary education track the government general built the Lycée Faidherbe de St. Louis. The pupils who successfully completed their studies at the Lycée Faidherbe could, if permission from Dakar was forthcoming, continue their studies in France with the possibility of attaining advanced university degrees. These students constituted the upper elite among the *évolués* and frequently acquired the status of French citizens while those trained in the technical schools often remained *sujets*, a source of friction within the French-educated elite throughout the period of imperial rule.[99]

Despite frequent statements and orders issued by governors general before the 1914–1918 war that set the education of all subjects of the empire as an unalterable goal of French colonialism, only a handful of the more than 14 million residents of French West Africa were receiving instruction in colonial schools by 1934. That year, the government general reported that 265 village schools, 75 regional schools, and 18 urban schools were functioning in the entire federation. At the elementary level less than 50,000 students were enrolled of which barely 4,500 were girls, none of who attended the urban schools. Throughout AOF only eight higher primary schools and 13 professional schools existed in 1934, catering to slightly more than 1,500 pupils. Finally, at the most advanced schools the numbers of students dropped to barely 100, with a mere handful tracked for advanced study in the metropole.[100]

André Maginot, minister of colonies, noted in 1929 that the "traditional elite…was too fragile" because of the gradual "disappearance of native customs" among the rural population as well as the "widened horizons" of *sujets* who were brought into "direct contact" with French civilization through schools, the army, or commercial activities. Furthermore, France had introduced European production methods ethnographers and administrators now asserted were unsuited to West African conditions and that contributed to the "disruption" of native culture and the local economy. Notwithstanding Maginot's insistence that "education and instruction" be reformed to "restore the prestige" of the "chiefs" and "native customs," Dakar did not take action until 1934.[101] Only after economic conditions had deteriorated to the point where political disturbances and strikes posed a threat to French business and the stability of imperial rule did Brévié order the formation of "rural popular schools" in every part of the federation. The government general contended that these institutions were designed to facilitate the "political and cultural evolution" of the indigenous population and, therefore, accorded with France's *mission civilisatrice*. In addition to the established curriculum— French, agriculture, commerce, and hygiene—these new schools "integrated [lessons in]…traditional native activities: crafts, rural life, [native] morality,

[and] the ways of the ancestors." Particular emphasis was placed on teaching "artisanal skills" to the pupils in rural West Africa "in order to preserve and renovate traditional native talents." In fact, the schools were physically designed to accentuate instruction in "native crafts." "*Maisons d'Artisans*" were added to the usual school building where special indoctrination in "African ways" was conducted. According to M. Charton, "The Artisan Houses strongly contribute to the evolution of native life and the traditional economy, they protect the character of traditional art and must be one of the most active furnaces [in which to forge] African culture." Dakar claimed the graduates of the rural popular schools constituted "an elite for the [African] race, but one that remains strongly rooted in the country."[102] Thus, the new schools were expected to avoid the worst effects of earlier education programs; the production of a class of people that aspired to be "French" and thought of themselves as the equals of colonial administrators.

In addition to training a new, more pliable elite than the earlier generation of *évolués*, the rural popular schools promised to rescue West Africa from the throws of the global economic crisis by restoring pre-colonial modes of production. The government general justified its encouragement of local industry, despite the objections of metropolitan business leaders and politicians, on the grounds that "long before the arrival of the whites, our African populations knew, by their own means, how to satisfy their personal needs." However, more was involved in Dakar's self-legitimization than the valorization pre-colonial African society. The Artisan Houses and the rural popular schools functioned as the structural bases for challenging earlier, more universal, versions of the *mission civilisatrice*. According to colonial governor and noted ethnographer Henri Labouret, "In destroying the economic way of life of our subjects we have created in them new needs, we have brought devastation to local industries. European influence," he continued, "by its permanent contact [with the natives] has reduced the artisanal elite to sterility and death."[103] For Labouret and other colonial officials, too direct a contact between Europe and the colonized peoples was the principle cause of the disturbances overseas in the 1930s, especially in Indochina where armed rebellion was ignited in 1930. Dakar, therefore, regarded the rural popular schools as the means whereby the cultural and social distance between French and West African society could be maintained and even widened while furnishing the means for more direct political control over the federation.[104]

To supplement the formal lessons at the new schools, as well as to provide first-hand experience at "being African," the government general orchestrated "traditional festivals" and dances. A 1937 report on native policy in AOF produced for the ministry of colonies maintained, "These celebrations demonstrate that our students observe and study native ways, that they remain in contact with their milieu, that they understand it, [and] that they love it."[105] Moreover, the colonial administration sponsored the construction of several museums, replete with *"salles d'ethnographie,"* in major urban centers like Dakar and Bamako.[106] In fact, some in the imperial hierarchy suggested that rural popular schools be founded in the cities of French West Africa as well.[107]

In the end, the rural popular schools did not lead to mass education or to greater affinity among the population for the French-sanctioned chiefs. By the time the Popular Front coalition of Socialists, Communists, and Radicals was elected to a majority in the Chamber of Deputies in 1936 the rural popular schools had only 25,506 students in the entire federation. Furthermore, the government general reported that only 290 such schools existed nearly three years after the program was inaugurated. Even these figures fail to reveal the extent to which Dakar fell short of its publicly stated objective to bring instruction to all West Africans. Many of the pre-existing village schools were simply renamed "rural popular schools" and their curriculum changed to conform to the new guidelines from the colonial administration. Therefore, of the 290 school buildings claimed in 1936, only 29 of them had been built in the previous three years. Subsequently, the enrollment recorded in 1936 marked an increase of about 4,500 students over figures for the village schools in 1933.[108]

The rural popular schools disappointed the government general in one other important regard: they did not undermine the place of the *évolués* in the colonial field. In fact, by the late 1930s the French-educated urban elite was in a stronger position within the imperial framework than it had been since the Great War. That enhanced stature resulted from a combination of factors associated with the economic crisis in the 1930s. One consequence of the Depression was a halt to recruitment of administrative personnel among the indigenous population.[109] This led to increased unemployment among the *évolués* and added to the volatile mix forming in the colonial cities. Consequently, the government general confronted the prospect of hundreds if not thousands of educated and skilled West Africans unoccupied in any profession and open to the "agitation of subversive elements among them." At the same time, Dakar realized that it lacked a sufficient number of trained teachers to staff the new schools and teach the new curriculum in "the bush." Ironically, the colonial administration turned to the very social element it feared most in the federation to carry out the "cultural regeneration" of African society—the *évolué*.[110]

Furthermore, political changes in the metropole undermined the agenda of conservatives within the imperial hierarchy. The Popular Front electoral victory followed by the massive strike wave in the summer of 1936 augured a change in direction for "native" policy as produced in Paris. The coalition partners of the new government took a more benign position on the status of *évolués* in the colonial field and regarded them as important contributors to imperial governance. In November 1936 Léon Blum, the socialist prime minister of France, and his minister of colonies, Marius Moutet, called a conference of all governors general to redefine the imperial mission and map the Popular Front's conception of the relationship between colonizers and colonized. The conference took two decisions of import: First, it established a "Committee for the study of native customs in the [French held] territories of continental Africa."[111] Significantly, the committee included not only leading French ethnographers—Lévy-Brulh, Labouret, and Marcel Griaule— as well as prominent representatives of the overseas administration—Robert Delavignette and M. Charton—it also drew upon the services of the *évolués* and in particular of the radicals among the French-educated elite through the person of Lamine Guèye. This leads to the second substantial resolution of the conference: The assembled representatives of the colonial administration made it a point of policy to engage the *évolués* directly in the administration of its overseas territories. In its final statement, the conference declared that all were agreed with "the view that the natives must be admitted to collaborate in the greatest measure possible in the administrative aspects of their country." By natives the governors general, led by the Popular Front government, made it clear that they meant the "elite" from both urban and rural centers.[112]

Moreover, the discourse practiced by the Popular Front as displayed in the resolution from the conference of governors for the first time announced that Africa belonged to "Africans," not France. While the subject populations might be associated with France, the territories over which the metropole ruled in the end still remained the possession of the native peoples. Therefore, the Blum government in effect renounced an important part of the *mission civilisatrice* and a key element used to legitimate colonial rule: the exclusive right of France to speak on behalf of the indigenous population and the metropole's sole prerogative to instruct Africans in their "authentic" culture. Accordingly, Moutet informed Dakar in 1937 that France's role in West Africa was to "assist...the evolution...of the black race," not to direct that development. Such assistance required the government general to seek the advice and opinions of the "native elite" on African customs and the needs of the population.[113] Furthermore, Moutet declared that the indigenous peoples were "free in the practice of their customs and in their evolution, but federated together in Overseas France."[114] In fact, Moutet re-circulated elements of the rhetoric practiced by Diagne during the 1914–1918 war and affirmed that "the man of the African and Madagascan bush, just like the man of the street in European France, has the right to be judged according to one's tradition and one's personality."[115] None of these pronouncements amounted to a renunciation of colonial rule, or even presented the prospect of a future where France did not exercise the final authority in Africa. However, they do mark a shift in the conception of imperial governance and the place of the educated elite in those structures. Also, while Moutet, Maurice Viollette, and Blum returned to certain universalist aspects of the *mission civilisatrice*, they did not seek a return to assimilation as a goal of France's colonial project. Rather, the notion of essential differences between European and African cultures was deeply embedded in the colonial field by the late 1930s and was practiced even by those on the political left who had once rejected such ideas. What the Popular Front proposed was a more "humanist" and "republican" relationship between the cultures, rather than the naked exploitation advocated by conservative colonial administrators in the 1920s and early 1930s.[116]

However, while there was general agreement among prominent figures of the French-educated elite that a cultural renaissance for West Africa was in order,[117] the *évolués* were sharply divided over whether to work with the colonial government to realize that end. Dismayed at the lack of response from the *évolués* to become instructors at the rural popular schools and support the government general's endeavor to teach African culture to the rural communities of the federation, Paris called an International Congress on the Cultural Evolution of Colonial Peoples in 1937. The conference marked the first time that the metropolitan government brought together representatives of ethnography, the colonial government, "native chiefs," and *évolués*. In a word, the congress was a meeting point of those social categories most directly engaged in the struggle for authority within the colonial field. Its purpose was to ease the level of conflict in the colonies by inviting the French-educated elite to cooperate in determining "native policy." Furthermore, the congress afforded the opportunity for Paris and Dakar to expose and exacerbate differences among the radical *évolués* by offering concessions to those willing to assist the colonial government in its projects, while refusing to acknowledge the position of those opposed to a working relationship with the imperial rulers.[118]

Among those willing to assist the government general in its rural education program was the Senegalese poet and *agrégé* Léopold Sédar

Senghor. Born in the trading center of Joal in the colony of Senegal on 9 October 1906, Léopold Senghor was the son of a merchant that acted as a liaison between peanut cultivators in rural West Africa and French concerns in the major port cities. Raised a Catholic and educated in French schools, Léopold Senghor was one of those rare *sujets* afforded the opportunity to complete his education in the metropole after attending the Lycée Faidherbe in St. Louis. After six years of study in Paris at the Lycée Louis-Le-Grand and the Sorbonne, in 1935 Léopold Senghor became the first African to pass his *agrégation*—the examinations that entitled one to teach at lycées. However, Léopold Senghor had to be naturalized since only French citizens were entitled to hold such positions. With help from Diagne, and despite promises that he would return to West Africa after completing his studies, Léopold Senghor became a citizen in 1934 and remained in France where he taught, with a brief interlude, until the end of the Second World War.[119]

Léopold Senghor attracted the attention of the government general and the ministry of colonies after he convened a conference in Dakar on "the cultural problem in French West Africa."[120] At that gathering Léopold Senghor spoke extensively about the need for a revival of African culture and the responsibility intellectuals from the federation had in that endeavor. Subsequently, Moutet invited Léopold Senghor to address the same question at a meeting planned to take place in Paris later that month, an overture welcomed by the young poet and teacher. In Paris Léopold Senghor chose as his theme support for the rural popular schools which he described as vehicles whereby a cultural renaissance would be affected in West Africa. In addition, Léopold Senghor outlined the basic reasons he alleged accounted for the opposition among some *évolués* to the new schools while also criticizing them for holding such positions. According to Léopold Senghor, most of the opposition to the rural popular schools among the French-educated elite in AOF derived from a deep-seated suspicion of the motives the government general had in encouraging the *évolués* to become teachers "in the bush." When Dakar approached the urban elite to take positions as instructors at the rural schools the colonial administration posed the question in economic terms, as a place where those with school diplomas could find work when none existed for them in the cities. Léopold Senghor asserted that this led many *évolués* to perceive the sole purpose of the schools as a means to siphon unemployment from the cities and reduce the potential for political confrontation in the urban centers of the federation. In other words, some *évolués* understood the rural popular schools to be a mechanism for breaking the political organizations and networks of the French-educated elite in the urban centers by isolating them in hostile rural communities where they would be subject to the exactions of the pre-colonial elite, and, perhaps, the hated *indigénat*.[121]

Léopold Senghor argued that the mistrust the urban elite had of Dakar's motives was based on statements made by the government general in justifying its new education program for the federation. At the outset, the government general advertised the new curriculum as a means to foster greater respect for the chiefs. Consequentially, the French-educated elite interpreted this measure as a new effort to marginalize them within the imperial framework and restrict their possibilities for social advancement within France and West Africa. Léopold Senghor, though, suggested that the rural popular schools could in the end be used to serve the cultural and political agendas of the *évolué* class. The lycée teacher explained that the new schools "were born of an entirely modern conception of culture. These [institutions] will serve to cultivate [cultural] difference [and] constituted [the basis for] a racial response of man in his own milieu that serves as an instrument of moral and intellectual perfection."[122] Rather than view the pre-colonial elite as rivals, Léopold Senghor urged the *évolués* to embrace them as "racial brothers," much as Diagne had done during his recruitment campaign in 1918.[123] This sentiment was echoed by Fily-Dabo-Sissoko, *chef de canton* of Bafoulabé in French Soudan, who insisted at the conference that "the Black must remain Black."[124]

Both Léopold Senghor and Sissoko cited Diagne and Delafosse as sources of inspiration for their cultural politics. In fact by the 1937 congress the deputy from Senegal and the ethnographer, political foes until Delafosse's death in 1926, had become linked in the rhetoric of cultural authenticity practiced by colonial administrators, the French-educated elite, metropolitan politicians, and the pre-colonial elite in West Africa. Upon the occasion of Diagne's death in 1934, the year the new school program was launched, Brévié wrote that the deputy from Senegal "had successfully assimilated ... French ideas and concepts without sacrificing any of the traditions of his country of birth." Brévié went on to remind Paris of the role Diagne played in the 1918 recruitment campaign and of his "ardent defense of French colonization." The governor general described Diagne as a "force for peace in the face of confused movements that sought to array the races of our colonies against us."[125]

Conclusion

However, the colonial mission that Diagne defended in 1918 as Commissaire of the Republic had been substantially undermined and reworked by the late 1930s. In fact, when Diagne campaigned for reelection in 1919 under the banner that "one could be both French and Muslim" he was bitterly attacked by the government general and his supporters were branded as subversive and dangerous. Armed with the knowledge produced by ethnographers like Delafosse, the colonial government denied not only the possibility of one being both French and Muslim (or African for that matter), it also disavowed the expectation that Africans could ever become "truly" French. Those practices of imperial rule that had produced an *évolué* class that aspired to "become French," Dakar asserted after 1918, had to be abandoned because they merely "uprooted" Africans from their "traditional culture," left them in "moral isolation," and exposed to the entreaties of "professional agitators."[126]

Anxious about the spread of "Bolshevik ideas" among the French-educated elite after the 1918 armistice, Dakar reached for new allies through which to preserve French authority in the federation. Prior to the Great War ethnographers had argued that West African society had its own "natural leaders" and "authentic" forms of social organization that must be respected if order was to be preserved in AOF. However, it was not until the circumstances of total war had exposed the fragility of French rule in West Africa that the government general was prepared to accept the conclusions reached by Delafosse and others concerning the "true nature" of indigenous society and France's mission overseas.

In his description of the "Negro-African Civilization," Delafosse presented a totalized and idealistic portrait of pre-colonial African society that informed practices of rule in AOF during the years between the two world wars. The rebellions of 1915–1916 and the subsequent radicalization of the French-educated elite provided proof to conservative and far-right officials within the imperial hierarchy that colonial rule could only be maintained if the rural native elite was restored to some degree of authority and associated with France in governing West Africa. As a result, Dakar embarked on a series of reforms in the administrative structure of the federation that organized and ossified native society into distinct tribal communities that were placed under the direct authority of a "chief" approved by the government general or its agents. Furthermore, since ethnographers and their sympathizers in Dakar and Paris claimed the African was "fundamentally a peasant," modernization of the local economy was deemed antithetical to maintaining order in the colonies and to the redifined *mission civilisatrice.* This reasoning justified the intensification of cash crop production and the increased use of forced labor in sub-Saharan Africa. Such policies furnished the bases for the development of a hegemonic bloc in the federation comprised of colonial administrators and native chiefs. By the late 1930s the position of the pre-colonial elite within the colonial field was dependent upon the survival of French rule in the region. Thus, as war clouds gathered in Europe after the 1938 Munich Pact delivered Czechoslovakia into the hands of Hitler's Germany, the chiefs of sub-Saharan Africa deluged the metropole with pledges to defend "French soil, its borders, [and] its colonial empire" in the event of a new conflict.[127]

However, the collapse of the global capitalist economy in 1929 revealed serious economic weaknesses in French West Africa and the fragile state of its administrative structures. Thousands of rural *sujets* migrated to neighboring British colonies and to the urban centers of the federation. This caused a further decline in cash crop production while the numbers of unemployed in the cities mounted. Yet, Dakar interpreted the discontent of the indigenous population as a sign that adequate attention had not been paid to the revival of autochthonous traditions. While the office of "chief" had been endowed with certain prerogatives it had been stripped of its prestige and divorced from "traditional" cultural practices. In response, the imperial government set out to teach the subject population how to be "African." The centerpiece of Dakar's project was the establishment of rural popular schools with a reformed curriculum that instructed the "natives" in their history, traditional farming techniques, folk music and art, as well as "customs" inherited from their "ancestors."[128]

Confronted with a shortage of teachers, though, Dakar turned to the *évolués* for assistance in the attempt to bring about a cultural renaissance in West Africa. Thus, a measure initially designed to enhance the position of the pre-colonial elite as a bulwark against the influence of the French-educated elite in the colonial field actually contributed to the increased stature of that social category. Instead of erecting a barrier between the urban elite and the rural masses, the government general was put in a position of encouraging the penetration of *évolués* into "the bush." However, the prospect of working in schools established for the express purpose of reinforcing the authority of rural chiefs and preserving French rule in the federation exposed new lines of division among the *évolués*. While some were prepared to use the institutions of the colonial state, including the ethnographic discourse espoused by Dakar and Paris, to serve their own objectives of producing a cultural renaissance in West Africa, many others greeted the proposal with skepticism and suspicion. In general, as Léopold

Senghor stated at the 1937 conference in Paris, those *évolués* who had taken up residence in the metropole generally supported cooperation with the rural popular school program. Meanwhile, those who remained in the colonized territories tended to be hostile toward any effort that removed them from the urban centers where their political base was situated.[129] Ultimately, the split within the French-educated elite also marked the emergence of a new generation of leaders that was characterized by their willingness to embrace the practices and discourse of colonial rule and wield them as weapons of resistance against imperial domination. It is to the rise of this new group of organic intellectuals among the *évolué* class and the metropolitan furnace wherein their ideas were forged that our attention now turns.

NOTES

1. CAOM, 3/SLOTFOM/53, letter from Kouyaté to Léon M'Ba, chief of the Pahouins in Libreville (Gabon), 6 July 1929. M'Ba later became the leader of independent Gabon.
2. Laitin, *Hegemony and Culture*, p. 171.
3. Laitin describes a similar process in the British colony of Nigeria where he argues that "an externally imposed hegemony became the decisive factor concerning the format of the politicization of culture." Ibid., p. 183.
4. CAOM, 1/AP/859, letter from the ministry of colonies to the governors general of the empire, "Administration Indigène," 9 October 1929.
5. CAOM, CG/107, letter from Emile Faure, leader of the *Rassemblement Colonial*, to the Guernut Commission, 27 April 1938, "Suggestions du groupe de l'Afrique noire du Rassemblement Colonial."
6. CAOM, 3/SLOTFOM/101, CAI report of 15 June 1923.
7. CAOM, CG/59, Jules Brévié, governor general of AOF, "Circulaire No. 128 A.P. sur la codification des coutumes indigènes," 19 March 1931.
8. A thorough study of the connection between far-right political movements in France and imperialism has yet to be undertaken. However, on several occasions Robert Soucy alludes to these links. See: Robert Soucy, *French Fascism: The Second Wave 1933–1939* (New Haven: Yale University Press, 1995), pp. 83–84, 255–256. According to Soucy, "Imperialism was a major ingredient in fascist solutions to the Depression...." (p. 84)
9. Georges Hardy, *L'Afrique Occidentale française* (Paris: Librairie Renouard, 1937), p. 53. Gustave Le Bon, "Psychological Laws of the Evolution of Peoples," in Alice Widener, ed., *Gustave Le Bon: The Man and His Works* (Indianapolis: Liberty Press, 1979), p. 49.
10. CAOM, 1/AP/838, Jules Carde, governor general of AOF, "Circulaire A/S du Commandement indigène," 11 October 1929.
11. CAOM, CG/52, speech by Brévié, December 1935.
12. CAOM, CG/52, report by Inspector General Charton, "L'Enseignement et l'Education en A.O.F.," 5 July 1936.
13. Soucy, *French Fascism: The Second Wave 1933–1939*, pp. 200, 202. Other important studies on the subject of fascism and French culture in the 1920s and 1930s include: Roberts, *Civilization Without Sexes*; Lebovics, *True France*; and Dan S. White, *Lost Comrades; Socialists of the Front Generation, 1918-1945* (Cambridge: Harvard University Press, 1992).
14. Mudimbe, *The Invention of Africa*, p. 20.
15. CAOM, 3/SLOTFOM/78, Kouyaté, "Principes directeurs d'une transformation de l'Outre-Mer," 27 May 1937.
16. CAOM, 1/AP/170, Van Vollenhoven, "Situation politique de la colonie," 20 December 1917.
17. CAOM, CG/59, Jules Brévié, "Circulaire No. 128 A.P. sur la codification des coutumes indigènes," 19 March 1931.
18. Much work remains to be done in exploring the relationship between French ethnography and systems of colonial rule. For some important recent studies on this subject see: Benoît de L'Estoile, "Africanisme & Africanism; Esquisse de

Comparaison Franco-Britannique," in A. Piriou et E. Sibeud, dir., *L'Africanisme en questions* (Paris: Dossiers Africains, 1997); Benoît de L'Estoile, "The 'Natural Preserve of Anthropologists': Social Anthropology, Scientific Planning and Development," in *Social Science Information*, 36:2 (1997); Benoît de L'Estoile, "Au nom des 'vrais Africains': Les élites scolarisées de l'Afrique coloniale face à l'anthropologie (1930-1950)," in *Terrain* (28 March 1997); Emmanuelle Sibeud, "Ethnographie africaniste et 'inauthenticité' coloniale," *French Politics, Culture, and Society* 20:2 (Summer 2002); and Alice Conklin, "The New 'Ethnology' and 'La Situation Coloniale' in Interwar France," *French Politics, Culture, and Society* 20:2 (Summer 2002).

19.   Louise Delafosse, *Maurice Delafosse: Le Berrichon conquis par l'Afrique* (Paris: Imprimerie F. Paillait, 1976), pp. 1, 7, and 106.

20.   See the "Circulaire relative à l'étude des coutumes indigènes," issued by Clozel, 12 January 1909, and the decree reorganizing the judicial system in AOF, 10 November 1903, cited in: Maurice Delafosse, *Haut-Sénégal-Niger*, V. I, (Paris: G.-P. Maisonneuve et Larose, 1972), pp. 18–20.

21.   Gallieni, *Gallieni au Tonkin*, p. 217. Ethnographers also insisted on their importance to the colonial mission. For example see: CAOM, 1/AP/838, Henri Labouret, "A la recherche d'une politique indigène dans l'Ouest Africain," in *L'Afrique Française*, January 1931; and Maurice Prouteaux, "Quelques exemples de l'utilité pratique des études ethnologiques," in *Journal de la Société des Africanistes*, Vol. 1, 1931.

22.   Maurice Delafosse, *Les civilisations disparues: Les civilisations négro-africaines* (Paris: Librairie Stock, 1925), pp. 5-6, 20. See also CAOM, 1/AP/170/3, M. Delafosse, "De la participation des Indigènes de l'A.O.F. à l'administration locale," in *Dépeche Coloniale*, 3, 5, 9 April 1918.

23.   Maurice Delafosse, *Participation élargi des colons européens et des indigènes à la confection des règlements locaux* (Marseille: Typographie et Lithographie Barlatier, 1922), pp. 6, 14.

24.   For a discussion of the *mission civilisatrice* as it was understood and as it informed practices of colonial rule during the early years of the Third French Republic see: Conklin, *A Mission to Civilize*, pp. 1–3. The quote was taken from Delafosse, *Les civilisations disparues*, p. 58.

25.   The decree that authorized the establishment of the Committee is cited by Hardy in *L'Afrique Occidentale française*, p. 14, and was dated 10 December 1915.

26.   Lucien Lévy-Bruhl, "L'Institut d'Ethnologie de l'Université de Paris," in *Revue d'Ethnographie et des Traditions Populaires*, No. 23–24 (1925). In 1931 Governor General Jules Brévié of AOF initiated an annual prize of 3,000 francs for the best scientific documentary work on the natives of the federation. That same year the *Journal de la Société des Africanistes* was founded in conjunction with the International Colonial Exposition held in Paris. For examples where officials in the colonial administration note the important contribution of ethnography to imperial rule see: CAOM, 5/SLOTFOM/2, Prof. Herman M. Bernelot-Moens, "L'Anthropologie Nouvelle et l'Avenir de la Civilisation," in *Dépêche Africaine*, February-March 1929; CAOM, 28/Papiers Moutet (PA)/5, letter from Marius Moutet, minister of colonies, to the government general for AOF, 9 July 1936, on the important contribution of the Institut Français d'Afrique Noire; CAOM, 28/PA/1, letter from Moutet to Radio-Cité, "Sur le Comité d'Étude des Coutumes Indigènes,"

1936; and CAOM, 5/Législation (Lég)/24, *arrêté* of the ministry of colonies that names Delafosse professor of languages and customs of AOF at the École Coloniale, 27 March 1920.

27. Maurice Delafosse, *Les Noirs de l'Afrique* (Paris: Payot et Cie., 1922), p. 157, 3, 138.

28. Important studies on the family, colonialism, natalism, and gender in France in the early decades of the twentieth century include: Jean Elisabeth Pedersen, "'Special Customs': Paternity Suits and Citizenship in France and the Colonies, 1870–1912," in Julia Clancy-Smith and Frances Gouda, eds., *Domesticating the Empire: Race, Gender, and Family Life in French and Dutch Colonialism* (Charlottesville: University Press of Virginia, 1998); Alice L. Conklin, "Redefining 'Frenchness': Citizenship, Race Regeneration, and Imperial Motherhood in France and West Africa, 1914-1940," ibid.; Andrés Horacio Reggiani, "Procreating France: The Politics of Demography, 1919-1945," in *French Historical Studies* 19:3 (Spring 1996); and Roberts, *Civilization Without Sexes*.

29. Delafosse, *Les civilisations disparues*, p. 39; and Delafosse, *Les Nègres* (Paris: Les Éditions Rieder, 1927), p. 36.

30. CAOM, 1/AP/541, "Le statut juridique de la femme dans les colonies françaises," anonymous note from Dakar to the ministry of colonies, probably written in 1939. The author cites "M. Delafosse" as the source for knowledge about the structure of the African family and marriage practices among the "natives" of the federation.

31. CAOM, CG/59, letter from the de Coppet to the ministry of colonies, "Mise en gage de personnes," 24 May 1937.

32. Delafosse, *Les Noirs de l'Afrique*, p. 140.

33. For examples see: Henri Labouret, *À la recherche d'une politique indigène dans l'ouest africain* (Paris: Editions du Comité de l'Afrique Française, 1931), p. 26; Labouret, "Le Paysannat Indigène en Afrique-Occidentale Française," speech given at the Congrès international et intercolonial de la société indigène, 5-10 October 1931, as part of the Exposition Coloniale Internationale de Paris 1931, p. 5; Hardy, *L'Afrique Occidentale française*, p. 69; Delafosse, *Les civilisations disparues*, pp. 8, 19; Delafosse, *Les Nègres*, pp. 38-39; Lucien Lévy-Bruhl, *L'Âme Primitive* (Paris: Librairie Félix Alcan, 1927), pp. 2, 107, 229.

34. Lévy-Bruhl, *L'Âme Primitive*, p. 71.

35. Georges Hardy, *L'Art Nègre: L'Art Anamiste des Noirs d'Afrique* (Paris: Henri Laurens, 1927), p. 2.

36. Delafosse, *Les Nègres*, pp. 49–50.

37. Delafosse, *Participation élargi*, p. 5.

38. For discussions of the "âme paysanne" of the West African see: Georges Hardy, *L'Art Nègre*, pp. 7–8; Robert Delavignette, *Les Paysans Noirs* (Paris: Éditions Stode, 1947), p. 12; and Delafosse, *Les Noirs de l'Afrique*, p. 93.

39. Jean Suret-Canale, *French Colonialism in Tropical Africa 1900–1945* (New York: Pica Press, 1971), p. 256. In fact, the colonial administration introduced the idea of "common land" that was assigned to various tribal groups. This had the effect of forcing mobile societies to become sedentary and it also divided the land according to tribal distinctions.

40. Ibid., p. 247. This issue is also explored in: Conklin, *A Mission to Civilize*, pp. 212–245.

41. CAOM, 7/AE/46, report of the government general for AOF, "La Production Agricole et Pastorale en Afrique Occidentale Française," November 1930.

42. CAOM, 7/AE/46, report of the government general for AOF, "La Production Agricole et Pastorale en Afrique Occidentale Française," November 1930; and ARS, Affaires Economiques (1Q), circulaire no. 087 from the government general to the lieutenant governors of the federation, 20 April 1926.

43. Henri Labouret, "Le Paysannat Indigène en Afrique-Occidentale Française," speech given at the Congrès international et intercolonial de la société indigène, 5–10 Octobre 1931, as part of the Exposition Coloniale Internationale de Paris 1931.

44. CAOM, 1/AP/665, government general for AEF to the ministry of colonies, "Situation Politique A.E.F.," 3 April 1936.

45. CAOM, 5/SLOTFOM/5, Francis Mury, "Encourageons le talent chez les noirs; mais ne crions pas des suite que génie; l'example de René Maran," in *Le Courrier Colonial*, 16 February 1934.

46. CAOM, 1/AP/838, Jules Carde, "Circulaire A/S du Commandement indigène," 11 October 1929.

47. For discussions of the disruptive effects of French penetration into West Africa during the last quarter of the nineteenth century see: Rabinow, *French Modern: Norms and Forms of the Social Environment* (Chicago: The University of Chicago Press, 1989); Cohen, *Rulers of Empire*; Cocquery-Vidrovitch, *Afrique Noire*; Donal B. Cruise O'Brien, *Saints and Politicians: Essays in the Organization of a Senegalese Peasant Society* (Cambridge: Cambridge University Press, 1975); Donal B. Cruise O'Brien, *The Mourides of Senegal: The Political and Economic Organization of an Islamic Brotherhood* (Oxford: Clarendon Press, 1971); Andrew F. Clark, *From Frontier to Backwater: Economy and Society in the Upper Senegal Valley (West Africa), 1850–1920* (New York: University Press of America, Inc., 1999); and Owen White, *Children of the French Empire: Miscegenation and Colonial Society in French West Africa, 1895–1960* (Oxford: Clarendon Press, 1999).

48. Gramsci, *Selections from the Prison Notebooks*, p. 12.

49. CAOM, 5/LEG/24, *Arrêté* promulgated by the ministry of colonies, 27 March 1920, signed by Albert Sarraut. The order also required the government general for AOF to pay Delafosse's salary out of its annual budget; and CAOM, 1/AP/3036, letter from Diagne to the ministry of colonies, "Compte rendu de l'action de la mission au Sénégal," 23 March 1918; telegram from Diagne in Bamako to the ministry of colonies, 26 April 1918; letter from Diagne to the ministry of colonies, "Prise de contact de la Mission avec les autorités," 16 February 1918. Furthermore, Maurice Delafosse's daughter, Louise, writes in her biography of the ethnographer that Angoulvant and Diagne conspired to end Delafosse's career in the colonial administration. She notes that the deputy from Senegal and the former governor general of AOF assiduously lobbied to prevent his return to the federation after the 1914-1918 war was concluded. Therefore, the only place the ethnographer could influence colonial affairs was as a teacher and an advisor in Paris. Louise Delafosse, *Maurice Delafosse*, pp. 297, 343.

50. Joe Lunn, *Memoirs of the Maelstrom*, p. 187.

51. CAOM, 1/AP/838, P.-C. Georges François, "Au sujet des chefferies noires en Afrique," in *Annales Coloniales*, 2 October 1930. François was honorary governor of colonies at the time.

52. CAOM, 1/AP/838, letter from the ministry of colonies to the Commissaire of the Republic of Togo, "Administration Indigène," written in 1930.

53. Examples include Jean Renaud, a former officer of the overseas army that served in Indochina and a leader of the *Solidarité Française,* and Colonel François de La Roque, an officer in Morocco and leader of the *Croix de Feu.* Soucy, *French Fascism: The Second Wave,* pp. 83-84, and 106.

54. Ibid., pp. 75, 256. Doriot by the late 1930s had emerged as one of the most important fascist leaders in France. During the Second World War he collaborated with Nazi Germany and volunteered to fight on the eastern front against the Soviet Union.

55. CAOM, CG/60, "Rapport Politique et Administatif," produced by the government general for AOF, 1932. In the report, the decrees of 18, 23 August, and 27, 28 September 1932 are cited as examples of colonial policy designed to create "l'organisation d'une administration purement autochtone." Also: ARS, 17G/234/108, correspondence of Merlin on the reorganization of indigenous administration.

56. CAOM, 1/AP/838, "Rapport à M. le directeur des affaires politiques," unsigned, 28 May 1943, citing earlier directives.

57. CAOM, 1/AP/838, "Arrêté portant réorganisation des communes mixtes et organisation des communes indigènes en Afrique Occidentale française," 16 January 1921, signed by Martial Merlin, governor general of AOF.

58. CAOM, 1/AP/2810/20, see the notes on discussions held throughout 1920 within the Conseil de Gouvernement for AOF on how to proceed with the reorganization of administrative authority in the federation. Similar discussions recurred in 1932 when Brévié carried the reforms even further during his tenure as governor general. On the latter reforms see: CAOM, 1/AP/2810/10, letter from the ministry of colonies to the government general for AOF, "Réorganisation territoriale des colonies de l'A.O.F.," 14 January 1932.

59. This point is also discussed in: Cohen, *Rulers of Empire,* p.12; Cocquery-Vidrovitch, *Afrique Noire,* p. 123; and Crowder and Ikime, "Introduction," in Crowder and Ikime, eds., *West African Chiefs,* p. XVII.

60. CAOM, 1/AP/2810/20, discussions of the Consiel de Gouvernement for AOF on the reorganization of native authority in 1920. See also: CAOM, 1/AP/170/6, note of 17 April 1920 by Merlin on the reorganization of the *communes mixtes* of AOF.

61. CAOM, 1/AP/542, letter from the "Délégues des Notables de la Ville de Rufisque" to the ministry of colonies, 8 September 1921.

62. CAOM, 1/AP/542, letter from Diagne to the ministry of colonies, 8 July 1922.

63. CAOM, 1/AP/838, "Arrêté local du 19 décembre 1930 réorganisant le commandement indigène au Dahomey," Article 7. After the government general reorganized the administration of the federation in the early 1920s, each of the individual colonies that comprised French West Africa promulgated separate measures to bring their administrative structures in line with the doctrines set forth by Dakar.

64. ARS, 17G/293/Fonds ministeriels (FM), "Note a.s. du rôle des chefs," from the government general, probably written in 1919 or 1920; ARS, 17G/293/FM, letter from the governor general to the ministry of colonies, 26 March 1921; and CAOM, CG/60, the first decrees were issued on 21 May 1919.

65.   CAOM, 1/AP/838, "Arrêté local du 19 décembre 1930 réorganisant le commandement indigène au Dahomey."

66.   Delafosse, *Les civilisations disparues*, pp. 5–6.

67.   *Journal de la Société des Africanistes*, Issue 1, 1931, report on a planning meeting for the Society of 10 December 1930, p. 294.

68.   CAOM, CG/59, "Circulaire No. 128 A.P. sur la codification des coutumes indigènes," 19 March 1931, issued by Jules Brévié, governor general of AOF.

69.   CAOM, 7/AE/46, letter from the ministry of colonies to the government general for AOF, "A.S. d'un plan de spécialisation des productions par colonies,"17 January 1927.

70.   CAOM, 7/AE/46, report of the government general for AOF, "La Production Agricole et Pastoral en Afrique Occidentale Française," November 1930.

71.   CAOM, 1/AP/838, "Arrêté local du 19 décembre 1930 réorganisant le commandement indigène au Dahomey," Article 3. See also in this regard: CAOM, 1/AP/2810/10, letter from the ministry of colonies to the government general for AOF, "Réorganisation territoriale des colonies de l'A.O.F.," 14 January 1932; CAOM, CG/60, "Rapport politique et administratif," 1932, which cites the "circulaires" of 18 and 23 August, and 27 and 28 September 1932 "défini le statut des chefs;" and CAOM, CG/59, decree "réorganisant la justice indigène en Afrique Occidentale française," 3 December 1931. This last decree extended the juridical authority of the chiefs making them responsible for adjudication "en matière civile et commercial." France retained the prerogative of ruling in all matters deemed to be of a criminal nature. For matters concerning the increased recourse to forced labor and Diagne's public support for it see: CAOM, 7/AE/31, the agency that supervised the practice of forced labor in AOF was called the *Service de la Main-d'oeuvre pour des Travaux d'Interêts general*, or SMOTIG; and CAOM, 7AE/33, "Conference International du Travail: Quatorzième Session: Juin 1930: Réponses au questionnaire préparatoire," signed by M. Besson.

72.   CAOM, 1/AP/1638, letter from the government general to the ministry of colonies and seconded by Georges Hardy, director of the École Coloniale, 8 October 1930.

73.   Xavier Yacono states that even within the trade union movement of the 1950s in AOF "les oppositions ethniques" superseded questions of "les intérêts de classe." Xavier Yacono, *Les Étapes de la décolonisation française* (Paris: Presses Universitaires de France, 1971), p. 42.

74.   Suret-Canale, *French Colonialism in Tropical Africa*, p. 79. See also: Cruise O'Brien, *The Mourides of Senegal*.

75.   This authority to make and unmake indigenous leaders dated to the earliest days of the federation and remained in effect until the 1950s when that power was transferred to the territorial assemblies created at the end of the Second World War. For early documentation of this ability to determine the composition and extent of native leadership see: CAOM, 1/AP/193, "Décret relatif à la création de communes mixtes en Afrique Occidentale Française," 15 May 1912, signed by William Ponty, governor general of AOF.

76.   CAOM, 7/AE/31, letter from the ministry of labor and social assistance to the ministry of colonies, "Secours de chômage aux coloniaux," 14 April 1933; and letter from the ministry of colonies to the ministry of labor and social assistance, "Coloniaux en chômage," 29 March 1932.

77. CAOM, 1/AP/148, "Conseil de Gouvernement; session de Novembre 1932; procès-verbaux des séances." See also: D. K. Fieldhouse, *The West and the Third World: Trade, Colonialism, Dependence and Development* (Oxford: Blackwell Publishers, 1999).

78. CAOM, 7/AE/46, report produced by the government general for AOF, "La Production Agricole et Pastorale en Afrique Occidentale Française," November 1930.

79. CAOM, CG/48, *Arrêté* of 11 January 1935.

80. CAOM, CG/48, "Rapport politique et administratif" for AOF, 1933. For earlier movements of people see, in the same carton, "Rapport Politique d'ensemble année 1928," "Les Exodes."

81. CAOM, 1/AP/148, "Conseil de Gouvernement; session de Novembre 1932; procès-verbaux des séances." This topic is treated at length by Suret-Canale, *French Colonialism in Tropical Africa*, pp. 244–55; Coquery-Vidrovitch, *Afrique Noire: Permanences et Ruptures*, pp. 10, 12; and John D. Hargreaves, *Decolonization in Africa* (London: Longman, 1994), p. 32.

82. Cruise O'Brien, *The Mourides of Senegal*, pp. 189-236.

83. Coquery-Vidrovitch, "Villes Coloniales," p. 55. In fact, Coquery-Vidrovitch argues that the origins of "l'hypertrophie urbaine charactéristique du Tiers Monde contemporain" are found in the Depression of the 1930s and this movement of peasants to the colonial cities. See also: Cruise O'Brien, *The Mourides of Senegal*, pp. 237–261.

84. For analysis on the strikes that affected not only Francophone Africa, but also many of the British African colonies in the 1930s see: Cooper, *Decolonization and African Society*.

85. CAOM, 1/AP/148, "Conseil de Gouvernement; session de Novembre 1932; procès-verbaux des séances."

86. CAOM, 1/AP/148, Brévié speech at the November 1932 meeting of the Government Council for AOF.

87. CAOM, CG/60, "Rapport politique et administratif" for AOF, 1930.

88. Suret-Canale, *French Colonialism in Tropical Africa*, p. 454.

89. CAOM, 1/AP/148, "Conseil de Gouvernement; session de Novembre 1932; procès-verbaux des séances."

90. CAOM, CG/52, "Arrêté No. 1427," 20 June 1934.

91. CAOM, 1/AP/873.

92. CAOM, CG/52, speech by Brévié, December 1935.

93. CAOM, CG/52, report by Inspector General Charton, "L'Enseignement et l'Education en A.O.F.," 5 July 1936.

94. CAOM, 1/AP/859, instructions sent by André Maginot, minister of colonies, to the governors general of AOF, AEF, Togo, and Cameroon, "Administration Indigène," 9 October 1929.

95. CAOM, CG/52, report by Inspector General Charton, "L'Enseignement et l'Education en A.O.F.," 5 July 1936.

96. Lebovics, *True France*, pp. 112–113, 128.

97. Cited in Soucy, *French Fascism: The Second Wave*, p. 252.

98. Conklin, *A Mission to Civilize*, p. 81.

99. CAOM, CG/52, "Rapport Statistique d'ensemble, année 1933–1934; Service de l'Enseignement."

100. CAOM, CG/52, "Rapport Statistique d'ensemble, année 1933–1934; Service de l'Enseignement."

101. CAOM, 1/AP/859, instructions from Maginot, minister of colonies, to the governors general of AOF, AEF, Togo, and Cameroon, "Administration Indigène," 9 October 1929.

102. CAOM, CG/52, report of Inspector General Charton, "L'Enseignement et l'Education en A.O.F.," 5 July 1936.

103. CAOM, CG/50, "L'Artisanat en Afrique Occidentale Française," in *Les Annales Coloniales*, 1937; and Governor Henri Labouret, "L'Artisanat exotique; son origine, son avenir," in the same edition.

104. CAOM, CG/52, "L'Enseignement en Afrique Occidentale Française; L'Ecole Normale William Ponty," in *Bulletin Presidence*, 21 September 1937.

105. CAOM, CG/52, "L'Enseignement en Afrique Occidentale Française; L'Ecole Normale William Ponty," in *Bulletin Presidence*, 21 September 1937.

106. CAOM, CG/52, "L'Institut de lAfrique Noire," in *Bulletin AOF*, 6 September 1937.

107. CAOM, CG/52, note for the ministry of colonies, "Enseignement Ecoles Urbaines," from A. Nègre, delegate to the colonial commission from Dahomey, 4 March 1937.

108. CAOM, CG/52, "Rapport statistique d'ensemble pour l'année scolaire 1935–1936."

109. CAOM, 1/AP/148, "Conseil de Gouvernement; session de Novembre 1932; procès-verbaux des séances," statement by M. Couillault, director of personnel.

110. CAOM, CG/52, "Du rôle de l'élite indigène," in *Bulletin d'Information et de renseignements*, 8 November 1937.

111. CAOM, CG/59, notice from the ministry of colonies, *Information D'Outre-Mer*, 22 October 1937. Even though the announcement of the committee was made before the conference convened, the meeting of the governors general sanctioned the committee and was instructed to work with it to provide a "more exact" knowledge of African culture.

112. CAOM, 1/AP/179/1, "Conférence des Gouverneurs Généraux—voeux adoptés," convened 5 November 1936.

113. CAOM, CG/59, letter from Marius Moutet, minister of colonies, to the director of political affairs for AOF, 15 September 1937.

114. CAOM, 28/PA/1, "Politique Républicaine Coloniale," undated draft of a speech, probably written in 1936.

115. CAOM, 28/PA/1, "Causerie de Monsieur Marius Moutet, Ministre de Colonies à Radio-Cité," "Sur le Comité d'Étude des Coutumes Indigènes," 1936.

116. CAOM, 28/PA/1, report from the ministry of colonies to the government general of AEF, "Conférence des Gouverneurs généraux," 12 August 1936. This letter outlined the purpose of the proposed conference and insisted that the new French government sought to move "all the branches of national life" in a "new direction." The conference would provide an opportunity to address the "grands problèmes que pose l'administration de nos territoires d'outre-mer."

117. CAOM, CG/107, letter from Léopold Sédar Senghor to the Guernut Commission in Paris, 28 October 1937.

118. *Congrès International de l'évolution culturelle des peuples coloniaux, 26-28 septembre 1937* (Paris: 1938), pp. 10–11.

119. Janet G. Vaillant, *Black, French, and African: A Life of Léopold Sédar Senghor* (Cambridge: Harvard University Press, 1990), pp. 5, 8, 87, 89, 107.

120. CAOM, CG/52, "Le Problème culturel en AOF; conference faite à Dakar le 4 septembre 1937 par M. Senghor, professeur au Lycée du Tours."

121. Léopold Sédar Senghor, "La Résistance de la Bourgeoisie Sénégalaise à l'École Rurale Populaire," in *Congrès International de l'évolution culturelle des peuples coloniaux*, pp. 43–44.

122. Ibid., p. 42.

123. CAOM, CG/52, letter from Léopold Senghor to the government general for AOF, "La Résistance de la Bourgeoisie Sénégalaise à l'École Rurale Populaire," 26 October 1937.

124. Fily-Dabo-Sissoko, "Les Noirs et la Culture," in *Congrès International de l'évolution culturelle des peuples coloniaux*, p. 122.

125. CAOM, 1/AP/595, telegram from Brévié to the ministry of colonies announcing the death of Diagne, 12 May 1934.

126. CAOM, 3/SLOTFOM/2, letter from R. Antonetti, governor general for AEF, to the ministry of colonies, "A/S du refoulement dans leur pays d'origine de certains indigènes habitant la Métropole," 8 July 1929.

127. CAOM, 1/AP/891/8, declaration by "Les chefs indigènes de l'Afrique Equatoriale Française à Monsieur le Gouverneur Général Reste," 4 October 1938. See also in the same carton, the letters from the chiefs of Goma-Tsetse of Brazzaville, Koubatika of Kinkala, Samba of Brazzaville, 24 February 1939; and the telegram from Governor General Reste of AEF to the ministry of colonies, 11 November 1938, that assured Paris the native chiefs displayed an "instense émotion patriotique et fervent loyalisme."

128. CAOM, CG/52, "L'Artisanat en Afrique Occidentale Française," in *Les Annales Coloniales*, 1937.

129. Léopold Sédar Senghor, "La Résistance de la Bourgeoisie Sénégalaise," in *Congrès International de l'évolution culturelle des peuples coloniaux*, p. 44.

Chapter Four

Returning to Native Lands: Cultural Authenticity, *Négritude*, and Anti-Fascism

The electoral triumph of the Popular Front coalition of Socialists, Communists, and Radicals in May 1936 "gave birth to immense hopes among [the colonized] indigenous populations" and metropolitan workers that their grievances would be redressed.[1] Even before Blum took office as France's first socialist premier on 4 June, news of the left's victory sparked an unprecedented wave of strikes throughout "Greater France." Within weeks over two million laborers had joined the work stoppages in France, many occupying their factories. Overseas, a militant urban labor movement that had been effectively checked after 1918 found new life. In French West Africa railroad and port workers disrupted the movement of raw materials and cash crops from rural areas to the coast, and consequently, their export to France. Laborers in the colonies pushed the same demands as those in the metropole: the 40-hour workweek, paid vacations, the right to collective bargaining, and, in some cases, state control of basic industry.[2] Most of the strikes were ended in France by the Matignon agreements that provided pay increases and collective bargaining rights for metropolitan workers. In the colonies, unrest led to subsequent legislation passed by Blum's government that legalized trade unions and afforded colonized workers protections similar to those enjoyed by laborers in France.[3] However, even though unions were legalized in the colonies by the decrees of 11 and 20 March 1937, and November 1937, Paris stipulated that only those who were "able to speak, read, and write French fluently" and who held a primary school degree could join the newly sanctioned organizations. As Frederick Cooper notes in his discussion of the "labor question" in sub-Saharan Africa, the Popular Front "sought to minimize the labor question" and constrain the growth of an urban proletariat in the colonies. However, persistent agitation among workers in West Africa forced the anti-fascist government to recognize the reality of a colonial working class and act to redress some of their grievances.[4]

For the *évolués* the Popular Front government promised an end to the new elite's marginal status within the colonial field. After nearly two decades of indifference or hostility on the part of Paris and Dakar toward the demands of the urban elite from French West Africa, Blum's government invited the *évolués* to once again participate in the governance of the federation. However, the French-educated elite was not asked to function as mere auxiliaries of the colonial administration, but "to collaborate in the greatest possible measure in the administrative life of their country."[5] According to the new minister of colonies, Marius Moutet, France's mission was "to develop and favor the *social and economic* evolution of the native peoples in their environment according to their own interests."[6] This change in imperial policy entailed alterations in the official perception of the *évolué* as well as the nature of indigenous society. While Paris retained the assumption that French and African societies were essentially different and accepted the ethnographic model of "authentic" cultures in AOF, the Popular Front government argued that France not only had an obligation to "revive" indigenous traditions, but also to assist in the "natural evolution" of native societies. Furthermore, Popular Front colonial policy legitimized *évolué* self-identity as it developed in the 1930s and accepted the new elite's claims to represent the "true" aspirations of the West African *sujets*. According to Charles Cutter, the new metropolitan administration secured the support of a significant sector of the French-educated elite from AOF because the notion of the *mission civilisatrice* embraced by Blum's government coincided with that held by many prominent *évolués* in the late 1930s.[7]

This chapter traces the development of a cultural movement among the French-educated elite from West Africa that prepared the ground for a political accommodation with the imperial power and provided the conceptual framework wherein the *évolués* emerged as a decisive and autonomous force in the colonial field. As the Depression took hold in France and its colonial empire, radicals among the *évolués* recast themselves as protectors of a vanishing African culture. Their mission, according to *La Dépêche Africaine*, one of the leading *évolué* journals in France between 1928 and 1933, was to "affirm the personality and originality of [the African] genius."[8] In fact, by the early 1930s many radical *évolués* had concluded that the West African colonies could not achieve the political independence sought by Kouyaté and the LDRN without first restoring the "natural dynamism" of indigenous cultures.[9] Therefore, the early years of the Depression were marked by a shift in the public activity of *évolués* who resided in the metropole away from the overt contest for state power in the colonial field and toward a struggle over the definition, preservation, production, and representation of "authentic" African culture.[10]

In part the diminution in the extra-parliamentary life of the French-educated elite reflected growing divisions within the *évolué* class. Those conflicts were manifested not only between radicals who resided in France, but also indicated a widening divergence of interest and self-identity that separated those *évolués* who lived in West Africa from those who resided primarily in the metropole. The disputes among the new urban elite from AOF were frequently couched in terms of a fight over who among them could rightfully claim to be "authentically" African and, therefore, lead the revival of indigenous society. In other words, *évolué* identity as it developed in the 1930s not only involved a claim to leadership of the *sujet* populations, it based this assertion upon a presumption that the new elite embodied the "real" African and therefore both represented and displayed the "African" before the world. This is an instance of what Michael Taussig calls the use of the "mimetic faculty" by the French-educated elite from AOF. According to Taussig, the crucial element of the mimetic faculty is "the two-layered notion of mimesis...[which is] a copying or imitation, and a palpable, sensuous connection between the very body of the perceiver and the perceived." Furthermore, he writes, "[I]t is useful to think of mimesis as the nature culture uses to create second nature." Taussig is referring to the process whereby certain worldviews, modes of production, and patterns of living become hegemonic in society. Thus, the *évolués* participated in a process whereby the ethnographic model of African society became hegemonic in the colonial field, but in that very development transformed the constitutive elements and popular conceptions of what comprised "authentic" indigenous culture.[11]

In the midst of this struggle a group of students from France's colonies in the Caribbean and West Africa founded a newspaper to "defend" the interests of a "minority in the metropole" that felt disconnected from the society in which they lived and alienated from their original cultures.[12] Although *L'Étudiant Noir* only appeared once, in March 1935, its contributors and the articles published in that edition provided the basis for a new movement among the *évolués* later called *Négritude* that infused earlier calls among the radicals for a cultural renaissance in sub-Saharan Africa with form and substance. Yet, the content for what Léopold Senghor described as "a cultural movement that has the black man as its goal" was largely derived from the work of ethnographers like Delafosse, the same source that provided the foundations for the hegemonic ideology used to validate French rule in West Africa.[13] In fact, the Martinican poet Aimé Césaire even accepted the colonial government's description of the *évolués* as "copies that are nothing but copies" of the French. He reproduced earlier attacks by conservatives in the imperial hierarchy and right-wing politicians in the metropole that argued "assimilation [was]…as dangerous for the colonizer as for the colonized."[14] At times this affinity between the discourse of the French-educated elite and that practiced by Dakar and Paris translated into a flirtation with fascism by some *évolués* in France.[15] Even Léopold Senghor testified to the influence Hitler fascism had among the educated elite from the colonies. Writing after the Second World War, the West African poet explained, "Hitlerian racism, adopted by Vichy…gave birth among the colonized peoples a deep race consciousness."[16]

However, international events curtailed the influence of fascism among the French-educated elite during the 1930s. Italy's invasion of Ethiopia just six months after *L'Étudiant Noir* was published provided the objective conditions whereby the political and cultural agendas of the *évolués* became linked to those of metropolitan anti-fascist movements. As "the last independent State in Africa" Ethiopia had long served as a symbol for those *évolués* who looked to the eventual end of colonial rule in Africa. Moreover, Haile Selassie's empire also signified the preservation of "authentic" African cultural values. Therefore, the invasion elicited apprehensions among the French-educated elite that "the cultural values of thousands of years [were] being destroyed in Ethiopia."[17] Since many *évolués* believed the right-wing government of Pierre Laval was complicit in the Italian adventure, the new elite from West Africa found allies in their struggle among the opposition forces that had recently come together in the Popular Front. In fact, the associations founded by *évolués* for the defense and aid of Ethiopia rapidly transformed themselves into self-styled "Popular Front[s] for the colonies."[18] The Colonial Popular Front brought cohesiveness to the revived extra-parliamentary life of the exiles from the colonies in ways that enhanced their ability to press claims to represent the subject population and contribute to shaping the Popular Front's colonial policies.

The electoral triumph of the Popular Front shortly after the defeat of Haile Selassie's armies brought the political allies of the French-educated elite from AOF to positions of direct influence in the colonial field. In the context of anti-fascist politics important elements within the *évolué* class were prepared to cooperate with the new metropolitan government to implement widespread reforms of the colonial system. Central to the reform agendas of the Popular Front and their allies among the colonized populations was the cultural development of the "rural populations" in West

Africa. Consequently, the anti-fascist government did not mark a rupture with general trends in colonialist discourse or strategies of governance as elaborated since the First World War. As Gary Wilder observes, the Popular Front's colonial policy was constrained by the hegemonic context in which it operated.[19]

However, Cooper cautions that "it is more useful to ask precisely where Popular Front colonial policy broke out of older frameworks, where it remained caught in them, and where it reshaped discourse for future regimes."[20] One area in which the anti-fascist government charted new ground in imperial policy was its insistence that a pre-condition for the success of the reform was the "formation of an educated elite" knowledgeable about local "traditions, mores, and customs" that was empowered to lead the "future evolution of the overseas [territories]."[21] According to Kouyaté, Léopold Senghor, and other radicals among the urban elite from West Africa, those *évolués* who remained in France throughout the 1930s were ideally suited to the task at hand since the "alienation" they experienced in the imperial center had forced them to confront their "authentic selves."[22] Having discovered the essence of Negro-African Civilization within them, Césaire asserted that the new elite was prepared to return to their "native lands" and take up the cause "of those who founder in the dungeons of despair."[23] That desire to return to their geographic place of origin was realized during the Second World War, which induced the mass repatriation of those *évolués* who had resided in France throughout much of the 20s and 30s. However, to reach that point our story must begin with an examination of the process whereby the *évolués* reinvented themselves as "authentically African" and redefined their role in the colonial field.

Strangers in a Strange Land:
The *Évolué* and the Search for True Culture

By 1928 relations between the West African community in France and the Communist Party (PCF) had soured to such a degree that many organizations founded by the Party had become virtually autonomous. In fact, several prominent *évolués* concluded that "Communism" posed as great a threat to native society as colonialism.[24] That year a group of dissidents and former members of the LDRN founded a rival journal in Paris dedicated "to establishing a universal correspondence between men of color."[25] *La Dépêche Africaine*, which first appeared in February 1928, rejected Lamine Senghor's assertion that racial unity was forged out of shared oppression at the hands of "European or American imperialism."[26] Rather, the circle around *La Dépêche Africaine* embraced assertions by ethnographers that "African Society" displayed a fundamental unity that pre-dated the European conquest and the slave trade by "thousands of years."[27] Accordingly, the dispute between the *Ligue* and the dissidents that gathered around the new journal centered on divergent conceptions of the "true" nature of African society and the "source" of their personal and collective identities.

Maurice Santineau, the political activist from Guadeloupe who founded and edited *La Dépêche Africaine*, argued that by placing the colonial experience at the center of African identity, the LDRN and the PCF denied the autonomous origins of indigenous culture and the uniqueness of the "ancestral traditions" practiced in West Africa. *La Dépêche Africaine* accused the Marxist *évolués* of presenting Europe as the sole starting point for human civilization when research by anthropologists and ethnographers suggested that Africa was the cradle of human culture.[28] The result, according to *La Dépêche Africaine*, was that the *Ligue* practiced a politics detrimental to African society because it sought to introduce notions of "class struggle" to West Africa that were alien to indigenous culture and that threatened the fundamental unity of the "black race." In language reminiscent of Delafosse a decade earlier, *La Dépêche Africaine* asserted that "collectivism is the highest moral principle of African society." However, "African collectivism...has nothing in common with European Marxism.... The African," the statement continued, "was born, lives and dies in collectivism." Satineau and his associates urged the *évolués* to focus their activities on the defense and preservation of indigenous culture in French West Africa from all "alien" influences, especially Marxism.[29] According to Satineau, such goals "permitted the elite of the Negro race to make its spiritual contribution to the common patrimony of humanity...[as well as] to affirm the personality and originality of its genius."[30]

Instead of independence for the French possessions, *La Dépêche Africaine* urged reforms in the structures of colonial government, expanded local self-rule in the colonies, and an easier naturalization process for the new urban elite.[31] Satineau and his associates found justification for their proposals in the same ethnographic discourse used by Dakar to justify continued French domination of AOF. *La Dépêche Africaine* lauded the work of Hardy, Delafosse, and others who "demonstrated" the "essential" cultural differences between African and European societies. Furthermore, Satineau's group pointed to "the very important work" of ethnographers in elucidating the contribution "authentic" African culture has made and could make to the common human patrimony.[32]

However, *La Dépêche Africaine* contended that indigenous society could only be protected and reinvigorated through the "formation of a [new] native elite," not, as Dakar asserted, through the empowerment of native chiefs.[33] Therefore, Satineau's journal advocated reforms in colonial education and urged Paris to concentrate greater resources on training the colonized population in basic skills as well as nurturing critical thinking abilities among the indigenous peoples. In addition, though, *La Dépêche Africaine* implored the *évolués* to engage in self-improvement by sharing their intellectual work and concerning themselves with enriching indigenous cultures. Accordingly, Satineau's publication presented itself as the center for the internal development of the "new elite" that was "urgently needed" "to save the Negro."[34] To facilitate that process the journal devoted substantial space to discussions about African culture, the publication of original literary works by *évolués*, and debates on the role of the intellectual in society. *La Dépêche Africaine* was aided in this task by some of the most prominent figures among the *évolué* community, including Maran, Jane Nardal, Georges Tovalou-Quenum, and Samuel Ralaimongo. In addition, important figures of the French left also lent their names to the new movement, foremost among them Léon Jouhaux, general secretary of France's largest trade union federation, the *Confédération Générale du Travail* (CGT).[35]

Thus, while *La Dépêche Africaine* shared a common discourse with Dakar, the journal deployed the findings of ethnography to decisively different ends and, as a result, contributed to the struggle for authority in the colonial field waged between the French-educated elite and colonial administrators. Governor General Carde regarded the new journal with suspicion and asked the ministry of colonies to monitor the activities of its contributors in France. Furthermore, the colonial government frequently interdicted the sale and distribution of *La Dépêche Africaine* in West Africa since Dakar claimed the journal posed a threat to "order" in the colonies and constituted a source of "dangerous ideas."[36] The government general found *La Dépêche Africaine's* willingness to accept "some measure of colonization" in Africa "as necessary" incredulous because the journal made that support conditional upon the new urban elite being accorded greater authority within the imperial hierarchy. In addition, Satineau's group urged that "the same legislative forms that [exist] in the metropole" be adopted in the colonies.[37] In other words, the circle around *La Dépêche Africaine* insisted that the *mission civilisatrice* as articulated by the French government prior to the Great War provide the guiding framework for the administration of the colonies, a position sharply at odds with Dakar's understanding of the colonial project after 1918. The end result, though, was not to be independence for the overseas possessions or even assimilation into the French Republic. Rather, *La Dépêche Africaine* argued that the reinvigoration of African cultures under the direction of the new urban elite provided the only means whereby the idea of *"La Plus Grande France"* then popular among metropolitan politicians and colonialists could be realized. In fact, the journal even received some support among fascist elements in the metropole and counted Pierre Taittinger, leader of the *Jeunesses Patriotes*, as one of its contributors.[38]

Despite its accommodation with imperial rule and occasional flirtations with French fascism, *La Dépêche Africaine* was, from its inception, an important force among the French-educated elite from West Africa. The monthly journal maintained a circulation of between 12,000 and 15,000 until it ceased publication in 1933 when Satineau was elected to the French Chamber of Deputies from Guadeloupe.[39] Part of the success enjoyed by *La Dépêche Africaine* resulted from its reaffirmation of a particular *évolué* self-identity that had emerged by then, which informed that community's political development and activities. *La Dépêche Africaine* perpetuated and enhanced the notion that the *évolués* constituted a unique social category within the colonial field, the role of which was to represent and lead the *sujet* population. However, Satineau's group challenged the Marxist understanding of imperialism that subsumed all colonized populations under the rubric of "oppressed proletariat" because they believed that assessment denied the importance of cultural difference and transformed the *évolués* into agents for the destruction of African culture.[40] The concern over the influence of Communism among the French-educated elite from AOF and its alleged negative consequences for African culture was reflected in the orientation of *La Dépêche Africaine* which increasingly turned to internal discussions among the *évolué* community resident in France. In the early 1930s *La Dépêche Africaine* published markedly fewer articles that highlighted abuses in the colonies and which advocated reform of the overseas administrative structure. Instead the journal concentrated its fire on Communism and especially the LDRN.

Despite such open hostility, their shared sense of isolation and marginality in relation to the major political struggles of the day led to secret meetings between Kouyaté's and Satineau's associates by 1929 where they discussed the prospect of concerted activity and the potential merger of the two groups.[41] While these encounters did not produce the tangible result of unified action, they did point to the increasing distance between Kouyaté and the PCF. Furthermore, Kouyaté's frequent attempts to meet with associates of *La Dépêche Africaine* resonated in the political direction of the LDRN itself, which was increasingly similar to that of Satineau's group. Even within the *Ligue* Kouyaté was criticized for taking "moderate" positions and abandoning the struggle of the working class. When in 1932 the schoolteacher from French Soudan proposed that the organization's mission statement be changed from advocating the "emancipation" of the "Negroes" to working toward "[their] cultural education," he was shouted down and the proposition was defeated.[42]

However, it was the conflicts that arose over the approach to be taken toward the 1931 International Colonial Exposition held in Paris that set in train the events that ended with a final rupture between the PCF and Kouyaté. More broadly, the divergent responses to the Exposition by the Communist Party and Kouyaté confirmed the turn within the *évolué* community away from the fight for political independence in West Africa and toward a struggle to define and "revive" African culture under a seemingly intractable colonialism. In part, the PCF's assessment of the Exposition was conditioned by the "left turn" taken by the international Communist movement in the late 1920s. That turn included sharper attacks on rival left-wing political organizations like the socialists and a concerted drive to attain unchallenged leadership of the organized working class.

The change in Communist politics also entailed a heightened emphasis on conformity with official Party positions, and the demand for acquiescence to the directives of the PCF leadership brought into sharp relief the increasingly incongruent appraisals made by the Party and the *évolués* of the situation in West Africa. In reaction to resolutions passed at the 1928 Congress of the Communist International, the Communist Party launched a series of attacks on the emergence of "bourgeois nationalism" among the French-educated elite from the colonies. The Party denounced suggestions that the struggle for "national liberation" took precedence over the class struggle, thereby reversing its 1925 decision to devote all resources overseas toward the achievement of "the independence of the colonies."[43] Instead, the *évolués* were encouraged to concentrate on "organiz[ing] the industrial proletariat" in the colonies so that "the unification of the revolutionary struggle of the colonial proletariat with that of the revolutionary worker's movement in the capitalist countries" could be realized. As in the early 1920s, the PCF asserted that the colonized populations and the metropolitan working class shared a "common enemy: imperialism."[44]

In the midst of this ideological shift within the Communist Party, France prepared to stage a celebration of its colonial achievements timed to coincide with the centennial of the 1830 conquest of Algeria. The PCF viewed the

1931 Colonial Exposition in Paris as an ostentatious display of the ill-gotten gains of "French imperialism [that has] ravaged thousands of villages in Africa and Asia" in pursuit of profit. To counter that celebration of colonialism, the Communist Party called on the "workers in France [and the] exploited from the colonies [to unite] against your common enemy, French capitalism, [for] the liberation and independence of the colonies."[45] The Party used the occasion of the Exposition as an opportunity to draw attention to the "imperialist terror" unleashed "in Indochina" by the French colonial administration against the nationalist and Communist forces agitating for independence in that colony.[46] The previous year non-Marxist anti-colonialist forces attempted an uprising against French imperial rule in Southeast Asia that was quickly repressed at the cost of thousands of lives. While the rebellion was contained, armed resistance continued in some areas and widespread discontent boiled just below a surface calm that was maintained by virtue of an overwhelming military presence. One result of the failed nationalist uprising of 1930–1931 was the emergence of Ho Chi Minh's Communist movement as the dominant anti-colonial force in Indochina. Consequently, the trajectory of decolonization in Southeast Asia diverged sharply from that of West Africa and other parts of the French empire since "the claims of Vietnamese political and cultural liberty were, [after 1931], wrapped up with [the idea of] socialist revolution." For the *évolués* from Indochina, the anti-colonial struggle included resistance to French attempts at "locking Vietnamese intellectuals into a colonized culture"[47] based upon ethnographic models of "primitive societies," unlike their counterparts from West Africa who were increasingly attracted to such imaginings of indigenous society.

In addition, the PCF was a major force behind the staging of a "Counter-Exposition" designed to present the truth of French imperialism elided by the official celebrations of empire. The idea for an "anti-imperialist exposition" was launched by the League Against Imperialism and for National Independence at a 1929 meeting in Berlin and was used to promote the Communist Party's position that cultural regeneration could only take place within the context of socialist reconstruction.[48] Initially, organizers had planned the opening of the counter-exposition to coincide with that of the official festivities in May. However, delays in funding, shortages of volunteers, and internal feuding over the design and purpose of the anti-colonial exposition precluded its being opened to the public before 24 September, when activities at the official exposition were winding down.[49] Once the doors to the counter-exposition did open, however, its few visitors were greeted with prominent displays of life in the Soviet Union, which "had restored freedom to their culture and [provided] wide autonomy" for cultural development.[50] Other displays depicted "the life of natives" in the French colonies, although these also reflected the Communist interpretation of the colonial condition in that they presented the colonized as workers toiling on railroads, in the mines, or building urban infrastructure. Captions under the photographs noted the 18,000 deaths caused by construction of the Congo railroad, the harsh treatment of forced laborers, and the extravagant lifestyle of colonial administrators. Separate rooms contained "objects of colonial art," demonstrating the vitality and potential of indigenous cultural production that could reach its fullest development through socialist reconstruction.[51] As Lebovics observes, this display of "native art" also reflected the "rage of French intellectuals and artists for the exotic primitive" then prevalent in Paris and embraced by the Surrealists who actively assisted in the organization of the counter-exposition.[52]

However, central to the projects of both the International Colonial Exposition and the counter-exposition was the claim to represent the "truth" about life in the colonies. Each sought to portray the "reality" of indigenous culture and articulate the aspirations of the colonized populations. As Taussig notes, "Colonial history too must be understood as spiritual politics in which image-power is an exceedingly valuable resource."[53] At Vincennes, site of the official exposition, native villages were (re)constructed in accordance with ethnographic expectations of "tribal" life, down to communal living quarters and visible hierarchies crowned by a "chiefly" presence.[54] To lend credence to the exhibitions, "authentic" natives were imported to Paris from the colonies and were made to perform "traditional" dances and rituals. The official exposition (re)confirmed for both the visitors and the French administrative establishment "that the colonizer was radically different from, and superior to, the colonized."[55] Furthermore, Vincennes offered visual "proof" of the success of France's mission overseas while it also realized the idea of *La Plus Grande France* in the capital of the empire. This is an example of what Jean Baudrillard calls the "hyperreal," or that which "is the generation of models of a real without origin or reality." Following Baudrillard, I read the Paris exposition as well as the counter-exposition as acts of "simulation" where it is "a question of substituting signs of the real for the real itself [that] begins with the liquidation of all referentials."[56] As Nicholas Mirzoeff writes, "[I]mperialism was never an undifferentiated phenomenon, repeating its maneuvers regardless of time and place, but was always constructed in regard to local specificities, the domestic agenda of the colonizing nation and with an eye to the other colonial powers."[57]

However, the attempt by organizers of the Paris exposition to flatten the colonial field and excise the conflicts then undermining French power overseas actually concentrated and intensified the tensions and divisions that continually destabilized imperial governance in the colonies. Vincennes became a new site where the struggle for authority in the colonial field was waged while it also contributed to shaping the imperial framework and further circumscribed the possible stances in opposition to French rule overseas. Vincennes served as a site of power/knowledge production about the colonies, the subject populations that resided therein, and France's mission overseas. As such, the Paris Exposition shaped and was shaped by resistance to the imperial project. As Gayatri Spivak writes, "[I]f the lines of making sense of something are laid down in a certain way, then you are able to do only those things with that something which are possible within and by arrangement of those lines. *Pouvoir-savoir*—being able to do something— only as you are able to make sense of it."[58]

The reproduction of the Cambodian temple Angkor Vat was a particular target of Communist Party action against the Paris exposition since it functioned metonymically for the colony of Indochina. The most celebrated disruption at the Angkor exhibit occurred on 4 July, when the power was cut at 10:30 p.m. and anti-colonial leaflets were dropped from trees overlooking the area where Indochinese soldiers and workers were quartered. In response, the director of the Paris municipal police ordered tightened security and prohibited all contact between the outside world and the Indochinese imported for the exposition.[59] Thus, in their attempt to produce a reality in France that was desired in the colonies, the organizers were forced to reproduce the conditions of struggle and repression operable within Indochina at the Angkor exhibit in Paris.

Inasmuch as Vincennes reinforced solidarity between the *évolués* from Indochina and the PCF, the Colonial Exposition also exacerbated tensions that were undermining the association of West African *évolués* with the Communist Party. In fact, the French-educated elite from AOF was notably absent from the campaign to disrupt the Paris exposition. Furthermore, while Kouyaté served on the organizing committee of the counter-exposition he took little interest in its operation and instead informed associates that he desired to "sell books and other works" that "reported on the colonies" at Vincennes.[60] While the *Ligue* had, at the request of the PCF, established in April a "Committee of Struggle" to agitate against the Paris exposition, the LDRN produced only one tract that denounced Vincennes while calling for the "liberation" of the colonies from "capitalist servitude."[61]

Throughout 1931 Kouyaté worked more closely with the circle around *La Dépêche Africaine* than with those who sought to undermine the official presentation of "authentic" African culture at Vincennes. Moreover, Kouyaté increased his criticism of the Communist Party for prioritizing the struggle of the Indochinese over that of the West Africans. In the "True Guide of the Colonial Exposition," printed by organizers of the counter-exposition, not one word was devoted to French West Africa, further evidence for Kouyaté and others in the *Ligue* that the PCF could not speak to the "reality" of life in the federation.[62] For Kouyaté, as for many West African *évolués* in the early1930s, the Communist Party's left turn threatened to further marginalize the new urban elite from AOF in their struggle for authority. The PCF's presentation of the indigenous population in the colonies as an undifferentiated working class with the same destiny and goals as that of the metropolitan proletariat left no room for the assertion of a unique African culture. In addition, it denied the profound structural changes induced in the federation by Dakar that forestalled the development of an urban proletariat in West Africa and, instead, reinforced patterns of rural production supervised by a largely compliant "traditional" elite.

Furthermore, the pressure applied on the LDRN to conform to the new directives of the Communist Party leadership in the wake of the left turn fueled resentment among West African *évolués* as it challenged the autonomy of action enjoyed by the *Ligue*. The new tactics embraced by the PCF also put the Party at odds with the self-identity of the *évolués* from AOF in that it denied the uniqueness of the *évolué* class within the colonial field, while also undermining the French-educated elite's exclusive claim to represent and lead the *sujet* populations. According to Kouyaté, the Communist Party had consistently demonstrated its "dislike of the intellectuals [from West Africa]" since 1925 and only sought their cooperation insofar as it "served" the interests of the metropolitan workers. He also accused the Party of having "destroyed" the organizations of West African *évolués* by its constant interference in their activities. By 1932 the dispute between Kouyaté and the PCF had reduced the *Ligue* to "a state of absolute inactivity." That year the Communist Party accused the schoolteacher from French Soudan of being a "bourgeois nationalist" who had sought "to sabotage the work of the *Ligue*." After a protracted series of hearings, Kouyaté was expelled from both the LDRN and the PCF in September 1933, although the ideological break had been consummated several years before.[63]

However, while the *évolués* found their presence and self-identity elided in the narratives on the "true" condition of life in the colonies articulated by

the PCF and evinced at the counter-exposition, the official presentation of
West African society at Vincennes also held no place for the new urban elite.
The public displays of "life in the bush" and the harmonious association of
distinctively different French and African cultures along the *Grande Avenue
des Colonies Françaises* in Paris left no room for those who claimed
participation in both worlds.[64] Furthermore, while both expositions provided
for the influence of French culture on the societies of Africa, they did not
allow for the reverse. Nevertheless, the dueling expositions did contribute to
the continued elaboration of a pattern of political engagement that placed
notions of "authentic" indigenous culture at the center of the struggle for
authority in the colonial field. In so doing, the organizers of both expositions
more tightly circumscribed the boundaries for sustained meaningful
participation in the imperial framework. Moreover, the occlusion of the
French-educated elite from the master and counter-narratives of indigenous
life operable in the metropole and in the colonies incited some *évolués* to
elaborate a model of "authentic" indigenous culture that not only secured a
prominent place for the new elite from West Africa, but also challenged
those archetypes presented at the expositions.

Ancestral Voices: Authenticity and the Cultural Politics of *Négritude*

The disappearance of *La Dépêche Africaine* early in 1933 after a year of
irregular publication combined with the public split between Kouyaté and the
Communist Party further weakened the already tenuous position of the
French-educated elite from AOF in the colonial field. However, the fractured
associational life of the *évolués* resident in France also opened a space for the
emergence of new leaders and organizations that not only called for a
regeneration of West African culture, but directly contributed to shaping
notions of what constituted "authentic" indigenous society. By 1934 the
évolués in France had founded several new collectivities, some of which
perpetuated the internationalist practices that had become familiar during
their sojourn in the Communist movement, though the new associations
situated racial solidarity or the shared experience of colonial subjugation
rather than class at the base of their organizational principles. Many others
functioned as aid agencies for those migrating from the colonies to the
metropole, where the recent arrivals not only received help to find shelter
and work, but were also given political education and lessons in
organizational life.[65]

Cut off from practical activity in the colonies by a combination of reform and repression initiated by Dakar and without an organized base in the metropole, Kouyaté and his supporters briefly associated with the Pan-Africanist movement based in Britain and the United States. As a result, the schoolteacher from French Soudan deepened his friendship with George Padmore, also recently expelled from the Communist Party in the United Kingdom for "bourgeois nationalist" positions that "tended to prefer racial unity over that of class unity."[66] Together, they concentrated their efforts on convening a "World Negro Congress" where ideas could be exchanged by representatives from throughout the African Diaspora and closer political relationships could be forged among the participants.[67] However, Pan-Africanism remained a tendency predominantly centered in the English-speaking world, despite early beginnings in Paris.[68] Similar to the LDRN's call for a single African state, Pan-Africanism asserted the fundamental unity of Africans and those of African descent as well as the necessity for political union in the post-colonial period. In the 1920s, Marcus Garvey's "back to Africa" movement had some influence among the *évolués* in France and supplied a link between the new elite from West Africa and the "black Diaspora" across the Atlantic. The Paris-based journal *Les Continents* had functioned as a center for Garvey's supporters in France until it ceased publication in 1924 after Diagne's victory in a slander suit against the editors. The subsequent absorption of the circle around *Les Continents* into Communist Party activities consequently choked off the influence of Pan-African ideas in France.

The regimes of power operable in the French colonial field as well as the specific conditions of command *sur place* in West Africa induced responses by the *évolués* that were at variance with those articulated by subjects of the British Empire or citizens of the United States. Whereas the idea of biological difference, enforced by various legal means, predominated in the British and American contexts, the French imperial framework privileged concepts of cultural uniqueness over corporeal markers of separateness and made citizenship conditional upon attainment of certain attributes of "French civilization." Each framework, therefore, induced resistance that corresponded to the hegemonic values that were viewed by those concerned as the basis of oppression. Consequently, in the United States and Britain oppositional politics were frequently organized along racial lines to defend or promote biologically defined communities against a force that subjugated them on those grounds.

Moreover, the French-educated elite had its own unique sense of self and political history that informed the structures and content of its public activity, which also differentiated it from those collectivities that emerged in the British imperial framework or within the context of American political culture. Bourdieu calls this the "habitus," which "is a socialized subjectivity.... Rationality is bounded not only because the available information is curtailed, and because the human mind is generically limited and does not have the means of fully figuring out all situations, especially in the urgency of action, but also because the human mind is *socially* bounded, socially structured. The individual is always...trapped...within the limits of the system of categories he owes to his upbringing and training." Thus, while activists in the United States and the British and French Empires occasionally joined forces and the various colonial empires held certain aspects in common, the *évolués* had to deploy the particular "species of capital (economic, social, cultural, symbolic)" sanctioned within the French colonial field in order to remain "players."[69] Consequently, *Négritude* as it emerged in the context of French imperialism is fundamentally distinct from the Pan-Africanism that developed in the British colonies. As Mudimbe observes, "Despite the importance of the *Négritude* movement, very little attention has been given to the relationships between its textual organization, its sources, and its expressions. We have known, for instance, that *Négritude* was a French invention but not how essentially French it was."[70]

The French-educated elite from West Africa, though, seemed to possess little of the cultural capital necessary to seriously influence developments in the colonies or the metropole by the mid-1930s. Neither Paris nor Dakar regarded the *évolués* as important to colonial governance and the new elite had yet to establish itself as the recognized leaders of the *sujet* population chafing under the domination of the pre-colonial elite and confined to labor on the plantations of rural West Africa. For the leading *évolués* resident in Paris, the problem centered on the need to articulate an identifiable conception of African society that satisfied their self-identity and mobilized the *sujets* as a force directed against the colonial administration and continued French rule overseas.

That challenge was taken up by a group of students from the French Caribbean and West Africa who founded the *Association des Étudiants Martiniquais en France* in 1934. The new organization claimed inspiration from the cultural politics practiced by Kouyaté and urged all *évolués* to "rally with enthusiasm to the work" of regenerating "the true black civilization."[71] While the student association's membership was much broader than the name indicated, migrants from the Caribbean dominated it. At its core were three student poets who had arrived in France in the late 1920s and early 1930s, Léon Gontran Damas from French Guyana, Aimé Césaire from

Martinique, and Léopold Sédar Senghor from Senegal. The three settled in Paris in the midst of the maelstrom that was *évolué* politics in the early 1930s and formed their impression of the established organizations as the fight between Communists, nationalists, and supporters of colonialism unfolded. While Philippe Dewitte argues that the *Négritude* movement constituted a synthesis of the various intellectual currents circulating among the "black" community in France during the 1930s, I suggest it marked a break with many of them and ushered in a new discourse among the exiles.[72]

The students were disheartened by what they called "the recent poor state of cultural affairs" among the *évolués*,[73] and sought to establish a basis for unified action in the colonial field that was not dependent upon the patronage or ideological efficaciousness of metropolitan parties or organizations. In fact, the circle that published the lone issue of *L'Étudiant Noir* in 1935 cited subservience to European parties, cultural forms, and intellectual trends as the root cause of the impotence that afflicted *évolué* politics. Césaire criticized previous generations of the French-educated elite for seeking "to become assimilated" to metropolitan culture. He asserted that those who had become like the colonizer "in the end believe that [they] had always been [like them, and, as a result, they] will mock those who have not assimilated, disavow [their] father[s] and abandon the Spirit of the Bush." Instead of "assimilation," the poet, much like Kouyaté before him, advocated "resurrection" as the basis for future cultural "creation."[74] Césaire demanded that the French-educated elite "accept…totally, without reserve…[their] race." It was up to the European to adjust to the indigenous cultures in the colonies, not for the *évolué* to "adapt to" French society. Furthermore, in their attempt to become assimilated, the French-educated elite had made themselves unrecognizable to the very people they claimed to represent. Instead of welcoming the leadership of the *évolués*, the *sujet* population "feared" them as intruders and surrogates for the colonizer.[75] To overcome this sense of double "alienation"—almost but not quite French and African—and reestablish a bond with the indigenous population in the colonies, the *évolué* had to be "cleanse[d] of the…contamination of being civilized."[76] According to Léopold Senghor, this entailed an intellectual and spiritual "pilgrimage to the sources" of African culture so that the *évolués* could discover their "authentic" selves and effectively lead their people in the "tradition of the *griots*." The *griots* were storytellers found in many West African societies, Muslim and non-Muslim alike, that functioned as organic intellectuals for those communities. The *griot* was the keeper of the local group's history as retold through oral performance from generation to generation. For Léopold Senghor, the *évolué* was the modern version of a *griot* that would not only bring the heritage of African culture to the Africans themselves, but also be the conduit whereby African cultural values and practices were introduced to European society as part of the achievement of a "civilization of the universal."[77]

Léopold Senghor asserted that this "voyage to ancestral sources" invariably ended with the affirmation of one's *"Négritude."*[78] However, as scholars of this cultural movement have noted, no consistent definition of *Négritude* was ever arrived at either among the founders of the tendency or even in Léopold Senghor's own descriptions.[79] The Senegalese poet often referred to *Négritude* as "the *collective personality of the Negro-African"* people. Accordingly, it was *"the ensemble of the cultural values of the black world*, [especially] those that are expressed in the *life*, the institutions and the works of the Blacks."[80] For Césaire, who first used the term in his celebrated 1939 poem *Cahier d'un Retour au Pays Natal*, *Négritude* was a living spirit that inhabited Africans and people of African descent. As such, it functioned as a "source of light…[that] thrusts into the red flesh of the soil/it thrusts into the warm flesh of the sky/it digs under the opaque dejection of its rightful patience."[81] According to Léopold Senghor, *Négritude* was also a weapon in the defense of "African culture under assault by that of Europe." In fact, Léopold Senghor made plain the trend among the *évolués* to "place the accent on cultural" activity rather than "politics" in 1930s France. He argued that it was through a concentration on political questions that Europe had subverted African society and diverted the French-educated elite from their task of reinvigorating indigenous culture and institutions in West Africa.[82]

As discussed earlier, the emergence of the *Négritude* movement in Paris coincided with the reform efforts by Dakar oriented toward reviving "traditional" institutions and practices among the native populations of West Africa. The colonial administration had situated the need for a cultural renaissance in AOF as a foundational element of France's *mission civilisatrice* as early as 1929, and had embarked on the "rural education program" in 1934 as a means to that end.[83] It was in that context, then, that the *Négritude* poets developed their ideas and articulated their conception of "authentic" African culture. This is an example of what Bourdieu describes as the nature of social reality. He writes, "Social reality exists, so to speak, twice, in things and in minds, in fields and in habitus, outside and inside of agents. And when habitus encounters a social world of which it is the product, it is like a 'fish in water:' it does not feel the weight of the water, and it takes the world about itself for granted."[84]

The structures of African society embraced by Léopold Senghor and others as "authentic" demonstrates the degree to which the hegemonic values operable within the French colonial field influenced the development of *Négritude*. Similar to Delafosse's presentation of "traditional" African social organization, the Senegalese poet described West African society as a series of "ever larger concentric circles...formed the same as that of a family." He added, also in line with the French ethnographic paradigm of "primitive" communities, that the family in West Africa included both descendents and ancestors, a model that placed "tradition" and the preservation of "authentic" indigenous practices at the center of African social organization.[85] Léopold Senghor asserted that "the head of the family [or group]...[was] the natural mediator between the living and the dead," a concept that provided the government general in Dakar with the justification for reifying tribal communities and basing governance on the authority of "chiefs." Moreover, Léopold Senghor shared Lévy-Bruhl's assessment that in such cultures the "individual does not really exist." Rather, the group was of paramount importance, a claim that allowed the Senegalese poet to declare that traditional African social institutions represented a "true form of socialism" and were, therefore, fundamentally "democratic."[86] Here he is building on the dual traditions of the *évolué* class: close proximity to imperial authority and radical politics.

The Senegalese poet's presentation of autochthonous tradition also reproduced hegemonic concepts of gender roles in West African society that included a separate spheres ideology, which situated women outside of public political life. Accordingly, Léopold Senghor declared, "Woman, because of the permanence of the family and as the giver of life, has been elevated [to the position] of a vital force and guardian of the home, that is to say, [she is] the holder of the past and [the] guarantor of the clan's future." He added that as "mother" the woman occupied a "prominent role within the family" that "surrounded" her with "respect" and allowed her to "exercise [many] liberties." Finally, the Senegalese poet declared that "the Negro-African woman, contrary to current opinion, does not need to be liberated: she has been *free* for millennia."[87]

Yet, complaints about the abuse of women in AOF mounted in the late 1930s that extended beyond earlier protests against the persistence of polygamy. Reformers that ranged from Catholic missionaries to the political left demanded that the government general take action to halt the traffic in women and the use of women as currency to pay off debts or to secure familial alliances.[88] Despite those protests, Dakar took no action to halt the maltreatment of women and insisted that since its mission was "to respect the customs and institutions" of the indigenous population it could not interfere.[89] Among the *évolués*, too, there was no concerted effort to include women or the issue of women's rights in the public activities of their various organizations. In fact, Kouyaté's organization denied "wives" of members the ability to participate in the "administrative" affairs of the *Ligue* and women who were not married to members could not even join the association.[90] Partly, this reflected the fact that nearly all of the *évolués* were male, a result of naturalization policies in the colonies that made citizenship for women contingent upon the status of their husbands and fathers and an educational system in which few women or girls participated. However, it also indicated a tendency among the *évolués* to embrace a model of public activity where women's involvement was highly restricted, thus providing the basis for the acceptance and propagation of a patriarchal model of social organization.

Léopold Senghor's presentation of women in African society also strongly resembled dominant paradigms of female participation in French society during the Third Republic. As Rachel Fuchs observes, republican ideology as it was articulated in the late nineteenth and early twentieth centuries "denied individualism to women" and "motherhood" was the criteria for women's entrance into the national community.[91] Additionally, Joan Scott writes, "The gendering of citizenship was a persistent theme in French political discourse.... [T]he common ground for individuality, as for citizenship, was masculinity." Yet, Scott also notes that "individuality was not only a masculine prerogative; it was also racially defined."[92] In effect, Léopold Senghor's discourse on autochthonous traditions in West Africa reproduced the feminization of African society characteristic of colonial domination[93] while it concomitantly valorized the patriarchal practices of rule exercised in the metropole that denied women the right to vote until 1944.

Yet, while the *Négritude* movement's conceptual framework approximated that through which the colonial administration and French state naturalized systems of rule in the metropole and colonies alike, Léopold Senghor and his associates deployed ethnographic discourse as a counter-hegemonic weapon in the struggle for authority within the imperial framework. For the Senegalese poet, Delafosse's concept of the "Negro-African Civilization" afforded the basis for an assault on French claims to rule West Africa and also the foundation for a thorough critique of the colonial administration's reform program that concentrated local command in the hands of "chiefs." Like Delafosse, Léopold Senghor regarded the "tribe" as the basic sociopolitical unit of West African society. The tribal community was comprised of "several families united...[under the leadership of] a chief [who is] the oldest descendent of a common ancestor."

However, the division of Negro-African Civilization along tribal lines did not disturb the fundamental unity of the culture. Rather, Léopold Senghor perpetuated the French tendency, valorized through ethnographic discourse, to homogenize African culture. For the *Négritude* movement, Negro-African Civilization was identified by a certain "style" that had "*image* and *rhythm*" as its "fundamental traits."[94] Damas insisted that even "an assimilated black American would spontaneously rediscover an original poetic vein [and that he had] conserved the original traditions of Africa."[95] Césaire also claimed the spirit of his "ancestors" inspired his work.[96] Tribal affiliations, accordingly, served primarily an administrative purpose and shared basic structural forms precisely because they developed out of the unified cultural base of the Negro-African Civilization.

The emphasis on rhythm and visual imagery as the markers of Negro-African culture legitimized poetry as the ideal form of expression for the French-educated elite from West Africa. According to Léopold Senghor, verse responded to a "vital necessity" for the *évolué* in that it allowed the "black soul" full range of its "passion." Unlike prose, Léopold Senghor claimed that poetry was not constrained by formal rules and did not require "technical" training.[97] Furthermore, verse continued the tradition of song and storytelling common to societies in the federation. Karin Barber explains that the custom of oral performance in West Africa linked past, present, and future generations in a continuous and ever-expanding community. These ceremonial acts were at the center of the legitimation process for many of the local ethnic communities, because they reaffirmed personal and political connections that spoke to power relationships operable between and within lineages.[98] Whereas Barber argues that women exercised great power through their role in "performing" lineage history, Catherine Coquery-Vidrovitch reminds us that very few women served as transmitters of "collective memory." Rather, the *griots* of West Africa, almost exclusively male "professional storyteller-musicians," tended to be more prominent in that vital social function.[99] For the *Négritude* circle, poetry marked the further development of Negro-African Civilization as it entered the "literate" world. Verse, consequently, allowed the "authentic" autochthonous cultures of West Africa to survive extinction in a world dominated by Europe, and to continue to grow within its own traditional parameters thereby giving expression to the inner "values" that animated the sociopolitical structures of Negro-African Civilization.[100]

However, while Léopold Senghor and his associates accepted the basic division of African society along tribal lines, they objected to the sweeping powers the colonial administration accorded to the pre-colonial elite over the *sujet* population.[101] Certainly, the Senegalese poet acknowledged, the "chief ... exercises authority.... However, he does so by delegation [of that power] from an [elected] council."[102] Léopold Senghor insisted that "Authentic" African tradition was "democratic" and the authority to command was rooted in the local population, as a collective entity, not as the government general imagined through the volition of an individual who ruled by virtue of inheritance or sanction from Dakar.[103] This conception of "true" indigenous society provided the framework for a renewed bid on the part of the *évolués* for support among the *sujet* population. *Négritude* ideology recognized the structural reality of rule in AOF, but offered the indigenous peoples the prospect of determining local authority and participating directly in the decision-making processes of their tribal community. The pre-colonial elite lacked legitimacy among the *sujet* population, Léopold Senghor and his associates argued, because they were not responsive to the needs of their people. Instead, the chiefs had become pawns in the system of colonial governance and were identified by the indigenous peoples more with French rule than "traditional" African society. Consequently, Dakar's ambition to revive African culture was inhibited by the administrative reforms enacted ostensibly as part of that mission.[104]

The solution, Léopold Senghor suggested, was for the *évolués*—the modern *griots*—to be permitted to carry out their "mission to restore *black values* in their truth and their excellence." This was to be accomplished, the Senegalese poet and his associates argued, through the "Artisanal Houses" and "rural popular schools" Dakar had established throughout the West African federation. However, the circle around Léopold Senghor insisted that the system of governance in AOF also had to be restructured to accord with "authentic" tradition in order to make the lessons learned in the new institutions meaningful for the indigenous people.[105] This position put the *Négritude* circle in opposition to both the colonial administration and the pre-colonial elite in West Africa.

Moreover, the conception of "authentic" African culture espoused by the *évolués* associated with *L'Étudiant Noir* and their proposed plan to rectify the "grave problems" that afflicted the overseas possessions rested upon the assertion that the French-educated elite held the exclusive right to speak on behalf of the colonized population. That prerogative derived from their having issued from African culture, but also having been forced to confront their "authentic" selves through "the alienation" experienced during their "exile" in the metropole.[106]

However, even among the *évolués* there were those who were construed as more authentic than others. Disputes arose among the *Négritude* poets not only about the nature of their movement, but also as to its translation into political activity in their respective locales. Generally, the division within the circle around *L'Étudiant Noir* was manifested between those from the Caribbean and the West Africans. One associate of Léopold Senghor and Kouyaté argued that the *évolués* from AOF had a distinct advantage over their friends from the Caribbean because the West Africans "had remained in contact with their ancestral land, with the African masses."[107] While Léopold Senghor and Aimé Césaire remained friends after the disappearance of *L'Étudiant Noir*, they did not frequently collaborate in organized politics and the West Africans went their separate way as they attempted to address the immediate concerns of life in AOF.

Despite the internal differences, the *Négritude* movement participated in the tradition of *évolué* self-identity that marked them as a distinct group within the colonial field founded upon their claimed participation in the cultural worlds of both Africa and Europe. However, under the circumstances of "exile" in France combined with the sense of "alterity"[108] thrust upon the French-educated elite from West Africa in the increasingly racist climate in France during the 1930s,[109] the *Négritude* circle contributed to the transformation of *évolué* identity through an assertion that they alone were "authentically" African. Whereas Delafosse had claimed that the new urban elite was no longer African because they had been contaminated by European culture, Léopold Senghor and his associates maintained that it was direct contact with French society that had created the conditions for the *évolué* to reclaim their veritable heritage. It was now the mission of the new *griots* "to preach" this notion of autochthonous tradition "as if it were the Gospel" to the *sujets* who had been deprived of their "real" culture through misguided colonial administrative policies.[110]

However, this assertion also indicated the degree to which divisions had arisen between the *évolués* that resided in the metropole and those that remained in West Africa. Léopold Senghor noted this discord in a 1937 letter to the ministry of colonies where he explained that the "*évolués*" in the federation had become protective of their status as bureaucrats in the cities and, in some cases, citizens of France. According to the Senegalese poet, the relentless assault conducted by the government general against the French-educated elite had created a climate of suspicion and eroded the West African *évolués'* commitment to a purpose greater than personal gain. Even the new urban elite in the federation, in dire need of "a more humane conception of culture," was construed as a target for the redefined mission of the modern *griots* based in Paris.[111] This divergence of interest was also evident in the ethnographic model of West African society embraced by

Léopold Senghor and his associates. Whereas the urban elite in the federation regarded Dakar's rural popular school program as another attempt to deny the *évolués* access to jobs in the colonial administration or urban wage-paying employment, the *Négritude* circle asserted that "authentic" indigenous culture was fundamentally rural.[112] Therefore, Léopold Senghor and his associates insisted that rural education was essential to the future viability of African culture and society.[113] In part, this reflected Léopold Senghor's own rural roots and indicated a shift in predominance among the *évolués* to those who originated in the smaller villages of the federation in contradistinction to the large urban centers.

While Césaire, Damas, Léopold Senghor, and their associates produced only one issue of their journal, *L'Étudiant Noir*, they significantly influenced *évolué* identity through participation in the extra-parliamentary life of the French-educated elite in the metropole. In fact, in addition to being one of its inspirations, Kouyaté was one of the earliest supporters of *Négritude*. He and Léopold Senghor founded the Association of West African Students after *L'Étudiant Noir* folded and together they embarked on the project of reconstituting "cultural solidarity" and political unity among the *évolués* from AOF.[114] Yet, it was Italy's invasion of Ethiopia just months after the appearance of *L'Etudiant Noir* that transformed *Négritude* from an obscure cultural movement based in Paris into a potent political force among the French-educated elite from West Africa. Italian dictator Benito Mussolini's assault on the last independent state in Africa provided the impetus for the resuscitation of *évolué* political life and created the basis for a new alliance between the French-educated elite from West Africa and the ideological left in the metropole.

Anti-Colonialism Is Anti-Fascism:
Ethiopia and the Colonial Popular Front

On 3 October 1935 Mussolini's army marched across the border of Italian Somaliland into Ethiopia, the only African state that escaped formal colonization. After seven months of aerial bombardment, poison gas attacks, summary execution, wholesale slaughter of civilians, and the destruction countless villages and cities, Ethiopia's army of 250,000 men was defeated and Emperor Haile Selassie fled into European exile. While resistance in the form of guerilla warfare persisted after the emperor departed, independence was not restored until British armies entered the country in 1941. In the meantime, the fascist rulers introduced forced labor to carry out public works projects designed to benefit Italians who were to be settled in the new addition to Mussolini's "Roman Empire." Throughout the period of Italian rule, mass executions were perpetrated against those suspected of aiding the guerilla armies. In one incident an estimated 10,000 to 30,000 people were killed when the Italian Viceroy, Marshal Graziani, ordered troops to open fire on a peaceful gathering of civilians lured into the open with the promise of a traditional distribution of food to the poor.[115]

The invasion of Ethiopia, however, was not a surprise, least of all to the *évolués* who had begun to establish organizations for the defense of "the Kingdom of the Negus" nearly one year before the attack.[116] In fact, the French-educated elite watched with trepidation as the metropolitan government entered into negotiations with Italy over the fate of Ethiopia. On 4 January 1935 Pierre Laval, France's premier, traveled to Rome where he and Mussolini signed an agreement that, according to Max Gallo, "left fascist Italy with 'free hands' in Ethiopia."[117] In addition to economic exchanges, the deal pledged Italy to respect France's colonial possessions, in particular the protectorate of Tunisia, in return for Paris' recognition of Italian claims to Ethiopia.

For the *évolués*, though, Laval's pact with Rome ended a brief flirtation with the fascist right in the metropole. In the confusion of *évolué* politics during the early 1930s a significant contingent of former Marxists and cultural nationalists among the French-educated elite had associated with movements on the far right such as *Solidarité Française* and the *Jeunesses Patriotes*.[118] Attracted by fascism's insistence on "national consciousness" and cultural purity, some *évolués* found their discourse had greater affinity with that practiced by the organized political right than among their former allies on the left. However, aside from a few migrants from the colonies that were hired by rightist associations as street brawlers and strikebreakers, the connections between *évolués* and fascism usually did not extend beyond contributions to each other's journals. Moreover, some of those same organizations on the political right provided the support that returned Pierre Laval to the office of premier in 1935. Robert Soucy notes, the French fascist movements "curtailed [their] antiparliamentary mobilization exercises to repay Laval for his [financial and judicial] support" when he was head of the government in the early 1930s.[119] Thus, when Laval reached the accord with Mussolini and the Italian dictator began amassing military forces on the Ethiopian border the *évolués* in France and West Africa reacted with hostility not only "against Italy...but against France as well."[120]

For the French-educated elite, especially that from West Africa, Ethiopia functioned as an important cultural signifier.[121] In fact, Léopold Senghor,

Kouyaté, and their associates placed greater weight on the idea of Ethiopia as a site of "authentic" African culture that had been preserved from the ravages of colonialism than they did on the empire's status as an independent polity. Political independence, accordingly, was significant only to the degree to which it protected and rested upon autochthonous cultural foundations. As one journal lamented when Italy launched its invasion, "Cultural values [that are] thousands of years old are being destroyed in Ethiopia."[122] In that context, the self-proclaimed mission of the *évolués* to lead a rival of "true" African society was wrapped up with the defense of that one region where it had continued to develop unimpeded by European rule.

Early in 1935 Kouyaté dispatched a letter to the Ethiopian emperor and his foreign minister in which he pledged his personal support as well as that of his associates. Kouyaté offered Haile Selassie all "practical, material" aid that the emperor would need in the event of aggressive action from Italy.[123] However, there is no evidence that the emperor ever received the letter. More likely than not, the correspondence was intercepted by the ministry of colonies and was promptly deposited in security files the CAI maintained on Kouyaté's activities. The government general for French West Africa had requested that Paris "attentively monitor the activities" of the *évolués* in the metropole as they pertained to the situation in Ethiopia. Furthermore, Dakar advised the ministry of colonies to interdict all information on the events unfolding in East Africa that was being circulated by the French-educated elite between AOF and the metropole.[124]

The colonial administration in West Africa recognized the symbolic importance Ethiopia held for the urban elite and expressed concern that the war in East Africa could result in political disturbances throughout the commercial and administrative centers of the federation. Dakar was particularly troubled about this prospect because the agitation in the rural areas that was induced by the Depression had only begun to taper off the previous year. Therefore, Italy's adventure in Ethiopia combined with economic distress furnished the context for a potential convergence of interests between the rural peasant population and the urban elite, a formula that filled the new governor general, Pierre Boisson, with anxiety about the ability of France to maintain control in the federation.[125] Furthermore, once the war had begun in October, the Italian government had its representatives in French West Africa meet with settlers from the metropole to raise money for the military effort. This exacerbated the tense atmosphere in the federation and incited protests against French rule in Dakar and other cities throughout AOF. These disturbances translated into a strong challenge to Diouf, the incumbent Senegalese deputy to the Chamber, who had succeeded

Diagne upon the latter's death in 1934. During the 1936 campaign, the radical opposition rallied behind Lamine Guèye, founder of the *Parti Socialiste Sénégalaise*, and lost solely due to the extensive patronage provided by Diouf and the strong support he received from the colonial administration.[126]

The 1936 election exposed the political gulf between the *évolués* based in the metropole and those who resided primarily in West Africa. While Diouf had inherited a powerful political base in the Four Communes of Senegal from Diagne and was protected by the government general, the radical *évolués* in France and those among the French-educated elite in AOF who had strong ties to the metropolitan "exiles" supported Guèye. However, it was Italy's invasion of Ethiopia that made Guèye's campaign as formidable as it was. The attack on Haile Selassie's empire had ignited renewed political life among the *évolués* that ultimately provided Guèye with the organizational base to sustain his candidacy. Significantly, the response to Italy's threats against Ethiopia was not initiated by the anti-fascist left in the metropole. Rather, it was the cultural nationalists, the modern *griots* associated with Kouyaté and Léopold Senghor, which urged the Socialists and Communists to join their cause in defense of Ethiopian independence.[127] This marked a new stage in *évolué* politics as the French-educated elite acted on their own behalf without connections to metropolitan parties or with integration into France's body politic as an end goal of their agitation.[128]

In August 1935, as Italian forces assembled on Ethiopia's border, a coalition of *évolué* associations based in Paris issued a call for a mass demonstration against the expected invasion and in "defense of the Negro race." The appeal urged migrants from colonized Africa to "come rally in defiance of the war [desired by] Mussolini, [the] declared enemy of our Race."[129] The most prominent organizers of the action included Kouyaté, his long-time associate in the LDRN Emile Faure, Léon Damas, and Léopold Senghor. On 21 August, at about 5 p.m., several thousand migrants from overseas gathered at the *Esplanade des Invalides* in Paris. However, the police had banned the demonstration and, in their attempt to disperse the assemblage, forced the marchers to head across the Seine River toward the *Place de la République*. The protesters, continually harassed by police, then made their way to the *Place de la Concorde* where Kouyaté and others delivered impassioned orations against the threatened aggression and France's complicity with it. Scuffles ensued that resulted in several arrests. Nevertheless, the following day, at an indoor rally in Paris organized by Kouyaté, up to 3,000 people assembled to voice their support for Ethiopia. One informant for the ministry of colonies noted, though, that at both actions "no revolutionary songs were sung, and the word 'communism' was not spoken once," indicative of how far the *évolués* had moved from their earlier association with the Marxist movement.[130]

By the end of 1935 the movement to support Ethiopia found coherence in a new journal, *Africa*, published by Kouyaté. *Africa* served as a vehicle for the mobilization of the French-educated elite not only against the war in Ethiopia, but also in the *évolués'* struggle for authority within the colonial field.[131] In January 1936 the ministry of colonies alerted the governors general of French West Africa and French Equatorial Africa that Kouyaté's publication was on its way from the metropole. Throughout the colonial hierarchy officials anxiously observed the success of the new journal, especially among "the evolved native population." While wary of Kouyaté's liaisons with "Ethiopian personalities," Gaston Joseph, the minister of colonies, called the attention of the colonial administrators to the ex-Communist's proposals on governance in the overseas possessions.[132] Kouyaté, like *La Dépêche Africaine* earlier in the decade, accepted a continued association between the African territories and France, with the latter in the role of "guiding nation." However, unlike Satineau's publication, Kouyaté insisted that this relationship be based upon mutual association where the colonies had been "elevated" to the status of "federated States…with autonomous and independent governments [each possessing] local Chambers of Representatives." Within this framework, the schoolteacher from French Soudan proposed that the peoples of the federated states would have "French nationality with citizenship in the local State." In social policy, the ex-Communist embraced the government general's program of basing local law upon the people's "traditions, mores, and customs." Moreover, Kouyaté welcomed Dakar's concentration of resources upon "the development of rural" production. However, this program could only be realized, Kouyaté insisted, through the deliberate "creation of an educated elite" that could direct this transformation to its completion.[133]

The reform agenda advanced by Kouyaté was a remarkable synthesis of the various political programs pushed by sectors of the French-educated elite from the earliest years of Diagne's electoral career, and was directly inspired by the model of "authentic" African culture articulated by the *Négritude* circle. Not only could the ambition of becoming "French" be achieved, but it would also be accomplished in the context of simultaneous independence or self-governance. In essence, the French-educated elite, under Kouyaté's plan, would be the acknowledged leaders of the African populations, while maintaining their links with the metropole, which would, in turn, support the *évolués* in their new capacity as the political authority in the federated states.

Moreover, the schoolteacher from French Soudan pledged to maintain the economic structure of the federation and its trade relationships with France. West Africa would, as a result, remain a predominantly agricultural society that produced cash crops and basic resources for export to the metropole. In turn, Kouyaté would have France guarantee the "protection of the imperial market," the very program promulgated by Paris in response to the Depression and bitterly opposed by Dakar.[134]

Kouyaté's reform agenda was an important intervention in the continued struggle for authority within the colonial field as it profoundly impacted the "rules of the game." The proposal published in *Africa* was directed explicitly at the hegemonic bloc forged between the colonial administration and the pre-colonial elite. The schoolteacher from French Soudan suggested an alliance between the metropolitan government and the *évolués* backed by the peasant masses as the solution to the perpetual crises of authority and production in West Africa. Since the *évolués* were the only social category within the colonial field that participated in a meaningful way in the cultural worlds of France and Africa, they were uniquely qualified to maintain the connections between the two societies in a non-colonial administrative environment. In such an arrangement, France was afforded the opportunity to perpetuate its influence in Africa, while the framework was established whereby "authentic" African culture could contribute to the common human patrimony as an equal and willing participant.[135]

However, Kouyaté's plan was contingent upon the willingness of the government in Paris to welcome the *évolués* as administrative allies. In the charged political atmosphere of 1936, those ideological friends were found on the anti-fascist left, the very forces from which Kouyaté and his associates had become estranged following the 1931 Colonial Exposition. As the war in Ethiopia continued and the mobilization of the *évolués* proceeded apace, an informant for the ministry of colonies noted laconically that the "anti-colonialist forces" among the French-educated elite from AOF were being "transformed into antifascist forces."[136] Objectively, Italy's invasion of Ethiopia, made possible by the collusion of the rightist government in France, had linked the struggle against fascism to the fight to end colonial oppression in the conceptual framework of many *évolués* from West Africa. This was made more apparent by the reactions of the organized right and left in France to the attack. On 4 October 1935, the day after the assault on Haile Selassie's empire, several prominent fascist intellectuals issued a statement in which they opposed sanctions against Italy and proclaimed that the immediate need was to preserve "peace in Europe." In response, the left produced a petition that called for Italy to be held accountable for having violated "international law." While sanctions were adopted by the League of Nations, they took effect after six weeks of fighting and were not enforced by any of the major powers, least of all France. Shortly after Haile Selassie fled to London the sanctions were dropped altogether.[137]

Meanwhile, between 1934 and 1936 the three major parties of the French left—Communists, Socialists, and Radicals—had agreed to a common anti-fascist electoral platform around which they mobilized as general elections neared in the spring of 1936. This "Popular Front" emerged in reaction to increased fascist activities in France as well as the aggressive posturing of Adolph Hitler in Germany and Mussolini's expansionist war in Africa. However, the *évolués* only joined the anti-fascist resistance when Italy attacked Ethiopia, much as the ideological left only became involved in opposition to Mussolini's actions in Africa after the invasion had begun.[138] The alliance between the French-educated elite from AOF and the metropolitan anti-fascists was not built upon shared ideological affinities any more than the Popular Front itself was based on common political objectives.[139] Rather, many *évolués* perceived the Popular Front as a means by which the French-educated elite could end its marginal status in the colonial field and improve conditions in the overseas territories. For the metropolitan parties, the support of the *évolués* from West Africa translated into greater resources with which to combat fascism in France as well as allies in the empire committed to a revised *mission civilisatrice* that had the democratization of indigenous society and greater local self-government at its core.[140]

In fact, the Popular Front's concept of "republican colonialism" closely resembled the reform proposal previously advanced by Kouyaté, and notions of authentic African society articulated among the *Négritude* circle. The leftist alliance accepted ethnographic assertions that "authentic" African society was "tribal" in nature, identity was "collective," not individual as in European cultures, and the "chief" was the legitimate authority within indigenous administrative structures. However, Moutet and his advisors asserted that native institutions were, "at base," "democratic" with a "council of Notables" that "represented the sentiments of the population" as the real source of authority in the village. The task of the French colonial administration was to further enhance those democratic characteristics through the development of local councils and the creation of "indigenous electoral colleges" that would choose the members of the village assemblies. Yet, nearly two decades of authoritarian rule by petty chiefs and colonial administrators had diminished the legitimacy of "traditional" forms of governance among the *sujet* populations, especially "chieftaincy." Therefore,

Moutet and others argued that the anti-fascist coalition had to use the *évolués* as "guides" to aid in the re-orientation of "native" society toward more "authentic" ways of life, thus affording the French-educated elite the opportunity to function in the custom of West African *griots*.[141]

Consequently, many prominent *évolués* expressed "immense hope" that the "colonial slaves" would be freed when the Popular Front won the elections of May 1936.[142] Throughout the colonial field the triumph of the anti-fascist left set off demonstrations, strikes, and factory occupations. When Moutet was named minister of colonies in the Blum government, he called upon Guèye, Léopold Senghor, and their allies for assistance to reform the system of governance in the colonies. Conspicuously absent from this circle of advisors was the elected deputy from Senegal, Galandou Diouf, as Moutet had actively campaigned on Guèye's behalf in 1936.[143] In addition, Brévié was replaced as governor general of the federation and the Socialist Marcel de Coppet appointed in his stead.

The close relationship between the Popular Front government and the *évolués* was reflected in the extra-parliamentary life of the modern *griots* as many of the groups that had formed to support Ethiopia coalesced in the *Rassemblement Colonial*, or "Popular Front for the Colonies," with Kouyaté as the guiding figure.[144] Along with the schoolteacher from French Soudan, the *Rassemblement Colonial* counted many of the most prominent figures in the metropolitan *évolué* community, including Léopold Senghor, among its active leaders. The Colonial Popular Front continued agitation in defense of beleaguered Ethiopia while it also served as a vehicle through which the *évolués* worked with the Blum government on the reform of the colonial administration in West Africa. In fact, the *Rassemblement Colonial* survived the Popular Front and continued to promote the political agendas of the French-educated elite until 1940, when all *évolué* organizations were outlawed by the Vichy regime.[145]

In November 1936 Moutet instructed the governors general of the colonies "to generously utilize the native elite...[who would be invited] to collaborate in the greatest measure possible in the administration of their country."[146] Within "native elite" Moutet included the *évolués* who he insisted were to be placed in positions of responsibility and deployed as "educators" to both the peasant masses and the pre-colonial elite, which was said to need instruction in "authentic" African practices of rule and cultural life. Moutet's policies were predicated upon acceptance of *évolué* identity and, consequently, the model of African society articulated by the *Négritude* circle. The claim by Léopold Senghor and his associates that they were the only legitimate representatives of "true" African culture was validated in the rhetoric and actions of the Popular Front, which embraced them as natural allies in the revised *mission civilisatrice*. In 1937 and 1938 Léopold Senghor, with the support of Paris, traveled throughout French West Africa to facilitate the revival of "traditional" indigenous ways of life and values and persuade the *évolués* resident in the Four Communes to end their objections to the rural popular schools. Moreover, those conferences, speeches, and meetings afforded a platform for the modern *griot* to expound upon his notion of Negro-African Civilization, one that resonated among a largely rural population sectioned into "tribal" administrative units and subject to the authority of "traditional" rulers.[147]

In addition to Léopold Senghor's public activities, Moutet named several prominent *évolués* to government commissions charged with the codification of "native custom" and the elaboration of systems of governance based upon those autochthonous traditions.[148] However, progress toward the development of a system of "customary law" was thwarted by objections that such a statute would inhibit the future evolution of native society. In opposition, Paul Rivet, a prominent ethnographer and curator of museums in France, asserted that Léopold Senghor, a supporter of the institutionalization of indigenous jurisprudence, wanted to "place Africa in a museum."[149] As a result, discussions on a "native statute" did not move beyond the preliminary stage during the Popular Front's brief tenure in government.

Nevertheless, deliberation on customary law implicitly raised the issue of the legal status of *évolués* in the colonial field. The *Rassemblement Colonial* urged the Popular Front to accord "political rights" to the French-educated elite "that would permit them [to] rapidly accede to power" in West Africa. Their responsibility, according to the Colonial Popular Front, would be to "direct the people toward their complete emancipation." The chiefs, though, were not to be left out of the new administrative order in the federation since they were an integral part of autochthonous social organization. The *Rassemblement Colonial* suggested that Paris "recognize the right of succession of the chiefs of the [various] races or tribes according to the [custom] established by the populations themselves." Yet, this custom could only be learnt, and chieftaincy could only gain legitimacy among the native peoples through the "generalization of the village schools [and the] creation of [additional] rural schools."[150]

Here, too, the Popular Front was unable to effectively address the concerns of their allies in the colonial field. Each attempt to expand the rights of native peoples in the colonies was defeated by an increasingly hostile Chamber of Deputies. In fact, the Popular Front itself began to fray as economic, political, and international pressures mounted in 1937 and 1938.

By the spring of 1938 the Popular Front government had officially collapsed. Within two years France itself was defeated and occupied by Hitler's military. Consequently, the struggles for authority within the imperial framework entered a new stage, one that found the new elite from AOF participating in a fight to save humanity from the horrors of fascist rule.

Conclusion

Instead of mitigating the conflicts that pervaded the colonial field, the Popular Front era brought into sharp relief the lines of division that continually undermined French rule in West Africa and eroded the stability of the Third Republic itself. By 1937 many of the gains secured by organized labor in the wake of the 1936 strikes had been rolled back, including the 40-hour workweek. The wage increases awarded through the Matignon agreements that ended the factory occupations were rendered inconsequential because of an inflation crisis partially engineered by manufacturing interests, which orchestrated a flight of capital from France. In June 1937 Blum was forced to resign as prime minister when the Senate denied a request that he be authorized to solve the economic crisis by decree. Furthermore, despite a ban on the activities of fascist leagues promulgated by Blum's government shortly after taking office, the radical right saw its fortunes improve as conservatives swelled the ranks of Colonel de La Roque's *Parti Social Française*, formerly the fascist *Croix de Feu*.[151] In less than two years, the Popular Front government had been replaced by a conservative administration headed by Edouard Daladier that ruled largely through decrees, the very administrative tool the Senate denied the anti-fascist coalition months earlier.

In West Africa, the Popular Front and its allies among the *évolués* resident in the metropole met resistance from the colonial administration, the pre-colonial elite, and the French-educated elite that had remained in the colonies. Imperial administrators objected to Moutet's plan to send the urban elite into the "villages" of the federation as teachers because this would create the structural means whereby enduring connections between the *évolués* and the "rural masses" could be established, the very association the colonial administration had worked to preclude since 1918. Those objections were dealt with through de Coppet's accession to the post of governor general in 1936, an act intended to bring the imperial hierarchy back under Paris' direction. De Coppet did encourage use of the new elite as liaisons with the bush and links were forged between *évolués* and rural communities throughout the federation during his tenure. By 1938 France had opened its first training school for teachers in AOF.[152] The collapse of the Popular Front, though, meant the end of Moutet's endeavors to reform colonial governance. News of Daladier's appointment to the office of premier induced a stream of letters from the pre-colonial elite in sub-Saharan Africa that pledged the chiefs' "fervent loyalty" to France and offered assistance to the imperial power in the event of any international crisis.[153] Thus, the hegemonic bloc forged between the pre-colonial elite and the colonial administration had survived the challenge from the anti-fascist left, albeit in a weakened state.

The fall of the Popular Front, though, did not mean a return to the margins of the colonial field for the *évolués*. By 1938 the French-educated elite had emerged as a powerful and autonomous force in the imperial framework and, in the process, *évolué* identity was transformed. Geographically isolated from the rural masses in West Africa and structurally precluded from access to positions of command in the colonial field, the French-educated elite resident in the metropole tended to abandon overt political objectives in favor of a cultural politics oriented around a struggle to represent "authentic" African culture. Through those discussions, Kouyaté and others among the *évolués* in France during the 1930s re-imagined themselves as protectors of "true" indigenous traditions that were threatened by all things European, including Marxism.

However, the debate over the "true nature" of African society necessitated that the *évolués* elaborate their own understanding of what it meant to be "authentically" African, one that had meaning in the colonial field. Accordingly, the French-educated elite was caught in a web of significance where notions of essential differences between "true" African and European societies were validated through ethnographic discourse. Nevertheless, the *Négritude* poets arrayed the language of ethnography against French rule and located themselves within "traditional" African society as modern *griots*. While Delafosse used his research to undermine the new urban elite's claims to be the legitimate representatives of the *sujet* population, Léopold Senghor and his associates argued that their experiences in the metropole had forced them to confront their "authentic" selves and discover the essence of Negro-African Civilization within themselves. Consequently, this "pilgrimage ... to ancestral sources" allowed the *évolués* to claim that they alone were "authentically" African since the *sujets* were trapped in a world that was administered and structured according to French misconceptions of autochthonous tradition.[154]

It was Italy's attack on Haile Selassie's empire in Ethiopia, though, that furnished the pretext for the revival of *évolué* associational life in Paris and the emergence of the *Négritude* ideology as a dominant force therein. The French right's tacit support of Mussolini's adventure provided the basis for a political alliance between the Popular Front coalition of Communists, Socialists, and Radicals and the French-educated elite from AOF. That congruence of interest was also reflected in shared conceptions of France's *mission civilisatrice* and agendas for the reform of colonial governance. Whereas the government general in Dakar deployed ethnographic discourse to justify the imposition of authoritarian rule in "the bush" through its agents among the pre-colonial elite, the Popular Front and its *évolué* allies insisted upon the fundamentally democratic character of indigenous society. Accordingly, Léopold Senghor and his associates challenged the authority of the pre-colonial elite among the rural population and were positioned as agents for the democratization of West African political culture. Through cooperation with the Popular Front government the modern *griots* were able to transform the rural popular schools from instruments designed to enhance the prestige of the pre-colonial elite and the power of the colonial administration into autonomous bases of influence for the *évolués* in rural West Africa.[155] In essence they became training grounds for a new generation of French-educated West Africans that would carry on the struggle against colonial rule. By 1938 the long "exile" of the *évolués* had ended and the modern *griots* were returning to their native lands to sing the praises of the Negro-African Civilization.

Yet, the precarious place of the *évolués* within the colonial field was exposed when Blum's government collapsed in 1938. Despite the assistance rendered by Léopold Senghor and his associates to the anti-fascist coalition, the *évolués* did not have clearly defined and uniform legal rights in the empire. Some were citizens of France, like Léopold Senghor after 1934, but most were classified *sujets* and, as such, were under the auspices of the *indigénat* and the authority of tribal rulers. Therefore, *évolué* cooperation with the Popular Front and their contribution to the articulation of France's *mission civilisatrice* in the late 1930s pointedly raised the question of native rights, especially the juridical status of the French-educated elite. Concomitantly, the colonial mission as elucidated during the Popular Front and the anti-fascist nature of Blum's regime advanced a notion of "French" identity that privileged egalitarian values and "universal" humanity over the hierarchical and particularist presentation of Frenchness associated with the far right. The Popular Front and its allies among the *évolués* maintained that it was possible to be both "French" and "African" while preserving the essential cultural traits of each society. This formula, though, had to await a second global conflagration before it was legislated into existence in the form of the French Union. Furthermore, the Second World War and France's rapid defeat induced a massive exodus of *évolués* from the metropole to their geographic places of origin. This "return to native lands" and the ideological nature of the fight against Hitler fascism provided the context wherein the "*sujets*" became "*citoyens*"—of a sort. Our narrative, therefore, moves to an examination of how the concept of citizenship was shaped in the French imperial framework.

NOTES

1. CAOM, 3/SLOTFOM/119, CAI note on the meeting of the "Association pour la Défense et l'Émancipation des Peuples Colonisés," 27 November 1936. This sentiment is also expressed in the statement of the *Comité d'entr'aide Indochinois*, 6 August 1936, located in CAOM, 3/SLOTFOM/43.

2. Cooper, *Decolonization and African Society*, pp. 93–94.

3. Suret-Canale, *French Colonialism in Tropical Africa*, pp. 449–450.

4. Cooper, *Decolonization and African Society*, p. 108.

5. CAOM, 1/AP/179/1, "Conférence des Gouverneurs Généraux—voeux adoptés," November 1936.

6. CAOM, 28/PA/1, Marius Moutet, "Politique Républicaine Coloniale," probably written in 1936. (Emphasis in the original.)

7. Cutter, "The Genesis of a Nationalist Elite," in Johnson, ed., *Double Impact*, p. 107.

8. CAOM, 5/SLOTFOM/2, "Notre but. – Notre Programme," in *La Dépêche Africaine*, February 1928.

9. CAOM, 3/SLOTFOM/109, L. Hanna-Charley, "Pour Notre Chère Race," open letter from *Le Groupe du Souvenir de Victor Schoelcher* to the *évolué* community in France, 6 July 1939.

10. CAOM, 5/SLOTFOM/23, "Rapport de Victor," 29 May 1932.

11. Michael Taussig, *Mimesis and Alterity: A Particular History of the Senses* (New York: Routledge, 1993), pp. 21, 252.

12. CAOM, 5/SLOTFOM/21, André Midas, "A Propos de l'Association," in *L'Étudiant Noir*, March 1935. The journal was described as the voice of the *Association des Étudiants Martiniquais en France*, although several members of its editorial board were from French West Africa.

13. CAOM, 5/SLOTFOM/21, Léopold Sédar Senghor, "L'Humanisme et Nous: René Maran," in *L'Étudiant Noir*, March 1935.

14. CAOM, 5/SLOTFOM/21, Aimé Césaire, "Nègreries: Jeunesse Noire et Assimilation," in *L'Étudiant Noir*, March 1935.

15. CAOM, 3/SLOTFOM/77, anonymous note by an agent of the CAI, 31 July 1934. The informant records "Rosso," a leader of the *Union des Travailleurs Nègres* (UTN—successor to the LDRN in 1933), as expressing concern over "le développement du fascisme dans les milieux coloniaux." This anxiety contributed to increased attacks on "nationalism" by the PCF-associated organizations among the French-educated elite. Robert Soucy also notes increased support among the colonized population for the organized fascist movements in France during the early and mid-1930s. Soucy, *French Fascism: The Second Wave*, pp. 65–66, and 220.

16. CAOM, 1/AP/2147, Léopold Sédar Senghor, "Illusions et Réalités Africaines," in *Temps Present*, 16 August 1946.

17. CAOM, 5/SLOTFOM/20, C. Ulrich, "La Guerre criminelle du fascisme," in *Front Mondial Contre Guerre et Fascisme*, October 1935.

18. CAOM, 3/SLOTFOM/78, CAI reports on the *Rassemblement Colonial*, founded on 13 April 1937 out of a fusion of several organizations devoted to the support of Ethiopia and the fight against "l'impérialisme française."

19. Gary Wilder, "The Politics of Failure: Historicising Popular Front Colonial Policy in French West Africa," in Tony Chafer and Amanda Sackur, eds. *French Colonial Empire and the Popular Front: Hope and Disillusion* (New York: St. Martin's Press, 1999), p. 51.

20. Cooper, *Decolonization and African Society*, p. 74.

21. CAOM, 3/SLOTFOM/78, Garan Kouyaté, "Principes Directeurs d'une Transformation de l'Outre-mer," in *Africa*, December 1935, and also forwarded as a letter to the ministry of colonies, 27 May 1937.

22. Léopold Sédar Senghor, "L'Apport de la poésie nègre au demi-siècle," in *Témoignages sur la Poésie du Demi-Siècle*, 1952, published in *Liberté I: Négritude et Humanisme* (Paris: Éditions du Seuil, 1964), pp. 138, 135.

23. Aimé Césaire, *Cahier d'un Retour au Pays Natal* (Paris: Présence Africaine, 1968), pp. 41-43 (English), 40-42 (French).

24. CAOM, 3/SLOTFOM/24, public letter from Maurice Satineau, secretary general of the *Comité de Defense des Interêts de la Race Nègre*, 30 March 1927. Satineau had split with Lamine Senghor in 1927 over the relationship between the PCF and the *Comité de Défense de la Race Nègre*.

25. CAOM, 5/SLOTFOM/2, Maurcie Satineau, "Notre but.—Notre Programme," in *La Dépêche Africaine*, February 1928.

26. CAOM, 5/SLOTFOM/3, Lamine Senghor, "Ce qu'est notre Comité de Défense de la Race Nègre," in *La Voix des Nègres*, January 1927.

27. CAOM, 5/SLOTFOM/2, Vincent Durand, "Le Collectivisme Africain," in *La Dépêche Africaine*, August 1928.

28. CAOM, 5/SLOTFOM/2, Roger Dévigne, "L'Adam des Races Blanches Était-il Africaine?" in *La Dépêche Africaine*, 15 April 1930. The article noted the importance of Prof. Louis Leakey's discoveries of human remains in East Africa and suggested that not only was Africa the site where human evolution commenced, but the continent also provided the foundations for all subsequent civilizations, a concept that became widespread among the new elite from West Africa by the 1950s through the work of Cheikh Anta Diop.

29. CAOM, 5/SLOTFOM/2, Vincent Durand, "Le Collectivisme Africain," in *La Dépêche Africaine*, August 1928.

30. CAOM, 5/SLOTFOM/2, Maurice Satineau, "Notre but.—Notre programme," in *La Dépêche Africaine*, February 1928.

31. CAOM, 5/SLOTFOM/2, "Rapport présenté par le Colonel Bernard à la Commission chargée d'étudier la Réforme du Conseil Supérieur des Colonies," in *La Dépêche Africaine*, August 1928.

32. CAOM, 5/SLOTFOM/2, review of Georges Hardy's *Vue Générale de l'Histoire d'Afrique* in *La Dépêche Africaine*, 15 September 1929.

33. CAOM, 5/SLOTFOM/2, Prof. Herman M. Bernelot-Moens, "L'Anthropologie Nouvelle et l'Avenir de la Civilisation," in *La Dépêche Africaine*, February-March 1929.

34. CAOM, 5/SLOTFOM/2, Robert Wibaux, "Elites Noires," in *La Dépêche Africaine*, April 1929, and a review of Albert Londres' *Terre d'Ébène*, in *La Dépêche Africaine*, August-September 1930.

35. CAOM, 5/SLOTFOM/2, *La Dépêche Africaine*, February 1928, list of contributors.

36. CAOM, 5/SLOTFOM/2, letter from Carde to the ministry of colonies, 26 June 1928. See also the letter from the ministry of the interior to the ministry of colonies, 29 January 1929. At the time, the government general and Paris tended to combine all critics of colonialism under the rubric of "Bolshevik" or "revolutionary." Therefore, even a moderate association like that headed by Satineau was objectively placed outside the parameter of those considered by the imperial hierarchy to be "legitimate representatives" of the colonized populations.

37. CAOM, 5/SLOTFOM/2, P. Baye-Salzmann, "L'Assimilation des Colonies aux mêmes formes législatives que la métropole est le seul moyen d'attacher foncièrement les Races autochtones à la France," in *La Dépêche Africaine*, February 1928.

38. CAOM, 5/SLOTFOM/2, Pierre Taittinger, "Pour la plus grande France," in *La Dépêche Africaine*, July 1928. In that edition, the editorial staff saluted Taittinger's election to the presidency of the Commission des Colonies in the Chamber of Deputies.

39. CAOM, 3/SLOTFOM/24, report of the CAI, January 1929; and 5/SLOTFOM/2, report of the CAI, January 1938.

40. CAOM, 5/SLOTFOM/2, "Le communisme et l'opinion indigène," editorial in *La Dépêche Africaine*, October-November 1930. The editorial protested the Communist International's decision that year to form a committee to oversee the "Black Revolution." *La Dépêche Africaine* called the decision "misguided" and asserted that the Third International's sights were set on the "wrong struggle."

41. CAOM, 5/SLOTFOM/3, "Rapport de Joe," agent of the CAI, 23 November 1929. Apparently, the Malgache *évolué* Ralaimongo acted as the liaison between Satineau's and Kouyaté's groups, with Maran coordinating the covert meetings.

42. CAOM, 3/SLOTFOM/53, "Rapport de Dubois" on the Assemblée Générale of the *Union des Travailleurs Nègres* (UTN—the successor to the LDRN when it changed names in 1932), 27 August 1932.

43. CAOM, 3/SLOTFOM/101, decision by the PCF colonial commission in 1925 to endorse the instructions received in a letter from Communist International leader Gregory Zinoviev, 12 January 1924.

44. CAOM, 5/SLOTFOM/45, *Méthodes et Tactiques Révolutionnaires: Thèses et Résolutions du 5e Congrès de l'I.S.R. Moscou Septembre 1930* (Moscou: Petite Bibliothèque de l'Internationale Syndicale Rouge, 1930), pp. 173, 182. These resolutions were adopted by a meeting of the Communist Party's Colonial Commission that year and confirmed at subsequent Party congresses.

45. CAOM, 3/SLOTFOM/5, leaflets printed by the PCF and distributed on the Exposition grounds as well as throughout Paris in the spring and summer of 1931.

46. CAOM, 3/SLOTFOM/5, undated statement of the *Comité de Lutte* formed by the PCF to conduct agitation during the period of the International Colonial Exposition. See also the slogans printed on numerous leaflets distributed at the Exposition and the "Counter-Exposition."

47. Lebovics, *True France*, p. 105, 119.

48. CAOM, 3/SLOTFOM/5, appeal by the *Ligue contre l'imperialisme et pour l'indépendance nationale*, 26 January 1929.

49. CAOM, 3/SLOTFOM/5, report of the CAI, "De l'exposition anti-coloniale," 20 November 1931.

50. CAOM, 3/SLOTFOM/5, "La Vertié sur les colonies: Petit guide pour visiter l'exposition de la Ligue anti-imperialiste," 1931. Only 14 visitors were reported by the police to have visited the counter-exposition on its opening day.

51. CAOM, 3/SLOTFOM/5, report of the CAI, "De l'exposition anti-impérialiste," 24 September 1931.

52. Lebovics, *True France*, p. 94.

53. Taussig, *Mimesis and Alterity*, p. 177.

54. Jacques Marseille has produced probably the most thorough pictorial analysis of the 1931 Paris exposition and graphically illustrates the attempt by the organizers to actualize "primitive society" in the streets of the metropolitan capital. Jacques Marseille, *L'Age d'Or de la France Coloniale* (Paris: Albin Michel, 1986), pp. 117-136.

55. Nicholas Mirzoeff, *Bodyscape: Art, Modernity and the Ideal Figure* (London and New York: Routledge, 1995), p. 136.

56. Jean Baudrillard, *Simulations* (New York: Semiotext[e], 1983), pp. 2, 4.

57. Mirzoeff, *Bodyscape*, p. 141.

58. Gayatri Chakravorty Spivak, "More on Power/Knowledge," in Donna Landry and Gerald MacLean, eds., *The Spivak Reader: Selected Works of Gayatri Chakravorty Spivak* (New York and London: Routledge, 1996), p. 151.

59. CAOM, 3/SLOTFOM/5, letter from "Le Commissaire Divisionnaire de l'Exposition Coloniale" to "le Directeur Général de la police municipale," 14 July 1931.

60. CAOM, 3/SLOTFOM/5, report of CAI agent "Joe" on a meeting with Kouyaté, 25 March 1931. See also the report of "Joe" dated 28 September 1931 that notes the absence of Kouyaté from meetings of the organizing committee for the counter-exposition.

61. CAOM, 3/SLOTFOM/111, report of the CAI, "LDRN," dated 2 May 1931, on the meeting of the executive committee of the *Ligue* held on 27 April. See also the Circular of the LDRN produced in August 1931 directed at the International Colonial Exposition contained in the same carton.

62. CAOM, 3/SLOTFOM/5, "Le Véritable Guide de l'Exposition Coloniale...L'Oeuvre civilisatrice magnifiée en quelques pages," 1931. Page one provides accounts of life in Madagascar and Guadeloupe, page two concerns the Congo railroad in AEF and the role of banking interests in Syria. Pages three and four, the centerfold, mark 100 years of French rule in North Africa, while pages five and six are devoted to the armed revolt and French repression in Indochina. Finally, page seven reports on conditions in French Guyana and contains an appeal to all workers to unite against imperialism.

63. CAOM, 5/SLOTFOM/23, reports by CAI agent "Paul" dated 8 November 1932 and 24 January 1933; CAOM, 3/SLOTFOM/53, report filed by "Paul," agent of the CAI, 7 March 1933; CAOM, 5/SLOTFOM/23, "Rapport de Victor," agent of the CAI, 29 May 1932; CAOM, 3/SLOTFOM/111, "Rapport de Victor," agent of the CAI, 17 February 1932; and CAOM, 3/SLOTFOM/53, report filed by "Joe," agent of the CAI, 30 September 1933.

64. For the plan of the 1931 International Colonial Exposition in Paris see: Marseille, *L'Age d'Or de la France Coloniale*, p. 121.

65. CAOM, 3/SLOTFOM/101. Some of the organizations established either along lines of inter-colonial solidarity, racial unity, or for mutual assistance included: *Association d'Entr'aide et de Culture des Indochinois, Solidarité Coloniale*, and the various *Comités de Secours* founded for West Africans, Martinicans, Algerians, and Madagascans.

66. CAOM, 3/SLOTFOM/77, see the anonymous note filed by an informant for the CAI, 30 June 1934.

67. CAOM, 2/SLOTFOM/3, "Rapport de Moïse," agent of the CAI, 3 February 1934.

68. Paris hosted the first Pan-African Congress in 1919. Thereafter, though, the major meetings of the Pan-Africanist movement took place in English-speaking countries and an overwhelming number of the participants at those conferences were from the U.S. or the British Empire. In fact, until 1945 few of the delegates to the Pan-African Congresses were even from Africa. The movement remained largely dominated by U.S. citizens and residents of the English-speaking Caribbean until the Manchester meeting in 1945 where the Gold Coast leader Kwame Nkrumah emerged as a leading force among Africans in the British empire with his calls for immediate independence. For further information on the Pan-African Congresses and movements see: P. Olisanwuche Esedebe, *Pan-Africanism: The Idea and Movement, 1776–1963* (Washington, D.C.: Howard University Press, 1982); and Tony Martin, *Race First: The Ideological and Organizational Struggles of Marcus Garvey and the Universal Negro Improvement Association* (Westport, Conn.: Greenwood Press, 1976).

69. Bourdieu and Wacquant, *An Invitation to Reflexive Sociology*, pp. 126, 98. (Emphasis in the original.)

70. Mudimbe, *The Invention of Africa*, p. 86.

71. CAOM, 5/SLOTFOM/21, Gilbert Gratiant, "Mulâtres...pour le bien et la mal," in *L'Étudiant Noir*, March 1935.

72. Dewitte, *Les Mouvements nègres en France, 1919-1939*, p. 358.

73. CAOM, 5/SLOTFOM/21, André Midas, "A propos de l'association," in *L'Étudiant Noir*, March 1935.

74. CAOM, 5/SLOTFOM/21, Aimé Césaire, "Nègreries; Jeunesse Noire et Assimilation," in *L'Étudiant Noir*, March 1935.

75. Césaire, *Cahier d'un Retour au Pays Natal*, pp. 40-42, 44, 68, 112.

76. Léopold Sédar Senghor, "Totem," in Léopold Sédar Senghor, *The Collected Poetry* trans. Melvin Dixon (Charlottesville: University Press of Virginia, 1991), p. 22. "Austere earth, land of purity, cleanse me of all/My petty desires and the contamination of being civilized." Written between October and December 1939.

77. Léopold Senghor, "L'Apport de la poésie nègre au demi-siècle," first published in *Témoignages sur la Poésie du Demi-Siècle*, 1952, and reprinted in Léopold Senghor, *Liberté I*, pp. 139, 135, 144.

78. Léopold Senghor, "Song of the Initiate," in *The Collected Poetry*, p. 136.

79. Some of the most significant studies of the *Négritude* movement in 1930s France are: Dewitte, *Les Mouvements nègres en France, 1919-1939*; Janheinz Jahn, *Muntu; An Outline of the New African Culture* trans. Marjorie Grene (New York: Grove Press, Inc., 1961); Kesteloot, *Black Writers in French*; Moro, *Négritude e Cultura*

Francese; Michel Hausser, *Essai sur la Poètique de la Négritude* (Paris: Éditions Silex, 1986); and Eleni Coundouriotis, *Claiming History: Colonialism, Ethnography, and the Novel* (New York: Columbia University Press, 1999).

80.   Léopold Senghor, "Introduction," *Liberté I*, pp. 8, 9. (Emphasis in the original.)

81.   Césaire, *Cahier d'un Retour au Pays Natal*, pp. 98–100.

82.   Léopold Sédar Senghor, "Introduction," in *Liberté III: Négritude et Civilisation de l'Universal* (Paris: Éditions du Seuil, 1977), p. 7.

83.   CAOM, 1/AP/859, André Maginot, minister of colonies, to the governors general of AOF, AEF, Togo, and Cameroon, "Administration Indigène," 9 October 1929. For information on the "écoles rurales populaires" see: CAOM, CG/52, especially the annual reports on education in Africa (1933–1937).

84.   Bourdieu and Wacquant, *An Invitation to Reflexive Sociology*, p. 127.

85.   Léopold Senghor, "Ce que l'homme noir apporte," first published in *L'Homme de Couleur* (Paris: Librairie Plon, 1939), and reprinted in *Liberté I*, pp. 27, 28-29.

86.   Lévy-Bruhl, *L'Âme Primitive*, p. 229; Léopold Senghor, "Éléments constitutifs d'une civilisation d'inspiration négro-africaine," first published in *Présence Africaine*, March-April 1959, and reprinted in *Liberté I*, pp. 284, 282–283, 270; and Léopold Senghor, "L'esthétique négro-africaine," first published in *Diogène* (October 1956), and reprinted in *Liberté I*, pp. 204, 205.

87.   Léopold Senghor, "Éléments constitutifs d'une civilisation d'inspiration négro-africaine," first published in *Présence Africaine*, March-April 1959, and reprinted in *Liberté I*, p. 269. (Emphasis in the original.)

88.   This issue is explored in: Ghislaine Lydon, "Women, Children and the Popular Front's Mission of Inquiry in French West Africa," in Chafer and Sackur, eds., *French Colonial Empire and the Popular Front*.

89.   CAOM, 1/AP/541, "Le statut juridique de la femme dans les colonies françaises," probably written in 1939. See also the report entitled, "Situation de la femme dans l'Afrique Noire," contained in the same carton and produced in the late 1930s.

90.   CAOM, 3/SLOTFOM/53, "Rapport de l'agent Joe," 29 August 1932, "Rapport de Dubois," 27 August 1932, and "Rapport de l'agent Joe," 5 September 1932.

91.   Rachel G. Fuchs, "Introduction" to the forum on "Population and the State in the Third Republic," *French Historical Studies* 19:3 (Spring 1996), pp. 636, 638. The articles by Joshua H. Cole, Jean Elisabeth Pedersen, Cheryl A. Coos, and Reggiani in the same issue explore the question of the construction of women's "place" in French society during the 70 years of the Third Republic's existence.

92.   Joan Wallach Scott, *Only Paradoxes to Offer: French Feminists and the Rights of Man* (Cambridge: Harvard University Press, 1996), pp. 9, and 10–11.

93.   Yaël Simpson Fletcher, "'Irresistible Seductions': Gendered Representations of Colonial Algeria around 1930," in Clancy-Smith and Gouda, eds., *Domesticating the Empire*, p. 209. In addition to the aforementioned collection, there is a growing literature that examines the role of gendered discourse in the articulation of colonial identities and the legitimization of imperial rule. For some recent examples see: Emily Apter, "Ethnographic Travesties: Colonial Realism, French Feminism, and the Case of Elissa Rhaïs," in Prakash, ed., *After Colonialism*; Gayatri Chakravorty Spivak, "Three Women's Texts and a Critique of Imperialism," in Ashcroft, et al., eds., *The Post-Colonial Studies Reader*; and Anne McClintock, *Imperial Leather: Race, Gender and Sexuality in the Colonial Contest* (New York: Routledge, 1995).

94. Léopold Senghor, "L'esthétique négro-africaine," in *Liberté I*, pp. 205, 204, 209. (Emphasis in the original.)
95. Léon-Gontran Damas, *Retour de Guyane* (Paris: Librairie José Corti, 1938), pp. 160, 176.
96. Aimé Césaire, "L'Irrémédiable," in *Les Arms Miraculeuses* (Paris: Gallimard, 1946), p. 46.
97. Léopold Senghor, "L'Apport de la poésie nègre au demi-siècle," in *Liberté I*, pp. 133, 135, 138, 134.
98. Karin Barber, *I Could Speak Until Tomorrow: Oriki, Women, and the Past in a Yoruba Town* (Washington, D.C.: Smithsonian Institution Press, 1991).
99. Catherine Coquery-Vidrovitch, *African Women: A Modern History* (Boulder, Co.: Westview Press, 1997), pp. 3-4.
100. Léopold Senghor, "Le Problème culturel en A.O.F.," in *Liberté I*, p. 19.
101. CAOM, 5/SLOTFOM/21, editorial in the *évolué* journal *Idéal et Réalité*, 1 October 1935.
102. Léopold Senghor, "Éléments constitutifs d'une civilisation d'inspiration négro-africaine," in *Présence Africaine* (March-April 1959), p. 270.
103. Léopold Senghor, "Ce que l'homme noir apporte," in *L'Homme de Couleur*, p. 30.
104. Léopold Senghor, "Le Problème culturel en A.O.F.," speech given at a conference organized by the Dakar Chamber of Commerce, 10 September 1937, reprinted in *Liberté I*, pp. 19 and 17.
105. Ibid. (Emphasis in the original.)
106. Léopold Senghor, "L'Apport de la poésie nègre au demi-siècle," in *Liberté I*, pp. 135, 138, 137.
107. CAOM, 3/SLOTFOM/109, L. Hanna-Charley, "Pour Notre Chère Race," 7 July 1939.
108. CAOM, 5/SLOTFOM/21, Césaire, "Nègreries; Jeunesse noire et Assimilation," in *L'Étudiant Noir*, March 1935.
109. CAOM, 5/SLOTFOM/51. In its March 1936 edition, the publication of the Guadeloupe Sudents' Organization in France reported that law students in the Latin Quarter of Paris had rioted against blacks. Such incidents were noted periodically throughout the 1930s and increased with frequency after 1935 in the wake of Mussolini's invasion of Ethiopia and the rise of the leftist Popular Front in the metropole.
110. Léopold Senghor, "L'Apport de la poésie nègre au demi-siècle," in *Liberté I*, p. 139.
111. CAOM, CG/52, Léopold Senghor to the Guernut Commission, "La Resistance de la Bourgeoisie Senegalaise à l'École Rurale Populaire," 26 October 1937.
112. Léopold Senghor, "L'Apport de la poésie nègre au demi-siècle," in *Liberté I*, p. 141.
113. Léopold Senghor, "Le problème de la culture," first printed in *Journées d'Etudes des Indépendants d'Outre-Mer*, July 1950, reprinted in *Liberté I*, pp. 93–97.
114. CAOM, 3/SLOTFOM/119, report of the CAI, 7 October 1938.
115. Ali A. Mazrui and Michael Tidy, *Nationalism and New States in Africa; From about 1935 to the Present* (Nairobi: Heinemann, 1984), pp. 5-6. The incident took place in 1937.
116. CAOM, 3/SLOTFOM/53, note by the CAI dated 27 February 1935.
117. Max Gallo, *L'Affaire d'Éthiopie aux origins de la guerre mondiale* (Paris: Éditions du Centurion, 1967), pp. 42–43, 59.

118. CAOM, 3/SLOTFOM/53, report by a CAI informant known only as "L.S.," 2 January 1935.

119. Soucy, *French Fascism: The Second Wave, 1933–1939*, p. 124.

120. CAOM, 1/AP/539/8, Pierre Jacquier, "Le Conflit Italo-Abyssin et l'Afrique Occidentale Française—1935–1936," in *Le Jour*, 5 January 1936.

121. CAOM, 3/SLOTFOM/43, speech by Emile Faure, close friend of Kouyaté, at a meeting of the *Comité d'assistance aux victimes de la guerre en Ethiopie*, 1 April 1936.

122. CAOM, 5/SLOTFOM/20, "La guerre criminelle du fascisme," in *Front Mondial Contre Guerre et fascisme*, 1–15 October 1935.

123. CAOM, 3/SLOTFOM/53, letter from Garan Tiémoko Kouyaté to the Ethiopian emperor, February 1935.

124. CAOM, 3/SLOTFOM/43, confidential report from Pierre Boisson, governor general of AOF, to the ministry of colonies, 21 November 1935.

125. CAOM, 1/AP/539/8, letter from Pierre Boisson, governor general of AOF, to the ministry of colonies, 11 September 1935.

126. CAOM, 1/AP/539/8, report by the government general, 11 January 1936, on the activities of the Italian consul, Mario Vattani, organizing collections in Dakar to support Italy's war effort in Ethiopia. See also: CAOM, 1/AP/539/5, "Rapport Politique du Gouvernement Général de l'A.O.F. (année 1936)." This document notes that the events in East Africa deeply affected the electoral campaign in May 1936 that nearly unseated the Senegalese deputy, Galandou Diouf. On the 1936 campaign see: CAOM, 1/AP/539/6, "Police et Sûreté de la Circonscription de Dakar et Dependances; Rapport annuel année 1937."

127. CAOM, 3/SLOTFOM/53, report by an informant of the CAI, "Les Critiques de Kouyaté," 7 February 1935.

128. CAOM, 5/SLOTFOM/20, "La guerre criminelle du fascisme," in *Front Mondial Contre Guerre et fascisme*, 1-15 October 1935.

129. CAOM, 3/SLOTFOM/43, call issued by various *évolué* organizations for a demonstration on 21 August 1935.

130. CAOM, 3/SLOTFOM/43, "Manifestation du 21 août 1935," report filed with the CAI on 23 August. See also, in the same carton, "Pour la Défense de l'Ethiopie," 22 August 1935.

131. CAOM, CG/60, note of 1935-1936 on the activities of Kouyaté that concerned Ethiopia and the publication of *Africa*.

132. CAOM, 5/SLOTFOM/21, letter from Gaston Joseph, minister of colonies, to the government general for AOF, "Le journal 'Africa' et le plan de réformes coloniales de Kouyate," 13 January 1936. See also in the same carton, letter from the government general for AEF to the ministry of colonies, 13 February 1936; letter from the government general for AOF to the ministry of colonies, 16 April 1937; and report from the government general for AOF, "Renseignements," 7 April 1937. In addition, for Dakar's assessment of Kouyaté's impact in West Africa, see: CAOM, 1/AP/542, "Rapport du Gouvernement General de l'Afrique Occidentale française," for the year 1935, written in 1936. For information on the circulation of *Africa* see: CAOM, CG/59, "Rapport Politique 1937," prepared by the governor of Senegal.

133. CAOM, 3/SLOTFOM/78, Garan Kouyaté, "Principes Directeurs d'une Transformation de l'Outre-mer," submitted to the ministry of colonies, 27 May 1937.

Kouyaté's plan was originally published in the first edition of *Africa*, 1 December 1935. See: CAOM, 5/SLOTFOM/21, Gaston Joseph, minister of colonies, to the governor general of AOF, "Le journal 'Africa' et le plan de réformes coloniales de Kouyate," 13 January 1936.

134. CAOM, 3/SLOTFOM/78, Kouyaté, "Principes Directeurs d'une Transformation de l'Outre-mer," 27 May 1937.

135. CAOM, 5/SLOTFOM/21, this goal is expressed by Césaire in his article, "Nègreries; Jeunesse Noire et Assimilation," in *L'Étudiant Noir*, March 1935.

136. CAOM, 3/SLOTFOM/53, undated anonymous report of the CAI, probably written in the spring of 1936.

137. Gallo, *L'Affaire d'Éthiopie*, pp. 19, 25, 110, 111.

138. Janet Vaillant observes that Léopold Senghor joined the Committee of Intellectuals Against Fascism after Italy invaded Ethiopia. Until that point, he had remained outside of politics. Vaillant, *Black, French, and African*, pp. 118–119.

139. One of the best studies of the Popular Front in France is: Julian Jackson, *The Popular Front in France: Defending Democracy, 1934–1938* (Cambridge: Cambridge University Press, 1990). Jackson argues that the only unifying factor that held the Popular Front together was a commitment to defend the constitution of the Third Republic from destruction at the hands of the radical right. Thus, when more substantive issues arose once the Popular Front was in government after 1936, the coalition frayed and conservative forces once again became dominant in France just prior to the advent of the Second World War.

140. CAOM, 3/SLOTFOM/43.

141. CAOM, CG/47, "Administration et langues Africaines," in *Bulletin d'Information et de Renseignements*, 8 November 1937. See also, in the same carton, Hubert Deschamps, "Note sur l'organisation administrative de l'Afrique noire," 23 February 1938; and the *Bulletin AEF*, July 1937.

142. CAOM, 3/SLOTFOM/119, report of the CAI on a meeting of the Association for the Defense and Emancipation of the Colonized Peoples, 27 November 1936. For further reactions among the *évolués* to the Popular Front victory see: CAOM, 3/SLOTFOM/43, minutes of the Mutual Aid Society for Indochinese in France, 6 August 1936.

143. CAOM, 1/AP/539/6, "Police et Sûreté de la Circonscription de Dakar et Dependances; Rapport annuel année 1937."

144. CAOM, 13/SLOTFOM/1, statutes of the *Rassemblement Colonial*, drafted on 11 April 1937 and adopted on 13 April 1937. See also the letter from the ministry of the interior to the ministry of colonies, "A/S de la convocation à Paris d'un Congrès intercolonial," 15 April 1937, in the same carton. Additional information is located in: CAOM, 3/SLOTFOM/78, note by an agent of the CAI, probably 1937, concerning the history and program of the *Rassemblement Colonial*. Information on Kouyaté's role in the *Rassemblement Colonial* is contained in: CAOM, 13/SLOTFOM/1, report by an agent of the CAI, written in late 1937.

145. CAOM, 13/SLOTFOM/1, letter from the executive committee of the *Rasemblement Colonial* to the ministry of colonies, 31 March 1939. Material on Vichy's actions against the *évolué* community, especially their associational life, is located in: CAOM, 3/SLOTFOM/97.

146.   CAOM, 1/AP/179/1, "Conférence des Gouverneurs Généraux—voeux adoptés," November 1936.

147.   CAOM, CG/52, "Le Problème Culturel en AOF; conference faite à Dakar le 4 Septembre 1937 par M. Senghor, professeur au Lycée du Tours;" and: CAOM, CG/107, letter from Léopold Senghor to the Guernut Commission, 28 October 1937.

148.   CAOM, CG/59, bulletin published by the ministry of colonies, *Informations D'Outre-Mer*, 22 October 1937. In that document Moutet names the *Comité d'Etudes des coutumes indigènes dans les territoires de l'Afrique continentale*. The Committee brought together many of the foremost French ethnographers and representatives of the French-educated elite, including Guèye.

149.   *Congrès International de l'évolution culturelle des peuples coloniaux*, p. 19, notes on the general discussion at the conference where Rivet and Léopold Senghor exchanged views on the most efficacious approach to devising indigenous legal codes.

150.   CAOM, CG/107, letter by Emile Faure, general secretary of the *Rassemblement Colonial*, to the Guernut Commission, "Suggestions du groupe de l'Afrique noire du Rassemblement Colonial," 27 April 1938.

151.   Soucy, *French Fascism: The Second Wave, 1933–1939*, pp. 113-115.

152.   Coquery-Vidrovitch, *African Women*, p. 75.

153.   CAOM, 1/AP/891/8, see especially the telegram from AEF to the ministry of colonies, 11 November 1938, and the declaration issued by "Les chefs indigènes de l'Afrique Equatoriale française à Monsieur le Gouverneur Général Reste," AEF, 4 October 1938. The letters were written at the time of the Munich Crisis and reflected increased fears of an immanent war with Germany. However, they also express a clear note of relief at the political changes in France after the demise of the Popular Front.

154.   Léopold Senghor, "Song of the Initiate," in *The Collected Poetry*, p. 136.

155.   Léopold Senghor, "La Résistance de la Bourgeoisie Sénégalaise à l'École Rurale Populaire," in *Congrès International de l'évolution culturelle des peuples coloniaux*, p. 44.

Chapter Five

Not Quite French:
Intermediate Spaces and Citizenship

In early 1946, during deliberations on a constitution for the Fourth French Republic, Henri Laurentie, minister of colonial affairs for the provisional government, explained, "It is with the *évolués* from throughout the [colonies] that [France] will succeed [in its mission]. [The French-educated elite] will be the scaffolding of the structure being erected in each of the territories. Therefore, it is not an exaggeration to say that [the *évolués*] are the vital center of the colonial question."[1] In fact, the French-educated elite—and its place within the imperial framework—had been at the core of the "colonial question" in West Africa since at least the 1914–1918 war, and, as such, had proved a constant source of disquiet for overseas administrators, metropolitan governments, and the pre-colonial elite alike.

However, it was a problem spawned by the very nature of France's *mission civilisatrice*, as variously interpreted in Dakar and Paris, and administrative practice in AOF. French rule in West Africa had produced what Mahmood Mamdani calls "a bifurcated world…inhabited by subjects on one side and citizens on the other."[2] That bipolar framework precluded the participation of the *évolués* as a stable and coherent force in the colonial field even though the hegemonic discourse practiced therein treated the French-educated elite as a unique social group that transcended the boundary separating *citoyen* from *sujet*. Thus, until the Second World War the French-educated elite was often the subject of administrative praxis and self-articulation without a clear definition of exactly who was considered to be part of that category, or a judicial framework that delineated the rights and obligations of those classified and self-identified as "*évolués*." This accords with Bourdieu's observation that "only rarely do [boundaries] take the form of juridical frontiers…even though they are always marked by more or less institutionalized 'barriers to entry.'"[3]

Laurentie's remarks, though, were made at a time when Paris had realized that an imperial structure erected on a foundation that opposed citizen to subject was no longer tenable. By then France had recognized the *évolués* as a distinct socio-juridical category within the colonial field. The decision to accord special status to the French-educated elite also sanctioned their emergence as co-administrators of West Africa with the metropolitan government.[4] In the process, the regimes of power operable in AOF underwent a radical transformation, one embodied in the metamorphosis of the colonial empire into the French Union through the constitution of the Fourth Republic. This chapter investigates how the French-educated elite from West Africa achieved its distinctive status within the colonial field that simultaneously situated them as a dominant social force within the federation. As a result, the struggle for authority in AOF entered a new phase wherein the hegemonic bloc of colonial administrators and the pre-colonial elite, many compromised by their wartime support of the collaborationist government based in Vichy, was displaced and increasingly marginalized. In fact, the fight against Nazi Germany and the supplicant French government headed by Marshal Henri Philippe Pétain had resurrected the pre-war alliance of *évolués* and the anti-fascist Popular Front in the form of the Resistance. Once "France had been liberated by its [colonial] empire,"[5] that partnership formed the basis for the new political order in the metropole and overseas territories.

However, the idea to create an "intermediate class" between citizen and subject did not originate with the Gaullist resistance.[6] Albert Sarraut, as part of his *mise en valeur* proposal in the early 1920s, recognized the "insufficiency" of French colonialism's bipolar framework and suggested that the new urban elite from overseas be considered as "half-French."[7] Such a designation pointed to the inability of the hegemonic discourse within the imperial framework to recognize any *other* terms than the binaries of "French" and "native"—not-French. Furthermore, the appellation "half-French" reaffirmed the primacy of the "civilizer" over the "primitive" while it simultaneously threatened France's dominance in the colonial field by the implication that it was possible for indigenous subjects to, eventually, become "French." As Bhabha writes, "The question of the representation of difference is…always a problem of authority."[8] In the political culture of the inter-war years, characterized by an insistence upon essential differences between "authentic" European and African cultures, the ascendant forces within France and AOF were predisposed to construe the creation of "intermediate classes" as a threat to the foundation of French rule in the federation. Accordingly, the binary world of citizens and subjects was at least formally preserved until the Second World War. Even the Popular Front failed to produce any meaningful change in the dominant power relations in West Africa or to expand citizenship rights in the colonies.[9] This was partly a consequence of the Popular Front's having embraced the hegemonic discourse practiced by Dakar and earlier conservative governments in Paris that presented the preservation of "authentic" African culture as a fundamental prerogative of the *mission civilisatrice.* As Wilder notes, "Its (the Popular Front's) policies must be recognized as having participated in the emergence after the First World War of a new form of colonial government."[10] Thus, the anti-fascist coalition was not inclined to challenge the basic division of the colonial field between citizens and subjects, nor was it amenable to a rapid increase in the number of indigenous subjects accorded French citizenship.[11] Moreover, by the mid-1930s there was not a strong push from below, as there had been in the past, for accession of the colonized to citizenship as the organized movements of the "modern *griots*" did not include that issue in their list of demands presented to the Popular Front. Instead, the *Rassemblement Colonial,* for example, asked Paris to accord the French-educated elite "political rights that will permit [their] rapid accession to power [in addition to] the institution of literary and artistic prizes and the orientation of the people toward a complete emancipation."[12]

France's defeat by Nazi Germany in the summer of 1940, though, profoundly altered the conditions in which the struggle for authority within the colonial field was waged. Initially, the actions of the new government installed at Vichy seemed to mark a continuation and intensification of established administrative practices. With one notable exception the colonial administration pledged its loyalty to Pétain's government, as did the pre-colonial elite. In the first months after the defeat, Vichy ordered overseas officials to inspect their territories and proselytize the new government's revised understanding of the *mission civilisatrice.* In the new order even the *originaires* of the Four Communes of Senegal were stripped of their status as citizens, elections to local assemblies were eliminated, and associational life among the colonized population was banned.[13]

Those circumstances produced widespread discontent among the *évolués* and presented an opportunity for the development of resistance activity in Africa. The decision by Félix Eboué, governor of Chad and himself an *évolué* from Guyana, to support General Charles de Gaulle not only gave Free France a geographic base of operations against Vichy, it also furnished the administrative foundation for a reordering of power relations in sub-Saharan Africa. To secure the support of the French-educated elite for de Gaulle's movement, Eboué decreed the formation of an intermediate category of "*notables évolués*" and the democratization of local command structures.[14] Subsequent decrees issued by de Gaulle and resolutions passed at the 1944 colonial conference in Brazzaville assured the modern *griots* an important place at the table in discussions of the post-war order in France and West Africa.

While there was general agreement among the various forces that had contributed to France's liberation that "the future of the country [and the empire] depend[ed] on a program of political and social renovation," no consensus emerged as to the form that reconstruction should take.[15] Furthermore, assertions by members of de Gaulle's entourage that the status of *notables évolués* was not a step toward full French citizenship escalated tensions between the metropole and the French-educated elite who now operated from a position of strength and had access to the machinery of government.[16] Thus, the alliance forged between the *évolués* and the Gaullist resistance in the context of the fight against Nazi Germany quickly frayed as discussions commenced on the nature of the Fourth French Republic and metropolitan/colonial relations therein. In the midst of those debates Lamine Guèye, the new deputy from Senegal and longtime activist in radical *évolué* politics, had the Constituent Assembly pass a law that declared "all the subjects of the overseas territories…citizen[s], with the same rights as French nationals in the metropole."[17] However, attempts to obstruct the implementation of the "Lamine Guèye Law" or to re-interpret it to the point of meaninglessness greeted its passage in both France and West Africa. Thus, the French Union was inaugurated in a sea of confusion and an atmosphere of increased hostility between the metropolitan government and the *évolués* from AOF. Once again, Paris posed as the defender of "authentic" African culture and turned to the pre-colonial elite to preserve French rule in West Africa. However, the dichotomous relationship of citizen and subject had been broken in the course of the Second World War and, in the process, the French-educated elite had secured the political and judicial basis from which to effectively challenge the metropole's authority in the federation. First, though, we must explore the antecedents to this development through an analysis of early indications that the binary framework of French colonialism could not be sustained.

Almost But Not Quite French:
The "Indigenous Elite," Mimicry, and Authority

"In native colonial society," read a 1927 proposal by the ministry of colonies, "certain individuals demonstrate a degree of culture, possessed of social value which, in fact, elevates them above the level of life of the other French subjects." The proposition continued, "Nevertheless, due to the short duration of their evolution, and the social and ethnic influences under which they have suffered, they are still profoundly different from the Europeans, profoundly native."[18] Since "everyone agree[d] that naturalization [of such individuals] was dangerous...because of the difficulty in acquiring the [French] mentality," and concurred that it was not desirable to "leave them in their normal condition," Bernard Lavergne, a member of the Conseil Superieur des Colonies and its legislative committee, suggested that France institute "a distinct category for the natives" called "*indigènes d'élite*," or "Native Elite." The new designation between citizen and subject, however, was not "to be considered as a step toward the acquisition of French citizenship." Rather, it was a "stable category" that was meant to "finally give legitimate satisfaction [to the demands of this group] without making them French citizens." Furthermore, those who had already been naturalized could not also have conferred on them the status of Native Elite.[19]

Lavergne's language betrayed a deep discomfort connected to the emergence of the *évolués* as a distinct social group within the colonial field. For the colonialist, the aspirations of the new urban elite to become citizens of France, a desire originally cultivated by the imperial power itself, threatened the distinctiveness of French identity. However, the decisions taken at the conclusion of the 1914–1918 war to restrict the naturalization rate and to marginalize the *évolués* only generated "discontent" among that important social class and, therefore, risked the future of French rule overseas. Furthermore, to merely leave them in their "normal state" as *sujets* endangered the stability of native society since the presence of the *évolués* disrupted "traditional" social structures and challenged the authority of the pre-colonial elite, one of the pillars of colonial governance.[20]

The debate over how to classify the French-educated elite from the colonies reveals what Bhabha calls the "ambivalence" and "indeterminacy" of "the [colonial] discourse of mimicry" deployed by imperial administrators based in Paris and Dakar.[21] In the political culture that dominated the French colonial field during the inter-war years, the *évolué* emerged in the conceptual framework of the colonial administration as a monstrous hybrid that was neither African nor French, but a threat to both. Sarraut's description of the new urban elite from West Africa as "half-French" was not only indicative of the "insufficiently determined...particular situation" of the *évolués*, it set the limits of the possible for the colonial subject while it simultaneously refused attainment of that potential.[22]

In fact, the suggestion to establish an "intermediate class" between citizen and subject grew out of the failure of either Paris or Dakar to enforce the citizenship legislation passed during the Great War or to honor the pledges made to those colonial subjects who fought for France in the conflict.[23] It also constituted part of the "wars over cultural identity" that dominated political discourse in France throughout the 1920s and 1930s and which centered on diverse presentations of the "true" nature of Frenchness.[24] After the 1914–1918 war many colonial officials expressed anxiety that the citizenship laws enacted during the conflict, if enforced, could "do great harm to the French" and create a situation wherein "the French would no longer represent the natives; the natives will represent the French."[25] After 1919, colonial administrators obstructed the naturalization process under the aegis of conducting "a very serious and rigorous examination of the intelligence, moral qualities, and loyalty of the candidates [in order] to provide the [metropolitan] administration the necessary assurances when it attributes the status of citizen to a native of our African colonies."[26] The naturalization rate had plummeted to such low levels that Sarraut joined protests by organizations founded to defend the interests of veterans from the overseas territories. When those complaints went unanswered Sarraut urged Paris to consider the recognition of the *évolués* as "half-French" to offset the possible growth of "nationalist" sentiment in the colonies, a suggestion quickly dismissed.[27]

The election of the *cartel des gauches* to a majority in the Chamber of Deputies in 1924, however, brought renewed interest in the naturalization question. The new minister of colonies, Edouard Daladier, viewed the low naturalization rate as a product of bureaucratic inconsistencies since each of the overseas federations had their own laws on citizenship. The separate administrative units of the empire deployed different criteria to determine who could rightfully be considered "French." Thus, there was no clear legal definition of what it meant to be "French," which only exacerbated and confirmed the trepidation expressed by many in the metropole that unless a single cultural idea of France was located its existence as a distinct civilization faced extinction.[28] That apprehension was also reflected in the various endeavors by Paris to create an immigration office after the First World War to control the flow of "foreign and colonial workers" into the metropole during a period of high unemployment and social unrest.[29]

Immigrant labor, which had been welcomed and encouraged during the war, underwent a transition similar to that of the colonial subjects and *évolués* in the discursive framework of the 1920s as migrants from beyond France's borders of all types were (re)presented as threats to French identity.[30]

In 1924 Daladier proposed to overcome the "incoherence" that dominated the question of "Frenchness" in the colonial field. After he reaffirmed that citizenship was "never accorded as a right, but as a favor" to those who were not the progeny of metropolitan citizens, the minister of colonies proffered "to codify...all the laws on naturalization" so that "only one category of citizens" would exist in the imperial framework. First, Daladier identified the aspects that all the laws shared. Those were that the candidate for citizenship should "be 21 years old, have rendered important services to French interests, especially during the war, prove[d] their knowledge of French, [and] renounce[d] their personal status." The minister of colonies then delineated the additional qualities necessary to be considered "sufficiently" French. The applicant had to have acquired "French sentiments" and be "in one of the following situations: to have received the Cross of the Legion of Honor; hold a professional or university degree; to have served in the French army and be a decorated officer or non-commissioned officer; to have a French wife; or to have been employed for at least ten years in the colonial administration or contributed in an exceptional way to the economic development of the country or given manifest proofs of their devotion to the French cause."[31]

While Daladier presented his plan as a means to make citizenship accessible to "all the natives born in a French colony or protectorate," it effectively restricted citizenship to soldiers, intellectuals, and the economic elite of the colonies, strata that encompassed only thousands out of the sixty million imperial subjects. Furthermore, Daladier's insistence that there be "only one category of citizen" and repeated references to the "special situation...of the *originaires* of the Four Free Communes of Senegal" suggested that the proposition was far less "liberal" than its author claimed. In fact, the proposal explicitly abrogated the unique protections won by the *originaires* through Diagne's efforts during the 1914–1918 conflict. If the measure had been approved it would have forced thousands of residents in Dakar, St. Louis, Rufisque, and Gorée to re-apply for a status many of them had enjoyed throughout their lives.[32] Accordingly, the most influential *évolué* organizations objected to Daladier's proposal and instead pressed for complete "equality" between "natives and French [citizens]," and enforcement of the decrees issued during the Great War.[33] Furthermore, Daladier's proposition continued the practice that made it more difficult for a subject of the French empire to become a citizen than a "foreigner."[34] This is evidenced in the case of two prospective students from Indochina denied admission to the École Coloniale because "these youth are not foreigners, but nor are they French citizens." Also the case of Salla Dialo bears witness to this dilemma. A decorated veteran of the Great War from AOF, Dialo also served in the French occupation army in Germany throughout the early 1920s and, while there, married a German woman with whom he had a son. The colonial administration repeatedly refused Dialo's request French citizenship, nor was he permitted to return to his homeland for fear of "contaminating" the local population since he had married a "white woman." This indicates that the colonial subject remained the extreme marker of difference between French and non-French, the radical "Other."[35]

In general, colonial administrators were averse to and suspicious of Daladier's project. One representative from India agreed to support the plan only if conclusive proof was presented that the *sujet* "had definitively evolved in the sense of [having acquired] the French mentality and the social and moral ideas that are the foundation of our [civilization]."[36] Others were more vehement in their opposition. Mario Roustan, vice president of the Senate's colonial commission, asserted that it was "dangerous" to accord colonial subjects French citizenship. He explained, "There are some people who are colonizers and some who are colonized." To breach that barrier by permitting the colonized to achieve equal status with the colonizers endangered "the authority of the mother country, without which [its] civilizing work would be ruined." Roustan mocked the notion that "to know how to write French" amounted to a measure of one's Frenchness and intimated that one was either French or not, but it was not possible *to become* French.[37]

Despite their differences, Daladier and his opponents within the imperial hierarchy shared a desire to preserve and strengthen the distinction between citizens and subjects. Daladier's measure was not designed as a vehicle whereby citizenship would be extended to all *sujets*. Rather, only an identified elite that had passed certain rigorous, and ambiguous, tests would be welcomed into the national patrimony. That did not, however, entail the acceptance of the *évolué* as a participant in colonial governance. In fact, Daladier's project was designed to eliminate the bases for the articulation of a distinct *évolué* identity through their absorption into the category "French." In that way, the minister of colonies shared Delafosse's judgment that the French-educated elite was "no longer native and could not be returned to their traditional society."[38] Yet, the concern voiced by many colonial administrators that the *évolué* "threatened" "traditional African society" did not lead them to endorse the proposition that the French-educated elite should be made citizens of the metropole any more than the imperial officials wanted them to remain in contact with "native cultures."[39] Thus, the defeat of Daladier's plan left the place of the *évolué* within the colonial field undecided, a circumstance that made the French-educated elite appear more ominous in the *imaginaire* of the colonial administration.

The solution, according to some in the imperial hierarchy, was "the creation...of a new juridical category" between citizen and subject. In 1927 the Conseil Superieur des Colonies proposed to institute the status of "*indigènes d'élite*" in order alleviate the "discontent...of those who have attained a certain degree of [French] culture and dignity...[but] to whom it did not appear at all desirable [to accord] the title of French citizen."[40] The status of Native Elite carried with it exemption from the *indigénat*, the right to participate in local elections, to present themselves as French (albeit not as equal citizens), and access to French schools.[41] Its supporters argued that the idea of an official designation such as "Native Elite" had an advantage in that it sanctioned the emergent self-identity of the *évolués* as being between two cultural worlds and participating in both. Accordingly, Lavergne and others on the Council asserted that the French-educated elite would welcome the new rank and, consequently, end their pressure to be accorded citizenship. This, in turn, would ultimately strengthen the authority of France in the colonies and, in particular, terminate the threat posed by the *évolués* to the colonial administration and the pre-colonial elite alike. To guarantee this outcome, the Council amended the proposition in 1928 to read that the status of *indigènes d'élite* was "a stable category...not a step toward the accession of citizenship." Instead, the new classification was to be understood as "a kind of aristocracy, of [native] hierarchy."[42]

While many of the *évolués* from West Africa certainly presented themselves as an "elite" destined to lead "the evolution of the Black Race," their goal was either "assimilation" to France through "naturalization," or a social revolution "to establish a Negro State in black Africa."[43] Furthermore, the category of Native Elite was founded upon the negation of what G. Wesley Johnson calls the "schizophrenic" identity of the *évolués*—both African and French, in the case of AOF. Johnson views *évolué* identity as comprised "of elements or qualities that are mutually contradictory or antagonistic."[44] While many within the colonial administration (and even figures like Léopold Senghor among the French-educated elite) held this view of the difference between French and African cultures, I suggest that it is precisely the supposed "contradictoriness" of European and non-European cultures that needs to be interrogated as a specific historical phenomenon with implications lasting beyond the colonial moment. Certainly Diagne did not subscribe to the notion that French and African cultures were antagonistic and even Léopold Senghor spent much of his active intellectual and political life attempting to demonstrate the "complementarity" of the two cultures— which, of course, still accepts the idea that there are such things as distinct "French" and "African" cultures.

For the architects of the proposed "intermediate class," the new urban elite was neither African nor French. The problem of the *évolué* lay precisely in the fact, often expressed by colonial administrators and ethnographers, that they were "uprooted" and "dislocated," which implied that they belonged nowhere in the colonial field, yet were a pervasive and disconcerting presence nonetheless.[45] The negative conception of *évolué* identity embedded in the classification Native Elite clashed with their own self-image since it sought to contain the French-educated elite in a colonial purgatory between citizen and subject and maintained the hegemonic image of the modern *griots* as "deformed." Thus, the new designation, suggested in a context where the language of cultural authenticity dominated the discourse practiced within the imperial framework, functioned as a sign of danger, a threat of permanent marginalization if a *sujet* transgressed the boundary that separated colonizer from colonized.[46]

Yet, even the suggestion that an intermediate category be instituted between citizen and subject elicited fierce objections from colonial administrators. Such a classification, the government general for AOF remonstrated, was "dangerous because it threatened...to compromise the happy equilibrium" of indigenous society and was "an offense to the traditional aristocracy" in West Africa. Moreover, Dakar added, "an autochthonous elite had already been solidly constituted" in the form of the "native chiefs."[47] For Dakar, the proposal to classify the *évolués* as a Native Elite undermined the basis of colonial governance as reconstructed after the Great War. The new status would provide the French-educated elite with a legal basis from which to challenge the authority of the colonial administration while it also, the argument ran, eroded the prestige of the pre-colonial elite upon which the government general relied to preserve France's domination in West Africa.[48]

By 1932 the proposal to form a Native Elite had been withdrawn. In fact, a final draft of the decree was never submitted to any of the legislative bodies in France or the overseas territories. Rather, the idea to create the status of *indigène d'élite* remained a nebulous concept floated to the governors general to gauge their reactions. Only Madagascar, French Equatorial Africa, and French Somalia were favorable toward the proposition.[49] Significantly, those were areas, especially in AEF, where the French education system and recruitment for the military was lowest. Therefore, the formation of a new category explicitly for the *évolués* in those territories did not imply the accreditation of special privileges to a noticeable portion of the population. However, in the other administrative units of the empire, especially AOF and Indochina, where the French-educated elite constituted a large and recognizable social group, opposition was most vehement.

The victory of the Popular Front in 1936 and Moutet's notion of "republican colonialism," however, threatened to bring about the imposition of a new native elite in West Africa without the supervision of the colonial administration, nor the special designation of a legal status between citizen and subject. Sending shudders throughout the imperial command structure, the anti-fascist coalition proclaimed that it was committed "to bring[ing] about a new way [of functioning in] all the branches of national life [including]…the administration of our overseas territories."[50] Nonetheless, the Popular Front passed from the political scene in 1938 without any fundamental change in the power relations operable within West Africa. No new attempts were made to expand citizenship in the federation and there was no formal suggestion that the bipolar framework of citizens and subjects should be done away with. Instead, the *évolués* were adopted by the anti-fascist coalition as allies in a re-imagined *mission civilisatrice* based on certain notions of "authentic" African culture that retained the core assertion that there were essential and immutable differences between "Europeans" and "colonial natives."

Yet, the Popular Front had gone further that any previous metropolitan government or overseas administration in the acceptance of *évolué* identity as self-articulated. It recognized their "Africanness" whereas Lavergne's Native Elite proposal still denied the French-educated elite that aspect of their sense of themselves. Furthermore, the Popular Front welcomed those among the *évolués* who were prepared to cooperate with French rule as full participants in the system of colonial governance, as a legitimate elite within West Africa. However, the anti-fascist coalition's inaction on the question of citizenship still reflected the refusal, even by the political left, to recognize the modern *griots* as French, another fundamental aspect of their identity. In part, this resulted from the rhetoric practiced by the French-educated elite that was more insistent during the 1930s on its African credentials than its "French" heritage.[51] The circumstances of the Second World War, though, induced a discursive shift within the colonial field whereby competing notions of the "true" France displaced earlier disputes over "authentic" African culture at the center of the struggle over claims to rule in West

Africa. In the process, the binary world of citizens and subjects was finally ruptured with the advent of a multiplicity of classifications for those caught within the French colonial field.

France That Is Not France:
Vichy, Resistance, and the *"Notables Évolués"*

In April 1940, one month before the German attack on France, Léopold Senghor, a soldier in the French army, expressed the ambivalent position of the *évolués* as they and thousands of others from the colonies were called upon, once again, to defend the metropole. In Paris the Senegalese poet wrote, "Ah! don't say I do not love France—I am not France, I know/I know that each time this fiery nation has freed her hands/She has written brotherhood on the front page of her monuments/She has spread a hunger for the intellect as well as for liberty." In conclusion, the modern *griot* pensively added, "Ah! am I not divided enough?"[52] Two months later Léopold Senghor was listed among the nearly two million French soldiers taken prisoner by Germany after its sudden victory in June. For the next eighteen months the Senegalese poet passed his time as an inmate of Stalag 230, until he was released for medical reasons.

The colonial exile community, like most people in France and the overseas empire, were stunned and disoriented by the swiftness with which the metropole had been subdued. Within a month of the defeat the Third Republic had ceased to exist and a new regime, guided by the amorphous program of the "National Revolution" and headed by the elderly Marshal Henri Philippe Pétain, was erected in its stead at the spa town of Vichy in central France. Under terms of the armistice, two-thirds of the metropole was occupied by Germany, an area which included Paris and the Atlantic seaboard, the southeastern third was left under Vichy's control, and Hitler's regime allowed Pétain's administration to retain possession of the colonial empire without interference from the occupation forces. Thus, while France was defeated and at the mercy of Nazi Germany, the overseas territories were left in the hands of a "French" government whose legitimacy was questionable at best. Furthermore, since "Africans provided almost nine percent of the French army in France, [including] some 100,000 troops...mobilized from AOF alone," by June 1940, the immediate fate of significant numbers of colonized subjects lay decidedly at the feet of Pétain's government.[53] In addition to the future of the POWs, those civilians from the colonies that resided in the metropole faced an equally uncertain future.[54]

However, it did not take long for the *évolués* in France to be made aware of the changed circumstances in a Europe dominated by Hitler's Nazi regime. The Vichy government, guided by a desire "not to provoke" the Germans on the "race question," not only failed to protect the colonized populations in either the "Occupied" or "Free" Zones, it resolutely undertook a program of repression against the "colonial natives" in general and the *évolués* in particular.[55] In Europe, Africans were banned from travel on the railway between the Free and Occupied Zones and, in 1941, were denied employment in France. As a result, Marseilles was transformed into a refugee center where thousands of people from the colonies assembled to be "repatriated...to their territory of origin, even those who had made their home in France."[56] Kouyaté was among those deported in the summer of 1940. In 1942 agents of the Nazi government in West Africa executed Kouyaté for resistance activity, bringing to an end the life of one of the most important figures in the history of anti-colonialism in the federation and radical politics among the French-educated elite in the metropole.[57]

Once in West Africa, though, those deported from France found no relief from the oppressive measures of the Vichy government. While Pétain and his supporters on the political right exacted revenge against leaders of the Popular Front and those on the political left in general, they also moved to decisively conclude the struggle for authority in AOF through the elimination of the *évolués* as a social group. Laws promulgated on 17 July and 14 August 1940 stripped the *originaires* of Senegal of their cherished special status in the colonial field. Henceforward, only children of "French" fathers were regarded as citizens, "indigenous" peoples were limited to employment at the lowest rungs of the colonial bureaucracy, the municipal councils of the Four Communes were abolished,[58] and Senegal's right to elect a deputy to the Chamber (now defunct) was rescinded, an act which ended Galandou Diouf's political life.[59] Furthermore, food, clothing, and other rations for "black" citizens in AOF during the war were set at far lower levels than those for "whites." As a result, the barriers that had separated the French-educated elite in West Africa from the rural *sujets* were breached since the various social groups in the federation were made "more conscious of common interests" with each other in the struggle for authority in AOF.[60]

As Philippe Burrin argues, Vichy based a large portion of its claim to legitimacy upon its retention of the overseas empire.[61] Therefore, the new government set out to win over the hegemonic bloc of colonial administrators and the pre-colonial elite to its "new" policies. Since those forces shared many of the ideological proclivities of Pétain's regime, it was not difficult to secure their allegiance. The entire colonial administration, with the important exception of Félix Eboué, the governor of Chad in Equatorial Africa, recognized the Vichy government and embraced its colonial policies. Subsequently, Pétain urged governors and governors general to tour the territories in their charge to explain to the indigenous populations the changed circumstances of the metropole and to proselytize the program of the "National Revolution," especially with regard to the ways in which it affected the empire. Throughout 1940 and 1941 Vichy received numerous telegrams from the African colonies that testified to the "native chiefs'…enthusiasm for the Marshal and [their] absolute loyalty to France."[62] Even some *évolués* were prepared to support Vichy, but only under the circumstances of continued resistance to Nazi Germany and the belief that Pétain's government was not ready to give up the fight.[63]

By late 1940 any illusions that Vichy would continue the war against Germany had vanished among the *évolués*. What was more apparent was the new regime's willingness to engage in unprecedented repression in the colonies and against migrants from overseas in the metropole, especially those among the French-educated elite. Despite the ban on associational life among the *évolués*, new organizations were founded and began to take on the form of nascent resistance movements. At first, those groups functioned as aid societies to those who were displaced from their former homes in the Occupied Zone. Others assisted in the repatriation of migrants from the colonies. Those few who remained in the "Free Zone" were urged by Vichy to join the National Union of French Students or the French Federation of Catholic Students. Among those who remained active in the official student movement were Léopold Senghor (after his release from a German POW camp in 1942), Alioune Diop, and Mamadou Racine Kane, all writers from Senegal and teachers in the French school system.[64]

However, membership in the government-sanctioned student organizations did not entail an ideological commitment to the new regime or the Nazi order in Europe. Rather, Pétain's administration was deluged with letters of protest against the racial and ethnic discrimination that was increasingly characteristic of life under Vichy. Some of the letters made explicit reference to the questionable legitimacy of the new government. For example, a petition against the discriminatory practices of both Pétain's regime and the occupation authorities read, "One is [either] France or one is not. When one has taken before the world and before a race the attitude which France has taken [since the defeat]…it is injurious for the country." The correspondent implored the government to reverse its repressive measures and protect the interests of its "black citizens" subject to the authority of the Germans in the Occupied Zone.[65] In addition, many members of the official Vichy student organizations were active participants in the Resistance from the earliest days of the conflict. Upon his release from a POW camp, Léopold Senghor joined the underground and remained an important contributor to the fight against Vichy and Nazi Germany throughout the war.[66]

In West Africa, resistance had also developed from the first months after the defeat. Demonstrations against the Vichy government erupted within weeks of the armistice agreement on 22 June 1940. Although they were repressed, the disturbances in West Africa were enough to attract the attention of General Charles de Gaulle in London. According to the leader of Free France, events in AOF "showed that...the continuation of the war appeared self-evident" to those in the federation. In addition, the general noted that a "fire was smoldering in most of our colonies."[67] Vichy also took notice of the discontent overseas, especially among the *évolués*. Admiral Platon, commander of the French fleet in West Africa, remarked, "It has come to my attention that a certain disquiet presently reigns among the *originaires* of AOF." According to the admiral, Vichy had to take measures "to calm the perturbations of the [*évolués*]" in order to avoid the growth of support for de Gaulle in the colonies.[68] Consequently, Vichy allowed the publication of *Dakar-Jeunes* in West Africa, a journal that provided a forum for the French-educated elite to debate the nature of "authentic" African culture and unintentionally cultivated local loyalties at the expense of fealty toward France. In addition, Pétain's regime sponsored special courses in the metropole for migrants from the colonies on topics such as "Africa and Civilization," "Is there a black soul?," and "African customs."[69]

The solutions to the discontent of the West African *évolués* proposed by Vichy were articulated within the framework of the "National Revolution" pronounced by Pétain after the defeat. That doctrine, however vaguely formulated, in many respects resembled the program carried out by colonial administrators in AOF since 1914–1918, often with the same language deployed to describe and justify the actions taken by Pétain's government. Accordingly, "The dominant note struck in National Revolution propaganda at Vichy...was the return to French roots." Those roots, however, were strikingly similar to the ones claimed for "authentic" West African culture in the 1920s and 1930s. On 11 October 1940 the Marshal declared that "family agriculture [would be] the principle economic and social base of France." Similar to French West Africa, France was to be a rural society "purged of debilitating urban and industrial excesses." Furthermore, in the words of Robert Paxton, "All [associated with the Vichy government] defended the virtues of social order, which they agreed was best maintained by authority and hierarchy," the same argument used to "resurrect" the pre-colonial elite after the Great War. Thus, one can expand Paxton's assessment that "continuities probably prevail over breaks between Vichy and subsequent regimes" and suggest that there were also many important continuities between Pétain's National Revolution and the language and practices characteristic of the inter-war French imperial framework.[70]

Yet, while Vichy reproduced much of the discourse of cultural authenticity that was hegemonic throughout the colonial field during the inter-war years, its rhetoric and praxis in the metropole and AOF undermined the notion that there were essential differences between French and African societies. Even if the particular cultural practices in France and Africa were different, the structural bases of each were presented as essentially the same. French and West African societies were both imagined as "authentically" agricultural with a mystical attachment to the land.[71] Each was presented as endowed with a "natural" elite with the prerogative to rule over obedient subjects. Furthermore, social hierarchies were reproduced within the male-dominated family, which was not only regarded as the foundation of society, but also as the model of the entire social structure. Finally, Vichy's aggressive appeal to the empire for support as an important basis of its claim to represent the "true" France also breached the boundaries designed to maintain the division between colonizers and colonized. The inspection tours launched by Vichy's supporters within the colonies in 1940 and 1941 invited the colonial subjects, through their sanctioned representatives among the pre-colonial elite, to participate in the debates over which forces constituted the "real" France after the defeat.

However, Vichy was not alone in its appeal to the colonial empire for legitimacy. General de Gaulle, from his base in London, also placed the colonized populations at the center of the struggle to determine which was the "true" France. On 18 June 1940, one day after Pétain announced that it was "necessary to stop the fighting,"[72] de Gaulle reminded his compatriots that France "is not isolated. Behind her is a vast empire." "In the vast spaces of Africa," the general wrote in his memoirs, "France could in fact re-create for herself an army and a sovereignty.... What was more, the national liberation, if accomplished one day thanks to the forces of the Empire, would establish links of solidarity between metropolitan France and the overseas territories. If, on the contrary, the war were to end without the Empire having made any effort to save the mother country, that would be the end, without a doubt, of the work of France in Africa." At stake was nothing less than French independence, France's *mission civilisatrice*, and the future of Franco-African relations. For de Gaulle, there was no question that the colonized populations were "French" and that the colonies were "a fragment of France" itself.[73] In other words, de Gaulle mobilized the rhetoric of *La Plus Grande France* to facilitate the continuation of the struggle against Nazi domination in Europe and legitimate his claims to represent the "real" France. That was at odds with Vichy's continued emphasis on African "authenticity" and its promotion of regionalism throughout the territories under its jurisdiction, a distancing that simultaneously subverted the barriers that separated colonized from colonizer.

Furthermore, whereas Pétain's government reaffirmed the bifurcation of the empire between *citoyens* and *sujets*, de Gaulle's supporters in Africa ruptured that categorical framework and, in so doing, prepared the ground for a fundamental re-ordering of the system of governance in colonies and metropole alike. While the Free French and Vichy asserted "the future of [France] depended upon the political and social renovation [of the country]," they moved in decidedly different directions to achieve that end.[74] For Vichy, reconstruction was to proceed along lines previously established for the resurrection of "authentic" African society during the inter-war years. For the Gaullists, however, the renewal of France was to commence with reform in the overseas territories, which, in turn, was also to serve as a precedent and precursor for the rebirth of metropolitan society after the liberation.[75]

However, that scenario was only possible because of Eboué's decision to support de Gaulle's appeal while all other colonial administrators raced to declare their loyalty to Vichy in the summer of 1940. Born on 26 December 1884 in the colony of Guyana on the northern coast of South America, Eboué, like many among the French-educated elite, passed through colonial schools, completed his education in Paris, and was subsequently admitted to the École Coloniale. From 1908 to 1930 he served in the administration of the colony Oubangui-Chari in French Equatorial Africa. After brief postings in French Soudan and Martinique during the 1930s, Eboué was appointed governor of Chad on 24 January 1939, the first *évolué* to achieve such high status. By mid-July 1940 Eboué was in contact with de Gaulle and on 26 August the governor of Chad became the first colonial administrator to side publicly with the London-based Resistance. Within days nearly all of AEF was brought under Eboué's control and placed at the disposal of de Gaulle. As compensation for that action, the leader of Free France named Eboué governor general of Equatorial Africa on 12 November 1940, the first "black" governor general in French colonial history.[76]

Eboué's declaration of support for de Gaulle was more than a calculated political or military choice. It represented a rejection of the idea of France presented by Vichy and the assertion of a counter-model of what it meant to be French, one inspired by the language of the Declaration of the Rights of Man and Citizen and the ill-defined and highly contested "spirit of 1789."[77] A master of ambiguous statements, though, de Gaulle gave few hints as to the content of his "certain idea of France." Rather, it was left to the followers of the general to articulate the substance of "Gaullism," a tendency that took its earliest form in the colonies. Like de Gaulle, Eboué recognized that the immediate future of the Free French movement rested upon the degree to which they could garner support in the colonies. However, as during the 1914-1918 war, the appeal to the colonized populations for assistance in the liberation of the metropole necessitated concessions to those elements within the overseas territories likely to contribute to such an endeavor. The identification of those forces was made easier by Vichy's repressive actions toward the French-educated elite and the enthusiastic response of many among the pre-colonial elite to Pétain's regime. Furthermore, since many of the colonial administrators were politically suspect and had compromised themselves through early declarations of loyalty to Vichy,[78] a framework was established wherein a fundamental transformation in the regimes of power operable within the colonial field was possible and imperative. However, that reorganization, based on the principle of equality among all peoples, necessitated the articulation of basic rights for the colonized populations within the context of "Greater France" and called into question the binary distinction between citizen and subject upon which French domination overseas was based.

On Eboué's recommendation, de Gaulle issued a decree on 29 July 1942 that introduced a third, legal term in the imperial framework—"*notables évolués*."[79] A report on the new rank noted that, under the circumstances of the Second World War, "the Governor General (Eboué) estimate[d] that the time ha[d] come to establish an intermediate status between the two existing categories [of citizen and subject], a status that allows [for] the elevation of the moral and judicial condition of the natives called '*évolués*,' without it being necessary to accord them citizenship."[80] The language used to describe the new status of *notables évolués* was nearly identical to that employed to depict the proposed category of *indigènes d'élite* between 1927 and 1932. There, too, the idea of an intermediate category was articulated around a reluctance to accord full French citizenship to the colonized populations. Yet, the criteria used to determine which subject qualified as a "*notable évolué*" was the same as that found in the naturalization laws in effect throughout French-controlled Africa. Accordingly, an aspirant to the rank of *notables évolués* had to have resided in the colony for ten years uninterrupted, "know how to speak, read, and write French fluently," never to have been convicted of a crime, and to have fulfilled all military obligations. The successful applicant was then eligible to participate in all local elections, was exempt from the *indigénat*, and their identity papers would record their new status.[81] Thus, the categories of citizen and *notables évolués* were conflated in the colonial field since the colonized were eligible to become "local or African citizens," but were still denied the prospect of becoming "French," the standards to become which were consequently left undifferentiated from the new rank.[82] In fact, even though Eboué and the Gaullists "reopened access to French citizenship for the natives" and asserted "there was no contradiction between that and the decree that created the status of *notables évolués*,"[83] they insisted that "individuals [must] develop gradually within their own culture."[84] Therefore, those accorded the new designation, similar to the proposed Native Elite, were slated to remain perpetually almost, but not quite, French.

However, the status of *notable évolué* differed in significant ways from the earlier attempt to form a Native Elite. Whereas the idea of *indigènes d'élite* was presented in the context of French dominance in Africa and was meant to counter the growth of radical political movements among the *évolués*, the creation of the *notable évolué* occurred while "France" was defeated and in a struggle to reclaim its sovereignty. Furthermore, the colonial administration had virtually disintegrated in AEF and in French West Africa it was firmly allied to Vichy. Thus, to reestablish French control in the colonies, the system of governance had to be entirely rebuilt with politically reliable cadres. According to Eboué and others in the Gaullist imperial hierarchy, only "the *évolués* had not been corrupted by Vichy propaganda"[85] and were capable of providing leadership in the colonies. Accordingly, all those identified as *notable évolué* were eligible to hold any position in the administrative hierarchy, except the post of governor general, and they were made "co-responsible" for the governance of the overseas territories with metropolitan citizens, which further conflated the two categories. In addition, the *mission civilisatrice* articulated by the Gaullist resistance closely resembled Moutet's earlier "republican colonialism" in that René Pleven, de Gaulle's head of colonial affairs, instructed the governors general to "progressively reserve the largest possible number of jobs [in the imperial administration] to the natives [of the colonies]."[86] In contradistinction to the mission pursued by Vichy, the Resistance presented the empire as a federation of equal peoples each charged with the exercise of authority in their respective territories.

However, whereas reform had proceeded from the top of the administrative hierarchy in Equatorial Africa under Eboué's leadership and was directed by de Gaulle's government-in-exile, events in West Africa had unfolded under vastly different circumstances. In AOF, Pierre Boisson, Vichy's high commissioner for Africa, instituted a veritable reign of terror against the French-educated elite and the colonial subjects. That repression was orchestrated around a racist imagining of the colonial field designed to promote divisions between the settler population, or *colons*, and the *originaires* who had been stripped of their rights and status. Accordingly, Boisson made administrative authority the exclusive preserve of the "white" population in West Africa, which forever precluded the possibility of self-governance for the African subjects.

Since all legal means of struggle were closed off to the colonized populations, underground organizations were formed and led by the French-educated elite.[87] Many of them were reincarnations of *évolué* political associations that had been proscribed by Vichy. Those movements included Guèye's Socialist Federation of Senegal and the LDRN, once headed by Kouyaté.[88]

Thus, when Boisson abandoned Vichy on 7 December 1942, a month after the Allied landings in North Africa,[89] and sided with a provisional government headed by Admiral Jean Louis Darlan, Pétain's former naval commander, the Resistance came in possession of a territory that had spawned its own autonomous underground movements. Those organizations had agendas and aspirations that did not always accord with the objectives of the government based in Algiers and created a volatile climate as the struggle for authority in the federation took the form of armed demonstrations and confrontations in the streets between supporters of contending factions. Unlike Eboué's decision to side with de Gaulle in 1940, Boisson's change of loyalty was an attempt to retain control over West Africa and to perpetuate Vichy politics under a new guise. Therefore, Boisson entered into negotiations with the United States and other forces to preserve his base at Dakar and secure a post in the new government to be assembled in Algiers. Even after Darlan was assassinated in late December 1942, Boisson supported General Henri Giraud, another late convert to resistance, in the dispute with de Gaulle over leadership of France.[90]

The Resistance forces led by the French-educated elite in AOF demanded that Boisson and the entire colonial administration in the federation be purged. In June 1943 the subterranean tensions became public as protests against Boisson erupted throughout West Africa. On 18 June 1943, the third anniversary of de Gaulle's broadcast from London, several thousand supporters of the Resistance marched in Dakar to demand that the imperial hierarchy be cleansed of collaborators. The government general met the assembly with force and disturbances continued for several days before Boisson was reassigned. Despite the departure of Boisson, though, the Gaullists still had not integrated the "indigenous" movements with the official Resistance organizations. Moreover, official reports suggested, "the leaders of the political groups" involved in the protests "were not masters of their troops."[91] After decades of repression and economic privation, the populace of West Africa utilized a period of administrative confusion to aggressively press their demands, however vaguely formulated. Not even long-time radicals like Guèye, regarded by the Gaullists as the foremost personality among the *évolués* and "the great hope" for future generations in the federation, could keep pace with the mobilization of the population by 1943.[92]

In that fluid situation, the provisional government had to act quickly to preserve some measure of authority in West Africa. To demonstrate their commitment to reform, the Gaullists rescinded Vichy's repressive measures, restored the local councils (with expanded authority), promised some measure of autonomy for the colonies, and assured the colonized populations that they would have significant representation in a Constituent Assembly convened to draft a new constitution for France.[93] In addition, the status of *notable évolué* was extended throughout the colonial empire as Pleven forced recalcitrant imperial officials to introduce the new rank in their territories with its attendant rights.[94]

Yet, these changes did not assuage the agitation in AOF. Rather, the seemingly contradictory demands for French citizenship and full autonomy for the colonies grew apace. By 1944 pressure from the colonized populations had forced de Gaulle to pronounce the demise of the colonial empire and the birth of a "French Community" wherein each constituent part was to be "interdependent."[95] However, the exact form that "Community" was to take remained an open question, one that further fueled the struggle for authority in West Africa as it entered its decisive stage. As the Allied victory approached in 1944 and the work of liberation neared its end, the task of reconstruction had hardly begun. While many acknowledged, "France had been liberated by its Empire,"[96] others wondered whether the metropole had not actually been conquered by its colonies.[97] Moreover, as Moutet remarked, "the Vichy regime had contributed to the destruction of [France's] moral prestige before the eyes of the indigenous population and ha[d] ruined [the metropole's] authority."[98] While de Gaulle entered Paris on 25 August 1944 at the head of Free French forces comprised primarily of recruits from Africa, the *évolués* extended their political networks throughout AOF and assumed control of what remained of the administrative structures in the federation. Therefore, when discussions began on the composition of the new Constituent Assembly the modern *griots* were able to press their agendas from positions of strength and held the keys to future Franco-African relations.

From Empire to Union:
Citizenship, National Identity, and the Fourth Republic

While it was apparent from the moment Eboué declared for de Gaulle that the fight against Vichy France and Nazi Germany would also entail a profound transformation in the regimes of power operable within the colonial field, discussion on the nature of those changes did not commence in earnest until 1943. Once the Allies had driven the Axis from North Africa and Boisson had deserted Pétain in AOF, victory no longer seemed distant for the Gaullists. The realization that the war had entered the endgame impelled the diverse forces of the Resistance to confront the issue of governance in a context where the former dominant groups were in disarray and previously marginalized elements had stepped into the vacuum. Thus, any solution to the question of authority in France and West Africa had to be arrived at through compromise and negotiation since no one group could command the situation. Within that framework, new alliances were formed and older relationships were ruptured in a struggle that centered on the very definition of "France" as a state and an identity. Furthermore, de Gaulle's early appeal to the empire to rescue the metropole from German occupation situated the "colonial question" at the vital core of deliberations on the nature of what it meant to be "French."

For the Gaullists, independence for the colonies was out of the question, a point confirmed in unambiguous terms at the conclusion of the 1944 Colonial Conference in Brazzaville, French Equatorial Africa.[99] In large measure, de Gaulle's actions during the war were driven by an intense desire to preserve the empire for France from all potential claimants—especially Germany, Italy, the United Kingdom, and the United States. Therefore, to lose the empire at the moment of liberation was "inadmissible."[100] However, the old relationship of metropole and colony was clearly out-dated and would not be accepted by the colonized populations who had rallied to the banner of Free France during the war. In fact, even the suggestion that West Africa would remain a colonial possession, a possibility evinced by the decisions taken at the Brazzaville Conference, elicited the ire of many among the *évolués*. Léopold Senghor, in a poem written only months after the liberation of Paris, implored, "Yet, Lord, forgive France, who hates occupying forces/And yet imposes such strict occupation on me...Oh, Lord, take from my memory France that is not France."[101] The language deployed by the modern *griot* indicated that he recognized the struggle for authority in West Africa had become, through the course of the Second World War, imbricated with the articulation of French identity. In addition, Léopold Senghor's rhetoric disclosed a resolve on the part of the French-educated elite and their allies in AOF to resist attempts to restore an imagined pre-war order, similar to what had occurred after the 1918 armistice.

Ultimately, the discourse practiced by the Gaullists during the fight against Nazi Germany and Pétain's regime circumscribed the possibilities for action in the colonial field once liberation had been achieved. In the clash over the "true" France between Vichy and the Resistance, the general's supporters articulated a vision of French identity that was the antithesis of that embodied in the National Revolution. Accordingly, Free France sought "to create a renovated France, more solid, greater and more fraternal" than before the war. Re-constructed France repudiated all forms of "racial discrimination," which "more than any other point distinguished [the Resistance's] ideas from those of Hitlerism and which justifie[d]...the sacrifices and the efforts demanded of the French Africans in order to contribute to the [final] victory."[102] Furthermore, since Vichy defended hierarchy and the rule of a "natural" elite that approximated a hereditary aristocracy, the Gaullists defended "Republican tradition" and "equality" where social distinctions were based solely on "merit," a notion of the veritable France that also informed the writings of Léopold Senghor and other prominent *évolués*.[103] Consequently, the official Resistance promoted a vision of the post-war order wherein the colonial empire was transformed into a "federation," "community," or some type of "union."[104] In order to develop the structural bases of the new relationship between the metropole and its colonies that reflected the changes induced by the war against fascism, the Gaullists called a conference of governors and governors general that met in Brazzaville between 30 January and 8 February 1944. The nature and importance of the Brazzaville Conference has received much comment, but little analysis in the scholarship of French colonialism. Some scholars, such as Coquery-Vidrovitch, dismiss Brazzaville as inconsequential to the history of decolonization while others, like Raymond-Marin Lemesle, argue that it charted the ideological trajectory of the end of French rule in Africa. In addition, the scholarly debate on the conference has frequently centered on whether or not it was at base "assimilationist" in intent, as Johnson suggests, or marked a definitive rejection of "assimilation" in French colonial policy, which is William Cohen's fundamental assertion.[105] I suggest that we situate the Brazzaville conference as one of a succession of "moments" in French colonial history that allows scholars to glimpse the conceptual framework within which decisions about governmental praxis were made. Furthermore, Brazzaville, like Moutet's conference in 1936, affords researchers the opportunity to identify the constellation of forces that were engaged in the process of delimiting the parameters of the field and the range of possibilities operable within that framework. Brazzaville was marked not just by whom was at the table, but also by the presence of those left out and in relation to whom choices were being made. Finally, the debate as to whether or not the conference represented the reassertion of assimilationist politics among French policymakers inadequately poses the questions for discussion about the place of Brazzaville in the history of colonial rule in Africa. Moreover, it locates the assimilation vs. association dispute at the core of strategies of imperial domination, which masks the complexity of the struggle for authority in West Africa and France. Rather, I suggest we examine the conceptual framework of the colonial field as an intricate matrix of conflicted and conflated positions that informed the choices made by historical agents enmeshed in objective relationships that were perpetually transformed in the process of their struggles within that context.

For all the pronouncements about "unity" and "France one and indivisible" made in connection with the convocation in AEF,[106] however, Cohen notes that Brazzaville "was more remarkable for its basic conservatism and its advocacy of the continuation of traditional policies."[107] In fact, the delegates assembled in the capital of Equatorial Africa, all of them colonial administrators, practiced the same hegemonic discourse that had informed imperial praxis between the two world wars. Accordingly, the final report on "native policy" for AOF concluded, "that the traditional authority of the Chief is or must be beyond discussion." The report called for a "serious investigation...of indigenous institutions...on the part of competent persons," which meant ethnographers. Officials from Dakar even repeated claims about the *évolués* that were characteristic of the post-1918 era. The French-educated elite was variously described in the document as "isolated, uprooted from their milieu" and "without hope of returning" to it.[108]

However, the circumstances of 1944 were vastly different than those of 1919. Unlike the previous period, Brazzaville attempted to find "a place" for the *évolués* in the new order. In 1944 the government general for AOF presented the French-educated elite as a "vanguard clearly situated above the masses by [virtue of] their knowledge, their intelligence, the influence they exercise and their potential for evolution.... [Therefore,] our attention is naturally fixed upon them." According to Dakar, "The question posed today is whether [or not] it is useful to go further down this path by conferring a special status, intermediate between that of 'subject' and 'French citizen,' and which could be called 'African citizenship' or 'local citizenship.'"[109] The solution reached at Brazzaville was to make the status of *notables évolués* a permanent feature of the colonial field, provide "greater autonomy to the colonies than in the past," and to increase the representation of the overseas territories in the new National Assembly in Paris. Administratively, however, the conference noted, "the traditional political institutions must be maintained, not as an end in itself, but in such a manner as to permit municipal and regional activity to function with maximum vigor. [T]hose institutions," the Gaullists asserted, "must be controlled and watched by the [colonial] administration."[110]

Brazzaville, then, marked a subtle reformulation of France's *mission civilisatrice* that attempted to preserve French authority in Africa, contain and utilize the prestige and influence of the *évolués* within the colonial field, curtail the aspiration to citizenship among the *sujet* population, and protect "autochthonous traditions" and "authentic" African culture. As one official from AOF noted, the result was "extreme confusion" throughout the empire. In West Africa, the proliferation of categories beyond the binary world of citizens and subjects meant that by 1944 there were at least four or five recognized special statuses in the federation. In addition to "French citizens" and "colonial subjects," there existed "native French citizens" naturalized on an individual basis in AOF, "French subjects [with] a privileged status" (the *notables évolués*), and the "traditional rulers" whose rank remained ambiguous, but were nonetheless a clearly identified social group with specific rights and responsibilities.[111] In the end, Brazzaville revealed that despite the universal recognition of Africa's contribution to the liberation of France, the metropolitan authorities were still not prepared to welcome the colonized subjects into the national patrimony. At best, the French-educated elite among indigenous peoples of West Africa could be regarded as "citizens of the empire" capable of further development toward a standard of "civilization" perpetually re-defined out of reach for non-Europeans. The rhetoric and actions of Brazzaville belied claims of a "Greater France" that had "110 million inhabitants."[112]

However, in some ways the 1944 conference was an important departure from earlier conceptual frameworks that informed imperial praxis. In fact, the notion of France's mission advanced by the Gaullists revived many of the aspects associated with Moutet's short-lived policy of "republican colonialism" during the Popular Front era. At Brazzaville, the report presented on behalf of the government general for AOF described "authentic" African society as fundamentally democratic. "Since the beginning of time," the document affirmed, "councils have existed in native society, [that] assisted the temporal chief; not elected but [which nevertheless] constituted a veritable representative assembly of notables." France's role was to prevent those native institutions from "atrophying in an increasingly bastardized form," as was allowed to happen under previous administrations in Dakar.[113]

This position accorded with the conception of "true" African culture articulated by Léopold Senghor and his associates in the *Négritude* movement during the 1930s and to which the Senegalese poet continued to adhere throughout the Second World War.[114] What had changed is that by the end of the World War II the *évolués* functioned as autonomous agents within the colonial field whose decisions profoundly affected the future of Franco-African relations. Thus, the organized movements of the French-educated elite, whose membership had swelled during the fight against Hitler fascism, virtually ignored the resolutions that came out of Brazzaville. Instead, they pressed demands for complete autonomy within a French Union and full citizenship status, identical to that enjoyed by metropolitans. For Guèye, Léopold Senghor, and other modern *griots* from West Africa, the struggle to liberate France had metamorphosed into a battle over the definition of "Frenchness" and access to that elusive identity for the colonized peoples. Representation in the new Constituent Assembly that was to be convened in 1945 and the deliberations on the constitution of the Fourth Republic became central arenas for that contest.

In April 1944 the provisional government based in Algiers issued guidelines for the election of members to a Constituent Assembly that for the first time granted the suffrage to women as well as the colonial populations, two groups that had been perpetually excluded from formal decision-making processes in France. Despite their overwhelming numerical strength, though, the colonial populations had far fewer representatives than their metropolitan counterparts. With a population of over 14 million, French West Africa was permitted to send only six delegates to Paris from five loosely delineated geographic regions, with the area "Senegal-Mauritania" granted two—one for "French citizens" mostly resident in the cities and the other for "French subjects" from rural West Africa. Votes were cast for party lists, which furnished an immense advantage to the organizations founded and led by the *évolués* since they were the most extensively developed and possessed the resources to mount successful campaigns on short notice.

The magnitude of the election that took place on 21 October 1945 for the Constituent Assembly cannot be exaggerated with regard to West Africa. For the first time under French rule the indigenous masses were asked to participate in a process where they chose their own representatives to an assembly convened in Paris to determine the future not only of the federation, but also France itself. The results confirmed what had become increasingly apparent toward the end of the war, that the modern *griots* were accepted, at least within the range of possibilities presented in 1945, as the legitimate spokespeople of the West African population. The six elected from AOF were; Sourou Apithy (Dahomey), Fily Dabo Sissoko (Soudan-Niger), Guèye (Senegal-Mauritania, citizens), Félix Houphouët-Boigny (Côte d'Ivoire), Léopold Senghor (Senegal-Mauritania, subjects), and Yacine Diallo (Guinea). All were associated with left-wing parties based in the metropole, but also directed local associations that functioned independently in the federation. Moreover, an analysis of the representatives from French Equatorial Africa, the Caribbean, and Madagascar reveals the strength of those among the *évolués* that had been active in France between the two world wars and who shared a perception of "authentic" African culture akin to Léopold Senghor's. Among the others chosen for the Constituent Assembly were Césaire (Martinique), Gaston Monnerville (Guyana), Ravoahangy (Madagascar), and Gabriel d'Arboussier (Gabon), who were all associates of the Senegalese poet and important figures in the cultural movements among the modern *griots* in France during the 1930s.[115]

Despite their limited numbers, the delegates from West Africa played a prominent role in the deliberations of the Assembly. That influence emanated from their participation on the Commission des territoires d'outre-mer at first presided over by Moutet. Comprised of Césaire, Gaston Defferre, Guèye, Monnerville, and Léopold Senghor,[116] in addition to Moutet, the commission was charged with the formulation of those elements of the constitution that concerned future relations between France and the former colonies, now called overseas territories or Overseas France. When Moutet was named minister of Overseas France, formerly the ministry of colonies, on 15 February 1946, Guèye was chosen as his successor at the head of the Commission of Overseas Territories. Thus, one of the most important committees of the Constituent Assembly was directed by a long-time activist in radical *évolué* politics and composed almost entirely of his supporters. Consequently, the Commission served as a powerful base from which the modern *griots* articulated their conception of French identity and asserted their prerogatives to authority in West Africa.

The debates within the commission and the Assembly focused on the relationship between France and the overseas territories and the status of the colonized populations in that framework. There was general agreement that a "French Union" was to be formed. However, the delegates divided over the nature of that association. Some, like Léopold Senghor, argued that "the colonies, other than those in the Antilles, [did] not demand assimilation" to France.[117] Rather, they insisted on extensive local autonomy and "free association" with France in a community of equal constituent parts. Others, led by Guèye, demanded full French citizenship without distinction between those from overseas and those from Europe. Guèye and his associates agitated for expanded representation of the former colonies in a single parliament for the entire French Union, or, failing that, a significant presence in a French Assembly and preponderant influence in a Chamber for the broader community.[118]

Thus, the deliberations over the nature of the Fourth Republic highlighted and sharpened divisions among the *évolués* at the precise moment when they were in a position to profoundly affect the structural bases of the new system of governance being articulated in France and West Africa. Moreover, the disagreements among the modern *griots* in 1946 confirmed that the limits of the possible within the colonial field had become circumscribed to two broad prospects—either assimilation or local autonomy. No other propositions on the relationship between France and its overseas possessions were entertained during the debates on the constitution. French authority had been gravely weakened in West Africa during the Second World War and could not be effectively reasserted after the liberation without the devolution of a large measure of the ability to command to the local population or its representatives. However, the notion of complete independence for the former colonies was also noticeably absent from the disputations on the constitution. The issue under consideration was what kind of relationship to have with France, not whether there should even be any connections in the post-liberation era.

The resignation of the Gaullists and the preponderant influence of the political left, especially that of the Communists and Socialists, in the Constituent Assembly favored Guèye's push for assimilation over arguments for local autonomy. Furthermore, "regionalism," which autonomy seemed to suggest, was too closely associated with the discredited and recently defeated Vichy regime and its program of the National Revolution. Therefore, the draft of the constitution presented to the public in a referendum on 5 May 1946 declared that "all the residents of the Union are free, equal and united; all, as a result, are citizens." Furthermore, the document proclaimed, "The citizens of all parts of the Union will be represented in a National Assembly." With regard to the Overseas Territories specifically, the constitution pronounced that "the administration of the [former colonies] will be clearly decentralized and the diverse territories will have their own governments with local liberties." Structurally, the Union was to have three tiers of government: the National Assembly, a High Council for the French Union, and local administrative bodies. Governors in the former colonies were to be replaced by "resident ministers" chosen at the Union level, and overseas residents were to have one delegate to the National Assembly for each 800,000 inhabitants, which would nearly triple the representation West Africa had at the Constituent Assembly.[119]

In the referendum only French citizens were permitted to cast ballots. Therefore, nearly 60 million people that might have witnessed their status suddenly improve within the colonial field were excluded from the process. Moreover, the political winds within France had also shifted. De Gaulle, in self-imposed political exile, urged a "no" vote because he objected to the unicameral structure of government embodied in the constitution and the preference given to political parties through the proportional representation system established for voting. In addition, the Gaullists and others on the political right warned against the dangers of "France" being overwhelmed by its former colonies in a framework that accorded citizenship to over 60 million residents overseas when there were only 42 million citizens of France at the time. Such a circumstance "confused the institutions of Metropolitan France and those of the French Union" and compromised particularist notions of "French nationality," or identity. Thus, any prospect that France's authority could be preserved in West Africa was, some argued, precluded in the draft of the constitution. Those anxieties, in the context of increased tensions between the Soviet Union and the United States in Europe, included assertions that the colonized populations would elect "Communists" to the National Assembly and the Communist Party would use support in the overseas territories to engineer a political takeover in the metropole.[120]

Although the vote was close, the constitution was defeated. In West Africa turnout was heavy among the few who were eligible to participate. In Senegal, which had the overwhelming majority of French citizens in the federation, 28,718 voted "*oui*" while only 2,522 chose "*non*." In the Caribbean, another area with a large population of *évolués* that had citizenship, the tallies were similar. Martinique decided yes by a margin of 23,166 to 4,720 and Guadeloupe did likewise by a count of 19,287 to 2,283.[121]

The setback, however, did not discourage Guèye and his supporters. Instead, only days after the referendum and weeks before elections to the Second Constituent Assembly, Guèye by-passed constitutional deliberations and won passage of a series of laws that radicalized the tensions within the colonial field and forced a final decision on the possibility for assimilation within the imperial framework. On 7 May 1946 the lame-duck Constituent Assembly passed a law sponsored by Guèye that "abolish[ed] all the remaining barriers between men that we wish to proclaim equal." The text of the act declared, "From the 1st of June 1946, all the residents of the overseas territories (Algeria included) have the status of citizen, of the same style as French nationals from the metropole or the overseas territories. Particular laws will establish the conditions in which they will exercise their rights as citizens."[122] In one stroke the binary division of citizens and subjects was swept aside. In addition, the timing of the resolution meant that in the elections to the next Constituent Assembly all residents of the Union were permitted to vote as equal citizens, under the same rules of representation operable within the metropole. Thus, the "Lamine Guèye Law," as it was called, attempted to implement the most fundamental aspects of the first draft of the constitution without further negotiations in the new assembly.

However, colonial administrators and their political allies within France reacted swiftly and with deep hostility to the new measure. A message from Saigon, capital of Indochina, expressed grave concern "over the repercussions" associated with "the result of the vote on the [Lamine Guèye Law] of 7 May 1946." Even Moutet equivocated in his support of the law. The Socialist minister for Overseas France claimed that the law "did not expressly state that the new citizens [were] French citizens." The act only proclaimed that "they [were] citizens of the same style as a French citizen, that is to say that they are permitted to enjoy the same liberties and to exercise the same rights as a French citizen." Moutet was confident that "the future Constitution [would] grant to the populations of the Overseas Territories the rights of French citizens...without conferring *French citizenship* [on them]." He noted that the most important aspect of the law was that it "assert[ed]...the great principle of equality: it turned French subjects into citizens, but it did not say that those citizens are French citizens."[123] While imperial officials and metropolitan politicians were prepared to regard the colonized populations as "equals" with natives of France, they were not willing to accept them as "French." Even a law designed to break down "all the barriers" that separated colonizer from colonized was not enough to overcome the notion that, however vaguely formulated, Africans and Europeans were essentially and immutably different.

The attack on Guèye's measure reinvigorated the confrontation between the modern *griots* and overseas administrators. Once again, claims were made that the *évolués* only "[gave] the impression that they have been freed of their original constraints," i.e., autochthonous traditions and "mysterious impulsions" carried with them since "the beginning of the world." Seemingly discredited conceptions of "authentic" African culture were revived in an effort to discredit the French-educated elite from West Africa. Chiefs, compromised by their support of Vichy during the war against Nazi Germany, were once more presented as the "guardians of tradition" and the "natural authorities" within indigenous society. Even slavery was defended as an intrinsic part of "true" native life. The *évolués* were chided for having abandoned "the lifestyle of their ancestors" in favor of "the modern world." Assertions that "all indigenous life was founded on the notion of the social group, not on individualism" were re-circulated to deny the wisdom and legitimacy of Guèye's law. Finally, imperial officials clamored for a resurrection of ethnography and a return to the work of such luminaries as Delafosse and Lévy-Bruhl to guide France in the articulation of policy for the overseas territories.[124] Even the Liberation could not free the modern *griots* from a conceptual framework that perpetuated their status as almost French, but not quite—and never can be.

If officials in the imperial hierarchy prevaricated over the exact meaning of the law and its terminology, though, the reaction among the population in West Africa was unambiguously enthusiastic. Leaders of the mass political movements in the federation petitioned Dakar for permission to hold large public celebrations on 1 June, the date the law was to take effect. The government general noted that "the application of the said law pose[d] a great number of problems" for the ability of the colonial administration to retain even a limited amount of authority in the federation.[125] Throughout 1945 and 1946 political disturbances mounted in the federation. Strikes proliferated as trade union rights were restored and the hated system of forced labor was finally abolished. In the countryside, the rural populations exerted pressure on local rulers for reform while urban organizations established bases across West Africa and elections politicized the tribal units upon which the structures of governance had been based in AOF.[126] Guèye's law, then, was promulgated in an atmosphere of intense struggle in the federation and contributed to the expectations held by the populace in that region.

However, since elections to the new Constituent Assembly were slated for 2 June immediate clarification on the Lamine Guèye Law was needed to determine who was eligible to vote and under what form of electoral system. Yet, Guèye refused comment on his measure, as did his lieutenant Léopold Senghor who declined to answer questions on whether the law meant the subjects were French citizens or citizens of the Union.[127] In the absence of an agreement on the act of 7 May 1946, established procedures were used in the selection of representatives to the new Constituent Assembly. Accordingly, all six who were selected for the First Constituent Assembly were returned for the Second. As before, the citizens of French West Africa elected Guèye and the "non-citizens" chose the others, including Léopold Senghor who was unopposed in Senegal-Mauritania.[128]

However, in France the election turned out quite differently. The *Mouvement Républicain Populaire* (MRP), the Christian Democratic party led by Georges Bidault, surpassed the Communist Party as the largest grouping in the Assembly, while the Socialists lost twenty seats. Thus, the new body was less radical than the first and met in an international climate where the superpower rivalry between the Soviet Union and the United States had begun to cast shadows across Europe. Those international tensions were also reflected inside France as the MRP forged alliances with the political right to forestall Communist influence in the draft of the constitution.

The document produced by the Assembly was more restrained than its predecessor was and the representatives from overseas were unable to play as prominent a role as they had during the earlier convocation. The new system of governance offered for public approval in the referendum of 13 October 1946 contained a bicameral legislature for the metropole, created an Assembly for the French Union in which metropolitan citizens retained a majority, and permitted the formation of local parliaments in the overseas territories.[129] However, the language of the document was much less generous than the one rejected in May. According to the new constitution, "The French Union [was] comprised, on one part, by the French Republic which encompasses metropolitan France, the overseas departments and territories, and, on the other part by territories and States associated [with France]."[130] No longer was the French Union formed by a free association of peoples. In the document eventually approved by the electorate the Union was merely formed.

Despite the loss of consent for the colonized peoples in the new order, Guèye's law was incorporated, unedited, as Article 80.[131] However, Article 80 was interpreted by Paris to mean that all residents of the French Union were citizens of the Union, not French citizens. Thus, two citzenships existed in the colonial field at the birth of the Fourth Republic—one for the "French" and another, lesser type, for the "others" of the new confederation.[132] Consequently, in the elections to the National Assembly on 10 November 1946 the West Africans were classified into two electoral colleges as they had been for selection of representatives to the Constituent Assemblies—one for French citizens and the other for citizens of the Union. In that election both Guèye and Léopold Senghor easily won seats as members of the SFIO. While the federation's representation to the Assembly was expanded from the single deputy allotted during the Third Republic, it remained proportionally disadvantaged when compared to the population of the metropole.

Conclusion

The new constitution, far from assuaging the discontent in West Africa, elicited vituperative responses from the modern *griots*. One *évolué* publication exclaimed, "No, Not this! ... The Project of the constitutional commission concerning the French Union is a monster." The constitution was berated for having betrayed the "republican tradition" and having abrogated "the rights of man."[133] The vision of the "true" France articulated during the Resistance had been abandoned and replaced with something that more approximated that offered by the reviled Third Republic.

Yet, as Delavignette noted a year after the second referendum, the colonial field had undergone a dramatic transformation in the preceding decade. "From 1936 to 1946," the colonial administrator noted, "under the double influence of the evolution in the ideas of the French governments on the subject of the colonial question, and of political and social changes in the overseas territories...significant reforms have profoundly modified the situation" in the former colonies. In fact, the language of colonizer and colonized itself had been discarded in favor of one with more egalitarian pretensions. Trade unions were permitted in West Africa and enjoyed the same rights as those in Europe. The despised *indigénat*, symbol of imperial repression, was eliminated. Forced labor, nearly two decades after the International Labor Organization ordered its suppression, was done away with. "Native justice," the source of authority exercised by the pre-colonial elite, was abandoned and French law was extended throughout West Africa in penal matters. Finally, the subjects had become citizens, albeit still not admitted to the French national patrimony.[134]

While much in the way of political and social rights had been won during the Second World War by the peoples of West Africa, the possibilities for action within the colonial field had become even more tightly circumscribed. In fact, an unintended effect of Guèye's 1946 law was that the option of becoming "French" was decisively closed off for the indigenous peoples of AOF. "Citizens of the French Union" marked the limit of what the imperial power would tolerate within a system of governance predicated upon the preservation of France's paramount status *vis–à–vis* the "diverse peoples of the overseas territories."[135]

Closed off from the prospect of full integration with the metropolitan power, the struggle for authority within West Africa shifted to a contest for dominance within the federation. Moreover, the structural changes embodied in the constitution of the Fourth Republic furnished the context for a re-centering of political engagement among the *évolués* from Paris to AOF. The establishment of territorial assemblies and the accreditation of citizenship rights to the autochthonous population meant that appeals to and support among the "local" residents counted for more than alliances with metropolitan political movements and the benevolence of French government officials. Accordingly, by 1946 France was engaged in a rearguard action to protect what little authority it retained after Vichy and the Liberation. The colonial state in West Africa was plagued by what Jean-François Bayart calls a "hegemonic crisis" where the prevailing discourse of cultural authenticity retained its efficacy, but the forces that had exercised hegemony between the two world wars had lost their ability to command in the situation.[136] In their stead the French-educated elite had emerged as the dominant social group within the federation and effectively commanded millions of supporters through mass political parties that continued to develop during the 1940s and 1950s.

Ironically, Guèye created the basis for his future political demise through the introduction of the 7 May 1946 law. The subsequent interpretation of that act, incorporated within the constitution of the Fourth Republic, limited Guèye's support base in West Africa to the narrow, and strictly bounded, community of French citizens and simultaneously placed the preponderance of influence in the federation in the hands of the rural population who were citizens of the Union. Thus, Guèye's lieutenant, Léopold Senghor, found himself in a stronger political position, with a boundless electoral base, than his mentor. Furthermore, as the debates within the Constituent Assemblies indicated, Léopold Senghor and Guèye embraced divergent notions of "authentic" African culture and Franco-African relations. The ultimate form of the French Union embodied in the constitution of the Fourth Republic actually sanctioned the Senegalese poet's perspective at the expense of Guèye's assimilationist position. Consequently, the stage was set for a shift in the struggle for authority in West Africa from a contest between colonized populations and the imperial power to a fight among divergent factions among the *évolués* themselves. Our narrative now turns to that dispute as it unfolded in the decade after the Fourth Republic was founded.

NOTES

1. CAOM, 1/AP/2147, Governor Henri Laurentie, "Le noeud du Problème Colonial: Les Évolués," in *Mensuel de Documentation*, February–March 1946.
2. Mamdani, *Citizen and Subject*, p. 61.
3. Bourdieu and Wacquant, *An Invitation to Reflexive Sociology*, p. 100.
4. CAOM, 1/AP/873, Decree 378, "Décret fixant les règles d'institution d'organisation et d'administration des communes indigènes en Afrique Equatoriale Française," signed by General Charles de Gaulle, 31 July 1942. That administrative order was later extended to all of Africa by a decision taken at the Colonial Conference convened in Brazzaville, 30 January–8 February 1944.
5. CAOM, 1/AP/214, Jean Gregoire, "Réformes de Structure; La Fédération Française," correspondence to the provisional government headed by General Charles de Gaulle, August 1944. A similar sentiment was expressed earlier by Pierre-Olivier Lapie, reporter general of the Overseas Commission to the consultative assembly, in an article titled, "Une Federation?" published in *La Marseillaise*, 25 December 1943, contained in the same carton.
6. CAOM, 1/AP/859, report of 15 April 1930 on the inaugural address of André Tardieu as prime minister delivered on 4 March 1929.
7. CAOM, 1/AP/1638, letter from Sarraut, minister of colonies, to the office of the prime minister, 19 June 1923.
8. Bhabha, *The Location of Culture*, p. 89.
9. CAOM, CG/48, "Renseignement de la population au 1er juillet 1936." According to this report prepared for the new Popular Front government, only 80,509 residents of AOF were recognized as "indigenous citizens," 17,148 were categorized as metropolitan natives, and another 14,580,655 were described as "indigenous subjects." Those numbers did not greatly change before the Second World War. In fact, the Popular Front reported that of the 21 people who petitioned for naturalization in 1935 only 6 were granted citizenship. In 1936 the government general in Dakar reported 22 requests for naturalization with only 1 accorded by the end of the year, 2 rejected outright, and another 19 tabled for future consideration. Report of the government general for AOF to the ministry of colonies, year ending 1936, in the same carton.
10. Wilder, "The Politics of Failure: Historicising Popular Front Colonial Policy in French West Africa," in Chafer and Sackur, eds., *French Colonial Empire and the Popular Front*, p. 51.
11. CAOM, 28/PA/1, Marius Moutet, "Politique Républicaine Coloniale," 1936.
12. CAOM, CG/107, letter from the *Rassemblement Colonial* to the Guernut Commission, "Suggestions du groupe de l'Afrique noire du Rassemblement Colonial," 27 April 1938.
13. CAOM, 3/SLOTFOM/97, see the note from Admiral Platon, secretary of state for colonial affairs, to the secretariat of state for the interior, "Objet: Application des lois des 17 juillet et 14 août 1940," 30 January 1941. That carton also contains many of the laws that were applied to the colonies as Vichy set out to implement its strategy of governance in the overseas territories.
14. CAOM, 1/AP/873. Eboué issued an *arrêté* in 1941 that created the status of *notables évolués* in French Equatorial Africa and de Gaulle issued "Décret 377" on 29 July

1942 that made the rank applicable to all of the colonies. That order was confirmed at the Colonial Conference held in Brazzaville from 30 January to 8 February 1944. See: CAOM, 1/AP/2288, for details on the Brazzaville Conference discussions on the "statut de notables évolués."

15. CAOM, 1/AP/873, correspondence from René Pleven to François de Menthon, 8 December 1943.

16. CAOM, 1/AP/873, "Projet de Décret fixant le Statut des indigènes évolués," presented by the Legislative Commission of the government general for AEF, 11 April 1942.

17. CAOM, 1/AP/3655, "Proposition de loi tendant à proclamer citoyens tous les ressortissants de la Métropole et des territoires d'outre-mer," passed by the Constituent Assembly on 7 May 1946 and put into effect on 1 June 1946.

18. CAOM, 1/AP/1638, proposition to institute a category of "*indigènes d'élite*" in the colonies, presented by Bernard Lavergne, member of the Conseil Superieur des Colonies, 15 June 1927.

19. CAOM, 1/AP/1638, Bernard Lavergne recorded in the "Procès-verbal de la séance du 13 juin 1928 [du] conseil de legislation coloniale," a division of the Conseil Superieur des Colonies.

20. CAOM, 1/AP/1638, Lavergne, "Procès-verbal de la séance du 13 juin 1928 [du] conseil de legislation coloniale."

21. Bhabha, *The Location of Culture*, p. 86.

22. CAOM, 1/AP/1638, letter from Sarraut to the office of the prime minister, 19 June 1923.

23. [23] CAOM, 1/AP/859, André Tardieu, inaugural address as prime minister, given on 4 March 1929 and recorded in a note contained in the files of the ministry of colonies dated 15 April 1930.

24. Lebovics, *True France*.

25. CAOM, 1/AP/1638, Albert de Pouvourville, "La Naturalisation des indigènes," in *Depêche Colonial*, 23 December 1924.

26. CAOM, 1/AP/1638, "Observations du Gouverneur Général – Naturalisations des indigènes," produced by the government general for AOF, 20 June 1923.

27. CAOM, 1/AP/1638, letter from Sarraut to the government general for Indochina, 15 June 1921; letter from Sarraut to the office of the prime minister, 19 June 1923. According to the ministry of colonies, only an average of 26 naturalizations a year occurred in the early 1920s out of the thousands eligible from service during the Great War and the hundreds of applications submitted each year.

28. Lebovics, *True France*.

29. CAOM, 7/AE/46, "Projet de loi relatif à la création d'un Office National de l'Immigration," 3 November 1921; see also, in the same carton, "Projet du loi portant création d'un Office National de l'Immigration," 12 October 1922; and "Décret instituant une commission permanente de l'immigration," in *Feuille d'Informations du Ministère de l'Agriculture*, 10 August 1920, contained in the same carton.

30. One of the best studies to date on the history of immigration and migrant communities in France is: Noiriel, *Le Creuset français*. Despite the frequent discussions about the formation of a National Immigration Office during the 1920s, it was not brought into existence until 2 November 1945, after the Second World War.

Marianne Amar et Pierre Milza, *L'Immigration en France au XXe siècle* (Paris: Armand Colin, 1990), p. 226. See also: Silverman, *Deconstructing the Nation*.

31. CAOM, 1/AP/1638, "Projet de Loi sur l'accession des indigènes des colonies et des pays protectorat, relevant du Ministère des Colonies, à la qualité de citoyen français," 24 November 1924.

32. CAOM, 1/AP/1638, "Projet de Loi sur l'accession des indigènes des colonies et des pays protectorat, relevant du Ministère des Colonies, à la qualité de citoyen français," 24 November 1924. See also: CAOM, 1/AP/2759, "Revue de la Presse," in *La Dépêche Coloniale*, 25 March 1925, in which the paper debates the merits and inadequacies of Daladier's proposal. Ultimately, the journal objected to the proposal and urged its defeat in the Chamber.

33. CAOM, 3/SLOTFOM/101, advance agenda of the "Congrès des peuples coloniaux de 1925," endorsed on 30 November 1924 by the *Union Intercoloniale* and the French Communist Party. The CAI agent noted that René Maran and the circle associated with *Les Continents* also supported the platform.

34. CAOM, 5/SLOTFOM/2, "Le Problème de la Naturalisation," in *La Dépêche Africaine*, April 1928.

35. CAOM, 1/AP/2759, letter from the École Coloniale to the ministry of colonies; and CAOM, 1/AP/2759.

36. CAOM, 1/AP/1638, unsigned letter from a deputy from India to Daladier, 17 February 1925.

37. CAOM, 1/AP/1638, Mario Roustan, "L'accession à la qualité de citoyen français," in *Annales Coloniales*, 17 September 1925.

38. CAOM, 1/AP/170, letter from the government general for AOF to the ministry of colonies, "Situation politique de la colonie," 20 December 1917.

39. CAOM, 1/AP/2147, Pierre Herbot, "Le problème des indigènes 'détribalisés,'" in *Bulletin du Comité de l'Afrique Française*, December 1937.

40. CAOM, 1/AP/1638, "Procès-verbal de la séance du 13 juin 1928" of the Conseil de Legislation Coloniale, a division of the Conseil Superieur des Colonies.

41. CAOM, 1/AP/1638, report from the ministry of colonies to the office of the prime minister, undated, but probably written in 1928 or 1929.

42. CAOM, 1/AP/1638, "Procès-verbal de la séance du 13 juin 1928" of the Conseil de Legislation Coloniale, a division of the Conseil Superieur des Colonies.

43. CAOM, 5/SLOTFOM/2, "La Revue des Idées sur la colonisation et l'evolution de la Race Noir; Formation d'une élite indigène," in *La Dépêche Africaine*, February-March 1929; Fritz Moutia, "La Question brûlante de la naturalisation des Indigènes," in *La Dépêche Africaine*, November 1928; CAOM, 3/SLOTFOM/111, letter from Kouyaté to W.E.B. Dubois, 29 April 1929.

44. G. Wesley Johnson, "Les Élites au Sénégal pendant la période d'indépendance," in Ageron and Michel, dir., *L'Afrique Noire Française*, p. 27.

45. CAOM, CG/60, political and administrative report produced by the government general for AOF for the year 1931.

46. It was assumed that no French citizen would aspire to become non-French. Thus, proponents of the designation Native Elite stated that this was a category designed for "natives" of the overseas possessions only.

47. CAOM, 1/AP/1638, unsigned letter from the government general for French West Africa to the ministry of colonies, 8 October 1930.

48. CAOM, 1/AP/859, letter from André Maginot, minister of colonies, "Administration Indigène," to the governors general of AOF, AEF, Togo, and Cameroon, 9 October 1929. Maginot based his opposition to the new status on the assertion that the structures of "traditional society" were "too fragile" to absorb such a change.

49. CAOM, 1/AP/1638, note on the responses of the governors general of the colonies, 8 July 1929.

50. CAOM, 28/PA/1, letter from Marius Moutet, minister of colonies, to the government general for AEF, "Conférence des Gouverneurs généraux," 12 August 1936.

51. CAOM, 5/SLOTFOM/2, Maurice Satineau, "Notre but.—Notre Programme," in *La Dépêche Africaine*, February 1928; and CAOM, 5/SLOTFOM/21, Aimé Césaire, "Nègreries: Jeunesse Noire et Assimilation," in *L'Étudiant Noir*, March 1935.

52. Léopold Senghor, "Liminary Poem," in Léopold Senghor, *The Collected Poetry*, p. 39, written in Paris, April 1940.

53. Hargreaves, *Decolonization in Africa*, p. 49.

54. Accurate figures on the numbers of people resident in France during the war that were originally from the colonies are not available. However, a document produced by the Vichy government reported that as late as 1942 there were still some 70,000 soldiers from the colonies in German POW camps. Furthermore, at the end of 1943 Pétain's government reported about 1,000 applications for family assistance from "indigènes" in France. CAOM, 1/AP/639, "Procès-Verbal No. 41," early 1942, on the situation of colonial POWs; CAOM, 3/SLOTFOM/50, internal Vichy correspondence, "Obtention de bons d'achats pour familles indigènes," 29 December 1943.

55. CAOM, 3/SLOTFOM/97, "Objet: Au sujet du retour en zone occupée des français de couleur, sang mélés et juifs," 18 August 1940.

56. CAOM, 3/SLOTFOM/97, "Les Conditions requises pour franchir la Zone de démarcation," in *Petit Parisien*, 27 August 1940. See also, in the same carton, General Charles Huntiziger, commander of the armed forces, "Note pour le ministre de la defense nationale; Objet: Rapatriement des militaires indigènes," 26 July 1940; letter from Gaston Joseph, secretary of state for colonies, to the secretariat of state for national education, 1 October 1940; and letter from Joseph to the head of the office of indigenous immigration, 28 September 1940.

57. CAOM, 3/SLOTFOM/ 97, undated and unsigned note on the evacuation of "students" and others from France to West Africa, probably written in late summer 1940. See also: Catherine Coquery-Vidrovitch, *Africa: Endurance and Change South of the Sahara* trans. David Maisel (Berkeley: University of California Press, 1988), pp. 274–275.

58. CAOM, 1/AP/639/9, correspondence from the secretariat of state for colonies, "Affaires Interessant le Haut Commissariat de l'Afrique Française," 15 September 1941. Even prior to the defeat elections to the assemblies and local councils in Senegal were suspended (decree dated 8 September 1939). On 28 September 1940 Pierre Boisson, posted as High Commissioner for Black Africa by Vichy and based in Dakar, issued an "arrêté de l'administration de la Circonscription de Dakar" in which he abolished municipal councils and replaced them with special delegations nominated by the colonial administration.

59. CAOM, 3/SLOTFOM/97, letter from Admiral Platon, secretary of state for colonies, to the secretary of state for the interior, "Objet: Application des lois des 17 juillet et 14 août 1940," 30 January 1941.

60. Hargreaves, *Decolonization in Africa*, p. 78.

61. Philippe Burrin, *France Under the Germans: Collaboration and Compromise* trans. Janet Lloyd (New York: The New Press, 1996). See especially the first section, "Reasons of State."

62. CAOM, 1/AP/639/9, telegram from AOF to the ministry of colonies, Vichy, 30 March 1941. See also the reports forwarded from West Africa to the metropole on 16 May 1941 that detailed the meetings between colonial administrators and the "chefs indigènes" contained in the same carton. While the degree to which those pledges were sincere and freely given can be questioned, earlier protestations on the part of the chiefs to Paris and Dakar, as well as statements during the Second World War of their willingness to use force to repress "the enemies of France," an action actually carried out at times, testify to their believability.

63. CAOM, 3/SLOTFOM/97, letter from Maurice Satineau, deputy from Guadeloupe and founder of *La Dépêche Africaine*, to Admiral Platon, 11 October 1940.

64. CAOM, 3/SLOTFOM/97. In 1940 the *Association d'Aide aux Etudiants Africains et Asiatique* and *Le Foyer des Etudiants Africains et Asiatiques* was founded. See also the list of members of the National Union of French Students produced by Vichy on 15 August 1941. Diop became the editor of the influential magazine *Présence Africaine* after the war, while Kane emerged as a widely respected writer in the 1950s.

65. CAOM, 3/SLOTFOM/97, letter from *Le Groupe du Souvenir de Victor Schoelcher* to the ministry of colonies, 5 September 1940. Attached to the message were several letters that attested to acts of discrimination (mostly on the railways) personally experienced.

66. To date little work has been done on the role of the *évolués* in the French Resistance. Only sketches of the Resistance activities undertaken by a few of the most prominent figures among the French-educated elite have been produced. For a discussion of Léopold Senghor's experiences during the Second World War see: Vaillant, *Black, French, and African*. The Senegalese poet's closest friend, Aimé Césaire, left France just prior to the outbreak of hostilities and spent the duration of the conflict in Martinique where he founded and edited the Resistance journal *Tropiques*.

67. Charles de Gaulle, *The Complete War Memoirs* trans. Jonathan Griffin and Richard Howard (New York: Carroll & Graf Publishers, Inc., 1998), p. 107.

68. CAOM, 3/SLOTFOM/97, letter from Platon to the secretariat of state for the interior, "Objet: Application des lois des 17 juillet et 14 août 1940," 30 January 1941; and letter from Platon to the secretariat of state for the interior, "Objet: Situation des originaires des territoires relevant du Secrétariat d'Etat aux colonies au regard des lois réglementant l'accès aux fonctions publiques," 12 March 1941.

69. CAOM, 3/SLOTFOM/97, "Objet: Cours sur l'Islam, le Monde Noir et l'Extrême Orient," 29 January 1942. See also, Vaillant, *Black, French, and African*, pp. 186–187. The promotion of local loyalties accorded with Vichy's support of "regionalism" in the metropole. See, for example: Eric T. Jennings, *Vichy in the Tropics: Pétain's National Revolution in Madagascar, Guadeloupe, and Indochina, 1940–1944* (Stanford: Stanford University Press, 2001). For a discussion of that aspect of the

National Revolution and the importance of folklorists therein, see: Lebovics, *True France*, p. 175.

70. Robert O. Paxton, *Vichy France: Old Guard and New Order, 1940–1944* (New York: Columbia University Press, 1982), pp. 145, 270, 142, and 331.

71. See the quote by Boisson where he describes the African as a "peasant in all his fibres." Found in: Cooper, *Decolonization and African Society*, p. 147.

72. Quoted in Paxton, *Vichy France*, p. 8.

73. De Gaulle, *The Complete War Memoirs*, pp. 84, 105–106.

74. CAOM, 1/AP/873, letter from René Pleven to François de Menthon, 8 December 1943.

75. CAOM, 1/AP/873, statement by *Le Groupement d'Action Patriotique et Républicaine*, a resistance organization that operated in West Africa, 3 October 1943. That association was among the first to call for a conference of governors general and representatives of all colonies in AOF and AEF, an event that took place early in 1944.

76. CAOM, 1/AP/873, "Les Realisations coloniales de la France combattante en Afrique Equatoriale Française," 1 March 1943, with a full biographical note on Eboué.

77. CAOM, 1/AP/873, "Les Realisations coloniales de la France combattante en Afrique Equatoriale Française," 1 March 1943.

78. CAOM, 1/AP/873, see the text of the address made to the people of Abidjan by the governor of Côte d'Ivoire, 26 September 1940.

79. CAOM, 1/AP/873, telegram from de Gaulle in London to Eboué in Brazzaville, 29 July 1942, in which the general notes that decree 377 on the "statut des notables évolués" has been signed.

80. CAOM, 1/AP/873, report of the legislative commission, "Projet de Décret fixant le Statut des indigènes évolués," 11 April 1942.

81. CAOM, 1/AP/873, Decree 377, signed by de Gaulle, 29 July 1942.

82. CAOM, 1/AP/2201, "Conference de Brazzaville – Afrique Occidentale Française – Politique Indigène – Rapport No. 1," February 1944.

83. CAOM, 1/AP/873, telegram from the National Liberation Committee to the government general for AEF, 3 March 1943. See, also, the letter from Brazzaville to the National Liberation Committee on the same subject, 24 February 1943, in the same carton.

84. CAOM, 1/AP/214, Pierre-Olivier Lapie, "Une Federation?" in *La Marseillaise*, 25 December 1943; Also, Pierre-Olivier Lapie, "Empire ou Fédération?" in *La Quatrième Republique*, 8 January 1944.

85. CAOM, 1/AP/873, letter from Eboué to de Gaulle, 7 September 1942.

86. CAOM, 1/AP/873, Decree 378, "Décret fixant les règles d'institution d'organisation et d'administration des communes indigènes en Afrique Equatoriale Française," 31 July 1942. See also: CAOM, 1/AP/878, letter from René Pleven to all governors general, "Objet: Inventaire des activités qui devront s'ouvrir aux indigènes," undated, probably written in 1944.

87. ARS, Rapports Annuels (2G), reports of the government general for AOF covering the years 1940, 1941, and 1943.

88. CAOM, 1/AP/872/18, report from the government general for AOF, "Expose Sommaire de la situation politique de l'Afrique Occidentale Française et du Togo pendant le mois d'Août 1944," 15 November 1944. Dossier 8 contains numerous

documents on the activities of other resistance organization in West Africa, including *Combat* and the *Croix de Lorraine*.

89.   CAOM, 1/AP/872/13, note on the decision by Boisson to abandon Vichy in favor of de Gaulle, 7 December 1942.

90.   For discussions of the convoluted negotiations among the various contenders for power in the "new" France during 1942 and 1943 that eventually ended in the triumph of de Gaulle, see: De Gaulle, *The Complete War Memoirs*; Burrin, *France Under the Germans*; and Paxton, *Vichy France*.

91.   CAOM, 1/AP/872/20, letter from Boisson to the Colonial Commission in Algiers, 25 June 1943; and, in the same dossier, a report produced for the provisional government, 21 June 1943.

92.   CAOM, 1/AP/872/18, report produced by the government general for AOF, "Expose Sommaire de la situation politique de l'Afrique Occidentale Française et du Togo pendant les mois d'Août 1944," 15 November 1944.

93.   CAOM, 1/AP/872/14, decree of 2 December 1943 that reestablished elected councils in AOF; measures on self-government by the natives in Dossier 9; CAOM, 1/AP/873, "Abrogation Decret Larminat du 21 avril 1941;" letter from Pleven that authorized the reestablishment of trade unions in West Africa and made the "Code du Travail métropolitain" applicable to the colonies; CAOM, 1/AP/878/8, "Abrogation des actes des 13 Août 1940 et subséquents relatifs aux sociétés secrètes," issued in 1943; and, the telegram from Pleven to Algiers that explains a recently-promulgated law "rétablissant légalité républicaine."

94.   CAOM, 1/AP/2288/9, see the letters from Pleven to the governors of Madagascar and Cameroon and the governor general of AOF written throughout 1944.

95.   CAOM, 1/AP/214, press conference of de Gaulle in Washington, D.C., "Quelques idées directrices pour l'action de T.A.M. en matière d'Empire," 10 July 1944.

96.   CAOM, 1/AP/214, Jean Gregoire, "Réformes de Structure; La Fédération Française," August 1944.

97.   CAOM, 1/AP/2146, René Moreux, councilor of the French Union, in *Marchés Coloniaux du Monde*, 19 May 1951.

98.   CAOM, 1/AP/2146, unsigned article, "L'Assemblee acclame la politique défini é par Marius Moutet; Emancipation politique et économique des indigènes," in *Le Populaire*, 24-25 March 1946.

99.   CAOM, 1/AP/2288/5, "Recommendations adoptées par la conference Africaine Française," 30 January 1944 – 8 February 1944.

100.   CAOM, 1/AP/2147, Paul-Émile Viard, "La Communauté Française," first written in February 1943 and republished in January 1946 during the debates on the constitution of the Fourth French Republic.

101.   Léopold Senghor, "Prayer for Peace," in *The Collected Poetry*, p. 71. The poem, written in January 1945, was dedicated to his long-time friends Georges and Claude Pompidou. Georges Pompidou would later serve as president of France from 1969 to 1974, after de Gaulle resigned for the second time in his political career.

102.   CAOM, 1/AP/2288/1, Hubert Deschamps, "Note sur la Politique Coloniale," 8 January 1944; and CAOM, 1/AP/2295/2, final report of the Brazzaville Conference given by Pleven, 8 February 1944.

103. CAOM, 1/AP/873, "Les Realisations coloniales de la France combattante en Afrique Equatoriale Française," 1 March 1943; Aimé Césaire, "Panorama," in *Tropiques*, No. 10, February 1944, p. 10.

104. CAOM, 1/AP/2201, message from the ministry of colonies to the government general for AOF, undated, but probably written in late 1944 or early 1945.

105. Catherine Coquery-Vidrovitch and Henri Moniot, *L'Afrique Noire de 1800 à nos jours* (Paris: Presses Universitaires de France, 1974), pp. 227–228; Raymond-Marin Lemesle, *La Conférence de Brazzaville de 1944: contexte et repères: Cinquantenaire des prémices de la decolonisation* (Paris: C.H.E.A.M., 1994), pp. 15, 106; G. Wesley Johnson, "The Triumph of Nationalism in French West Africa," p. 311; Cohen, *Rulers of Empire*, p. 169.

106. CAOM, 1/AP/2201/5, "Contribution à une doctrine de politique imperiale," written in early 1944.

107. Cohen, *Rulers of Empire*, p. 169.

108. CAOM, 1/AP/2201, "Conference de Brazzaville—Afrique Occidentale Française—Politique Indigène—Rapport No. 1," delivered at the conference between 30 January and 8 February 1944.

109. CAOM, 1/AP/2201, "Conference de Brazzaville—Afrique Occidentale Française—Politique Indigène—Rapport No. 1," delivered at the conference between 30 January and 8 February 1944.

110. CAOM, 1/AP/2201/5, recommendations of the Brazzaville Conference; Dossier 10 on the administrative reforms that emanated from the meeting; CAOM, 1/AP/2288, telegram from Brazzaville to Algiers, 7 February 1944; and Dossier 5, "Recommendations adoptées par la conference Africaine Française," 30 January–8 February 1944.

111. CAOM, 1/AP/2288, "Note sur le programme de la Conférence Imperiale de Brazzaville," from the government general for AOF, 21 October 1943.

112. CAOM, 1/AP/214, "La France a 110 millions d'Habitants," undated and unsigned note present in the file that contains discussions about the composition of the Constituent Assembly.

113. CAOM, 1/AP/2201, "Conference de Brazzaville—Afrique Occidentale Française—Politique Indigène—Rapport No. 1," presented at the meeting between 30 January and 8 February 1944.

114. CAOM, 1/AP/2147, Léopold Senghor, "Illusions et Réalités Africaines," in *Temps Present*, 16 August 1944.

115. CAOM, 1/AP/2146, list of deputies from overseas to the Constituent Assembly, 15 February 1946.

116. CAOM, 1/AP/2146, composition of the Commission des territoires d'outre-mer, December 1945.

117. CAOM, 1/AP/2147/1, Léopold Senghor in the *Journal Officiel*, 20 March 1946.

118. CAOM, 1/AP/2146, "La Constitution de l'Union Française," in *Bulletin Hebdomadaire*, 25 February 1946.

119. CAOM, 1/AP/2146, "La Constitution de l'Union Française," in *Bulletin Hebdomadaire*, 25 February 1946; untitled article in *Le Figaro*, 8 February 1946, in the same carton; and *Loi No. 46-680*, published in the *Journal Officiel*, 14 April 1946, and promulgated the previous day.

120. CAOM, 1/AP/216/4, "Rapport du groupe d'Etudes du Statut de l'Union Française," written in the spring of 1946. The group included Laurentie among its members. See also: CAOM, 1/AP/3655, Noel Henry, "Objet: nationalité et citoyenneté des 'ressortissants français,'" 29 August 1946.

121. CAOM, 1/AP2146, election results published in *Bulletin d'Information*, 20 May 1946.

122. CAOM, 1/AP/3655, "Proposition de loi tendant à proclamer citoyens tous les ressortissants de la Métropole et des territoires d'outre-mer," 7 May 1946.

123. CAOM, 1/AP/3655, telegram from the government general for Indochina to the ministry of overseas territories, 8 May 1946; and, in the same carton, letter from Moutet to the government general for AOF, "Application de la loi du 7 mai 1946," written in June 1946. (Emphasis in the original.)

124. CAOM, 1/AP/2147, see the series of articles written by Pierre Singly and published in *Marchés Coloniaux*, entitled, "La Personalité des populations indigènes," that ran from 30 November 1946 to 2 August 1947. In particular, see the editions of 30 November 1946, 21 December 1946, 1 February 1947, 15 February 1947, 1 March 1947, and 2 August 1947. The discourse practiced by Singly was picked up and re-produced throughout the colonial field by administrators, French politicians, and even some among the French-educated elite from West Africa.

125. CAOM, 1/AP/3655, "Note pour Monsieur le ministre," from the government general for AOF to the ministry of Overseas France, 22 May 1946.

126. CAOM, 1/AP/3655, letter from Robert Delavignette to the ministry for Overseas France, "Sur le statut des originaires des territoires d'Outre-Mer dans l'Union Française," 23 October 1947. For a discussion on the turmoil in AOF during 1945 and 1946 see: Cooper, *Decolonization and African Society*, pp. 227–233.

127. CAOM, 1/AP/3655, letter from Yvon Gouet inserted in the file on citizenship legislation maintained by the ministry for Overseas France, 25 May 1946.

128. CAOM, 1/AP/2146, election results published in *Bulletin d'Information*, 17 June 1946.

129. CAOM, 1/AP/216/1, records of the discussions on the draft for the second constitution of 1946.

130. CAOM, 1/AP/2146, "Constitution de la République Française," published on 29 September 1946 and put to a referendum on 13 October 1946.

131. CAOM, 1/AP/3655, Marius Moutet, "Objet: Conséquences Juridiques des articles 80, 81 et 82 de la Constitution," 13 June 1947.

132. CAOM, 1/AP/3655, "Situation au 1er avril 1948," report to the National Assembly.

133. CAOM, 1/AP/2146, unsigned article published in *L'Africain*, 21 August 1946.

134. CAOM, 1/AP/3655, letter from Delavignette, "Sur le statut des originaires des territoires d'Outre-Mer dans l'Union Française," 23 October 1947. The *indigénat* was abolished on 20 February 1946, forced labor on 18 April 1946, and "Native justice" on 30 April 1946. Those changes are treated below.

135. CAOM, 1/AP/214, François Bernard, "L'Union Française: Illusions et Réalités," in *Cahiers du Monde Nouveau*, June 1946.

136. Bayart, *The State in Africa*, p. 108.

Chapter Six

The New Missionaries: Reform, Rebellion, and the Crisis of Authority in the 1950s

"One could observe, at the end of the 1939–1945 war," a report produced by the government general for French West Africa noted, "an alarming disaffection with regard to authority, [directed at] the customary [chiefs] as much as toward the [colonial] administration." The source of that discontent, according to Dakar, was "*an evolved elite*" that had been "*given access to public life...by the end of 1946 [through] the establishment of elected assemblies....* Those elected [representatives], in many places, have supplanted the chiefs in the loyalties of the masses."[1] In fact, France faced serious crises throughout the empire after the Second World War, in addition to those in French West Africa discussed above. In Algeria, on 8 May 1945, the day victory was declared in Europe, a mass protest in Sétif against French rule ended in street confrontations that left thousands dead in revenge attacks by imperial subjects and *colons* alike. After the retreat of Japan from Indochina, Ho Chi Minh, leader of the Viet-minh and former head of the French Communist Party's *Union Intercoloniale* in the 1920s, emerged from his long underground struggle and proclaimed Vietnam's independence on 2 September 1945. Finally, in Madagascar rebellion swept many rural areas in 1947 and was brutally repressed by France at the cost of an estimated 40,000 lives and a military occupation of the island continued into the 1950s.

Dakar's presentation of the challenges to French authority as the work of *évolués* in command of naïve masses perpetuated ethnographic notions about "authentic" African society that had functioned as a hegemonic discourse since at least the 1914–1918 war. Despite Boisson's claim that the 1943 disturbances in AOF showed "the leaders of the political groups which participated in the Commemoration of 18 June [were] not the masters of their [own] troops,"[2] the colonial administration was discursively precluded from the acknowledgement of the autonomous agency of "subaltern groups," defined by Gramsci as those classes whose actions are characterized by "spontaneity" and "have not achieved any consciousness of the class 'for itself.'"[3] Rather, the government general interpreted the 1943 clashes as well as subsequent confrontations as signs that the French-educated elite could not exercise authority in the federation. Dakar reminded Paris, in a gesture of self-consolation, that the *évolués* and urban workers constituted only a small fragment of the West African population, no more than two to three percent of the more than fifteen million residents of the federation as late as 1958.[4] The government general commented, "The peasant masses have generally remained, despite all that had happened, more attached to their customary institutions than [has] the urban proletariat." Since the peasants constituted the overwhelming majority of the indigenous population, it was necessary to base administrative policy on "the preservation of the traditional leaders in reinvigorated chieftaincies." The result, Dakar surmised, would be that "the vote of the peasant masses should turn to the disadvantage of those presently elected, [who were] functionaries and city dwellers."[5]

This chapter analyzes some of the ways in which the battle to represent the "veritable" African in the decade after France's Liberation shaped the decolonization process in West Africa and contributed to the ascendancy of a certain faction of *évolués* in government by 1956. To reassert its authority in West Africa and undermine demands for equal rights with metropolitan citizens, the colonial administration attempted to re-orient political debate around questions of the "authentic" Africa and away from deliberations about the "true" France. Toward that end Paris created the *Fonds pour l'Investissement en Développement Economique et Social* (FIDES) in 1946 to "modernize" the basic infrastructure and productive capacity of West Africa. Money was dispensed for road construction, communications development, and improvement in urban sanitation and housing. As a corollary to FIDES, the "high commissioner of AOF," formerly the governor general, launched the *Fonds d'Equipement Rural et de Développement Économique et Social* (FERDES) in 1949 "to aid the rural collectivities in the realization of work [that is] of local interest." The objective of both plans was to simultaneously increase the attachment of the West African population to France and preserve "traditional" autochthonous society, which once more re-produced the tension that underlay the metropole's *mission civilisatrice* since at least the Great War.[6] As Cooper notes, "The point of metropolitan investment in colonial infrastructure, then, was not to extract Africans from their rural, communitarian ways, but to allow economic growth to take place with less disturbance of African society."[7]

Administratively, the government general turned to the pre-colonial elite for the maintenance of order. Funds from FERDES were only dispensed through "rural collectives"—a euphemism for "tribes"—which preserved the economic power of the pre-colonial elite after the system of forced labor was abolished in 1946.[8] Furthermore, Dakar introduced elections for "tribal" assemblies as a means to assuage demands for increased political rights among the population and concurrently "protect" "traditional" institutions.[9] While the "democratization" of "indigenous" society was presented as the fulfillment of France's pledge to revive "authentic" African culture, it effectively politicized the office of "chief" and tribal communities in ways that transformed the pre-colonial elite into local party bosses allied with contending factions among the *évolués*. Dakar's reforms embedded debates over the exact nature of "traditional" authority in West Africa and the specific functions of the "chief" into the electoral politics of the federation and made chieftaincies new sites of contention between colonial administrators and the modern *griots* in the struggle for authority within the colonial field. Consequently, social mobilization based on ethnic differences was legitimized and communal institutions were entrenched as the foundation of governance in the federation.

Concomitantly, the organized movements of the *évolués* were transformed from small groups of the French-educated elite that recruited mostly in urban centers into mass parties based on the adherence of ethnic or tribal groups. Also, Dakar's attempt to minimize the influence of the trade unions and *évolué* political organizations sanctioned the entrance of rural West Africans into the political arena and enhanced the appeal of modern *griots* like Léopold Senghor who embraced an image of the "authentic" African as fundamentally peasant, collectivist, and ethnic. As a result, disputes among the French-educated elite over the veritable nature of autochthonous society and its future intensified along lines similar to that evidenced during the rural popular school campaign of the 1930s and the debates in the colonial commission of the Constituent Assembly in 1946.[10] The struggle between Guèye and Léopold Senghor in Senegal was exemplary in that regard. After his unexpected victory in the 1951 elections Léopold Senghor and the *Bloc Démocratique Sénégalaise* (BDS) launched a revolution "in the bush" that fundamentally undermined the French administration's ability to govern in West Africa. Tribal leaders compromised by their association with the colonial state or those who supported Léopold Senghor's political rivals were toppled and replaced by supporters of the BDS.[11] Similar actions transpired throughout AOF where the *Rassemblement Démocratique Africain* (RDA) and its affiliates dominated the political scene.[12]

The success of parties like the BDS and RDA not only reflected a shift within *évolué* politics it also pointed to the colonial administration's weakened position in West Africa. In response to that precarious situation, Dakar called for "a vast decentralization" of the system of governance in the federation.[13] Throughout the 1950s the government general and Paris floated various reform measures designed to provide "administrative autonomy for the diverse collectivities" bounded according to "ethnic affinities."[14] Those proposals culminated in the *Loi Cadre* of 1956 that dissolved AOF and permitted the formation of ministerial cabinets for each of the territories that comprised the former federation, an act that effectively ended French rule in West Africa. However, by 1956 Paris had realized that the termination of direct governance over the federation did not necessarily imply the elimination of France's influence in the region. Rather, *évolué* identity as articulated by Léopold Senghor and his associates, as well as their particular notions of "authentic" African and French culture, afforded the former metropole the possibility to relinquish administrative dominance in West Africa while remaining an important cultural and economic force in the area after formal independence in 1960. That prospect accorded with France's re-defined mission subsequent to de Gaulle's return to power in 1958 and was embodied in the transformation of the ministry for Overseas France into the ministry of culture headed by the former anti-colonialist and writer André Malraux.[15]

How was it possible for decolonization to be imagined and accepted by those very elements in Paris who in the previous decade had "dismissed any idea of autonomy, any possibility for development outside the French imperial framework?"[16] Moreover, what factors enabled certain elements among the *évolué* class and not others to realize their aspiration to become the "legitimate rulers" of the former West African colonies and to simultaneously maintain their intricate connections with the ex-metropole? To address those questions we begin with a discussion of the ways in which France attempted to reassert its ability to command in AOF after 1946.

Equal But Different:
Development, Democracy, and the Civilizing Mission

French authority in West Africa was tenuous at best in the years that immediately followed the metropole's liberation from German occupation.[17] Accordingly, the provisional government born of the Resistance had to (re)construct France's image and re-define its mission in West Africa if it hoped to retain dominance in the region. Curiously, Moutet and others within the imperial hierarchy asserted that could only be done through the "political and economic emancipation of the natives."[18] What Paris and Dakar imagined as the "political and economic emancipation" of the peoples of West Africa was articulated within a framework bounded by the circumstances of the fight against Hitler fascism and hegemonic discourses of cultural authenticity and essential difference operable throughout the colonial field. One of the earliest systematic statements of Gaullist colonial policy captured what Stoler and Cooper describe as "the tensions between the exclusionary practices and universalizing claims of bourgeois culture [that] were crucial to shaping the age of empire."[19] In 1943 the provisional government in Algiers proclaimed that "the foundation of French native policy [is] the first article of the Declaration of the Rights of Man and Citizen which it is more than ever necessary to recall: [All] men are born and remain free and equal in their rights. Social distinctions are only based upon common utility. However," the statement continued, "this principle, too often misunderstood, has also often been applied too rashly, without taking account of the local living conditions." France's mission in Africa, according to the Gaullists, was "to aid" in "social" development "without disrupting ... traditional institutions."[20] Later, Pierre-Olivier Lapie asserted that "it [was] necessary...to raise [the colonized peoples] to the level of French civilization without destroying their autochthonous institutions."[21]

France, though, confronted a crisis of its identity as a colonial power in a global context that did not favor expressions of cultural or racial superiority and that was dominated by political forces inimical to the preservation of extraterritorial empires.[22] As Moutet expressed it, "The real problem...is to know how the [colonized] populations will evolve, how they will be able to attain a higher degree of civilization, how their representatives will be listened to and how [France] will establish a climate that will reject conscious or unconscious racism."[23] Thus, the socialist minister for Overseas France articulated the fundamental dilemma that ensnared metropolitan politicians and imperial officials alike. How was it possible for Paris to fulfill its mission to "civilize" populations deemed still to be in need of "elevation" to some higher plane of existence while at the same time respecting the basic equality of all peoples? Moutet's rhetoric simultaneously affirmed the universal rights of man *and* the superiority of French culture over those "others" it ruled. That discursive web constrained the possibilities for imperial action in West Africa while it opened spaces for the colonized population to challenge the legitimacy of France's dominance in the federation.

›

The solution to Moutet's "real problem" devised by the Fourth Republic and its overseas administrators was embodied in the twin policies of "economic progress," or development, and "cultural preservation." That agenda concomitantly furnished a new basis upon which France legitimized its rule in West Africa while the program itself was valorized through ethnographic discourses about the "authentic" nature of indigenous society in AOF that were resurrected in the post-Liberation period. The metropole presented itself as a financial benefactor for the colonized populations and as their sole protection against forces bent on the destruction of their traditions. Officials in Paris and Dakar expected the economic programs would assuage the agitation of urban workers and increase rural production while political reform was designed to militate against the increased prestige and authority of the *évolués* through popular participation in the selection of "tribal" leaders.

A report prepared by the ministry for Overseas France recounted the degree to which the federation had "suffered from the war." "Forced production, [use of] forced labor, extreme taxation, [and] military recruitment" during the conflict had profoundly dislocated the local economy and left in its wake a deep sense of "malaise" among the people.[24] De Gaulle and others used similar language to describe the condition of the metropole after four long years of occupation. The general noted that France suffered from a widespread lack of food "to satisfy the barest needs of existence," an "exhausted population...on a ravaged territory," and the absence of basic services like electricity, transportation, and heat.

However, while the Gaullists and other politicians of the early Fourth Republic measured "progress" for Europe in terms of "technology" and the "modernization" of the "manufacturing sector,"[25] for West Africa advancement was gauged according to improvements in "commercial [and] agricultural" activity.[26] Accordingly, the Constituent Assembly voted the creation of the *Fonds d'Investissement et de Développement Économique et Social des Territoires d'Outre-Mer* (FIDES) in April 1946 for which the National Assembly implemented funding in 1947. Over the next ten years Paris provided approximately $542 million (in contemporary value) to West Africa to build roads, expand railroads, develop communications systems, construct urban housing and sanitation, establish schools, and repair and expand ports like Dakar, Conakry, and Abidjan. While FIDES was the greatest financial commitment of the metropole to the economy of AOF in the history of French rule in the region and was the only concerted effort toward the achievement of some of the earliest stated objectives of the *mission civilisatrice*, it was sharply criticized by many among the French-educated elite on two counts. First, the amount of money invested was judged inadequate for the needs of the more than 17 million people in the federation. Second, and more importantly for the modern *griots*, FIDES risked the transformation of Africa into a permanent "appendix of Europe" that operated as a "reservoir of primary resources and an outlet for Europe's surplus production."[27] In fact, as Cooper argues, one of the primary goals of the investment program was the formation of an identifiable, disciplined labor force that would increase the efficiency of already established industries and, therefore, aid in the recovery of France's economy after the devastation of the Second World War.[28] Thus, the elected representatives from West Africa recognized that the aid programs devised in Paris would not lead to the "autonomous economic development" of the federation, but served to maintain French economic hegemony in AOF.[29]

However, the development programs enacted for French West Africa by the Fourth Republic proceeded not only from the self-interest of metropolitan businesses and financiers, they also accorded with certain conceptions of the nature of African society held by Dakar and Paris and their perception of the "limits of the possible" for indigenous economic activity.[30] France's mission was not merely to ameliorate local living conditions, but to do so in a way that preserved autochthonous traditions. Thus, the idea of "industrializing" Africa was precluded by the discursive framework within which metropolitan politicians and overseas administrators operated. Instead, investment had to be oriented toward the enhancement of "local characteristics" and systems of production. This was most clearly evidenced by the government general's supplemental economic program, the *Fonds d'Equipment Rural et de Développement Économique et Social en A.O.F.* (FERDES), created by an *arrêté général* issued by the high commissioner for AOF, Paul Béchard, on 23 March 1949, just two years after FIDES was put in operation.[31] In its justification for the new program, the government general noted that FIDES did not provide money for investment in the productive capacity of the federation. Rather, the 1947 fund was designed to facilitate the more efficient movement of goods and materials throughout the region and especially toward the ports where they would be exported to France. Yet, in order for FIDES to achieve its goals, money had to be set aside specifically to encourage agricultural production, which was presented as the "natural profession" of the African. Therefore, FERDES was established in order "to help rural collectivities realize works of [seemingly] limited importance and localized interest."

FERDES, though, was not simply an aid package. It required the active collaboration of the overseas administration and clearly defined "collectivities" on commonly agreed to programs. Dakar set up the fund, but the West African population had to initiate the projects and it entailed a lengthy bureaucratic process for sanction. Accordingly, "A rural collectivity (village, association, agricultural union, cooperative, etc.) propose[d] the completion of a project of local interest which it ha[d] decided to finance in part." The local government official studied the plan and transmitted it with an opinion to the territorial administration. If the colonial governor approved its utility, the "technical service" was requested to make studies about its implementation. The findings were then forwarded to a permanent commission of the Conseil Général and a special committee on development. If they were favorable, the project was then funded out of a local pool of capital. If, on the other hand, the Conseil Général did not support it, the entire idea was scrapped and barred from being carried out. In its first year, FERDES provided 142 million CFA francs for 260 separate projects that required the petitioners to cover the initial expenses and one-third of the total cost.[32]

Significantly, any request for money through FERDES had to emanate from some "collectivity," not from potential individual entrepreneurs or private businessmen. That accorded with hegemonic conceptions of "authentic" indigenous culture that presented the "true" African as a "collective personality." Consequently, "it [was] the group that decide[d] for the individual; it [was] in the group that the individual [found] inspiration for his conduct." Furthermore, the "African" style of work was "fundamentally different from that of the metropole." "Labor [in Africa]," the argument ran, "was performed collectively [and even] property [was] collective." However, that should not be confused with Communist forms of social organization, a confusion of which Léopold Senghor was accused at the time. Rather, "The peasant[s] of the savanna consent[ed] (sic) to be guided, directed...[by] the authority of their chiefs."[33] While Dakar allowed for the possibility that agricultural unions and rural cooperatives could conduct such development projects, the expected financial contribution of the group in need of the assistance militated against all but "tribal" associations and other organizations directed by the pre-colonial elite from access to the fund. Thus, economic development was intimately connected to administrative reforms that strengthened "tribal" foundations of governance in the federation and attempted to enhance the prestige and authority of the "chief" amidst increased challenges to French rule from the *évolués* and urban workers.

However, the sudden accession to citizenship on the part of the *sujets* following passage of the Lamine Guèye Law on 7 May 1946 vastly complicated Dakar's endeavors to reassert its authority as well as any attempts to revive the pre-colonial elite as meaningful agents of governance. Moutet and Governor General Cournarie immediately set out to regain the initiative usurped by Guèye and the modern *griots* in the struggle for authority in the colonial field through attempts to limit the efficacy of the law. While Guèye asserted his act was intended to "abolish all the barriers that still remain between men that we like to call equal," Paris and Dakar countered that there was a difference between "citizenship" and "nationality." Moutet argued that citizenship meant access to a set of basic, shared rights, while "nationality" represented an unspoken cultural affinity that could not be clearly articulated and did not necessarily correspond to juridical status. In that way, the metropole negated the crisis over "naturalization" for colonial subjects by making them citizens of the French Union and simultaneously denying them the possibility of ever becoming "truly" French. Accordingly, the former *sujets* had the right to vote in local and Union-wide elections, participate in public life, the *Code du Travail* was applicable overseas, and the *indigénat* was suppressed.[34] However, the residents of Overseas France were "not permitted to exercise the rights" of citizens when they were "in the metropole."[35] The West Africans were described as citizens of their particular locality and of the French Union, not as citizens of France. In addition, while the constitution of the Fourth Republic for the first time enshrined women's suffrage and declared them equal citizens with men, women in the former colonies still could only achieve citizenship status through "association with the request of the husband or the father."[36] Consequently, the colonial subjects were defined as "equal" to but "separate" from the French, a policy that in the United States was being challenged through the Civil Rights Movement at that time. It is also significant that women and children, even adult children, in the colonies remained linked in the *imaginaire* of colonial administrators at a time when French civil law had begun to de-link them. It suggests that the notion "traditional" was becoming more exclusively associated with the emergent "Third World" while Europe was "modernizing" and moving away from "traditional" forms of life. This represents an act of imperial fantasy similar to those discussed by Anne McClintock in the case of England.[37]

Since the residents of French West Africa were entitled to the same rights as "Frenchmen," but were not "French," the government general argued that those rights should be exercised within "traditional" institutions that corresponded to their separate and distinct "nationality." René Pleven, France's prime minister in 1951, proclaimed that "the existence of the customary or traditional chiefs...constitutes one of the original traits of African societies" which the metropole was committed to defend against those unnamed forces that threatened "authentic" indigenous culture. The stated function of the pre-colonial elite was to "officially represent the autochthonous collectivities,"[38] an assertion that directly challenged the *évolués'* claims to leadership among the West African population. Officials in Paris and Dakar warned against "creating a disequilibrium [of political power in the federation] to the advantage of the urban centers [that are] of recent development...[and that] express the very exclusive interests of a minority of *évolués* and detribalized persons to the detriment of the great mass of the rural populations."[39]

The imperial administration posed not only as the protector of "traditional" African culture, but also as the champion of the peasants' interests against attempts by urban politicians and workers to monopolize authority in AOF. In a discursive framework that privileged notions of "democracy," "equality," and "freedom," Dakar sought to reclaim the advantage in the struggle for authority within the colonial field through reinventing itself as an agent of democratic reform that opposed the pretensions of "demagogues" from the cities to become tyrants over the West African masses.[40] Accordingly, the government general "proceed[ed] to reorganize the chieftaincies" to bring them line with "authentic tradition."[41] The model for the "true" African society that guided the decisions Dakar made with regard to colonial governance after the Liberation was derived from Moutet's notion of "republican colonialism" propounded during the Popular Front. Native communities were democratic and command was exercised through an elected council that selected a "chief" to represent the interests of the collectivity, defined as an "ethnic or tribal group." Therefore, in 1947 Dakar decreed the "introduction of an electoral system for the choice of chiefs." Other reforms the same year created "tribal assemblies," composed of individuals chosen by means of "quasi-universal suffrage" similar to the method used to elect representatives to the National Assembly and Assembly of the French Union (*Assemblée de l'Union Française*— AUF).

Dakar hoped that such measures would stem the migration of peoples from rural areas to the urban centers, a movement enhanced by acts promulgated in 1946 that provided for "freedom of association, [and]...of movement." The declaration of the right of indigenous peoples to move freely throughout the federation reversed one of the pillars of imperial governance in the 1920s and 1930s that "required" all residents of West Africa to be "attached to his village of origin," and to remain under the authority of "his chief."[42] The government general held that such changes risked the "detribalization" of the entire region and furnished a pool of disgruntled urban unemployed susceptible to the agitation of "provocateurs" among the modern *griots*. Thus, the combination of economic investment in agriculture and administrative democratization in the rural areas was designed to make life "in the bush" more attractive to the indigenous peoples and undercut the appeal of those *évolués* elected to the metropolitan government or the AUF.[43]

The West African representatives seated in Paris responded to Dakar's reform measures with attempts to limit the authority of cheiftaincies. While their own conception of "authentic" African society generally accorded with that presented by the metropolitan government and imperial administration, the *évolués* were not prepared to allow the pre-colonial elite to exercise the preponderance of power in the federation. Therefore, Fily-Dabo Sissoko (himself a chief), Léopold Senghor, Guèye, Yacine Diallo, and other modern *griots* within the National Assembly introduced resolutions that called upon the government to "clearly define the status of the native chiefs of AOF, AEF, Togo, and Cameroon," especially with regard to the range of their responsibilities and prerogatives in relation to "the masses." Moreover, the *évolués* challenged France's and the colonial administration's "right" to represent the "interests" of the West African population and their ability to "intervene" in matters of "custom."[44] Implicit in their argument was an assumption by the modern *griots* that they alone were capable of understanding the "true" nature of African society and of fulfilling the desires of the indigenous peoples in the federation. That position was legitimated through their having been elected by those they claimed to represent whereas the government general was composed of appointees from Paris with no evident organic connection to the West African people.

However, Dakar's reform of the command structures in AOF threatened to create a similar base of legitimacy for the pre-colonial elite as they could subsequently claim to have been chosen by the people over whom they governed. In fact, the pre-colonial elite began to organize itself into associations to defend their interests against the urban-based parties led by the French-educated elite. While the modern *griots* introduced resolutions in Paris to sharply delimit the authority of "native rulers," the "chiefs" protested against the erosion of their influence since the end of the Second World War. Amidst professions of loyalty to France, the *Syndicat des Chefs de Canton de la Guinée Française* argued for the "creation, according to ethnic region, of a disciplinary council composed singly of canton chiefs elected by their comrades."[45] The Chiefs' Union suggested that the pre-colonial elite, since their position derived from "custom," had to have its "role...in Africa...guaranteed for the future," a perspective shared by the ministry for

Overseas France and officials in Dakar.[46] The "native" rulers proclaimed themselves "guardians of local traditions" and asserted that such a status necessitated that their ability to command according to "custom" should not be infringed by legislation from Paris sponsored by the *évolués*. Accordingly, the pre-colonial elite insisted that they alone knew what constituted "authentic" African culture. Therefore, the various Chiefs' Unions announced that "the moment ha[d] come for us, Canton Chiefs, to protect ourselves from all militant politics and to solemnly affirm our independence with regard to all the political formations."[47]

Despite the aggressive response on the part of the pre-colonial elite to the actions of Léopold Senghor and his associates in Paris, appeals to legitimacy based exclusively on "tradition" and claims to unbounded power over their charges could not mobilize significant support in a discursive context that prized notions of democracy, reform, and equality. In fact, the Senegalese poet disputed the degree to which the position of the chiefs was really based on "custom." In a report to the National Assembly in 1954 Léopold Senghor stated that the units over which the pre-colonial elite governed were the "creation of the French Administration." Moreover, the "subjects" they ruled were "French citizens," entitled to the full liberties of citizens as embodied in the constitution. "The question posed, therefore, is to know to what degree one can impose on French citizens a chief that they have not freely chosen."[48] The colonial administration and metropolitan government had become trapped by their own rhetoric. While Dakar might sympathize with the chiefs and lament their weakened position in the colonial field, the government general could not retreat on its promises to democratize West African society. In addition, the residents of the federation could not be refused the status of citizens of the French Union, which provided a basis for claims to entitlements under the provisions of the constitution that included the right to vote for their own representatives and participation in the choice of local officials.[49] Thus, in May 1951 the National Assembly, just prior to the second general elections under the Fourth Republic, passed a law that "considerably expanded the right to vote and permitted the rural populations to enter the electoral process."[50] The government general's attempts to outflank the *évolués* through reform had not led to the revival of the pre-colonial elite, nor had it significantly strengthened France's authority in the federation.

Nevertheless, the failure to reproduce a new version of the old hegemonic bloc of "traditional" rulers and colonial administrators did not entail the displacement of the ethnographic discourse of cultural "authenticity" and essential differences between Europeans and Africans that had dominated the colonial field since at least the 1914–1918 war. Instead, Léopold Senghor and his associates mobilized the ethnographers' language to legitimate their stance in the struggle for authority within the imperial framework and to undermine the claims of both the pre-colonial elite and imperial officials to speak on behalf of "true" native custom. Moreover, Léopold Senghor's presentation of the "real" African society wedded ethnographic assertions about the nature of autochthonous practices in AOF to the egalitarian rhetoric of the Resistance to forge a potent discourse that allowed the *évolués* associated with the Senegalese poet to gain command of the political situation in West Africa and to do so with the support or at least quiescence of Paris.

Léopold Senghor accused the French government, through "profound ignorance" of "authentic" custom, of having "greatly disorganized African society."[51] In his speech before the National Assembly on 2 June 1954, the deputy from Senegal instructed the metropolitan politicians on the "real" nature of "Negro-African Civilization" in terms lifted directly from Delafosse's writings. Like the ethnographer, the *Négritude* poet explained that "Negro-African political society...is formed by ever-larger concentric circles...[and] forms a kind of family.... [S]everal families which speak the same dialect and who share a common origin form a tribe." "However," the deputy from Senegal asked rhetorically, "what is the Negro-African family? It is not a European type household, composed only of parents and their children. It includes all persons, living or deceased, who share a common ancestor." The chief, as head of this family, was the "link between the dead and the living." However, Léopold Senghor cautioned that real authority resided with a "council of elders whose decisions...were executed by the head of the family." The largest expression of the Negro-African political community was akin to "a small kingdom" of which the chiefs were "functionaries," like "village mayors." That entity was fundamentally "collective" in nature with an extensive "separation of powers" and checks on the authority of all representatives of the community. Therefore, Léopold Senghor argued for the introduction of the "secret ballot" in the election of local assemblies and chiefs, and the complete "democratization of [the pre-colonial elite's] functions." West African society was to continue to be organized according to "ethnicity," which formed the "natural" unit of social cohesion and from which "custom" was derived. However, universal suffrage "of the two sexes" would restore prestige and "authenticity" to the administrative structures of the federation.[52]

Officials in Dakar or Paris could do little in response to Léopold Senghor's position. First, the government general and ministry for Overseas

France regarded the image of African society presented by the pre-colonial elite as "dangerous for the evolution of Africa and even for the chieftaincies themselves." A note produced by the commission for the overseas territories days after Léopold Senghor's lesson on Negro-African Civilization before the assembled deputies in Paris warned that the suggestions of the "traditional" rulers were "retrograde" and would ultimately induce bitter reactions among the people. Second, though, the metropole charged that "*Senghor's project* [went] much farther than the government's own project and sacrifice[d] the traditional aspects of chieftaincy in favor of its modern aspects." That too was "dangerous" because it "perilously politicized" the office of chief making it susceptible to take-over by the *évolués* through their political parties.[53] However, Léopold Senghor's presentation of "authentic" African society more closely accorded with that advanced by the colonial administration and Paris and did so through the deployment of the same language practiced by the imperial rulers themselves. Moreover, by the early 1950s Dakar had lost control of the situation on the ground in West Africa and authority had shifted decisively to the French-educated elite and its parties. Thus, even if the government general had endorsed the proposals of the pre-colonial elite its ability to engage effectively in the struggle was significantly limited. In the end, the overseas administration and Parisian officials opted to pose as mediators in the disputes that engulfed the federation.

Nonetheless, Dakar's measures helped to reorient debates within the colonial field that effectively closed off discussions about the "true" France within AOF and re-centered questions of rights and governmental praxis on disputes over the "real" African culture. More fundamentally, the urban centers where political activity was most developed and contentious were displaced as the focus of the fight for leadership in West Africa as the village or "tribal" group was transformed into the primary site where authority was contested and from whence it derived. In the process, bitter confrontations erupted among the French-educated elite that further complicated the struggle for authority within AOF. Those disagreements, which often ended in violence among the contending forces, were articulated around divergent conceptions of "authentic" African culture and the self-identity of the modern *griots* as palpable authority passed to their hands in the federation during the 1950s.

The West African Revolution:
Parties, Tradition, and Authority, 1946–1955

Despite the general unity of the West African delegates to the Constituent Assemblies in Paris during 1945 and 1946, they remained organized in separate associations, most of which had minimal memberships and were concentrated in the cities of the federation. In addition, the political movements in French West Africa tended to be either affiliated with one of the major metropolitan parties or an incarnation of various Resistance groups formed during the fight against Vichy and Nazi Germany. However, disappointment with the second draft of the constitution for the Fourth Republic and the hostility that greeted passage of the Lamine Guèye Law of 7 May 1946 convinced many West Africans seated in Paris that "the principal task in [1946 was to] unite all the anticolonialist forces within each territory." The form that unity took was the *Rassemblement Démocratique Africain* (RDA), born at a congress in Bamako, French Soudan, on 19-21 October 1946, a week after the referendum that approved the Fourth Republic's constitution.[54]

The main force behind the RDA, and its elected president, was Félix Houphouët-Boigny. Born on 19 October 1905 in Yamoussoukro, Ivory Coast, one year before Léopold Senghor, Houpouët-Boigny graduated from the École William Ponty and the Dakar School of Medicine where he was licensed as a doctor. He was the son of a chief and became a Canton Chief in his own right during the inter-war years. By the 1930s Houphouët-Boigny was a prosperous cocoa planter in the Ivory Coast and in 1944 founded the *Syndicat des planteurs africains*, which challenged the dominance of the settler community over cash crop production in the region.[55] The following year he was elected to the First Constituent Assembly in Paris where he sponsored the law that ended forced labor in the colonies, an act consequently known as the "Houphouët-Boigny Law."[56]

Even though nearly all the West African representatives seated in Paris endorsed Houphouët-Boigny's call to found the RDA in order to resist "the reactionary counter-offensive of the Second Constituent Assembly,"[57] disputes soon arose over the political orientation of the new organization. While Houphouët-Boigny was not a member of the Communist Party and had never participated in any of the Communist-inspired or sponsored groups among the *évolués*, he urged the RDA to affiliate with the Communists in the National Assembly since the PCF constituted "the vanguard of the struggle against colonialism." Houphouët-Boigny asserted that the Communists were natural allies with the colonized populations because of objective circumstances brought about by the world capitalist system. "In effect," the RDA president explained, "if it is true that the colonialist attitude finds nourishment in racial prejudice and the differences between civilization[s], it is not any less true that the origin of colonialism is the result of the imperialist and tentacular development of capitalism for the last three-quarters of a century."[58] Thus, the cocoa planter furnished an analysis of colonialism and the nature of the anti-colonialist struggle nearly identical to that articulated by Lamine Senghor and Garan Kouyaté in the late 1920s during the ascendancy of the LDRN among the *évolués* in the metropole.[59]

However, Houphouët-Boigny's decision to ally the RDA with the PCF did not signify that the new party was "Communist" or that it desired full assimilation of the West African population to France. On the contrary, the first resolution of the 1946 Bamako congress declared that the RDA's political objectives were to "recognize and favor the free expression of African originality [and] rejects all the shackles of a false assimilation." Houphouët-Boigny told his supporters in early 1947, "We (the RDA) believe … in the value of the Negro-African Civilization and we intend to maintain the contribution that it is want to make to human civilization."[60] The RDA president's rhetoric was, in fact, more closely aligned with that practiced by Léopold Senghor and the *Négritude* circle than the position of the Communist Party, which at the time had returned to its advocacy of full assimilation and equal citizenship throughout the French Union.[61]

Despite the general discursive unity among the prominent *évolués*, Houphouët-Boigny's insistence on an alliance between the RDA and the PCF provided the pretext for divisions to arise among the initial signatories to the call for the Bamako congress. The emergent tensions of the Cold War, which included the end of Communist participation in the French government by May 1947, had begun to erode the basis for cooperation between Socialists and Communists characteristic of the Resistance and Popular Front eras. In that context, Moutet urged members of the SFIO section in West Africa, headed by Guèye, to boycott the proceedings at Bamako. As a consequence, many of the most prominent *évolués* either absented themselves from the birth of the RDA or soon thereafter dropped out and distanced themselves from its activities. Among those who adhered to Moutet's injunction or left the RDA within the next year were Guèye, Léopold Senghor, Fily-Dabo Sissoko (the presiding president at Bamako), Sourou Apithy, and Yacine Diallo.[62]

However, Moutet's actions were not solely governed by emergent Cold War considerations. The primary concern of the Minister for Overseas France was the anti-colonialist rhetoric of the new party, which pledged to wage a "struggle" against the "1946 Constitution" and the "assimilationist theories that aspire to transform the French African territories into an 'Overseas France.'"[63] Accordingly, the RDA posed a potentially serious threat to French authority in West Africa even as it embraced the rhetoric of cultural authenticity and essential difference promoted by Moutet and the colonial administration. Moutet was caught between his denial of full equality among imperial subjects and French nationals and the desire to maintain metropolitan command in the federation. The actions of *évolués* like Guèye and Houphouët-Boigny precluded the possibility that France could achieve both aims. Consequently, the metropole would either have to accord full French citizenship to the overseas population or eventually relinquish control of the federation.

While Moutet was not prepared to choose, his insistence that supporters of the SFIO in the federation boycott the RDA forced many among the *évolués* to decide between a complete break with metropolitan politics or continued struggle for the extension of French citizenship to the former colonial subjects. Guèye had staked his political reputation on the idea of assimilation through the law on citizenship that bore his name. Therefore, the deputy from Senegal had little room for maneuver and opted for "obedience" to the injunctions of the metropolitan party. In his wake, he carried Léopold Senghor and others who were not as committed to the idea of French citizenship. However, the *Négritude* poet was not comfortable with Guèye's direction and later publicly expressed regret at "the fault committed by the Senegalese deputies...in refusing to attend the Bamako Congress of the RDA.... My error was in obeying orders which were imposed on me from outside."[64]

Léopold Senghor's ambivalence as well as declarations by leaders of the RDA that "they love[d] France" highlighted the conflicted identity articulated by many among the French-educated elite as they attempted to maintain their claims to being both French and African in a context that increasingly demanded that they assume one or the other.[65] Moreover, the discussions over attendance at Bamako forced into the open a long-smoldering dispute among the *évolués* over their place within the imperial framework that was oriented around contrasting notions of the "real" African society and its future manifestation. Accordingly, the central political conflict in West Africa throughout the 1950s was not that between Léopold Senghor and Houphouët-Boigny, or Senegal and the Ivory Coast. Rather the formative confrontation during the period of decolonization was that which erupted between the *Négritude* poet and Guèye.

The argument that West African decolonization was fundamentally characterized by the struggle for influence and dominance between Léopold Senghor and Houphouët-Boigny, or the RDA and the bloc directed from Senegal results from a narrow focus on the 1956 *Loi Cadre*, the subject of the next section of this chapter. The political debate in AOF, accordingly, has been presented as a dispute between supporters of federation or "Balkanization," a word associated with the Senegalese poet's critique of the aforementioned law. However, such analyses ignore the basic discursive and conceptual unity between the leaders of Ivory Coast and Senegal. They shared similar notions of "authentic" African culture and engaged in nearly identical political practices in their rise to ascendancy. Léopold Senghor's later regret at the decision taken by his party in 1946 indicates the depth of the affinity between the two leaders of post-colonial West Africa. Cooper's focus on the "labor question" in French West Africa enables him to avoid viewing the political disputes in the federation in terms of a rivalry between Houphouët-Boigny and Léopold Senghor. In fact, Cooper notes that Mamadou Dia, Léopold Senghor's able assistant in Senegal, deployed the same language used by colonial administrators and Houphouët-Boigny in their advocacy of the *Loi Cadre* shortly after it was passed in 1956.[66]

By 1948 Léopold Senghor and Guèye had become bitter political rivals. That year Léopold Senghor intimated that the metropolitan party only viewed the West Africans as votes to preserve the SFIO's seats in the National Assembly. In a letter to the Socialist Party's general secretary, Guy Mollet, in which the junior deputy from Senegal announced his resignation from the metropolitan organization, Léopold Senghor wrote, "The truth [was] that the [Socialist] Party [was] using the overseas territories not as ends but as means." Consequently, he had now "founded a purely African party, the *Bloc Démocratique Sénégalais* (BDS)," the goal of which was to lead the federation "toward an African socialism." The new association announced that it would "base [its] action...on the survival of our old agrarian economy, singularly derived from the underlying communitarian spirit [of the people]." That meant active "support for the agricultural cooperatives [organized around] production and consumption."[67] Guèye was cast in the role of the "West African bourgeoisie" that Léopold Senghor derided in the 1930s during the debates over the rural popular schools. As in the Popular Front era, the *Négritude* poet urged the *évolués* to take up the leadership of rural AOF and embrace a model of "authentic" Africa that was peasant, collectivist, and tribal. As a result, Léopold Senghor and the BDS, along with Houphouët-Boigny and the RDA, deepened the turn within the colonial field away from claims about the "true" France and toward arguments over the "veritable" nature of African society and its future incarnation.

Léopold Senghor's decision to split with Guèye, though, was not only informed by pre-conceived notions of "authentic" African culture, it also reflected significant transformations in the nature of the struggle for authority in West Africa. On 10 October 1947 over 20,000 workers on the Dakar-Niger railway line went on strike in perhaps the most dramatic labor action in the history of the federation and one immortalized in Sembène Ousmane's novel *Les Bouts de bois de Dieu: Banty mam yal.* The strike began over demands by the workers for the abolition of separate racial hierarchies in the railway and equal benefits for the employees of the line.[68] As Cooper notes, the rhetoric deployed by union officials closely resembled the assimilationist discourse of the Resistance period and one embedded in the Lamine Guèye Law of 1946. Ibrahima Sarr, one of the strike leaders, even appealed to the "new and true France" for full equality among all the residents of the French Union.[69]

By the time the strike ended on 19 March 1948 many thousands more people beyond the actual strikers had been drawn into a struggle that quickly took on the aura of an anti-colonial action, even if the union leaders made no such claims. However, the *évolués* and their political organizations were caught off guard and played no meaningful role in a fight that exposed the weakness of the government general and forced significant concessions from Dakar.[70] Once again, it appeared that the self-proclaimed leaders of the West African people "were not in command of their troops." Houphouët-Boigny and Sissoko urged the laborers at various times during the strike to return to work, with limited success. Guèye was virtually invisible during the entire struggle as he was closely allied with the Socialist governor general and the SFIO-led government in Paris. Léopold Senghor met privately with strike leaders and expressed sympathy, but never made public pronouncements in favor of the action. Nevertheless, the *Négritude* poet was convinced by the 1947-1948 strike that the time had come for a break from metropolitan parties. Only then could the modern *griots* assume their role a "legitimate leaders" of the West African people.[71]

Officials in French West Africa greeted the formation of the BDS, like the RDA, with initial hostility as the new "African" parties posed direct threats to the colonial administration's ability to command in the federation.[72] Yet, it was the very reform measures promulgated by the government general in order to strengthen France's authority in AOF that opened the structural space for the new challenges to French dominance in West Africa. In the conceptual framework within which the BDS and RDA operated, the peasants constituted the natural constituency of a "truly African party." The democratization of "tribal" structures after the Second World War, intended to restore prestige and authenticity to the pre-colonial elite after its dubious wartime record, provided the means for the realization of their ambitions to become the accepted representatives of the indigenous peoples of the federation. Léopold Senghor and the BDS insisted that the government general honor its commitment to revive "authentic" democratic African political practices and permit secret ballot elections for all "tribal" offices. Throughout 1949 the BDS deluged the ministry for Overseas France with protests against the "illegal" appointment of chiefs, a practice that had become routine since at least the 1914-1918 war and against which Diagne had remonstrated in the early 1920s.[73]

In 1949 a succession crisis among the Lébou in Senegal provided the context for the first serious confrontation between the SFIO, BDS, colonial administration, and the pre-colonial elite over authority in the federation and France's commitment to its recast *mission civilisatrice*. The Lébou resided mainly in the urban centers of Senegal and had long claimed a "democratic" tradition for the selection of its leadership. In fact, in the middle of the nineteenth century the Lébou had proclaimed a republic and did away with the office of chief, a political system ironically destroyed by the French later that century. In 1949 El Hadj Moussa Diop, the "grand sérigne" of the Lébou, fell ill and delegated his functions to El Hadj Ibrahima Diop, a relative. According to reports produced by the government general and letters from various factions among the Lébou, dissent emerged within the community over this "hereditary succession" and the pro-SFIO stance of the leadership. When Ibrahima Diop left on a pilgrimage to Mecca, the dissidents, backed by the BDS, proclaimed his dethronement and held elections for a new leadership, an action in defiance of Dakar's decision that year to cease the practice of electing chiefs.[74] The SFIO, which depended on the votes of the Lébou to remain the dominant party in the Four Communes of Senegal, complained of the BDS's tactics and urged the government general to intervene. However, officials in Dakar pleaded "ignorance of customary law" and declared that it had to remain "neutral" in tribal politics, a rare, although increasingly common, admission of the colonial administration's weakness in the federation after the Second World War.[75] The government general described the feud among the Lébou as a product of tensions internal to the group exacerbated by the machinations of "external" forces. A report written on the dispute surmised, "Certain malcontents and envious elements among the Lébou were able to find a powerful ally [in the BDS] in order to satisfy their ambitions. For their part, this new political party saw the occasion to detach the Lébou bloc from its political alliance with the SFIO." The government general's account predicted that more such actions were to be expected in the future, an indication that discontent was widespread in the federation and that "African" political parties had become powerful forces in the region.[76]

By 1953 Dakar proclaimed that a "general climate of social agitation reigned" throughout French West Africa which "required the [immediate] attention" of the administration.[77] Despite covert and official support for Guèye's Socialists, the BDS and RDA had increased their strength in the disgruntled rural communities of West Africa and even among the urban trade unions.[78] In 1952 Senegal's territorial assembly, dominated by the BDS after the 1951 elections, adopted a resolution that called for the "reform of chieftaincies in the sense of 'democratizing' those traditional institutions." The measure restricted the size of each group over which a chief had authority to "20,000 inhabitants." Once the population exceeded that "fixed" number, it was to be divided and a new "tribal" community formed under a separate chief elected by universal suffrage and a secret ballot.[79] The BDS had maneuvered Dakar into a trap from which it could not escape. It either had to carry out that aspect of its mission dedicated to the preservation of "traditional structures" and defend the pre-colonial elite from the actions of the French-educated elite, or it had to fulfill its promises to democratize the command structures of the federation, which invariably opened the door to penetration of the bush by the urban-based political parties of the *évolués*. The actions taken by the "African" parties precluded the possibility that the colonial administration could do both. When Dakar attempted to circumvent the territorial assembly's resolution and refused to divide a tribal unit headed by N'Doulte N'Diassane, Mamadou Dia, deputy leader of the BDS, threatened that the decision "could have serious political repercussions."[80]

In the city of Thiès, center of the 1947–1948 rail strike, a bitter fight erupted between the SFIO and BDS in 1953 that further demonstrated the government general's loss of command as well as the greater influence of Léopold Senghor's party in communities that transcended the boundaries between rural and urban discontent. In 1953 the territorial assembly by-passed the government general and ordered the division of an ethnic community in Thiès led by Massamba Sall, a strong supporter of Guèye. The BDS argued that Sall's community was "not ethnically homogeneous," which violated the basis of governance in West Africa and subjected people to the authority of an individual not of their own tribal background. Despite accusations from the Socialist leader that the action was singly "motivated by the political agenda of the present majority party (BDS)," Dakar could not reverse the decision for fear such interventions in "customary matters" would provoke a general revolt.[81] Moreover, the BDS based its actions on the same principles used by Dakar since the Great War to justify its system of rule in West Africa. Consequently, the government general absolved itself of responsibility in such matters and delegated the authority to decide all issues concerned with cheiftaincies and tribal politics to the territorial assemblies.[82]

While the dispute over Sall's community unfolded, a crisis erupted among the Tidjani in Thiès.[83] A disagreement between Babakar Sy, caliph of the Tidjani and an important Muslim leader in Senegal, and his brother El Hadj Mansour Sy, described by Dakar as the "legitimate successor to Babakar Sy," provided the pretext for Cheikh Tidjani Sy, Babakar's son, to proclaim himself heir to the caliph. The BDS immediately declared in favor of Tidjani Sy since Mansour was a militant of the SFIO. Léopold Senghor's party mobilized the local trade unions in support of its candidate for caliph and launched a strike on 13 October 1953 that brought the city to a standstill.[84] Once again, Guèye's complaints that the actions of the BDS "created a dangerous [and] anarchic situation for public order" and resulted from a "declared hostility" on the part of the new party "to the chiefs, [in particular those] who support the minority party" (SFIO), failed to receive satisfaction from Dakar or Paris.[85]

The fight between the SFIO and the BDS in Senegal reflected broader trends in West Africa as demands for fulfillment of the post-Liberation reforms that promised "equality" and "democracy" simultaneously deepened the rift between France and its overseas possessions.[86] As in the 1947-1948 Dakar-Niger rail strike, the succession crises among the Lébou and Tidjani enhanced the prestige and position of the "purely African" parties who shared the government general's imagination of "authentic" indigenous society in the federation, but challenged their prerogative to govern it. By the early 1950s a pattern had emerged in the struggle for authority in French West Africa that progressively eroded the imperial administration's ability to effectively set the rules of engagement in the colonial field. Citizens of the French Union demanded the realization of expectations raised by the fight against Hitler fascism and Vichy while Paris and Dakar hesitated or attempted to deflect those appeals. The confrontation usually concluded with minor concessions and greater support for organizations that pressed for political autonomy or independence.

In an attempt to prevent the latter result, François Mitterrand, minister for Overseas France and leader of the *Union Démocratique et Social de la Résistance* (UDSR), initiated a dialogue with Houphouët-Boigny and the RDA in advance of the 1951 general elections. As a result, Houphouët-

Boigny agreed to drop his organization's formal affiliation with the Communist Party, always a matter of convenience more than of ideological principle, and work with the UDSR in the National Assembly and the AUF. While the UDSR was one of the smaller parties in France, it was strategically important to the formation of many of the coalitions that governed during the Fourth Republic. Thus, an alliance with the UDSR afforded the RDA greater influence in the decision-making process at the imperial center than did a relationship with the ostracized PCF. Furthermore, Mitterrand, as the price for RDA support, agreed to broad administrative changes in West Africa. Those reforms included the replacement of the Socialist Béchard as governor general, associated with anti-RDA activities in the 1940s, and a law on 24 May 1951 that eliminated the dual electoral college system and created near universal suffrage in the federation just weeks before the 17 June general elections.[87]

While the government general anticipated the changes would result in an increased presence of the RDA in the Second National Assembly, it did not expect the overwhelming rejection of "metropolitan" parties like the SFIO, even in strongholds such as Senegal. In fact, the major beneficiary of the expanded suffrage was not the RDA, but a coalition led by Léopold Senghor called the *Indépendants d'Outre-mer* (IOM), of which the BDS was the dominant force.[88] Bernard Cornut-Gentille, governor general of AOF after Béchard's removal, informed Louis Jacquinot, Mitterrand's successor at the Overseas France ministry, that "the results of the 17 June elections constituted a very great surprise: no one could have predicted the triumph of the BDS." So thorough was Léopold Senghor's victory over Guèye and the SFIO that the Senegalese Socialist leader lost his seat in the National Assembly to the *Négritude* poet by more than a two-to-one margin.[89]

Dakar attributed the IOM's achievements to the support it received from trade unions and Islamic leaders, or Marabouts, who exercised significant influence in the region.[90] In fact, the BDS campaigned in "defense of Islam" in some areas, a curious slogan since the Party's leader was a devout Catholic and not part of the dominant Wolof ethnic group.[91] To secure the support of organized labor, which had demonstrated its strength during the 1947-1948 strike, the BDS provided "financial subsidies" to the unions and placed Abbas Guèye, one of the most prominent trade union officials in the federation, second on its electoral list, behind only Léopold Senghor. They both won election to the National Assembly. Dakar noted that such an arrangement "created real discontent and excited the spirits ... of the Marabouts [who] descended into the [political] arena and incited their followers to go on strike and follow the example of the unions." As a result, the BDS also provided funds to the religious orders and incorporated their leaders into the upper echelons of the party.[92]

The political maneuvering in Senegal, reproduced throughout West Africa, indicated an important change in the regimes of power operable in the federation. By the 1951 elections the various social forces and discontented elements of AOF no longer sought redress of their grievances through appeals to the colonial administration. Rather, they looked to the "African" parties for the achievement of their aspirations. Those parties cast themselves as "anti-colonial" and, as such, directed the struggles that gripped West Africa away from demands for full equality with France and toward autonomy. Accordingly, the discourses and political agendas of the colonial administration and the *évolués'* parties converged in a way that undermined French authority in the region even while it further entrenched tribal groups as the basis for governance in the federation.

The ability of the BDS and RDA to mobilize the discontent of rural and urban communities pressured the pre-colonial elite to come to terms with the new parties of the modern *griots* in order to preserve their place in West African society. Consequently, the accommodation of some "chiefs" with the *évolués* furnished important electoral support for the BDS and RDA, which enhanced their position *vis-à-vis* Paris and Dakar. Michael Crowder and Obaro Ikime write, "In French West Africa the chief has only been important in the period of effective African rule at times when there has been a struggle for power between two parties.... [W]hile the chief could be given a temporary political role by identifying him with one party or another and thus adding to the weapons at the politicians' disposal, he was dispensable after he had been used successfully, for having no continuing power base of his own, he was no longer of any use to them."[93] While that statement portrays one aspect of the relationship between the pre-colonial elite and the *évolués*, it does not account for the endurance of the institution of chieftaincy after independence and the continued role of "tribal" politics in the "national" context. I suggest that there was a continuous process of negotiation and mutual manipulation involved in the relationship between the two social groups, with the French-educated elite, at least during the 1950s, in the dominant position.[94]

Those among the pre-colonial elite that did not align with the new parties were "often replaced and cut off by a council of notables [dominated] by the BDS."[95] Despite "warnings" sent to Paris by associations that represented the interests of the pre-colonial elite that the "authority of the traditional chiefs [was] being eroded"[96] and protests against the "politicization of the chieftaincies," the government general only promised to "look into the matter" and subsequently failed to take action.[97] Even a committee convened by the government general on administrative reform in 1954 alerted Dakar of the "dangerous possibilities [contained] in the election of chiefs by universal suffrage and secret ballot" because it undermined "traditional practices," but offered no basis for action to preclude such practices.[98] "In effect," Dakar observed in 1954, "a complete change in the [political] situation [of West Africa] had taken place. The electoral law of May 1951 considerably expanded the right to vote and permitted the rural populations to enter into the electoral game. The overwhelming majority of their votes in 1951...went to M. Senghor."[99]

While the government general accused the BDS and RDA of "skipping steps in the political evolution of Black Africa...[through] the transformation of traditional chieftaincies into modern and purely democratic institutions," the colonial administration's possibilities for action were tightly circumscribed within the colonial field by the mid-1950s.[100] The "rapid evolution of the political situation" in the federation, though, did not occasion a revision of France's *mission civilisatrice* in sub-Saharan Africa.[101] To ensure that "authentic" African culture was not swept away by "extremists" among the *évolués* and to "guarantee that the chiefs would not cease to play a role in [Africa's] future as it had in the past," the imperial hierarchy overhauled the administrative structures of French West Africa and then divested itself of political rule.[102]

Decolonization?
Administrative Reform, Balkanization, and the Demise of AOF

By the mid-1950s conditions in France and West Africa had reached a crisis point. After the military debacle at Dien Bien Phu in 1954 Indochina gained its independence as North and South Vietnam, Laos, and Cambodia. That same year a revolt began in Algeria that soon involved the commitment of nearly a million soldiers and brought the colonial wars home to the metropole in the form of bombings, protests, and ultimately a coup that returned de Gaulle to power. As Maurice Agulhon understates it, events overseas were "not without consequences in internal politics" for France.[103] In the midst of those crises Paris sent Pierre Sanner on an inspection tour of AOF the purpose of which was to form recommendations on "the institutional reform of French West Africa." While he urged caution on the speed with which the structural bases of governance were changed, Sanner suggested that the fundamental goal of that transformation should be the accentuation of "the individuality" of each constituent territory in the federation. Locally, administration was to remain "based on ethnic affinities," but those "collectivities" were to be accorded greater "autonomy" from the various centers, whether it was the government general in Dakar or territorial capitals like Abidjan and Conakry.[104] One official anticipated that such reforms would stem the "exodus of the rural populations" toward the cities where "those masses [became] detribalized [and] disoriented." Furthermore, Sanner's proposals contributed to the actualization of France's mission in that they assisted Africa in "the transition from feudalism to democracy" while they simultaneously acknowledged the "regional variation of customary practices," which afforded the means to protect "authentic" cultural institutions in the process.[105]

By the end of 1954 Sanner's suggestions began to circulate as a draft administrative reform law, or *Loi Cadre*. The version that was submitted to the National Assembly in March 1956, though, went much further than the modest changes advanced by Sanner. According to the bill put before the assembled representatives in Paris, the government general for AOF was to be "suppressed. Each of the territories of French West Africa," the document proclaimed, "constitute[d] a public collectivity endowed [with its distinct] moral personality and financial autonomy."[106] Article two asserted that "the *Loi Cadre* recognized the ability of the [native] inhabitants to administer themselves." In order to realize that capacity, the act called for the expansion of the powers vested in the territorial assemblies, to the point where they functioned "as a parliament" with the right to modify or overturn laws promulgated in the metropole. Each territory was to form "a cabinet bestowed with real authority." Article three urged the "Africanization" of "all levels of the [governmental] hierarchy." All matters adjudicated by the government general to that point, which included budget allocations, public works projects, commercial law, public hygiene, housing, tourism, and justice, were transferred to the purview of the territorial assemblies and their ministerial cabinets. Only matters of national defense remained out of their hands. In addition, all foreign policy questions fell under the jurisdiction of the government in Paris.[107]

The Gaston Defferre Law, as the *Loi Cadre* became known, also had provision for changes in local administration within each of the territories. In recognition of the "great difference in the situation and mentality between the populations in the bush and those in the urban centers,"[108] Paris ordered the formation of distinct administrative bodies that reflected, and consequently preserved those idiosyncrasies. While the cities were accorded town governments based on geographic residence, complete with mayors, "rural collectivities" formed local councils constituted from "cohesive economic, political, and ethnic" groups.[109] This is the nature of what Mamdani identifies as the "bifurcated State," "two forms of power under a single hegemonic authority. Urban power spoke the language of civil society and civil rights, rural power of community and culture." Mamdani regards this as "the most important institutional legacy of colonial rule."[110] The imperial administration justified the separate bases for governance between rural and urban communities on the claim that, despite the concerted efforts of the government general, the majority of city residents were "detribalized Africans."[111] Significantly, even though the inhabitants of West Africa's cities were presumed to no longer have connections with their tribal group, they remained "African" and did not become any more "French" in the process. While urban workers might resemble Europeans, they remained perpetually and fundamentally African, albeit not as "authentically" African as those who continued to reside in their rural communities under the supervision of chiefs.[112]

Defferre, the minister for Overseas France after the 2 January 1956 elections, masked the radical nature of the reform in his explanation of the motives behind the *Loi Cadre*. According to the Socialist minister, "The *Loi Cadre* [was] situated in the evolution [of overseas policy that can be] traced from the preamble of the Constitution [of the Fourth Republic and] constitute[d], in effect, a decisive stage, in that it consecrate[d] the capacity of the overseas inhabitants to govern themselves." Defferre cited a laundry list of measures taken on that road to self-government, which commenced with Brazzaville and included FIDES and FERDES, the Lamine Guèye Law, and the application of the *Code du Travail* in the territories of the French Union.[113] The minister for Overseas France confidently announced that the *Loi Cadre* indicated that the long "political apprenticeship" of the West African population had been "achieved." France had fulfilled its *mission civilisatrice* and was prepared to devolve authority on those leaders who represented "the fullest expression of public opinion."[114]

However, Defferre did not explain how what had begun as an investigation into reform of the government general for French West Africa in 1953 had, within three years, concluded with a law to abolish the federation and allow the constituent territories virtual independence. The silence in Defferre's speech marked a refusal on the part of the metropolitan government and colonial administration to recognize their inability to command in West Africa. Even as France proclaimed the accomplishment of its mission in language that suggested a planned progression, the *évolués* had seized the very foundations of colonial governance while the government general bemoaned its incapacitation. By the time the *Loi Cadre* was placed before the members of the National Assembly the terms of the struggle for authority within the colonial field had been altered to the point that what was "politically...unsayable...unthinkable" a few years prior had become imperative if France was to avoid a confrontation in West Africa on a scale experienced in Indochina between 1946 and 1954, or that in which it was then engaged in Algeria.[115] The tenuous coalition of centrist parties that governed the Fourth Republic found itself trapped in a vice between the political right that urged the government to resist "centrifugal forces" that threatened the future of French power overseas and elements of the left and some business circles that argued the time had arrived to end the colonial adventure.[116]

Nevertheless, the most decisive factor in the promulgation of the Gaston Defferre Law was the ascendancy of the *évolués* as the dominant social force in West Africa. Elections to the Third National Assembly on 2 January 1956 resulted in impressive victories for the "African" parties of the modern *griots*. Houphouët-Boigny's RDA and Léopold Senghor's BDS/IOM won all but a handful of the seats to the National Assembly as well as clear majorities in most local assemblies. In addition to the two party leaders, those elected to seats in Paris included Mamadou Dia (IOM, Senegal), Mobido Keïta (RDA, Soudan), Sissoko (SFIO, Soudan), Hamani Diori (RDA, Niger), Sékou Touré (RDA, Guinea), Apithy (independent, Dahomey), and Hubert Maga (IOM, Dahomey).[117] Unlike the 1951 vote, the success of the RDA and BDS/IOM did not surprise officials in Dakar or Paris. However, the outcome in France transformed those achievements from matters of local or regional importance into developments that significantly affected politics in the metropole and the nature of the French state itself. The Communist Party gained nearly fifty seats to become the largest party in the Assembly, while the right, organized around Pierre Poujade and his regionalist anti-tax, anti-state movement that also embraced the cause of *Algérie Française*, emerged as a potent force in the new parliament. Thus, the coalition of socialists, radicals, and Christian Democrats that had dominated the Fourth Republic since its inception was more dependent than at any previous time on the votes of overseas parties like the RDA and BDS/IOM. That reliance was confirmed when the new Socialist premier, Guy Mollet, named Houphouët-Boigny to the cabinet, the first African to hold such a post in the French government. Other members of the RDA were appointed to influential positions in the National Assembly and as under-secretaries in various ministries.[118]

In West Africa, the 1956 vote combined with discussions of the *Loi Cadre* signaled a new phase in the struggle for authority in the federation. In that contest, though, the colonial administration was largely absent and Paris served as a distant referent and, at best, as an arbiter of last resort. By the spring of 1956, the fight to pose as the legitimate leaders of the indigenous population had devolved into an internal competition among the *évolués* themselves. That change was explicitly acknowledged by Houphouët-Boigny in a speech delivered before supporters in Cotonou, Dahomey, in which he declared, "The *Loi Cadre* will be what we make of it, that is to say its [substance] will be of our own [determination]."[119] That assertion at once dismissed France as a serious player in the political field within West Africa and proclaimed the French-educated elite as the adjudicator of the region's destiny.

However, the modern *griots* differed in their notions of the proper institutional bases for administrative authority in the federation. In that dispute the principle protagonists were Houphouët-Boigny and Léopold Senghor as each attempted to realize their *imaginaires* of "authentic" African forms of political and social organization. The *Négritude* poet embraced the *Loi Cadre* as an important "first step toward internal autonomy,"[120] but accused Paris of the "Balkanization of black Africa [that, consequently, would continue to be] under French influence."[121] Furthermore, Léopold Senghor and Dia protested the articulation of separate administrative structures for rural and urban communities and informed Defferre that the decrees to implement the *Loi Cadre* had to provide for "complete democracy" in all communities, especially the tribal assemblies.[122] Léopold Senghor's greatest concern, though, was article one, which abolished the federation. Even though the reform act enhanced the authority of the territorial assemblies, it did not provide for the creation of a "federal" assembly that would maintain the territorial unity established by France in 1895. For the Senegalese leader that meant the formation of socio-political "entities without [historical] reality. To accept the *balkanization* of Africa would [amount to] acceptance, [along] with our misery, of the alienation of our reasons for living."[123] In addition, the Gaston Defferre Law transferred budgetary control to each of the separate territories, which essentially wound up FIDES and FERDES since they were federally administered. Thus, the "autonomous" political units had no means by which to coordinate their economic activity, a serious problem for a region whose economy was organized on the basis of a unified federal administrative structure.[124]

While Léopold Senghor regarded separate ethnic or tribal groups as a "natural" part of "authentic" African society and its basic unit of governance, he also maintained that the diverse communities were bound together by a shared "Negro-African culture" rooted in the primordial past.[125] Accordingly,

French West Africa, despite its colonial origins, could be considered a legitimate and "authentic" form of administrative organization for Africans. For Léopold Senghor and his supporters the "regeneration" of "real" African culture could only proceed on the basis of political unity.[126] Gabriel d'Arboussier, vice president of the RDA and long-time Communist, echoed that sentiment at a press conference in 1958 when he contended that "federation [was] the institutional form of the expression and the aspiration of the unity of the peoples of Black Africa."[127]

However, Paris insisted that "decentralization" of the federal administrative structure, even to the point of its abrogation, better conformed to the "natural" forms of social organization in Africa. Accordingly, the law passed by the National Assembly on 19 June 1956 by a margin of 446 to 98 and the Assembly of the French Union four days later, 124–1, provided for its implementation by "particular decrees for each territory." Furthermore, the "heads of the territories" were provisioned with absolute authority "to constitute rural collectivities" and take all other measures necessary for the restructuring of the governmental system in their areas of control.[128]

Léopold Senghor noted the contradiction manifested in France's international relations in the late 1950s. To a meeting of the BPS—*Bloc Populaire Sénegalais*, successor to the BDS in 1956—the Senegalese leader affirmed, "They are correct, the French, the Germans, the English, or [for that matter] all the other good Europeans to desire to unite Europe, but how are we to accept that they are trying to unite Europe while they are attempting to disunite Africa?"[129] At the moment when Defferre insisted that Africa could only achieve its potential in economic, cultural, and political development through the dismemberment of AOF and the empowerment of local, tribal collectivities France had taken the lead in the formation of the European Economic Community, consecrated by the Treaty of Rome in 1957. Even as the metropole's ability to command in West Africa evaporated it continued to uphold, through its rhetoric and praxis, notions of essential differences between Europeans and Africans.

However, important forces among the *évolués* shared Paris' conception of the "true" expression of African social organization and welcomed the *Loi Cadre* as the road to real political power. Foremost among them was Houphouët-Boigny who, as a cabinet member, participated in the draft of the final version of the law presented to the National Assembly.[130] He and his associates within the RDA embraced the idea that the separate territories were legitimate forms of social organization within Africa that allowed the "traditional wisdom" of its peoples effective influence on local policy and contributed to the "evolution" of indigenous societies.[131]

Houphouët-Boigny's stance reflected divisions among the modern *griots* that dated from the period when the Four Communes of Senegal enjoyed a special status within the colonial field as French citizens and, through Diagne's activities, claimed a leadership role in relation to the entire West African population. Already by the 1920s conflicts had emerged between those among the French-educated elite who were *citoyens* and those who were *sujets*, each of which tended to articulate divergent stances in the struggle for authority within the colonial field.[132] Even though all imperial subjects had been transformed into citizens of the French Union in 1946, the divisions and animosities that arose between the "Senegalese" and the rest of West Africa persisted. Thus, Houphouët-Boigny and others interpreted Léopold Senghor's calls for maintenance of the federation as attempts by the Senegalese to sustain their pre-eminent position among the *évolués* of the region, a perception seemingly confirmed by Senegal's absence at the founding congress of the RDA in 1946.

In addition, Houphouët-Boigny's stance continued a practice born of the confrontation between the colonial administration and the *évolués* where the federal authorities were deemed the primary opposition to African self-rule and Paris occasionally functioned as a source of support for the French-educated elite's demands. Consequently, Houphouët-Boigny argued that the *Loi Cadre*, since it removed the obstructive presence of the federation, enabled the "different" peoples of West Africa to construct a more direct relationship with France that was mutually beneficial. In language nearly identical to that practiced by Moutet after the Lamine Guèye Law was passed in 1946, the Ivory Coast planter and doctor told supporters that his goal was the creation "of a community of men [that were] different but equal in rights and responsibilities." He added, "We need France for our human and social emancipation, France needs us in order to ensure the durability of its grandeur, of its genius in the world.... [In that relationship] we, Africans, [would be] able to make our contribution to the construction of a new world, to the greater understanding between men." According to Houphouët-Boigny, the *Loi Cadre's* devolution and decentralization of authority provided the institutional basis for the realization of that vision.[133]

The discourse practiced by Houphouët-Boigny legitimized France's assertion that it had a *mission civilisatrice* in West Africa and concomitantly authorized the vital place of the *évolué* in the relationship between the two areas even after decolonization. At the moment when the French presence appeared to have become superfluous in West Africa the leaders of Ivory Coast provided the metropole with the possibility of a role in the region after the territories had achieved self-governance. In fact, at no point during the debate on the *Loi Cadre* or over its implementation did the *évolués* associated with Léopold Senghor or Houphouët-Boigny express a desire for complete independence. Instead, they imagined the elaboration of a "federal republic" with France or a "Eurafrican federation" that achieved the model propounded in Article 41 of the first draft of the constitution for the Fourth Republic which stated that "France form[ed] with the overseas territories ... a voluntary union."[134]

However, the French-educated elite was concerned that France wanted to sever all ties with West Africa if it could no longer administer the region. That trepidation was fueled by a series of article in *Paris-Match* written by Raymond Cartier shortly after the *Loi Cadre* was passed. Cartier asserted that the metropole had "little need of Africa, [but] it has an immense need for us."[135] Rather than a re-statement of the *mission civilisatrice* that claimed France had a purpose in West Africa, Cartierism, as it became known, argued that since the imperial center had little to gain from a relationship with Africa it should give up the overseas territories and cultivate liaisons in Europe and with North America. Jacques Marseille suggests that the emergence of Cartierism signaled the end of France's overseas adventure since French business interests not connected to the colonial trade had gained ascendancy in the metropole and forced a shift in international policy toward more "modern" and lucrative ventures in Europe and North America.[136] While Marseille has highlighted an important aspect of the decolonization process, I suggest we also look at the important cultural and social contexts in which decisions about rule and the relationship between metropole and colony were made. French colonialism was rarely imagined as primarily an economic association between France and the colonies. Rather, even the economics of imperialism were couched in terms of a "mission," which implied a wide-ranging beneficent connection between metropole and colony. Furthermore, Marseille's economistic reading of decolonization cannot account for the enduring connections between France and its former colonies after independence. Additionally, its does not allow the researcher to understand why de Gaulle and subsequent French leaders believed it to be so important to maintain close relations with, in particular, its former African colonies.

Gaston Cusin, the high commissioner of AOF, informed Defferre that "the African *évolués*...were extremely upset...by Cartier's articles."[137] Thus, while French authority waned in West Africa, the modern *griots* struggled to formulate a basis whereby the territories of the federation could maintain close, even symbiotic relations with the metropole. In that endeavor, the *évolués*, ensconced as the dominant political class in most of AOF, induced a discursive shift within the colonial field as they insisted that France would not be France without Africa. Léopold Senghor and others argued that Africa had distinct contributions to make to the "development" of French culture and a French presence in the world, while an enduring connection with France enabled the continued evolution of "our own Negro-African personality."[138] It was an argument that some within the colonial administration also embraced. Cusin informed the Ivory Coast's territorial assembly in August 1956 that "Franco-African cooperation" afforded France "the means whereby it could recover its grandeur and [Africa could receive] the benefits of our evolution."[139] Moreover, de Gaulle adopted that position after he was returned to power in 1958 and it became the basis of the Fifth Republic's foreign policy almost continuously from that point to the present.[140]

The notion of a "Eurafrican federation" and the concern to maintain close relations with France even if the territories became politically independent represented an institutional manifestation of the self-identity articulated by the *évolués* since at least the Great War. Despite the rhetorical change within the colonial field after the Liberation to an emphasis on disputes over "authentic" forms of African social organization, the French-educated elite continued to present itself as simultaneously "French" and "African." In fact, assertions by the *évolués* that they constituted the "legitimate leaders" of the West African people were founded upon their claims to participate in the cultural worlds of both Europe and Africa. That circumstance afforded them access to influential positions in Paris as well as direct contact with the indigenous communities of the federation, a connection that was claimed to benefit both communities. The end of colonialism merely furnished the context wherein the modern *griots* could fulfill their mission in Africa and the larger world. According to Léopold Senghor, "It [was] in the Latin Quarter … that [the *évolués*] became conscious of their authenticity, that they began to preach *Négritude* as the gospel. Today, they are the best writers in the French Union; they are the heads of [governmental] departments, pioneers in the heart of the metropole or in Africa; they are not politicians, but political people, men [whose purpose is] to serve and who serve [their people]."[141] Ouezzin Coulibaly, member of the RDA and vice president of Upper Volta's territorial assembly in 1958, explained that "the African elite," which he described as "the intellectual[s]," "constitute[d] a sort of investment for the country." They had "the task" to direct "the evolution of the territory" and preserve its unity. However, Coulibaly did not call for independence. He merely asserted the need for "real autonomy," which implied a continued relationship with

France in a context where the new African states had achieved self-government.[142]

Thus, the positions adopted by the French-educated elite as the imperial system crumbled between 1955 and 1960 were consistent with long-held notions of their place in the colonial field and emanated from their particular identity. Contrary to assertions by some scholars, there was no "conversion of African elites and politicians from a pro-assimilationist perspective to a pro-nationalist approach" during the fifteen years between the end of the Second World War and independence in 1960. Furthermore, in the meetings of the various forces that attempted to rescue some federal structure for West Africa between 1957 and 1960, and in the resolutions of those parties that opposed such efforts there is little indication of an "emotional attachment to the nation-state [by] the assimilated Africans," especially to the "French" nation.[143] The modern *griots* were attached to a particular institutional and conceptual framework in which they constituted the "vital core." Consequently, their ambition, in general, was "to form...an autonomous State within the French Republic, a State that would accordingly accede to the status of a State associated in a confederal structure."[144] However, events in the metropole conspired to shift discussion from an association with France as self-governing states to the reconstruction of that link as independent entities.

Conclusion

Barely a year after the first elections took place in West Africa under the provisions of the *Loi Cadre* reforms through which new territorial presidents took office and cabinets were formed,[145] the Fourth Republic itself collapsed. While France had accepted by 1956 that it could no longer effectively govern West Africa, had accorded independence to Tunisia and Morocco the previous year, and in 1954 was driven from Southeast Asia, it waged a brutal war to prevent Algeria from attainment of similar status. As debates raged over implementation of the *Loi Cadre*, the French, in association with Israel and Britain, launched an attack against Egypt whose government had nationalized the Suez Canal in July, one month after Defferre's law was voted into effect. In part, that assault was in retaliation for Egypt's support of the rebels in Algeria. Additionally, France intercepted a Moroccan plane headed for Tunisia that carried Ahmed Ben Bella, one of the leaders of Algeria's *Front de libération national* (FLN) just prior to the invasion of the Suez Canal Zone. The following year witnessed the "Battle of Algiers," an intense and vicious struggle ultimately won by General Jacques Massu. However, Massu's "victory" produced outrage in France at the widespread use of torture against suspected members of the FLN. The circulation of Henri Alleg's *La Question* in February 1958, a personal account of his experiences as a torture victim at the hands of French forces in Algeria, further galvanized opposition in France to the war and intensified pressure on the West African politicians to break with a country that seemed not to have learned the lessons of its own history under Nazi occupation.[146]

However, protest over Algeria was not confined to the political left. The vocal forces in favor of *Algérie Française*, concerned that Paris was prepared to "abandon" Algeria as it had other parts of the empire, staged a coup in Algiers on 13 May 1958. A "Committee of Public Safety" was formed of leading rightists, many of them supporters of Poujade with fascist connections that dated to the 1930s, and Gaullists that included Massu, Jacques Soustelle, Raoul Salan, Jacques Chaban-Delmas, and Léon Delbecque. On 24 May the conspirators attacked and occupied Corsica, which was planned as a base for the ultimate invasion of Paris. In the meantime de Gaulle offered to take the reigns of state, if so asked, but refused to condemn the actions in Algeria, despite pleas by Paris to do so. On the day the coup plotters had set for its assault on Paris, the former leader of Free France proclaimed that negotiations were in the works to form a new government, presumably with him at its head. Somber protests in the French capital organized by the political left in opposition to the coup, de Gaulle's machinations, and the government's refusal to defend the Republic were of no avail. On 1 June, in a move eerily reminiscent of the dark days in June 1940, the National Assembly invested de Gaulle as head of state. The next day, the retired general was given unlimited governmental authority and the right to elaborate a new constitution. The Fourth Republic, born in the excited atmosphere of the Liberation, had died in the morass of colonial wars.

The events of May and June 1958 accelerated agitation in West Africa for complete independence from France and the reconstruction of relations on the basis of a "free association" of peoples. The constitution presented by de Gaulle in September permitted just such a possibility. In a whirlwind tour of Africa by the new head of state and his trusted aid André Malraux, de Gaulle offered the peoples of the overseas territories the option of immediate independence, if they voted "no" in the 28 September constitutional referendum, or association with France in a "federal community," if they chose "yes." In essence, de Gaulle provided the prospect for the *évolués* to realize their imagined relationship with France. Accordingly, the RDA,

Léopold Senghor and his associates in Senegal, and the "religious leaders and traditional chiefs" who had attained their office during the agitation of the mid-1950s all declared for "*oui*" in the balloting. However, organized labor and the political parties that depended on working class support opted for "*non*."[147] Only Guinea's territorial government was directed by elements not from the class of the French-educated elite. Led by the trade unionist Sékou Touré and backed by the *Union Générale des Travailleurs d'Afrique Noire* (UGTAN), founded in January 1957 after a break with the metropolitan CGT, Guinea was the only territory to vote "no." On 29 September 1958 Touré declared Guinea an independent state outside the "French Community."[148]

Despite the overwhelming "yes" vote in the other seven territories of the federation, they too began to declare their independence as early as January 1959. By 1960 all the former members of AOF had become sovereign states and the "French Community" had suffered a swift, silent death. That demise was largely precipitated by unrest that engulfed West Africa after the referendum. Angered by the alliance between *évolués* and "traditional" rulers in the rural areas, a combination that provided the turnout in favor of the constitution and also furnished the votes for the parties led by the modern *griots*, organized labor and the radical student movement engaged in a series of strikes that often ended in violence.[149] Their demands were nearly identical to those put forth against the colonial administration earlier in the decade—higher wages, family allowances, union rights, and access to the decision-making process.[150] In response, the new leaders of the territories instructed UGTAN that "the time had come [for workers] to take a 'national consciousness' in order to obtain real independence and the complete freedom of Africa." Furthermore, Niger's leader Hamani Diori explained, in the midst of a general strike in his territory, that "the government's" goal was "the realization of continuous social peace in the country [which was] necessary for the influx of private and public investment."[151]

By the late 1950s a new hegemonic bloc had been constituted in West Africa, one that brought together the French-educated elite and the pre-colonial elite, albeit one reconstituted after the revolution in the rural areas between 1949 and 1955. The government general's attempt to forestall the *évolués*' rise to administrative authority through a redirection of the struggle for dominance in the federation toward notions of "authentic" African forms of social organization actually weakened the colonial administration's ability to command. Its economic and political reforms, designed to revive native chieftaincies, opened conceptual and institutional spaces for the emergence of powerful "African" parties that also adhered to the ethnographic paradigm of "natural" indigenous political practices advanced by Dakar. In a contest over which force was best qualified to "lead" the West African people, imperial officials were outmatched by modern *griots* that asserted an "organic" connection with autochthonous communities and claimed the ability to effectively represent their wishes in Paris. Trapped between a desire to use the pre-colonial elite as a bulwark against the *évolués* and pledges to "democratize" the federation's command structure, the government general's room for engagement in the struggles within the colonial field was tightly circumscribed. In the end, it opted for reform and, consequently, furnished the means for the French-educated elite to transform its organizations from small urban groups into mass parties. In that context, Defferre's law in 1956 merely confirmed a reality that had already been achieved. Even without a formal resolution from Paris, the territories of AOF had become self-governing through the aggressive actions of the modern *griots* and their ability to mobilize the vast discontent of rural West Africa.

However, the process whereby the *évolués* became the ruling class throughout much of West Africa in the 1950s touched off a vigorous debate about the nature of "decolonization." Léopold Senghor and others among the French-educated elite stated flatly that decolonization meant, "in a word, nothing but independence."[152] That provided the modern *griots* with the means to fulfill their mission to regenerate "authentic" African culture and forge a new relationship with France as "equals" in a "free association." Anything that precluded the achievement of those ends, as witnessed in the case of the trade unions, was fought as relentlessly as had the colonial administration against those forces that obstructed France's *mission civilisatrice*. Moreover, the accession of the French-educated elite to leadership in West Africa did not result in a revolutionary transformation of the command structures in the region, merely an alteration in the relations of power operable between contending social forces. The authority of the ruling parties after 1956 was dependent upon the support of tribal rulers who mobilized their constituents to turn out for elections in exchange for patronage from the state, a practice that recalled the days of French ascendancy. While the chiefs and religious leaders were generally supportive of the parties directed by *évolués* such as Houphouët-Boigny and Léopold Senghor, the fundamental referent in the construction of local identities and the foundation of the system of governance in West Africa remained that of the tribal group. As authority devolved to the modern *griots* they confronted increased rivalries among those communities for the resources of the state. Already by the late 1950s "fratricidal violence" had erupted in Guinea, Niger, Upper Volta, and French Soudan (Mali).[153] The rivalry between

Guèye and Léopold Senghor in Senegal earlier that decade adumbrated a pattern of political struggle among tribal groups associated with different parties or factions within parties that became generalized in West Africa by 1960. Significantly, only Guinea, led by a trade unionist, passed laws that abolished chieftaincy and set out to revolutionize the basis of governance. However, calls for "real" decolonization mounted even as the modern *griots* consolidated their position in the new states. In the conclusion to our narrative we examine the different interpretations of the meaning of the end of empire in the ex-metropole and former AOF, and assess the legacy of French rule in West Africa.

NOTES

1. CAOM, 1/AP/2153, unsigned report from AOF to the ministry for Overseas France, "Note: Chefferies—formation des cadres et des élites," 4 May 1953. (Emphasis in the original.)

2. CAOM, 1/AP/872/20, telegram from Boisson to the colonial commission of the provisional government in Algiers, 25 June 1943.

3. Gramsci, *Selections from the Prison Notebooks*, p. 196. For the past two decades there has been a rich, and growing literature that studies the "history" of subaltern groups and seeks to demonstrate their important presence in the narratives that have generally been constructed from the "top down." Such works have added complexity to and deepened the theoretical and empirical approaches to understanding social change from directions previously not explored. See: Ranajit Guha, *Elementary Aspects of Peasant Insurgency in Colonial India* (Delhi: Oxford University Press, 1983); Dipesh Chakrabarty, "Postcoloniality and the Artifice of History: Who Speaks for 'Indian' Pasts?" in *Representations* 37 (Winter 1992); and Spivak, "Can the Subaltern Speak?" in Nelson and Grossberg, eds., *Marxism and the Interpretation of Culture*.

4. CAOM, 1/AP/2130/3, "Note: Les Collectivités urbaines et le prolétariat," 1952. See also: CAOM, 1/AP/2198/3, report by Afrika Youjnée Sakhary at the Institut Orientaliste de l'Académie des Sciences de l'URSS, Moscow 1958.

5. CAOM, 1/AP/2130/5, report produced by the government general for AOF, "Les Collectivités rurales et le paysannat," written in 1953.

6. CAOM, 1/AP/2130/5, "Plan de developpement economique et social 1948–1952;" "Note au sujet des Fonds d'Equipement Rural et de Développement Économique et Social en A.O.F.," 12 May 1950; "Les collectivités rurales et le paysannat," 1953.

7. Cooper, *Decolonization and African Society*, p. 195.

8. In fact, as Cooper notes, FIDES was created the same month the decree that abolished forced labor was passed by the Constituent Assembly, April 1946. Cooper, *Decolonization and African Society*, p. 195.

9. CAOM, 1/AP/3638/1, "rapport" produced by the Assembly of the French Union (AUF), 25 November 1953, on the creation of local councils in AOF.

10. CAOM, 1/AP/2153, "Travaux de la Commission des T.O.M. et avant-rapport de M. Senghor," 1954.

11. CAOM, 1/AP/2177, letter from the government general for AOF to the ministry for Overseas France, "Objet: Critiques formulées par Me. Lamine Guèye à l'encontre de l'Administration du Sénégal," 9 January 1954.

12. CAOM, 1/AP/2188, letter from Mohamed Mahouud Mahmoud Ould Cheikh Cadi de Tombouctou to the ministry for Overseas France, 24 March 1955, in which he complains of interference in tribal affairs by militants of the RDA from Soudan, Senegal, and even Morocco.

13. CAOM, 1/AP/2130/5, "Plan de developpement ecnomique et social 1948-1952."

14. CAOM, 1/AP/491, "Memoire sur la réforme des structures de l'A.O.F.," produced by the government general in Dakar, 11 July 1955.

15. For a thorough analysis of the formation of the ministry of culture in France after 1958 and its relation to the end of formal empire overseas see: Lebovics, *Mona Lisa's Escort*.

16. CAOM, 1/AP/2288/5, "Recommendations adoptées par la conference Africaine Française," 30 January–8 February 1944, at Brazzaville.

17. ARS, Esclavage et Travail (K)/328/26, "Renseignements, 11 January 1946, which documents the strikes by clerical, manual, and metal workers in French West Africa that began in January 1946.

18. CAOM, 1/AP/2146, "L'Assemblée acclame la politique définié par Marius Moutet; Emancipation politique et économique des indigènes," in *Le Populaire*, 24-25 March 1946.

19. Stoler and Cooper, "Between Metropole and Colony," in Cooper and Stoler eds., *Tensions of Empire*, p. 37.

20. CAOM, 1/AP/873, "Les Realisations coloniales de la France combattante en Afrique Equatoriale Française," 1 March 1943.

21. CAOM, 1/AP/214, Lapie, "Empire ou Fédération?" in *La Quatrième Republique*, 8 January 1944.

22. There has been a great deal of important research recently on the internationalization of the colonial question after the Second World War and the role of the Cold War in the facilitation of decolonization. In this regard see: Marc Michel, *Décolonisations et émergence du tiers monde* (Paris: Hachette, 1993); Hargreaves, *Decolonization in Africa*; Grimal, *Decolonization*; and Cooper, *Decolonization and African Society*. Also, there has been a resurgence of interest in decolonization in general. See, in this regard: Martin Thomas, *The French Empire at War, 1940–1945* (Manchester: Manchester University Press, 1998); Martin Shipway, *The Road to War: France and Vietnam, 1944–1947* (Oxford: Berghahn, 1996); and Tony Chafer, *The End of Empire in French West Africa: France's Successful Decolonization?* (Oxford: Berg, 2002).

23. CAOM, 1/AP/2147, Marius Moutet, "Politique d'Association," 15 September 1946.

24. CAOM, 1/AP/2130/5, "Les collectivités rurales et le paysannat," 1953. See especially the section headed, "Situation en 1946."

25. De Gaulle, *The Complete War Memoirs*, pp. 716, 772, 773, 775, 777.

26. CAOM, 1/AP/2130/5, "Les collectivités rurales et le paysannat," 1953. See especially the section headed. "Objectifs poursuivis."

27. CAOM, 1/AP/2130/5, "Une resolution du groupe interparlementaire des Indépendants d'Outre-Mer à propos des decisions de la conference de Londres," 16 May 1950. The *Indépendants d'Outre-Mer* (IOM) was a grouping of deputies to the National Assembly and the Assembly of the French Union from Africa, for the most part, headed by Léopold Senghor and usually associated with the Christian Democratic MRP in French politics. It represented an opposition tendency to the *Rassemblement Démocratique Africain* (RDA) founded by Félix Houphouët-Boigny and associated with the PCF in French politics until 1950.

28. Cooper, *Decolonization and African Society*, pp. 194–195.

29. CAOM, 1/AP/2130/5, "Qui faut-il penser de sociétés Africaines de prevoyance?" 1952, report contained in the files of the ministry for Overseas France.

30. The concept of "the limits of the possible" is associated with the Annales School of history developed in France through the works of Lucien Febvre, Marc Bloch, and Fernand Braudel. For a fuller discussion of the concept and examples of its use in historical writing see: Fernand Braudel, *Civilization and Capitalism, Fifteenth to*

Eighteenth Centuries, Volume 1, The Structures of Everyday Life: The Limits of the Possible trans. Siân Reynolds (Berkeley: University of California Press, 1992).

31. CAOM, 1/AP/2130/5, "Note au sujet des Fonds d'Equipement Rural et de Développement Économique et Social en A.O.F.," 12 May 1950.

32. CAOM, 1/AP/2130/5, "Note au sujet des Fonds d'Equipement Rural et de Développement Économique et Social en A.O.F.," 12 May 1950. See also in the same carton, "Les collectivités rurales et le paysannat," 1953; and "Note sur les principes generaux de l'etablissement du plan quadriennal de developpement economique," 1953. The Plan was to cover the years 1953–1957.

33. CAOM, 1/AP/2147, Pierre Singly, "La personalité des populations indigènes," in *Marchés Coloniaux*, a series of articles published between 30 November 1946 and 2 August 1947.

34. CAOM, 1/AP/3655, letter from Moutet to the governors general of all overseas territories, 13 June 1947.

35. CAOM, 1/AP/3655, speech before the Assemblée de l'Union Française by Pierre Boisdon, "Citoyenneté de l'Union Française," 4 September 1952.

36. CAOM, 1/AP/3655, letter from Moutet to the governors general of all overseas territories, 13 June 1947.

37. Anne McClintock, *Imperial Leather*.

38. CAOM, 1/AP/2153/1, *Décret* issued by René Pleven (prime minister) and Louis Jacquinot (minister for Overseas France), 2 November 1951; and, in the same carton, Decree on the status of chiefs in West Africa, submitted to the Assemblée de l'Union Française in 1952.

39. CAOM, 1/AP/2128, note produced by the ministry for Overseas France, 4 July 1953.

40. CAOM, 1/AP/3638, "Rapport" submitted to the AUF by the general political commission, 25 November 1953.

41. CAOM, 1/AP/2152/1, "séance" of 9 August 1947 in the National Assembly, published in the *Journal Officiel* the following day.

42. CAOM, 1/AP/2153, "Note: Chefferies – formation des cadres et des élites," 4 May 1953, produced by the ministry for Overseas France. The decree on the election of "chiefs" was issued on 12 February 1947.

43. CAOM, 1/AP/3638/1, "Organisation politique et administrative de la Brousse," produced by the government general for AOF, August 1955.

44. CAOM, 1/AP/2152/1, "Proposition de Résolution tendant à inviter le Gouvernement à préciser le statut des chefs indigènes en Afrique occidentale française, en Afrique équatoriale française, au Togo et au Cameroun," presented by Yacine Diallo, Aubame, Horma Ould Babana, Ninine, Lamine Guèye, Fily-Dabo Sissoko, Léopold Senghor, and Sylvandre, deputies of the National Assembly, 17 June 1947. See also, in the same carton, "Proposition de Loi relative au statut des chefs coutumiers en Afrique occidentale française, au Togo, au Cameroun et en Afrique équatoriale française," presented by Deputies Aku, Apithy, Aubame, Condat Mahaman, Guissou, Laribi, Mamba Sano, Martine, Nazi Boni, Mamadou Ouedraogo, Savarane Lambert, and Léopold Senghor, 16 May 1950.

45. CAOM, 1/AP/2152/1, "Doléances des Chefs de Canton de la Guinée Française," directed by Diallo Ousmane, 15 October 1947. See also, in the same carton, letters from Diallo Ousmane to the ministry for Overseas France, 31 October 1947; letter from the *Syndicat des Chefs de Canton de la Guinée Française* (headed by El Hadj

Almamy Ibrahima Sory Dara Barry at that time) to the ministry for Overseas France, 10 April 1953; and letter from Barry to the president of France and the French Union, 28 May 1956.

46. CAOM, 1/AP/2152/1, letter from the ministry for Overseas France to El Hadj Barry, 28 May 1956.

47. CAOM, 1/AP/2153, "Proclamation du Prince Adingia Président de l'Association des Chefs Coutumiers de la Côte d'Ivoire," in *France-Afrique*, 20 August 1954.

48. CAOM, 1/AP/2152/1, Léopold Senghor, "Rapport" to the Assemblée Nationale, 2 June 1954.

49. The argument that post-war discourses of equality tightly circumscribed the room for maneuver on the part of the colonial administration and greatly empowered the residents of West Africa is extensively and effectively developed with regard to the "labor question" and trade union politics in the 1940s and 1950s in: Cooper, *Decolonization and African Society*.

50. CAOM, 1/AP/2143, "Note sur le Sénégal," October 1954, produced by the government general for AOF.

51. CAOM, 1/AP/2152/1, "Proposition de Loi relative au statut des chefs coutumiers en Afrique occidentale française, au Togo, au Cameroun et en Afrique équatoriale française," presented by the deputies from French-ruled sub-Saharan Africa, 16 May 1950.

52. CAOM, 1/AP/2152/1, Léopold Senghor, "Rapport" to the Assemblée Nationale, 2 June 1954. See also: CAOM, 1/AP/2153, Max Jalade, "M. Senghor présente le rapport sur le statut des chefs coutumiers," in *La Rene de Guinée*, 12 April 1954, where excerpts of Léopold Senghor's speech before the National Assembly were published and analyzed in advance of the formal presentation to the deputies in Paris.

53. CAOM, 1/AP/2153, "Travaux de la Commission des T.O.M. et avant-rapport de M. Senghor," June 1954. (Emphasis in the original.)

54. CAOM, 1/AP/2712, speech by Félix Houphouët-Boigny, president of the RDA, before supporters in Paris, 6-10 February 1947.

55. For brief biographical sketches of Houphouët-Boigny and other prominent West African politicians during the 1950s see: Djibril Tamsir Niane and Jean Suret-Canale, *Histoire de l'Afrique Occidentale* (Conakry-Paris: Présence Africaine, 1961).

56. For a more thorough discussion of Houphouët-Boigny's role in the campaign to end forced labor see: Cooper, *Decolonization and African Society*, pp. 186–191.

57. Félix Houphouët-Boigny, "Le R.D.A. dans la lutte anti-impérialiste," quoted in Niane and Suret-Canale, *Histoire de l'Afrique Occidentale*, pp. 191–192.

58. CAOM, 1/AP/2712, speech by Houphouët-Boigny at a meeting of the RDA in Paris, 6-10 February 1947.

59. CAOM, 3/SLOTFOM/101, statement published in *Cahiers du Bolshevisme*, No. 36, 21 January 1926.

60. CAOM, 1/AP/2712, speech by Houphouët-Boigny to a meeting of the RDA in Paris, 6-10 February 1947.

61. See Henri Lozeray, "La Question Coloniale," in *Cahiers du Communisme*, No. 6, April 1945, reproduced in: Monéta, *La Politique du Parti communiste français*, pp. 150-152.

62. The Cold War influence on Moutet's attitude toward the Bamako Congress is discussed in: Ruth Schachter Morgenthau, *Political Parties in French-Speaking West Africa* (London: Clarendon Oxford University Press, 1967), p. 89.

63. CAOM, 1/AP/2712, "Resolutions du Congrès Constitutif du Rassemblement Démocratique Africain, Bamako, Octobre 1946."

64. Speech by Léopold Senghor in January 1957 at the founding congress of the *Convention Africaine* held in Dakar. Quoted in: Morgenthau, *Political Parties in French-Speaking West Africa*, p. 89.

65. CAOM, 1/AP/2712, "Le Rassemblement Africain à Bamako," in *Bulletin d'Information*, November 1946.

66. For discussions about the disputes between Senghor and Houphouët-Boigny see: Mazrui and Tidy, *Nationalism and New States in Africa*; Morgenthau, *Political Parties in French-Speaking West Africa*; and Cooper, *Decolonization and African Society*.

67. Léopold Sédar Senghor, "Vers un socialisme africain," letter to Guy Mollet of the SFIO, 27 September 1948, published in: Léopold Sédar Senghor, *Liberté II: Nation et Voie Africaine du Socialisme* (Paris: Editions du Seuil, 1971), p. 50; Léopold Sédar Senghor, "Introduction," *Liberté II*, p. 8; Léopold Sédar Senghor, "Naissance du Bloc démocratique sénégalais," *Rapport sur la méthode* au 1er congrès du B.D.S., 15–17 avril 1949 à Thiès, *Liberté II*, 57.

68. ARS, K/457/179, "Renseignements," 29 October 1947.

69. Quoted in: Cooper, *Decolonization and African Society*, p. 242. A thorough study of the 1947-1948 Dakar-Niger Railway strike has yet to be written, although Cooper's work is among the best treatments to date. Even if highly romanticized and written in the decade after the strike, Sembène's novel is also an excellent account of this "epic event." Sembène Ousmane, *Les Bouts de bois de Dieu: Banty mam yal* (Saint-Amand, France: Le Livre Contemporain, 1960).

70. ARS, K/458/179, "Renseignements," 16 March 1948.

71. CAOM, 1/AP/2177, letter from Mamadou Dia and Léopold Senghor to the ministry for Overseas France, 26 February 1949.

72. CAOM, 1/AP/3641/1, letter from Léopold Senghor to the ministry for Overseas France, 9 June 1949. See also: CAOM, 1/AP/2177, letter from Léopold Senghor to the ministry for Overseas France, 20 January 1950.

73. CAOM, 1/AP/2143, letters from Léopold Senghor to the ministry for Overseas France, 14 and 17 January, 10 February, and 16 June 1949. For Diagne's criticisms see: CAOM, 1/AP/542, letter from Diagne to the ministry of colonies, 8 July 1922, and the letter from "Délégues des Notables de la ville de Rufisque," led by Diagne, to the ministry of colonies, 8 September 1921.

74. CAOM, 1/AP/2153, "Note: Chefferies—formation des cadres et des élites," produced by the government general for AOF, 4 May 1953. On 12 February 1947 the governor of Senegal issued an *arrêté* "introduisant le système électif dans le choix des chefs de canton et de province." On 2 March 1949 after "des troubles en résultèrent," the *arrêté* was rescinded by a new order that declared the selection of tribal leadership "revint au régime antérieur."

75. CAOM, 1/AP/2177, letter from the high commissioner of AOF to the ministry for Overseas France, "Grand Sérigne de Dakar," 6 March 1950; letter from the ministry for Overseas France to the government general for AOF, "Plainte des notables lebous

a/s attitude de la municipalité de Dakar dans élections coutumières," 4 April 1950; letter from Paul Coste-Floret, minister of Overseas France, to Léopold Senghor, 29 June 1949.

76. CAOM, 1/AP/2177, letter from the government general for AOF to the ministry for Overseas France, "Grand Sérigne de Dakar," 6 March 1950.

77. CAOM, 1/AP/2143, "Note sur la situation au Sénégal," 17 November 1953.

78. CAOM, 1/AP/2177/7, letter from Léopold Senghor to the ministry for Overseas France, 20 January 1950. See also, in the same carton, the letter from Léopold Senghor and Abbas Guèye (trade union leader and deputy from the BDS after 1951) to the ministry for Overseas France, 6 December 1951.

79. CAOM, 1/AP/2143, report from the director of political affairs for AOF to the government general, "Critiques formulées par M. Lamine Guèye à l'encontre de l'Administration du Sénégal," 9 January 1954. The resolution was adopted on 26 May 1952.

80. CAOM, 1/AP/2177/7, letter from Mamadou Dia to the ministry for Overseas France, 31 July 1953.

81. CAOM, 1/AP/2143, letter from the ministry for Overseas France to the high commissioner of AOF, "Critiques formulées par M. Lamine Guèye, ancien ministre, à l'encontre de l'Administration du Sénégal," January 1954.

82. CAOM, 1/AP/2153, "Note—Avis du Groupe d'Etude sur la Réorganisation Administrative de l'A.O.F.," 5 November 1954.

83. Similar fights erupted at the same time within the Mouride Brotherhood of Senegal. For a discussion of that subject see: Cruise O'Brien, *The Mourides of Senegal*, pp. 269–270.

84. CAOM, 1/AP/2143, "Note sur la situation au Sénégal," 17 November 1953.

85. CAOM, 1/AP/2177/7, letter from Guèye to the ministry for Overseas France, 6 January 1954.

86. CAOM, 1/AP/2188, letter from Mohamed Mahmoud Mahmoud Ould Cheikh Cadi de Tombouctou to the ministry for Overseas France, 24 March 1954. See also, in the same carton, the letter from Amadou Doucoure, senator from Soudan and Chef de Canton du Ouagadou.

87. Morgenthau, *Political Parties in French-Speaking West Africa*, pp. 101–102.

88. CAOM, 1/AP/2201/10, list of deputies to the Second National Assembly. The results of the 17 June 1951 election returned eight members of the IOM, five SFIO, five RDA/UDSR, and one RPF (*Rassemblement du Peuple Français*), de Gaulle's new party, which posted the most impressive gains in the new National Assembly in France.

89. CAOM, 1/AP/2143, letter from the government general for AOF to the ministry for Overseas France, "Perspective électorale au Sénégal," 13 March 1952.

90. Cruise O'Brien, *The Mourides of Senegal*, p. 268; Cruise O'Brien, *Saints and Politicians*, p. 163.

91. CAOM, 1/AP/2143, letter from the government general for AOF to the ministry for Overseas France, "Perspective électorale au Sénégal," 13 March 1952.

92. CAOM, 1/AP/2143, letter from the government general for AOF to the ministry of Overseas France, "Situation politique et sociale du Sénégal," 12 December 1953. See also: Cruise O'Brien, *The Mourides of Senegal*, p. 270.

93. Crowder and Ikime, "Introduction," in Crowder and Ikime, eds., *West African Chiefs*, p. XXVII.

94. This point is also confirmed by Cruise O'Brien's work on the subject. Cruise O'Brien, *The Mourides of Senegal*; Cruise O'Brien, *Saints and Politicians*.

95. CAOM, 1/AP/2143, "Note sur la situation politique au Sénégal et dans le cercle de Thiès en Particulier," 25 October 1953.

96. CAOM, 1/AP/2152/1, letter from *Le Syndicat des Chefs de Canton de la Guinée Française* to the ministry for Overseas France, 10 April 1953.

97. CAOM, 1/AP/2153, "Question Ecrite No. 6735 du 29 mai 1956 posée à Monsieur le Ministre de la France d'Outre-Mer par Monsieur Gontchome Sahcuiba, Sénateur du Tchad." See also, in the same carton, "Note sur le statut des Chefs coutumiérs," 28 October 1952, produced by the ministry for Overseas France.

98. CAOM, 1/AP/2153, "Note—Avis du Groupe d'Etude sur la Réorganisation Administrative de l'A.O.F.," 5 November 1954.

99. CAOM, 1/AP/2143. "Note sur Sénégal," October 1954.

100. CAOM, 1/AP/2153, note from the government general for AOF to the ministry for Overseas France, "Statut des Chefs Coutumiers," undated, but probably written in 1954.

101. CAOM, 1/AP/2292, "Note pour Monsieur le Chef du Bureau du Cabinet; Objet: A/S demand d'interpellation de M. Dia Mamadou," 6 January 1958, produced by the office of political affairs for AOF.

102. CAOM, 1/AP/2152, letter from the ministry for Overseas France to the *Association des Chefs de la Guinée*, May 1956.

103. Agulhon, *The French Republic*, p. 355.

104. CAOM, 1/AP/491, "Notes sur la réforme des institutions de l'Afrique Occidentale française par M. l'inspecteur de la France d'outre-mer P. Sanner," 24 October 1955. Sanner conducted his tour in 1953 and 1954. See also, in the same carton, "Note au sujet des suggestions faites par M. l'inspecteur Sanner sur la réforme de structure de l'Afrique Occidentale Française," 12 August 1955; and "Memoire sur la réforme des structures de l'A.O.F.," 11 July 1955.

105. CAOM, 1/AP/3638/1, "Rapport" produced by the general political commission of the AUF, 25 November 1953. While the report was made in the midst of Sanner's tour of AOF, the metropolitan administrative bodies were kept informed of his progress and received regular correspondence from the inspector for Overseas France. Thus, the report was based on preliminary suggestions made by Sanner while he was still on mission.

106. CAOM, 1/AP/492, "Avant-Projet de loi relatif aux institutions des territoires de l'Afrique Occidentale Française," 30 November 1955.

107. CAOM, 1/AP/2292, "Le Contenu de la Loi-Cadre," adopted by the National Assembly on 19 June 1956. CAOM, 1/AP/492, letter from the ministry for Overseas France to the high commissioner of AOF, Gaston Cusin, "Projet de Loi-Cadre autorisant le gouvernement à mettre en oeuvre des réformes dans les Territories d'Outre-mer," June 1956. See also, in the same carton, "Decret fixant les attributions des assemblées territoriales de l'A.O.F. et de l'A.E.F.," issued in the fall of 1956. CAOM, 1/AP/2292, "Loi-Cadre; Loi No. 56–619 du 23 juin 1956."

108. CAOM, 1/AP/2292/7, "Le contenu de la Loi-Cadre," adopted by the National Assembly on 19 June 1956.

109. CAOM, 1/AP/492, letter from Defferre to Cusin, "Projet de Loi-Cadre autorisant le Gouvernement à mettre en oeuvre des réforms dans les Territoires d'Outre-mer," June 1956.

110. Mamdani, *Citizen and Subject*, pp. 18, 25.

111. CAOM, 1/AP/492, "Organisation Politique et Administrative de la Brousse," produced by the government general for AOF, August 1955.

112. CAOM, 1/AP/2131, "Note sur l'Institut Musulman de Boutilimit en Mauritanie," 9 February 1955. For a more detailed discussion of the French administration's refusal to recognize the West African workers as "equal" to Europeans see: Cooper, *Decolonization and African Society*.

113. CAOM, 1/AP/2292/6, "Eléments pour le discours du ministre de la France d'Outre-mer à la commission permanente du Grand Conseil de l'A.O.F.," 21 July 1956. CAOM, 1/AP/492, letter from Defferre to Cusin, "Projet du Loi-Cadre autorisant le Gouvernement à mettre en oeuvre des réformes dans les Territoires d'Outre-mer," June 1956.

114. CAOM, 1/AP/2189/7, "Reformes apportées dans les territoires relevant du ministère de la France d'Outre-Mer par la loi No. 56–619 du 23 juin 1956, dite loi-Cadre, et par les decrets pris pour son application."

115. Bourdieu, *Language and Symbolic Power*, pp. 172–173.

116. For an analysis of colonial politics in the metropole during the 1950s see: Chafer, *The End of Empire in French West Africa*; Jacques Marseille, *Empire colonial et capitalisme français: Histoire d'un divorce* (Paris: Éditions Albin Michel, 1984); Paul Clay Sorum, *Intellectuals and Decolonization in France* (Chapel Hill: University of North Carolina Press, 1977); Anthony Clayton, *The Wars of French Decolonization* (London: Longman, 1994); John Talbot, *The War Without a Name: France in Algeria, 1954-1962* (New York: Alfred A. Knopf, 1980); and Jean-Pierre Rioux, *The Fourth Republic, 1944-1958* (Cambridge: Cambridge University Press, 1987).

117. CAOM, 1/AP/2201/10, list of elected representatives from West Africa during the 1950s and their professions. A survey of the occupations and social backgrounds of those elected to the AN or AUF indicates the ascendancy of the *évolués* as a social class in the federation. The most frequently represented occupation was that of "instituteur," or schoolteacher, followed by doctors, a very distant second. Other prominent professions included administration workers and commercial agents. Sékou Touré was the only trade unionist, or worker, elected from West Africa, and only one chief was sent to Paris. The teachers included Léopold Senghor, Dia, Këita, and Diori, while Houphouët-Boigny was cross-listed as a doctor and planter. No peasants were elected, nor were any women seated in Paris or the territorial assemblies.

118. Morgenthau, *Political Parties in French-Speaking West Africa*, pp. 106–111.

119. CAOM, 1/AP/2197/9, "Declaration de M. Houphouët-Boigny à Cotonou," 25 February 1957.

120. Léopold Sédar Senghor, "La Loi-Cadre, première étape vers l'autonomie interne," in *L'Economie: Journal d'Informations industrielles, financières et agricoles du monde entier*, 27 June 1957, p. 8.

121. CAOM, 1/AP/2197, notes on a press conference given by Léopold Senghor in Dakar on 19 November 1958. The records of that public statement are also contained in:

CAOM, 1/AP/2198. ARS, Affaires Administratives (18G)/273, letter from the government general for AOF to the ministry for Overseas France, 12 May 1956.

122. CAOM, 1/AP/492, letter from Dia and Léopold Senghor to Defferre, 2 May 1956.

123. Léopold Sédar Senghor, "Balkanization ou Fédération," in *Afrique Nouvelle*, December 1956, and reproduced in *Liberté II*, p. 181. (Emphasis in the original.)

124. Léopold Sédar Senghor, "Les décrets d'application de la loi-cadre ou 'donner et retirer ne vaut,'" in *L'Unité Africaine*, 5 March 1957, re-printed in *Liberté II*, p. 211.

125. Léopold Sédar Senghor, "L'esthetique négro-africaine," in *Diogène*, October 1956, and re-printed in *Liberté I*, p. 205. Léopold Sédar Senghor, "Le problème des langues vernaculaires ou le bilinguisme comme solution," in *Afrique Nouvelle*, 3 January 1958, and re-printed in *Liberté I*, p. 229.

126. CAOM, 1/AP/2292, speech by Dia to supporters of the BPS (*Bloc Populaire Sénégalais*—the re-named BDS after a merger between it and several dissident factions of the RDA in 1956), published in *Paris-Dakar*, 20 December 1957.

127. CAOM, 1/AP/2198/9, statement made by d'Arboussier at a press conference in Dakar, 22 November 1958.

128. CAOM, 1/AP/2292, "Loi-Cadre; Loi No. 56–619 du 23 juin 1956;"CAOM, 1/AP/492, letter from the ministry for Overseas France to the high commissioner of AOF, "Projet de Loi-Cadre autorisant le Gouvernement à mettre en oeuvre des réformes dans les Territoires d'Outre-mer," June 1956; CAOM, 1/AP/2189/3, "Reformes apportées dans les territoires relevant du Ministère de la France d'Outre-Mer par la loi No. 56.619 du 23 juin 1956, dite loi-Cadre, et par des decrets pris pour son application."

129. CAOM, 1/AP/2198/3, speech by Léopold Senghor to a meeting of the BPS in St. Louis, Senegal, 19 March 1957.

130. CAOM, 1/AP/2292/6, "Loi-Cadre; Loi No. 56-619 du 23 juin 1956." In the section headed, "Les caractères de la Loi-Cadre," Houphouët-Boigny was acknowledged as having provided "indispensable aid" in the formulation of the act and in its ultimate passage. Other members of the RDA like Hamani Diori of Niger, quoted in the section, proclaimed it the "acte de la plus grande porte."

131. CAOM, 1/AP/2197, speech by Apithy on the occasion of his election as president of the territorial assembly of Dahomey, 15 May 1957. See also, in the same carton, "Declaration de M. Houphouët-Boigny à Cotonou," 25 February 1957.

132. CAOM, 3/SLOTFOM/53, letter from Garan Kouyaté, leader of the LDRN, to Léon M'Ba, chief of the Pahouins in Libreville (Gabon, AEF), 6 July 1929.

133. CAOM, 1/AP/2292/6, speech by Houphouët-Boigny to RDA militants in Abidjan, Ivory Coast, 8 March 1957.

134. CAOM, 1/AP/2292, "Le Comité Directeur de la Convention s'est réuni à Dakar les 10 et 11 novembre," in *Afrique Nouvelle*, 12 November 1957; and speech by Houphouët-Boigny to supporters of the RDA in Abidjan, 8 March 1957, in dossier 5 of the same carton. CAOM, 1/AP/2146, "Le Texte de la Nouvelle Constitution," in *Le Monde*, 21-22 April 1946.

135. CAOM, 1/AP/2186/3, Raymond Cartier in *Paris-Match*, 18 August 1956.

136. Marseille, *L'Empire colonial et capitalisme français*, pp. 11–15.

137. CAOM, 1/AP/2186/3, letter from Cusin to Defferre, 15 December 1956.

138. Léopold Senghor, "Naissance du Bloc démocratique sénégalias," in *Rapport sur la méthode*, 15–17 April 1949, reproduced in *Liberté II*, p. 53.

139.   CAOM, 1/AP/2292/6, speech by Cusin before the Ivory Coast's territorial assembly, 23 August 1956.

140.   Stanislas Adotevi has provided an important study in the development of de Gaulle's colonial policy during the period of decolonization in which this point is made. Stanislas Spero Adotevi, *De Gaulle et les Africaines* (Paris: Editions Chaka, 1990), p. 175.

141.   Léopold Sédar Senghor, "Les Élites de l'Union Française au service de leurs peuples," in *Marchés Coloniaux du Monde*, 27 February 1954, p. 573.

142.   CAOM, 1/AP/2197, "Le vice president du conseil de Haute Volta M. Ouezzin Coulibaly fait le point de la situation politique à Bobo-Dioulasso," 31 March 1958.

143.   Johnson, "The Triumph of Nationalism in French West Africa," in *Décolonisations européennes*, pp. 314, 313. For information on the attempts by Léopold Senghor and others to forge a new basis for federation in West Africa after the *Loi Cadre* was put in effect in 1957 see: CAOM, 1/AP/2198/9, notes on a conference convened by "partisans de la création d'une 'fédération primaire' en A.O.F.," November 1958. Supporters of the *Négritude* poet directed that meeting. For information on the attempts by RDA dissidents from Houphouët-Boigny's position to push for federation see: CAOM, 1/AP/2292, "Creation d'un Parti federal?" in *Abidjan Matin*, 19 February 1958. Sékou Touré (Guinea) and Hamani Diori (Niger) led the dissidents. In the end, only the Mali Federation of Senegal and French Soudan emerged from those efforts and that too failed by 1961.

144.   CAOM, 1/AP/2198/3, speech by Léopold Senghor to supporters of the BPS in St. Louis, Senegal, 19 March 1957.

145.   CAOM, 1/AP/2197/9, see the reports on the campaigns by the multitude of political parties for the March 1957 elections throughout West Africa. Those elected president after 31 March 1957 were: Houphouët-Boigny (Ivory Coast), Apithy (Dahomey, replaced by Maga in 1960), Sékou Touré (Guinea), Coulibaly (Upper Volta, died 7 September 1958, succeeded by Maurice Yameogo), Kéita (Soudan/Mali), Diori (Niger), Léopold Senghor (Senegal), and Sidi el Mokhtar (Mauritania).

146.   CAOM, 1/AP/2292/6, resolutions of the *Congrès des Jeunes de la Haute Volta*, held in Ouagadougou, 26-28 October 1957. Dissidents within the RDA demanded Houphouët-Boigny's resignation for his failure to take a "positive" stand on Algeria. See: CAOM, 1/AP/2197, "Le congres du R.D.A. n'aura vraisemblablement pas lieu," 30 January 1957. The signatories to the call for the Ivory Coast's leader to resign included; Sékou Touré, Saifoulaye Diallo, Hamani Diori, and Ouezzin Coulibaly.

147.   CAOM, 1/AP/2198/3, notes on the positions of the African parties and public associations on the referendum of 28 September 1958.

148.   CAOM, 1/AP/2198/3, "M. Sékou Touré se prononce pour l'indépendance nationale de la Guinée," 29 September 1958. See also, in the same carton, the "Revue des évènements politiques A.O.F. octobre 1958," and notes on a press conference held by Léopold Senghor on 19 November 1958.

149.   ARS, Affaires Politiques (17G)/633, "Service de Sécurité," in *Bulletin d'Information*, February 1958, accounting for the violence throughout 1957 and 1958.

150.   CAOM, 1/AP/2198, press reports that discuss the strikes that swept Senegal, Niger, and Upper Volta in January 1959.

151. CAOM, 1/AP/2189/3, "Le ministre du travail du Niger reprend à son compte les revendication de l'U.G.T.A.N.," 31 March 1958. See also: CAOM, 1/AP/2198/9, radio speech by Diori, 2 January 1959.

152. CAOM, 1/AP/2197, Oumar Bâ, vice president of the *Union des Originaires de Mauritanie*, in response to an article that appeared in the official paper of the Moroccan nationalist party, Istiqlal, 6 November 1957. "Qu'est-ce que la décolonisation? La gestion intégrale de ses affaires par l'autochtone. En un mot c'est l'indépendance tout court."

153. CAOM, 1/AP/2189/3, "Resolution du secretariat du comite directeur de l'U.G.T.A.N. sur les recents incidents qui ont endeuille l'Afrique noire," Dakar, 16 May 1958.

Conclusion
The Politics of Cultural Authenticity and Imperial Legacies

Between 1958 and 1960 nine post-colonies emerged within the colonial field that has served as our analytical framework. The former federation of French West Africa had metamorphosed into eight independent states—Senegal, Guinea, Mali (former French Soudan), Mauritania, Niger, Upper Volta (today Burkina Faso), Dahomey (today Benin), and Ivory Coast—while France had passed from the Fourth to the Fifth Republic. The *évolués* had emerged as the dominant social group within former AOF, in command of the system of governance and ensconced in the upper echelons of the new state structures. For that class, the end of French rule marked the culmination of a protracted struggle for authority with colonial administrators and the pre-colonial elite that began to take shape during the First World War. In the course of that contest a hegemonic framework emerged that privileged the idea of cultural "authenticity" and particular notions of the "true" forms of French and African social organization that were based on assumptions of essential and immutable differences between the two. That political culture was reflected in the institutions of empire as well as colonial discourse. Consequently, the possibilities for effective engagement in the colonial field were strictly limited as the participants became locked in a realm of meaning that operated according to its own logic; a regulatory system that authorized some stances while it marginalized others.

That arena of encounters and confrontations provided the context wherein a particular *évolué* identity was articulated, one that points to the colonial specificity of the forms of struggle and social organization elaborated in France and West Africa during the twentieth century. By the end of the 1914–1918 war the French-educated elite had developed from what Bourdieu calls a "theoretical class" into a "real" class. The experiences of that conflict and the apperception of those events transformed "sets of agents who occupy similar positions and who, being placed in similar conditions and submitted to similar types of conditioning, have every chance of having similar dispositions and interests, and thus of producing similar practices and adopting similar stances" into "a group mobilized for struggle...[capable] of mobilization into organized movements, endowed with an apparatus and a spokesperson, etc."[1] *Évolué* class-consciousness was organized around assertions of their unique position within the colonial field, astride the divide between French and African cultures, between citizen and subject. That self-awareness was promoted by the praxis and discourse of imperial rulers who at times embraced the French-educated elite as necessary allies in the *mission civilisatrice* and at others rebuked them as "dangerous," "uprooted," "detribalized," and "confused."[2]

For the *évolués*, though, existence between European and African societies and within both functioned as a basis for claims to authority—the prerogative to speak on behalf of the *sujet* population and to represent French culture to the indigenous communities of AOF. Such assertions entailed the acceptance of the idea that there were such things as identifiable and distinct "French" and "African" societies. Moreover, that committed the new urban elite to the perpetuation (and realization) of those differences in a framework that required a permanent connection to the imperial power.

Consequently, both the colonial rulers and the *évolués* from West Africa were reluctant decolonizers in the 1950s. At the moment when France could no longer effectively govern in the region, metropolitan leaders and the modern *griots* assiduously avoided discussion of "independence" and, instead, sought the means whereby a new "fraternal" relationship could be forged in the post-colonial era.[3] That association was embodied in the concept and institutions of *La Francophonie* as developed through the initiative of Léopold Senghor and other leaders of the West African states in the 1960s. "*La Francophonie*," according to Léopold Senghor, president of Senegal, was the fulfillment of France's mission overseas, "the main reason for [its] expansion beyond the hexagon." He described it as a "symbiosis" of metropolitan and overseas cultures expressed through the "French language" which Léopold Senghor called "the language of culture."[4] However, that symbiotic connection depended upon the continued presence of the West African educated class at the "vital core" of the new international order, just as Laurentie had earlier asserted that the *évolués* constituted the "essential center of the colonial question."[5] Houphouët-Boigny and others argued that both France and West Africa benefited from such an arrangement. Through the continued leadership of the French-educated elite in ex-AOF the former metropole retained its sense of "grandeur" and a means whereby its cultural influence remained potent in a world dominated by the two superpowers, the

Soviet Union and the United States. For West Africans, the *évolués* posed as conduits for economic assistance from France and as representatives of the region's people on the world stage, especially in the halls of French government where they had personal friendships and political alliances.[6]

However, as Coquery-Vidrovitch and Moniot observe, the French-educated elite's presentation of the new post-colonial order "impli[ed] an unconditional economic subordination [of West Africa] to the former metropole."[7] Léopold Senghor, Houphouët-Boigny, and their associates presented the revamped relationship between France and former AOF as part of a global division of labor wherein each community was endowed with clearly defined roles that contributed to the prosperity of a greater whole. Those niches arose from the "essential natures" of each society. Since "White reason [was] analytical [and] practical, [while] Negro reason [was] intuitive and active,"[8] Senegal's president explained, "Science and Technology" belonged to Europe, which functioned as the "engineer," and the "Negro-African Civilization," fundamentally peasant, collectivist, and tribal, played the part of "farmer" and aided in the "spiritual" development of humanity."[9]

Léopold Senghor's assertion that "authentic" Africa must be "agricultural" and "tribal" did not result entirely from abstract ideas gleaned from the writings of ethnographers, though. It also reflected the political and economic structures operable in West Africa as French rule receded in the 1950s. The rise of the "African" parties to prominence after the Second World War was based on their ability to secure control of ethnic or tribal communities through having their supporters elected to village assemblies and the office of chief. The reform programs launched by France and the government general after the defeat of Nazi Germany contributed to the transformation of "tribal" communities, already the foundation of colonial governance and cash-crop production, into sites of intense conflict for authority in the federation. As a result, the mobilization of ethnic-based constituencies, in the absence of federal deliberative structures open to African participation, became a primary vehicle whereby political influence accrued in French West Africa. In the process, the parties founded by *évolués* developed into mass organizations that depended on the loyalty and continued support of distinct tribal associations, each of which expected to gain from its connections to the electoral group.[10] That arrangement furnished the basis for a patronage system in West African politics, the early development of which was encouraged by the actions of colonial administrators, that has turned many post-colonial systems of governance in

Africa into what scholars have labeled "vampire States," "kleptocracies," or "piratical regimes."[11]

The rapid emergence of "African" parties such as the BDS or RDA in West Africa owed more to their ability to tap the discontent of rural communities and direct it toward the replacement of chiefs sanctioned by French rulers or associated with "metropolitan" parties like the SFIO than to the widespread endorsement of any ideological programs. In addition, the new parties drew upon the previously established links of their leaders with prominent religious figures,[12] family or lineage connections, and the support of their particular ethnic or tribal community.[13] French officials and rival political associations documented numerous instances of tribal or religious leaders distributing "party membership" cards to their communities that created the appearance of mass support for a certain group. The distribution of those papers provided the basis for the amount of "subsidies" awarded by the party to that collectivity's leadership and promises of future economic investment after state authority had passed from French hands. That pattern of political engagement was only enhanced by the provisions of the *Loi Cadre* that turned budgetary control over to the territorial assemblies dominated by those parties. Moreover, the colonial administration's economic programs FIDES and especially FERDES prepared the ground for such financial practices since it organized economic assistance, or fiduciary allocations, on the basis of petitions by rural collectivities. Thus, the budgetary structures inherited by the new rulers of West Africa accorded with established political praxis and furnished the basis for the perpetuation of those activities into the post-colonial era. In addition, the *évolués* were, in general, willing to maintain such structures after having acquired political authority because they accorded with the ethnographic paradigm of "authentic" African forms of socioeconomic organization embraced by Léopold Senghor and others in the course of their struggles with colonial administrators, the pre-colonial elite, and metropolitan politicians.[14]

In fact, Léopold Senghor, Houphouët-Boigny, and their associates presented "national *independence*" or self-government as an end in itself. Political liberty was, accordingly, the only necessary precondition for the "recovery and affirmation, defense and illustration of the collective personality of the black peoples: of *Négritude*."[15] In other words, "authentic" African cultural and social practices required only that they be freed from the constraints of colonial rule in order to flourish and resume their "natural evolution."[16] The conflation of liberation with political independence reflected the narrow agendas of the new ruling class in West Africa that denigrated the "social question" in preference for concerns about control of state institutions. That, too, had been born of the struggle for authority within the colonial field. As that contest unfolded, a substantial divide had emerged between the *évolués* and the bulk of the West African population that was exacerbated by the actions of the colonial administration and the particular self-identity articulated among the French-educated elite. That self-conception situated the modern *griots* perpetually as "leaders" of the indigenous population and as missionaries charged with the revival of "real" autochthonous cultures. The French-educated elite, consequently, claimed for themselves direction of a *mission civilisatrice*, a role France had attempted to reserve for itself. As Chatterjee writes, "An elitism now becomes inescapable. Because the act of cultural synthesis can, in fact, be performed only by a supremely cultivated and refined intellect. It [nationalism] is a project of national-cultural regeneration in which the intelligentsia lead and the nation follows."[17]

The model of the "veritable" Negro-African Civilization adopted by the new West African leaders denied the need for any significant social reforms, in particular with regard to the condition of labor and women. Léopold Senghor proclaimed, "In Africa...classes [were] recently invented [and], therefore, artificial." Accordingly, the BDS leader continued, "our political objective is...not to suppress inequalities born of class differences, but of those which result[ed] from race and geography."[18] At a March 1958 meeting of the UGTAN, West Africa's largest trade union federation, Niger's new secretary of labor and an RDA member, Saloum Traore, instructed the workers that "it was time [for them] to take a 'nationalist consciousness' in order to obtain real independence and complete freedom for Africa."[19] In the years before 1960 the territorial governments of Niger and Upper Volta had put down strikes, imprisoned working class leaders, and had begun a process that culminated in the general destruction of autonomous trade union movements after political sovereignty was achieved.[20]

On the question of female emancipation, the new leaders of West Africa were generally dismissive. Just months before he declared Senegal independent as part of the Mali Federation, Léopold Senghor, at the Second International Congress of Black Writers and Artists in Rome, announced that, "contrary to current opinion, the Negro-African woman does not need to be liberated: she has been *free* for millennia." The Senegalese leader said that freedom resulted from the woman's role as "giver of life" and "guardian of the home." As wife and mother, a "permanent" position for women in Léopold Senghor's conceptual universe, the female members of the household actually occupied the "highest position" in the family. Since the family was the foundation of everything in "authentic" African society, women enjoyed "wide-ranging authority and liberty."[21] Consequently, the rise of the *évolués* as leaders of West Africa, a class almost devoid of females, did not include provision for the enhancement of women's living conditions or their place in society. In fact, the American author Richard Wright noticed the utter absence of women among the French-educated elite at the moment when they claimed for themselves the prerogative to direct the affairs of West African society. At the First International Congress of Black Writers and Artists in Paris Wright suggested that this reflected, and perhaps contributed to the "backward" thinking of people like Léopold Senghor, who he singled out for criticism at the meeting.[22] The resurrection of "real" African culture after independence, according to Léopold Senghor's *imaginaire*, entailed the perpetuation of established patriarchal power structures into the post-colonial order.

However, the new regimes of power operable in West Africa after 1960 were inherently unstable and the position of the *évolués* at the apex tenuous at best. They had become the leaders in the region on the basis of connections with sympathetic elements among the pre-colonial elite and the inability of French administrators to significantly direct events in the federation after the Second World War. Independence, then, did not entail a "resolution" of what Bayart had identified in a general context as the "hegemonic crisis"[23] that had plagued the federation throughout the period of imperial domination. Rather, the vital support of the "new" chiefs for the parties of the French-educated elite transformed those organizations into arenas of competition for influence and resources just as the earlier administrative reforms had politicized the chieftaincies and exacerbated internal tribal rivalries.[24] The difference, though, was that the struggle within the parties was between separate communities, not internal to them. Those rivalries, which had already exploded in Upper Volta after 1956 and spread throughout West Africa in subsequent years, threatened to tear the neoteric states of ex-AOF apart along communal lines and make the new rulers hostage to the vicissitudes of ethnic conflict, or end in their removal from political power entirely.[25] Such prospects reinforced the *évolués'* sense of connection to France, and their ultimate dependence upon the former metropole to remain in office, a tendency that became more pronounced as the years passed.[26]

However, the West African leaders' affinity was for a particular idea of France, one that closely approximated the vision propounded by de Gaulle and other architects of the new Fifth Republic. Whereas the Third Republic had construed the acquisition of an overseas empire as a basis for French grandeur, de Gaulle asserted that France's "renewal" and its place as a great nation depended upon its "independence" not only from the two superpower blocs, but also from "the constraints imposed upon her by her empire."[27] Ironically, de Gaulle's preparedness to accept the former colonies' decision to opt for independence, which he could not have prevented anyway, recalled an older conception of French republicanism articulated in the course of the Revolution of 1789. At that time the First Republic had made the overseas possessions integral parts of France and accorded the residents citizenship, an act repeated by the Second Republic in 1848.[28] The colonial experience, though, had fundamentally altered the "republican idea" in France and notions of Frenchness with which it was associated.[29] Whereas earlier Republics had sought to integrate all the peoples of the metropole and the colonies into a "Greater France," de Gaulle "excluded from the realm of possibility all idea of the assimilation of the [subject peoples] into the French population," and into a common political entity.[30] In the struggles for authority that shaped the imperial framework a particularist French identity had emerged based on the assumption of essential and immutable cultural differences between Europeans and Africans. The hostile reactions to and (re)interpretations of the Lamine Guèye Law in 1946, spearheaded by Moutet, confirmed the dominance of the idea of a "true" France that was insular, exclusive, and defensive. It was significant that the campaign by colonial administrators and French politicians to undermine the reach of Guèye's act deployed the rhetoric of "cultural preservation" and played on fears that "in the near future" France would be absorbed by its empire and turned into a colony itself.[31]

The long history of imperial officials' obstruction of the naturalization process and attempts to find some juridical status for the *évolués* that avoided their accession to citizenship pointed to the articulation of increasingly narrow definitions of Frenchness. Such practices and the language used to justify them contributed to the development of racist and anti-immigrant politics in France during the twentieth century, a process that has fueled the rise of Jean-Marie Le Pen's *Front National* since the 1980s. As Virginie Guiraudon observes, such movements do not generally target migrants from other parts of Europe. Rather, the "foreigner" in their rhetoric refers to people "of North and West African origin. Paradoxically," she notes, "they are not very foreign…they are ex-colonial migrants."[32] The infamous "scarf affair" of 1989 where three Muslim girls were expelled from a high school in Creil highlighted the continued importance of the (ex)colonial "other" as a marker of difference in the delineation of French identity.[33] Diagne's assertion in 1919 that "one could be French and Muslim" continues to meet fierce resistance in France today and is a focal point in discussions about the "crisis" of national identity said to be afflicting the former metropole.[34]

However, the defense of "true" French culture was not limited to battles within the Hexagon. Rather, cultural politics was, and remains, a fundamental element of the Fifth Republic's foreign policy, the key to the maintenance of the country's grandeur. Even before most of the West African territories had announced their independence the staff of the crumbling ministry for Overseas France found employment in a new ministry of culture, created by Malraux. The new office was designed to wage the war to preserve and revive "real" French culture within Europe as well as overseas. It was to pick up the cause of a *mission civilisatrice* that could no longer be carried out by possession of a colonial empire. Lebovics writes, "When...Malraux needed staff for his new ministry, he recruited as the majority of his senior officers men who had learned their craft as colonial administrators. When he wanted to create a network of Houses of Culture all over metropolitan France, he asked his aide, the former African administrator Emile Biasini, to head the effort: 'What you did with the Africans, why not do the same in France?'"[35] Moreover, the new agency and the subsequent formation of the institutions of *La Francophonie* at a 1970 conference in Niamey, Niger, at which Malraux was the French delegate, furnished the structural bases for cooperation between former adversaries—ex-colonial administrators and the West African *évolués*. While differences persisted between them in discussions about cultural aid and technical assistance, the question of political authority was no longer at issue and relations were rarely strained.[36]

Over forty years after the territories of AOF gained their independence and France acquired a new regime the former metropole remains an important presence in West Africa. On a visit to the region in July 1999 French President Jacques Chirac, leader of the party founded by de Gaulle, noted that African democracy "had its own special rhythm," which implied a willingness to embrace regimes otherwise construed as dictatorial. That statement enraged those in the area who have suffered at the hands of the post-colonial regimes France has consistently supported, in particular the people of Ivory Coast where he made the statement. Five months later, in December 1999, a military coup, in part provoked by the ethnic and "nationalist" politics promoted by the Ivorian government, ended the regime of President Henri Konan Bédié.[37] The deposed president fled to Togo and subsequently to France where he has received refuge. Since then Côte d'Ivoire has sunk deeper into civil war and anti-French sentiments flared into rioting following France's military intervention in 2003 and a peace deal it brokered, which at this writing has yet to resolve the conflict. Chirac's claim for a "special" brand of "African" democracy indicates that the politics of cultural authenticity, based on the assumption of essential and immutable differences between Europeans and Africans, endures as an integral part of French foreign policy and conceptions of the world. It is also an approach long promoted by the leaders of post-colonial Africa in their attempts to deflect charges of authoritarian rule within those countries.[38]

However, it has become increasingly difficult for the rulers of France and West Africa to persist on the course they have chosen. Challenges to the hegemonic conceptions of "authentic" French and African societies articulated during the colonial period have mounted. Assertions of a "true" national or cultural identity appear more archaic as European unity proceeds along its rocky path, "anglicisms" threaten the "purity" of the French language, and the peoples of West Africa suffer in a global capitalist system in which they are marginal players. Conklin notes that even the continued use of "French" among West African intellectuals and rulers has come into question, a development met with increased defensiveness by Paris.[39] Such reactions contributed to France's willingness to do nothing to stop the genocide that occurred in Rwanda and to shelter those responsible for the slaughter of 800,000 people in 1994. Moreover, the obsession with the defense of "French culture" in Africa against the march of "Americanization" informed choices made to support the tyrannical regime of Mobutu Sese Seko in Zaire to its bitter end in 1997.[40]

In 1955 Alioune Diop wrote that "colonialism [was] the mortal enemy of native cultures [in Africa] and also the enemy of culture in Europe." The following year Frantz Fanon objected to Léopold Senghor's assertion that there was an "authentic" African culture and warned that such positions contributed to the "vegetation" and "mummification" of those societies. He argued that the end result of Léopold Senghor's stance would be the "valorization" of the position occupied by the imperial power. In a heated exchange at the 1956 First International Congress of Black Writers and Artists in Paris, Richard Wright also took exception to the Senegalese leader's claims about Africa. The American author said of Léopold Senghor's presentation, "It was a brilliant speech...a brilliance poured out in impeccable, limpid French, about the mentality and sensitivity of the African.... Yet, as I admired it, a sense of uneasiness developed in me.... Must we make a circumference around [African culture], a western fort to protect it and leave it intact, with all the manifold political implications in that?"[41]

That statement and Fanon's premonitory objection could also be applied to presentations of the "true" France that have situated language purity, geographic place of origin, and ethnic background as criteria for "Frenchness." If it is necessary to have a clearly defined idea of the "veritable" France or Africa, more useful models than those propounded by ethnographers in a colonial context abound. Those include the notion that the "authentic" France is that of 1789, a position often invoked during the 1920s and early 1930s as the struggle for authority within the imperial framework intensified. The idea of a "universal humanism," propounded by Léopold Senghor with decidedly anti-universalist characteristics, where all are "free and equal in their rights and obligations" was also made available during the fight for dominance within the colonial field.[42] Those possibilities were not expunged when France and West Africa obtained their independence from colonial rule; they were merely subsumed in a rush for control of the "political kingdom."[43] It is perhaps not too late to embrace such alternative notions of "authenticity," ones not based on ideas of essential and immutable differences with their attendant hierarchical and exploitative implications. On many occasions throughout this narrative we have noted the diversity of options available for struggle against imperial rule and its effects in France and West Africa. The eventual dominance of a particular discourse and praxis was the product of numerous factors, among them the conflict between "players" within the colonial field, the structural realities of imperial governance, and the accumulated and interpreted history of Franco-African relations. Today France and West Africa continue to wrestle with the legacies of colonialism while people in both locales persist in their search for a meaningful decolonization. As Fanon writes, "In decolonization there is, therefore, the need of a complete calling into question of the colonial situation."[44] That need remains present over forty years after the end of formal French rule in West Africa.

NOTES

1. Bourdieu, *Language and Symbolic Power*, pp. 231-232.

2. CAOM, 3/SLOTFOM/2, letter from the government general for AEF to the ministry of colonies, "A/s du refoulement dans leur pays d'origine de certains indigènes habitant la Métropole," 8 July 1929.

3. Léopold Sédar Senghor, "La Loi-Cadre, première étape vers l'autonomie interne," in *L'Économie*, 27 June 1957, p. 8; CAOM, 1/AP/2292, "Abidjan reçoit M. Gaston Cusin, Haut Commissaire de la République en A.O.F.," 22 August 1956, speech by Cusin before the territorial assembly in Ivory Coast; and speech by Houphouët-Boigny before supporters of the RDA in Abidjan, 8 March 1957, contained in the same carton.

4. Léopold Sédar Senghor, "Le Français langue de culture," published in *Esprit*, November 1962, and reprinted in *Liberté I*, pp. 359, 363.

5. CAOM, 1/AP/2147, Governor Henri Laurentie, "Le noeud du Problème Colonial: Les Évolués," in *Mensuel de Documentation*, February–March 1946.

6. CAOM, 1/AP/2292/6, speech by Houphouët-Boigny before supporters of the RDA in Abidjan, 8 March 1957; and "Abidjan reçoit M. Gaston Cusin, Haut Commissaire de la République en A.O.F.," 22 August 1956, in the same carton.

7. Coquery-Vidrovitch and Moniot, *L'Afrique Noire de 1800 à nos jours*, p. 391.

8. Léopold Sédar Senghor, "L'esprit de la civilisation ou les lois de la culture négro-africaine," in *Présence Africaine*, June–November 1956, Vols. 8-10, pp. 52, 58. The article was a reprinted speech that the Senegalese leader gave at the First International Congress of Black Writers and Artists, convened in Paris, 19–22 September 1956, just three months after the National Assembly passed Defferre's Loi Cadre.

9. Léopold Senghor, "L'apporte de la poésie nègre au demi-siècle," in *Témoignages sur la Poésie du Demi-Siècle*, 1952, and reprinted in *Liberté I*, pp. 141, 134.

10. CAOM, 1/AP/2153, report from the ministry for Overseas France, "Note sur le statut des Chefs coutumiérs," 28 October 1952.

11. Those who have written extensively on the "crisis" of the African state include: Bayart, *The State in Africa*; Davidson, *The Black Man's Burden*; Ayittey, *Africa in Chaos*; Achille Mbembe, "The Banality of Power and the Aesthetics of Vulgarity in the Postcolony," *Public Culture* 4:2, Spring 1992; and Young, *The African Colonial State in Comparative Perspective*.

12. See: Cruise O'Brien, *Saints and Politicians*; and Cruise O'Brien, *The Mourides of Senegal*.

13. CAOM, 1/AP/2143, letter from the government general for AOF to the ministry for Overseas France, "Perspective électorale au Sénégal," 13 March 1952.

14. CAOM, 1/AP/2143, note from Dakar to the ministry for Overseas France, "Situation politique et sociale du Sénégal," 12 December 1953; CAOM, 1/AP/2131/5, "Plan de developpement economique et social 1948–1952;" "Note au sujet des Fonds d'Equipement Rural et de Développement Économique et Social en A.O.F.," 12 May 1950, in the same carton; and CAOM, 1/AP/492, "Decret fixant les attributions des assemblées territoriales de l'A.O.F. et de l'A.E.F.," December 1956.

15. Léopold Senghor, "Introduction," in *Liberté I*, p. 7. (Emphasis in the original.)

16.   CAOM, 1/AP/2189/6, "Note pour le chef du 3ème bureau," records of the AUF, unsigned, written in 1952. Alioune Diop, "Liminaire – en retard," in *Présence Africaine*, August-September 1955, No. 3, p. 3. Alioune Diop, "Liminaire; entre l'est et l'ouest," in *Présence Africaine*, October-November 1955, No. 4, p. 4.

17.   Chatterjee, *Nationalist Thought and the Colonial World*, p. 73.

18.   CAOM, 1/AP/2146, Léopold Sédar Senghor, "La République Fédérale Française; Contre le Courant Centrifuge de l'Etat Associé, une Seule Solution," in *Marchés Coloniaux du Monde*, 4 April 1953.

19.   CAOM, 1/AP/2189/3, "Le ministre de travail du Niger reprend à son compte les revendications de l'U.G.T.A.N.," in *Bulletin de renseignements*, 31 March 1958. The meeting was held in Niamey on 17 March.

20.   CAOM, 1/AP/2198/9, see the documents relating to the strikes that swept many of the urban centers in Niger and Upper Volta throughout 1958 and 1959. Of particular interest is the radio speech delivered by Hamani Diori, leader of Niger, on 2 January 1959, as a general strike was declared throughout West Africa.

21.   Léopold Senghor, "Éléments constitutifs d'une civilisation d'inspiration négro-africaine," in *Présence Africaine*, March–April 1959, and reprinted in *Liberté I*, p. 269. (Emphasis in the original.)

22.   Richard Wright, "Tradition and Industrialization," in *Présence Africaine*, June–November 1956, p. 347, 354.

23.   Bayart, *The State in Africa*.

24.   Cruise O'Brien, *Saints and Politicians*.

25.   CAOM, 1/AP/2197/9, "Le vice president du conseil de Haute Volta M. Ouezzin Coulibaly fait le point de la situation politique à Bobo-Dioulasso," 31 March 1958; and CAOM, 1/AP/2189/3, "Resolution du secretariat du comité directeur de l'U.G.T.A.N. sur les recents incidents qui ont endeuille l'Afrique noire," 16 May 1958.

26.   Vaillant points to Léopold Senghor's "decision in 1962 to oust [his Prime Minister] Mamadou Dia...[as] the fatal moment at which he chose the French" over the people of Senegal. From that period forward the President of Senegal relied upon a French military presence to maintain control until he retired on 1 January 1981 and moved back to France. Only months after the arrest of Dia, Léopold Senghor published his article in Esprit that proclaimed French as the language of culture. Vaillant, *Black, French, and African*, p. 335.

27.   Charles de Gaulle, *Memoirs of Hope: Renewal and Endeavor* trans. Terence Kilmartin (New York: Simon and Schuster, 1971), pp. 36, 37. While this is certainly a retroactive explanation for the actions associated with the collapse of the French overseas empire that allows de Gaulle to maintain the fiction that he and officials in Paris were in firm control of the situation, directing the process each step of the way, it does convey the sense of Frenchness embraced by de Gaulle and that was reflected in the policies pursued by his government throughout the 1960s and perpetuated by successors to the present.

28.   CAOM, Gén/237, "Constitution An III (5 Fructidor An III, 22 août 1795)," Law of 16 pluviose An II (4 February 1794); and CAOM, Gén/119, decree of 29 April 1848 that abolished slavery and made the former slaves eligible for participation in the National Assembly.

29. Wilder, "Framing Greater France Between the Wars," *Journal of Historical Sociology* 14:2.

30. De Gaulle, *Memoirs of Hope*, p. 45.

31. CAOM, 1/AP/2146, see the articles that appeared in *Marchés Coloniaux du Monde* throughout 1951 on the interpretation of the Fourth Republic's constitution.

32. Guiraudon, "The Reaffirmation of the Republican Model of Integration," in *French Politics and Society* 14:2 (Spring 1996), pp. 47–48.

33. For a discussion of the scarf affair and its connection to nationality codes and debates on French identity see: Ireland, "Vive le jacobinisme," in *French Politics and Society* 14:2 (Spring 1996), pp. 33–46.

34. CAOM, 1/AP/595, "Profession de foi de Citoyen Blaise Diagne," in *L'Ouest-Africain français*, 20 November 1919.

35. Lebovics, *Mona Lisa's Escort*, p. 7.

36. One possible exception could be the 1974 coup that overthrew Niger's president and one of the founders of La Francophonie Hamani Diori. While conclusive evidence has yet to surface, it has long been rumored that France was behind the military takeover, speculation given some encouragement by the quick support France accorded the new regime and bitter disputes between the former metropole and Diori in the months prior to the action.

37. See the articles in: *The New York Times*, 24 July 1999; 24 December 1999; 26 December 1999; 27 December 1999. The coup occurred on 23 December 1999 and started with troops looting the capital of Abidjan in response to their not having been paid for some time. The next day General Robert Gueï proclaimed himself the head of state.

38. Léopold Senghor, "Éléments constitutifs d'une civilisation d'inspiration négro-africaine," in *Présence Africaine*, March-April 1959, reprinted in *Liberté I*, pp. 282–284.

39. Conklin, *A Mission to Civilize*, p. 247.

40. One of the best studies to date on French anxieties over the threat posed by "Americanization" is that by Kuisel, *Seducing the French*.

41. Alioune Diop, "Liminaire; entre l'est et l'ouest," in *Présence Africaine*, October-November 1955, No. 4, p. 4. Frantz Fanon, "Racisme et Culture," in *Présence Africaine*, June–November 1956, pp. 130, 123. Richard Wright, "Débats" of 19 September 1956, the opening session of the Congress, in *Présence Africaine*, June-November 1956, pp. 67, 68.

42. CAOM, 1/AP/3655, "Proposition de la loi tendant à proclamer citoyens tous les ressortissants de la Métropole et des territoires d'outre-mer," 7 May 1946; and CAOM, 1/AP/524/2, discussions in the Chamber of Deputies in 1916 on implementation of the 19 October 1915 Diagne Law; and the letter presented to the Senate on 14 September 1916 from Senegalese soldiers that proclaimed their willingness "participer courageusement à la grande guerre" as equal citizens of France, signed by Dakhourou-Koulynguidiane, printed in Presse Coloniale, 13 September 1916, contained in the same carton.

43. Kwame Nkrumah, the first president of independent Ghana, was the most vocal proponent of the idea that Africans should seek the political kingdom first, implying that all other ills would be dealt with or disappear once colonial rule was ended.

44. Fanon, *The Wretched of the Earth* (New York: Grove Press, 1963), p. 37.

Bibliography

Archives

Le Centre des Archives d'Outre-mer (CAOM), Aix-en-Provence, France
Records of the Ministries of Colonies and Overseas France, and Colonial Officials:
Affaires Politiques, Affaires Économiques, Commission Guernut, Généralités, Législation, Télégrammes

Records of the *Service de Contrôle et d'Assistance en France des Indigènes des Colonies* (CAI):
Service de Liaison entre les Originaires des Territoires d'Outre-mer (SLOTFOM)

Personal Papers:
Papiers Administratives (Series 28, Marius Moutet)

Official Proceedings and Acts:
Journal des Débats
Journal Officiel (Paris)

Les Archives de la République du Sénégal (ARS), Dakar, Senegal
Les Archives de l'Afrique occidentale française (AOF):
Actes officiels (1817–1959) (1A), *Dossiers de personnel* (1C), *Opérations militaires (1823–1934)* (1D), *Périodes de guerre (1914–1948)* (2D), *Personnel militaire* (4D), *Assemblée territoriale* (4E), *Grand conseil de l'AOF (1947–1959)* (22E), *Rapports périodiques* (2G), *Inspection, missions d'inspection des colonies (1874–1958)* (4G), *Affaires politiques AOF (1895–1918)* (17G), *Affaires administratives: AOF [1840]—(1893–1958)* (18G), *Elections (1841–1958)* (20G), *Police et sûreté (1825–1959)* (21G), *Travail, main-d'oeuvre et esclavage (1807–1958)* (K), *Enseignement après 1920 (1895–1958)* (O), *Affaires économiques: Généralités (1920–1959)* (1Q)

Official Proceedings and Acts:
Journal Officiel (AOF)

Depositories of Published Sources

Bibliothèque Administrative d'Outre-mer (AOM) in CAOM
Bibliothèque National de France (BNF) in Paris, France

Bibliothèque Section d'Outre-mer (SOM) in CAOM
La Bibliothèque des Archives du Sénégal (BAS) in ARS

Secondary Works

Adotevi, Stanislas Spero. *De Gaulle et les Africaines*. Paris: Editions Chaka, 1990.

Ageron, Charles-Robert, and Michel, Marc, Directeurs. *L'Afrique Noire Française: L'heure des Indépendances, acts du colloque 'La France et les indépendances des pays d'Afrique noire et de Madagascar,' Aix-en-Provence 26–29 avril 1990*. Paris: CNRS éditions, 1992.

Agulhon, Maurice. *The French Republic 1879–1992*. Translated by Antonia Nevill. Cambridge: Blackwell, 1993.

Ayittey, George B. N. *Africa Betrayed*. New York: St. Martin's Press, 1992.

———. *Africa in Chaos*. New York: St. Martin's Griffin, 1999.

Bach, Daniel C., editor. *Regionalisation in Africa: Integration and Disintegration*. Bloomington: Indiana University Press, 1999.

Barber, Karin. *I Could Speak Until Tomorrow: Oriki, Women, and the Past in a Yoruba Town*. Washington, D.C.: Smithsonian Institution Press, 1991.

Baudrillard, Jean. *Simulations*. New York: Semiotext[e], 1983.

Bayart, Jean-François. *The State in Africa: The Politics of the Belly*. Translated by Mary Harper, Christopher and Elizabeth Harrison. London and New York: Longman, 1993.

Benoist, Joseph Roger de. *L'Afrique Occidentale Française de la Conférence de Brazzaville (1944) à l'Indépendance (1960)*. Dakar: Les Nouvelles Éditions Africaines, 1982.

Betts, Raymond F. *Assimilation and Association in French Colonial Theory, 1890–1914*. New York: Columbia University Press, 1961.

Bhabha, Homi K. *The Location of Culture*. London and New York: Routledge, 1995.

———, editor. *Nation and Narration*. London: Routledge, 1995.

Bourdieu, Pierre. *Language and Symbolic Power*. Translated by Gino Raymond and Matthew Adamson. Cambridge: Harvard University Press, 1991.

———, and Wacquant, Loïc J. D. *An Invitation to Reflexive Sociology*. Chicago: The University of Chicago Press, 1992.

Burrin, Philippe. *France Under the Germans: Collaboration and Compromise*. Translated by Janet Lloyd. New York: the New Press, 1996.

Certeau, Michel de. *Heterologies: Discourse on the Other*. Translated by Brian Massumi. Minneapolis: University of Minnesota Press, 1986.

Chafer, Tony. *The End of Empire in French West Africa: France's Successful Decolonization?* Oxford: Berg, 2002.

———, and Sackur, Amanda, editors. *French Colonial Empire and the Popular Front: Hope and Disillusion*. New York: St. Martin's Press, 1999.

Chakrabarty, Dipesh. "Postcoloniality and the Artifice of History: Who Speaks for 'Indian' Pasts?" In *Representations*, 37 (Winter 1992).

Chapman, Herrick. *State Capitalism and Working-Class Radicalism in the French Aircraft Industry*. Berkeley: University of California Press, 1991.

Chatterjee, Partha. *Nationalist Thought and the Colonial World: A Derivative Discourse?* Minneapolis: University of Minnesota Press, 1998).

Clancy-Smith, Julia A. *Rebel and Saint: Muslim Notables, Populist Protest, Colonial Encounters (Algeria and Tunisia, 1800-1904)*. Berkeley: University of California Press, 1997.

————, and Gouda, Frances, editors. *Domesticating the Empire: Race, Gender, and Family Life in French and Dutch Colonialism*. Charlottesville: University Press of Virginia, 1998.

Clark, Andrew F. *From Frontier to Backwater: Economy and Society in the Upper Senegal Valley (West Africa), 1850–1920*. New York: University Press of America, Inc., 1999.

Clayton, Anthony. *The Wars of French Decolonization*. London: Longman, 1994.

Cohen, William B. *Rulers of Empire: The French Colonial Service in Africa*. Stanford: Hoover Institution Press, 1971.

————. *The French Encounters with Africans: White Response to Blacks, 1530–1880*. Bloomington: Indiana University Press, 1980.

Comte, Gilbert. *L'Empire Triomphante (1871–1936): 1. Afrique occidentale et équatoriale*. Paris: Denoël, 1988.

Conklin, Alice L. *A Mission to Civilize: The Republican Idea of Empire in France and West Africa, 1895-1930*. Stanford: Stanford University Press, 1997.

————. "Redefining Frenchness: Citizenship, Imperial Motherhood and Race Regeneration in France and West Africa, 1914–1940." In Clancy-Smith, Julia A., and Gouda, Frances. *Domesticating the Empire: Race, Gender and Family Life in French and Dutch Colonialism*. Charlottesville: University Press of Virginia, 1998.

————. "The New 'Ethnology' and 'La Situation Coloniale' in Interwar France." In *French Politics, Culture, and Society*, 20:2 (Summer 2002).

Cooper, Frederick. *Decolonization and African Society: The Labor Question in French and British Africa*. Cambridge: Cambridge University Press, 1996.

————, and Stoler, Ann Laura, editors. *Tensions of Empire: Colonial Cultures in a Bourgeois World*. Berkeley: University of California Press, 1997.

Coquery-Vidrovitch, Catherine. "Villes Coloniales et Histoire des Africains." In *XXe Siècle*, 20 (October–December 1988).

————. *Afrique Noire: Permanences et Ruptures*. Paris: Payot, 1985.

Coundouriotis, Eleni. *Claiming History: Colonialism, Ethnography, and the Novel*. New York: Columbia University Press, 1999.

Crowder, Michael. *Senegal: A Study in French Assimilation Policy*. London: Methuen, 1967.

————. *Colonial West Africa: Collected Essays*. London: Frank Cass, 1978.

————, and Ikime, Obaro, editors. *West African Chiefs: Their Changing Status under Colonial Rule and Independence*. New York: Africana Publishing Corporation, 1970.

Cruise O'Brien, Donal. *Saints and Politicians: Essays in the Organization of a Senegalese Peasant Society*. Cambridge: Cambridge University Press, 1975.

————. *The Mourides of Senegal: The Political and Economic Organization of an Islamic Brotherhood*. Oxford: Clarendon Press, 1971.

Cutter, Charles H. "The Genesis of a Nationalist Elite: The Role of the Popular Front in the French Soudan (1936-1939)." In Johnson, G. Wesley, jr. editor. *Double Impact: France and Africa in the Age of Imperialism*. Westport, Conn.: Greenwood Press, 1985.

Davidson, Basil. *The Black Man's Burden: Africa and the Curse of the Nation-State*. New York: Times Books, 1992.

Dewitte. Philippe. *Les Mouvements nègres en France, 1919–1939*. Paris: L'Harmattan, 1985.

Dubois, Laurent. "La République Metisée: Citizenship, Colonialism, and the Borders of French History." In *Cultural Studies*, 14:1 (2000).

Fanon, Frantz. *Black Skin, White Masks*. Translated by Charles Lam Markmann. New York: Grove Press, 1967.

———. *A Dying Colonialism*. Translated by Hoakon Chevalier. Middlesex, England: Penguin Books, 1970.

———. *The Wretched of the Earth*. Translated by Constance Farrington. New York: Grove Press, 1963.

Fieldhouse, D.K. *The West and the Third World: Trade, Colonialism, Dependence and Development*. Oxford: Blackwell Publishers, 1999.

Fields, Karen E. *Revival and Rebellion in Colonial Central Africa*. Portsmouth, N.H.: Heinemann, 1997.

Foucault, Michel. *The History of Sexuality: Volume I: An Introduction*. New York: Vintage Books, 1990.

———. *Discipline and Punish: The Birth of the Prison*. Translated by Alan Sheridan. New York: Vintage Books, 1995.

Fussell, Paul. *The Great War and Modern Memory*. London: Oxford University Press, 1977.

Gallo, Max. *L'Affaire d'Éthiopie aux origines de la guerre mondiale*. Paris: Éditions du Centurion, 1967.

Geertz, Clifford. *The Interpretation of Cultures*. New York: Basic Books, Inc., 1973.

Genova, James E. "The Empire Within: The Colonial Popular Front in France, 1934–1938." In *Alternatives*, 26 (2001): 175–209.

Gilroy, Paul. *The Black Atlantic: Modernity and Double Consciousness*. Cambridge: Harvard University Press, 1996.

Girardet, Raoul. *L'Idée coloniale en France de 1871 à 1962*. Paris: La Table Ronde, 1972.

Gramsci, Antonio. *Selections from the Prison Notebooks of Antonio Gramsci*. Translated and Edited by Quintin Hoare and Geoffrey Nowell Smith. New York: International Publishers, 1992.

Grazia, Victoria de. *How Fascism Ruled Women; Italy, 1922–1945*. Berkeley: University of California Press, 1992.

Grimal, Henri. *Decolonization: The British, French, Dutch, and Belgian Empires 1919–1963*. Boulder: Westview Press, 1978.

Guha, Ranajit. *Elementary Aspects of Peasant Insurgency in Colonial India*. Delhi: Oxford University Press, 1983.

Guiraudon, Virginie. "The Reaffirmation of the Republican Model of Integration: Ten Years of Identity Politics in France." In *French Politics and Society*, 14:2 (Spring 1996): 47–57.

Habermas, Jürgen. *Jürgen Habermas on Society and Politics*. Translated and Edited by Steven Seidman. Boston: Beacon Press, 1989.

Hargreaves, Alec G. *Voices from the North African Immigrant Community in France: Immigration and Identity in Beur Fiction*. New York: Berg, 1991.

Hargreaves, John D. *West Africa: The Former French States*. Englewood Cliffs, N.J.: Prentice Hall, Inc., 1967.

———. *Decolonization in Africa*. London: Longman, 1994.

Hausser, Michel. *Essai sur la Poétique de la Négritude*. Paris: Éditions Silex, 1986.

Hendrickson, Hildi, editor. *Clothing and Difference; Embodied Identities in Colonial and Post Colonial Africa*. Durham: Duke University Press, 1996.

Horowitz, Donald L., and Noiriel, Gérard, editors. *Immigrants in Two Democracies: French and American Experiences*. New York: New York University Press, 1992.

Houtondji, Paulin J. *African Philosophy: Myth & Reality.* Bloomington: Indiana University Press, 1996.

Hunt, Lynn. *Politics, Culture, and Class in the French Revolution.* Berkeley: University of California Press, 1984.

Hunt, Nancy Rose. *A Colonial Lexicon: Of Birth Ritual, Medicalization, and Mobility in the Congo.* Durham: Duke University Press, 1999.

Huntington, Samuel P. "The Clash of Civilizations?" In *Foreign Affairs* (Summer 1993): 22–49.

Iliffe, John. *Africans: The History of a Continent.* Cambridge: Cambridge University Press, 1995.

Ireland, Patrick. "Vive le jacobinisme: Les étrangers and the Durability of the Assimilationist Model in France." In *French Politics and Society,* 14:2 (Spring 1996): 33–46.

Jackson, Julian. *The Popular Front in France: Defending Democracy, 1934–1938.* Cambridge: Cambridge University Press, 1990.

Jahn, Janheinz. *Muntu: An Outline of the New African Culture.* Translated by Marjorie Grene. New York: Grove Press, Inc., 1961.

Jennings, Eric T. *Vichy in the Tropics: Pétain's National Revolution in Madagascar, Guadeloupe, and Indochina, 1940–1944.* Stanford: Stanford University Press, 2001.

Johnson, G. Wesley, jr. *The Emergence of Black Politics in Senegal: The Struggle for Power in the Four Communes, 1900–1920.* Stanford: Stanford University Press, 1971.

———. "The Ascendancy of Blaise Diagne and the Beginnings of African Politics in Senegal." In *Africa,* 3 (July 1966).

———, editor. *Double Impact: France and Africa in the Age of Imperialism.* Westport, Conn.: Greenwood Press, 1985.

July, Robert W. *The Origins of Modern African Thought: Its Development in West Africa During the Nineteenth and Twentieth Centuries.* New York: Frederick A. Praeger, 1967.

Kastoryano, Riva. "Immigration and Identities in France: The War of Words." In *French Politics and Society,* 14:3 (Spring 1996): 58–66.

Kesteloot, Lylian. *Intellectual Origins of the African Revolution.* Washington, D.C.: Black Orpheus Press, 1972.

———. *Black Writers in French: A Literary History of Negritude.* Translated by Ellen Conroy Kennedy. Philadelphia: Temple University Press, 1974.

Kristeva, Julia. *Strangers to Ourselves.* New York: Columbia University Press, 1991.

Kuisel, Richard F. *Seducing the French: The Dilemma of Americanization.* Berkeley: University of California Press, 1996.

Laitin, David D. *Hegemony and Culture: Politics and Religious Change among the Yoruba.* Chicago: The University of Chicago Press, 1986.

Landry, Donna, and MacLean, Gerald, editors. *The Spivak Reader: Selected Works of Gayatri Chakravorty Spivak.* New York and London: Routledge, 1996.

Lebovics, Herman. *Mona Lisa's Escort: André Malraux and the Reinvention of French Culture.* Ithaca and London: Cornell University Press, 1999).

———. *True France: The Wars over Cultural Identity, 1900–1945.* Ithaca and London: Cornell University Press, 1992.

———. *The Alliance of Iron and Wheat in the Third French Republic, 1860–1914: Origins of the New Conservatism.* Baton Rouge: Louisiana State University Press, 1988.

Lemesle, Raymond-Marin. *La Conférence de Brazzaville de 1944: contexte et repères: Cinquantenaire des prémices de la decolonisation.* Paris: C.H.E.A.M., 1994).

Lequin, Yves, director. *Histoire des étrangers et de l'immigration en France*. Paris: Larousse, 1992.

L'Estoile, Benoît de. "Au nom des 'vrais Africains': Les élites scolarisées de l'Afrique coloniale face à l'anthropologie (1930-1950)." In *Terrain* (298 March 1997).

Liauzu, Claude. *Aux Origines des Tiers-Mondismes: Colonisés et Anticolonialistes en France (1919-1939)*. Paris: Éditions L'Harmattan, 1982.

Lunn, Joe. *Memoirs of the Maelstrom: A Senegalese Oral History of the First World War*. Portsmouth, N.H.: Heinemann, 1999.

Mamdani, Mahmood. *Citizen and Subject: Contemporary Africa and the Legacy of Late Colonialism*. Princeton, New Jersey: Princeton University Press, 1996.

Manschuelle, François. "Assimilé ou patriote africains? Naissance du nationalisme culturel en Afrique française (1853–1931)." In *Cahiers d'Études Africaines*, 2-3 (1995).

Marseille, Jacques. *L'Age d'Or de la France Coloniale*. Paris: Albin Michel, 1986.

———. *Empire colonial et capitalisme français: Histoire d'un divorce*. Paris: Éditions Albin Michel, 1984.

Mbembe, Achille. "The Banality of Power and the Aesthetics of Vulgarity in the Postcolony." In *Public Culture*, 4:2 (Spring 1992).

———. *On The Postcolony*. Berkeley: University of California Press, 2001.

McClintock, Anne. *Imperial Leather: Race, Gender and Sexuality in the Colonial Contest*. New York: Routledge, 1995.

Memmi, Albert. *The Colonizer and the Colonized*. Boston: Beacon Press, 1991.

Michel, Marc. *L'Appel à l'Afrique: Contributions et réactions à l'effort de guerre en A.O.F., 1914–1919*. Paris: Publications de la Sorbonne, 1982.

———. *Décolonisations et émergence du tiers monde*. Paris: Hachette, 1993.

Mirzoeff, Nicholas. *Bodyscape: Art, Modernity and the Ideal Figure*. London and New York: Routledge, 1995.

Mommsen, Wolfgang J. *Theories of Imperialism*. Translated by P. S. Falla. Chicago: University of Chicago Press, 1982.

Monéta, Jakob. *La politique du parti communiste français dans la question coloniale, 1920-1963*. Paris: F. Maspéro, 1971.

Morgenthau, Ruth Schachter. *Political Parties in French-Speaking West Africa*. London: Clarendon Oxford University Press, 1967.

Moro, Adriana. *Négritude e Cultura Francese. Surrealismo Chiave della Négritude?* Torino: Edizioni dell'Orso, 1992.

Mortimer, Mildred. *Journeys Through the French African Novel*. Portsmouth, N.H.: Heinemann, 1990.

Mudimbe, V. Y. *The Invention of Africa: Gnosis, Philosophy, and the Order of Knowledge*. Bloomington and Indianapolis: Indiana University Press, 1988.

———. *The Idea of Africa*. Bloomington: Indiana University Press, 1994.

———, editor. *Nations, Identities, Cultures*. Durham: Duke University Press, 1997.

Naylor, Phillip C. *France and Algeria: A History of Decolonization and Transformation*. Gainesville: University Press of Florida, 2000.

Ngugi wa Thiong'o. *Decolonising the Mind: The Politics of Language in African Literature*. Portsmouth, N.H.: Heinemann, 1997.

Nicolet, Claude. *L'Idée républicaine en France, 1789–1924: Essai d'histoire critique*. Paris: Gallimard, 1982.

Noiriel, Gérard. *Le Creuset français: Histoire de l'immigration XIXe—XXe siècles*. Paris: Seuil, 1988.

————. *Workers in French Society in the 19ᵗʰ and 20ᵗʰ Centuries.* New York: Berg, 1990.

Nord, Philip. *The Republican Moment: Struggles for Democracy in Nineteenth-Century France.* Cambridge: Harvard University Press, 1995.

Paxton, Robert O. *Vichy France: Old Guard and New Order, 1940–1944.* New York: Columbia University Press, 1982.

Pilbeam, Pamela M. *Republicanism in Nineteenth-Century France, 1814–1871.* New York: St. Martin's Press, 1995.

Prakash, Gyan, editor. *After Colonialism: Imperial Histories and Postcolonial Displacements.* Princeton: Princeton University Press, 1995.

Rabinow, Paul. *French Modern: Norms and Forms of the Social Environment.* Cambridge: MIT Press, 1989.

Ranger, Terrence, and Vaughan, Olufemi, editors. *Legitimacy and the State in Twentieth Century Africa: Essays in Honour of A. H. M. Kirk-Greene.* Oxford: The Macmillan Press Ltd., 1993.

Reggiani, Andrés Horacio. "Procreating France: The Politics of Demography, 1919–1945." In *French Historical Studies*, 19:3 (Spring 1996).

Rioux, Jean-Pierre. *The Fourth Republic, 1944–1958.* Cambridge: Cambridge University Press, 1987.

Roberts, Mary Louise. *Civilization Without Sexes: Reconstructing Gender in Postwar France, 1917-1927.* Chicago and London: The University of Chicago Press, 1994.

Ross, Kristin. *Fast Cars, Clean Bodies: Decolonization and the Reordering of French Culture.* Cambridge: The MIT Press, 1996.

Said, Edward W. *Culture and Imperialism.* New York: Vintage books, 1994.

————. *Orientalism.* New York: Vintage, 1979.

Shipway, Martin. *The Road to War: France and Vietnam, 1944–1947.* Oxford: Berghahn, 1996.

Sibeud, Emmanuelle. "Ethnographie africaniste et 'inauthenticité' coloniale." In *French Politics, Culture, and Society*, 20:2 (Summer 2002).

Silverman, Maxim. *Deconstructing the Nation: Immigration, Racism, and Citizenship in Modern France.* London and New York: Routledge, 1992.

Simmel, Georg. *The Sociology of Georg Simmel.* Translated by Kurt H. Wolff. New York: The Free Press of Glencoe, 1964.

Sorum, Paul Clay. *Intellectuals and Decolonization in France.* Chapel Hill: University of North Carolina Press, 1977.

Soucy, Robert. *French Fascism: The Second Wave 1933–1939.* New Haven: Yale University Press, 1995.

Spillman, George. *De l'Empire à l'Hexagon.* Paris: Librairie Académique Perrin, 1981.

Spivak, Gayatri Chakravorty. "Can the Subaltern Speak?" In Nelson, Cary, and Grossberg, Larry, editors. *Marxism and the Interpretation of Culture.* Urbana: University of Illinois Press, 1988.

————. *In Other Worlds: Essays in Cultural Politics.* New York and London: Routledge, 1988.

————. "More on Power/Knowledge." In Landry, Donna, and MacLean, Gerald, editors. *The Spivak Reader: Selected Works of Gayatri Chakravorty Spivak.* New York and London: Routledge, 1996.

Stoler, Ann Laura. "Sexual Affronts and Racial Frontiers; European Identities and the Cultural Politics of Exclusion in Colonial Southeast Asia." In Cooper, Frederick, and Stoler, Ann

Laura. *Tensions of Empire: Colonial Cultures in a Bourgeois World*. Berkeley: University of California Press, 1997.

———, and Cooper, Frederick. "Between Metropole and Colony; Rethinking a Research Agenda." In Cooper, Frederick, and Stoler, Ann Laura, editors. *Tensions of Empire: Colonial Culture in a Bourgeois World*. Berkeley: University of California Press, 1997.

Stone, Judith F. *Sons of the Revolution: Radical Democrats in France, 1862-1914*. Baton Rouge: Louisiana State University Press, 1996.

Suret-Canale, Jean. *L'Afrique noire: L'ère coloniale 1900–1945*. Paris: Éditions Sociales, 1962.

Talbot, John. *The War Without a Name: France in Algeria, 1954–1962*. New York: Alfred A. Knopf, 1980.

Taussig, Michael. *Mimesis and Alterity: A Particular History of the Senses*. New York: Routledge, 1993).

Thomas, Martin. *The French Empire at War, 1940–1945*. Manchester: University of Manchester Press, 1998.

Vaillant, Janet G. *Black, French, and African: A Life of Léopold Sédar Senghor*. Cambridge: Harvard University Press, 1990.

Vaughan, Olufemi. "Assessing Grassroots Politics and Community Development in Nigeria." In *African Affairs*, 94 (1995): 501–518.

———. *Nigerian Chiefs: Traditional Power in Modern Politics, 1890s–1990s (Rochester Studies in African History and the Diaspora, V. 7)*. Rochester: University of Rochester Press, 2000.

White, Dan S. *Lost Comrades: Socialists of the Front Generation, 1918–1945*. Cambridge: Harvard University Press, 1992.

White, Owen. *Children of the French Empire: Miscegenation and Colonial Society in French West Africa, 1895–1960*. Oxford: Clarendon Press, 1999.

Wilder, Gary. "Framing Greater France Between the Wars." In *Journal of Historical Sociology*, 14:2 (June 2001).

———. "The Politics of Failure: Historicising Popular Front Colonial Policy in French West Africa." In Chafer, Tony, and Sackur, Amanda, editors. *French Colonial Empire and the Popular Front*. New York: St. Martin's Press, 1999.

Wilson, Kathleen. *The Sense of the People: Politics, Culture and Imperialism in England, 1715–1785*. Cambridge: Cambridge University Press, 1998.

Winichakul, Thongchai. *Siam Mapped: A History of the Geo-Body of a Nation*. Honolulu: University of Hawaii Press, 1994.

Yacono, Xavier. *Les Étapes de la décolonisation française*. Paris: Presses Universitaires de France, 1971.

Young, Crawford. *The African Colonial State in Comparative Perspective*. New Haven and London: Yale University Press, 1994.

Young, Robert J. C. *Colonial Desire: Hybridity in Theory, Culture and Race*. London and New York: Routledge, 1995.

Index

FRANCOPHONE CULTURES
& LITERATURES

General Editors: Michael G. Paulson & Tamara Alvarez-Detrell

The Francophone Cultures and Literatures series encompasses studies about the literature, culture, and civilization of the Francophone areas of Africa, Asia, Europe, the Americas, the French-speaking islands in the Caribbean, as well as French Canada. Cross-cultural studies between and among these geographic areas are encouraged. The book-length manuscripts may be written in either English or French.

For further information about the Francophone Cultures and Literatures series and for the submission of manuscripts, contact:

> Michael G. Paulson
> Tamara Alvarez-Detrell
> c/o Dr. Heidi Burns
> Peter Lang Publishing, Inc.
> P.O. Box 1246
> Bel Air, MD 21014-1246

To order other books in this series, please contact our Customer Service Department:

> (800) 770-LANG (within the U.S.)
> (212) 647-7706 (outside the U.S.)
> (212) 647-7707 FAX

or browse online by series at:

WWW.PETERLANGUSA.COM